T0335735

Introduction to
Windows® and Graphics
Programming with Visual C++®

with Companion Media Pack

Second Edition

Introduction to
Windows® and Graphics
Programming with Visual C++®

with Companion Media Pack

Second Edition

Roger Mayne

University at Buffalo
State University of New York, USA

World Scientific

NEW JERSEY · LONDON · SINGAPORE · BEIJING · SHANGHAI · HONG KONG · TAIPEI · CHENNAI

Published by

World Scientific Publishing Co. Pte. Ltd.

5 Toh Tuck Link, Singapore 596224

USA office: 27 Warren Street, Suite 401-402, Hackensack, NJ 07601

UK office: 57 Shelton Street, Covent Garden, London WC2H 9HE

Library of Congress Cataloging-in-Publication Data
Mayne, Roger, 1942–
    [Windows and graphics programming with Visual C++.NET]
    Introduction to Windows and graphics programming with Visual C++ : (with companion media
pack) / Roger Mayne, University at Buffalo, State University of New York, USA. -- 2nd edition.
        pages cm
    Revision of: Introduction to Windows and graphics programming with Visual C++.NET. ©2005.
    ISBN 978-9814641869 (hardback : alk. paper) -- ISBN 978-9814699402 (pbk : alk. paper)
    1. Microsoft Visual C++ 2. C++ (Computer program language) 3. Microsoft .NET Framework.
I. Title.
    QA76.73.C153M3284 2015
    006.7'882--dc23

                                    2015008114

British Library Cataloguing-in-Publication Data
A catalogue record for this book is available from the British Library.

In-house Editor: Amanda Yun

Printed in Singapore

Preface

This is the second edition of a book originally developed from a set of programming examples for the introduction of Microsoft's Visual C++ to engineering students studying computer graphics. The book has also been found useful for engineers and scientists interested in writing their own computer programs for stand-alone personal computing in the Windows environment. The step-by-step sequence of examples used in the book and the tutorial presentation have proven to be especially effective for teaching Visual C++ programming and the basic ideas of computer graphics. This second edition continues the spirit of those original example programs while covering many features of Visual C++ and the Microsoft Foundation Classes (MFC). All of the examples in the book have been updated to the current version of Visual C++ at this writing (Version 2013). We have also added two new chapters to provide coverage of touch screen programming. The presentation requires only a modest level of mathematical and programming expertise and should provide a useful learning experience for anyone with a serious interest in Visual C++ and MFC Applications.

We begin only with the assumption that the reader has a basic familiarity with C/C++ programming. A traditional "Hello World" program serves as a starting point. And the sequence of example programs proceeds from relatively simple programming to arrays and pointers and on to object-oriented concepts before entering the "Windows World". Each example program is discussed completely and in the early chapters every line of program code is listed and numbered so it can be easily discussed. If you have had only modest exposure to C/C++ you should be able to follow the material but you will find it helpful to have an introductory programming book at hand to review syntax and language details.

The focus of this work is on programming with Visual C++ to develop computer programs which include the Windows graphical interface, graphics components and the touch screen. We attempt to move through these topics with just the right amount of detail. We emphasize the presentation of concepts and program code to accomplish programming tasks. We also try to avoid the detailed discussions of computer language typically present in texts on computer programming. By striking this balance, we are able to progress quickly from the alphanumeric world to the Windows environment and on to touch screen programming. The Microsoft Foundation Classes and the programming tools which are part of MFC are an important part of the presentation. This provides an approach to Windows programming and touch screen operations that should be easily understandable. And that can be extended to a wide range of applications, including tablets, as your programming skill increases.

Chapters 1–3 begin this adventure with the introduction of Visual C++ organization and a review of C++ programming including arrays, pointers, data structures and classes. These later topics form the basis of the object-oriented concepts at the heart of C++ and Windows programming. Chapters 4–7 move the focus to Windows programming with MFC Applications. We consider the document/view architecture, mouse drawn graphics, file storage and printing of drawings. A step-by-step presentation is used to describe programming for the user interface including menu items, tool bar buttons, dialog windows, scrolling, etc. Chapters 8 and 9 develop object-oriented programming to introduce customized classes for two-dimensional objects and graphs in MFC Applications. Animation examples, including a robot simulation, are presented. A strategy for color contour plotting is also described and demonstrated. Chapters 10 and 11 are new chapters on the touch screen interface and introduce the basic gesture and touch input functions available in MFC. Drawing, animation, graphs and tablet friendly examples are included.

When you finish your study of this book and our collection of example programs, you should be well equipped to continue your own exploration of the extensive capabilities of Visual C++. The example programs have been selected to cover many common tasks of interest in

Windows programming and you should find them useful for a variety of applications. The program files included with the book are available as templates for you to adapt to your own purposes, and the various classes and functions for handling two-dimensional objects, graphs and touch screen programming may be used directly in your own programs.

Writing a book about modern computing environments is much like shooting at a moving target since trends change quickly. Considering these dynamics, however, the Visual C++ and MFC programming environments have been remarkably stable. Our introductory level programs have operated in many versions of Visual C++ with only modest modifications needed as new versions have been introduced. Certainly, the basic programming concepts of Visual C++ and MFC applications are now well established and have persisted as Visual C++ has evolved. This second edition presents fully updated projects for Visual C++ Version 2013. Based on our experience for more than a decade, we expect that this full update will be useful for several years to come. The additional chapters provided on the touch screen should be especially important for programs including this now familiar interface.

All of book's projects are contained in its "Companion Media Pack" available on the World Scientific website. Instructions for accessing the media pack and downloading the projects are described in the Appendix. We anticipate that the example programs available in the media package will be upward compatible and that readers will readily adapt to modest changes in the environment. In the event that new versions of Visual C++ do require adjustments of the example projects we intend to provide that information and, if necessary, access to updated versions of the projects. Information on updating may be found on the World Scientific website or obtained by Email to the author at mayne@buffalo.edu.

Acknowledgments

I would like to acknowledge the patience and valuable comments of the students here at Buffalo who worked with my instructional material during its development. The congenial atmosphere and support provided by my colleagues in the Department of Mechanical and Aerospace

Engineering have also been very much appreciated. The first drafts of this book began during a sabbatical visit to the University of Genoa, Italy in the Dipartimento di Ingegneria Meccanica. I would like to thank Professor Rinaldo Michelini for his extended hospitality there. I would also like to acknowledge Professors Jianzhong Cha and Gary Shen for their help in organizing short courses on this material at Beijing Jiaotong University, Huazhong University of Science and Technology and Group T at KU Leuven. Those experiences have been very helpful in the development of this new edition. Finally, I am happy to thank my wife, Rosemary, for her patience and companionship throughout this project.

Roger Mayne
Buffalo, NY
January, 2015

Contents

Chapter 1

Basic Concepts

Microsoft's Visual Studio provides a full package of tools for Windows and web programming within a comprehensive development environment. Visual C++ is one of the component languages of Visual Studio along with Visual Basic, Visual C# and Visual F#. It is the most standard of the Visual Studio languages and is reasonably, but not fully, compatible with ISO/ANSI C++ standards. The C++ language contained in Visual C++ produces the fast and efficient programs that are often required for use in scientific, engineering and computer graphics applications. These applications typically involve repetitive computations, iterative calculations, extensive data sorting and graphics operations that are all handled well by C++. At this time, and for the foreseeable future, C++ is the most generally useful programming language for scientific and engineering applications ranging from interactive graphics and automated design to numerical simulation.

This book is focused on the use of Visual C++ and the Microsoft Foundation Classes for the development of Windows programs — that is, for programs intended to operate on a personal computer using the Windows operating system. The book introduces Windows programming at a level that is accessible to people of many technical backgrounds. Through its eleven chapters and an extended series of examples, you can expect to learn how to write your own programs combining the convenience and graphics capabilities of Windows with the utility of C++ programming. You should become well prepared to develop programs for engineering or scientific applications or to move on to more advanced topics in computer graphics programming.

The Companion Media Pack that accompanies this book is available from the publisher's web page following the directions shown in the

Appendix. The media pack contains the complete project files for all of the example projects in the book and also a series of selected executable files which illustrate the scope of the book's contents. The project files are used in each chapter and provide all of the programming code necessary to compile and build the projects. The code for each project is discussed in detail in the text. The example projects provide the basis for developing competency with Visual C++ and the ability to write meaningful programs including graphics and touch screen capability. The selected executables presented in the media pack are organized by chapter and may be executed directly, with or without the installation of Visual C++ on your computer. They illustrate the step-by-step progress that takes place as we move from chapter to chapter.

Before discussing the example projects of the media pack in more detail, the sections below introduce Visual C++ and provide an initial introduction to programming in the Visual C++ environment. Readers interested in a quick-start can page forward to Section 1.7 where the media pack is more thoroughly described.

1.1 Background

Within Microsoft's Visual Studio, the Visual C++ module makes the management of Windows programming a convenient task. It provides an organizational structure, as well as editing, compiling, linking and debugging capabilities in a single package. Of course, library functions, the Microsoft Foundation Classes (MFC) and a wide range of resources are also part of the package. These make it possible for an application programmer to produce extensive programs with full Windows functionality while having less than a complete mastery of the computer science behind the Windows operating system. The organizational features and available programming tools offered within Visual C++ have made it the environment of choice for an impressive number of engineering application programs including, for example, computer aided design packages.

Compared to the dynamics of the computing world in past years, the programming environment offered by Visual C++ and MFC

Applications has been notably stable. Many of the example programs included here originally began in Version 5.0 of Visual C++. Without change, they compiled and executed in Visual C++ 6.0 and have since functioned with only modest adjustments in newer versions of Visual C++. The basic programming concepts of Visual C++ and MFC applications have become well established and have persisted as Visual C++ has evolved over many years. Considering this history and the evolutionary process, learning the basic concepts and programming strategies presented here will remain valuable as Visual C++ continues to develop in the future.

The purpose of the introductory material in this chapter is to provide an initial familiarity with the Visual C++ environment and to begin its use for simple programming tasks. We assume that the reader has had some previous exposure to C/C++ programming — either through a programming course or through self-study. In this introduction and throughout the book you will find that our emphasis is on presenting concepts and strategies to accomplish programming tasks. The intention here is not to provide the full language detail present in most books on computer programming. Although we may occasionally stray into discussions of programming language and syntax, our focus is on the use of Visual C++ for developing computer programs including basic graphics and Windows functionality. We expect to move in that direction with just the right amount of detail. That is, enough detail to learn and understand the programming tasks at hand but not so much detail that we get bogged down in programming intricacies. If you have only a modest background in C/C++, you may find it helpful to have a standard C/C++ textbook at hand as you proceed through our examples. The excellent "help" tools readily available for Visual C++ will also assist you with any details that are not included here.

This chapter introduces the fundamentals of Visual C++ and simultaneously provides a review of C/C++ programming. The chapter is divided into a set of subsections that begin with the simplest of "Hello World" programs to familiarize you with the Visual C++ programming environment. We then present a series of programs using: "while" loops and "for" loops for program control, functions for repeated operations, and keyboard inputs for user interaction. The final section of the chapter includes several programming examples for simple calculations, especially illustrating the basic user interaction needed to control a calculation process. After completing this chapter, you should be ready to move on to Chapters 2 and 3 where arrays, pointers and object-oriented programming are considered. We initially work with programming for the simple console format and its alphanumeric mode. Then, beginning in Chapter 4, we move on to Windows programming and graphics using MFC Applications.

1.2 Getting Started with Visual C++

The programs and example files used throughout this book and contained in the accompanying media pack were developed using a full installation of the now current Professional Edition of Visual Studio (Version 2013) working in Windows 8.1. Visual C++ operates within the Visual Studio environment but is not the only available language. Program development with Visual C++ takes place within Microsoft's Integrated Development Environment (IDE) and it contains many options and possibilities that are outside the scope of this book (in fact, way outside the scope of this book). We will focus exclusively on the set of possibilities that will allow us to move quickly into the use of Visual C++ and MFC Applications for writing Windows programs and using computer graphics in personal computing.

We start by considering Figure 1.1 which shows the typical screen seen as Visual Studio is executed by clicking on its icon from your PC desktop. Of course, we're assuming here that you have successfully installed Visual Studio (with Visual C++) and that you have created a shortcut on the desktop. This basic Visual Studio screen will appear before you begin any program development. The screen will take on this form once you have closed the Visual Studio "Start Page" by clicking on its "X". The Start Page is a very useful organizational tool and you will figure it out easily as you begin to accumulate some Visual C++ experience. As shown in Figure 1.1, Visual Studio contains the familiar menu bar and toolbar structure typical of programs that run every day on

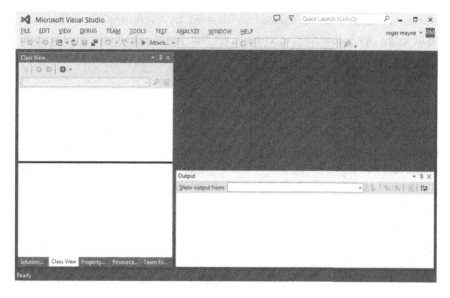

Figure 1.1 Opening Screen of Visual Studio

your PC. If your screen doesn't initially appear exactly as in Figure 1.1, a few clicks on file tabs, pins and "Xs" can put it in this form. If you get lost in arranging windows, clicking on the menu item **Window** and then **Reset Window Layout** in the dropdown menu list (**Window > Reset Window Layout**) provides a return to the default arrangement.

The basic screen arrangement of Visual Studio contains three windows for use in writing and compiling programs. The largest window on the upper right is an edit window that displays the active text files in which you may be writing and editing code (if more than one file is active, tabs appear which allow convenient switching from one file to another). The window to the left in Figure 1.1 is a workspace area which allows you to display and control the overall arrangement of the programming project that you have active. At various times, the space may be occupied by the Solution Explorer, a Class View window, a Properties window, etc. This space divides into two or more windows as needed and its contents may be controlled by the tabs beneath it and also by entries under the View menu bar item, by buttons on the toolbar, and by pins and "Xs" which are found in the individual windows. The workspace area can be resized as desired by exploring the window's right edge with the mouse cursor. At the point where the resize icon replaces the mouse cursor, click and drag the window edge to adjust its size.

In Figure 1.1, the window at the bottom of the screen is the "Output" window where Visual Studio communicates with you. Results from compiling and linking are displayed there — including, of course, compiling errors and warnings. As desired, other information can be displayed as output by making an entry into the "output from" text box. As shown in Figure 1.2, both individual windows can be "undocked" from their positions on the left and bottom edges of the screen. Just click and drag at the title bar on the upper edge of the window. The windows can also be re-docked at one of the other edges of the display if desired. Also, in case you'd like another window to study, a Toolbox window can be displayed on the right of the screen. Just click on the menu item **View**

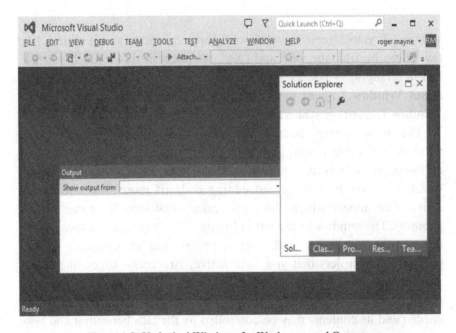

Figure 1.2 Undocked Windows for Workspace and Output

and then **Toolbox** in the dropdown menu list (**View > Toolbox**) or click the appropriate toolbar button (which may have to be added to the toolbar — look for the "add" arrow on the right). Finally, the edit window can be viewed in full screen by clicking on **View > Full Screen**. The full screen presentation is particularly helpful when editing a complex program or multiple files. When finished with full screen editing, clicking on **View > Full Screen** serves as a "toggle" which will return you to the regular window arrangement.

As you can see, there are many possibilities for arranging and managing the development environment. You will find the arrangement most convenient for you as you begin writing and editing Visual C++ programs. Of course, remember that if needed, the command "Reset Window Layout" under the "Window" menu bar item will return you to the default configuration.

1.3 A First Program

It has become an established tradition to write a "Hello World" program as a first step in using a new programming environment. The purpose of such a program is to furnish an introduction to the environment and allow you to produce your first executing program. Of course, we will follow that tradition with our own introduction to the "world" of programming with Visual C++. This program is the most direct possible requiring only the few lines of code below:

```
/*Hello World Example
Writes "Hello World" to the screen*/
#include <stdio.h>
void main (void)
{
printf ("\nHello World !\n\n");
}
```

The above statements use very straight forward C/C++ language. The program begins with the two explanatory "comment" lines between the comment indicator /* at the beginning and concluding with the */ at the end. The program itself is based on the standard screen output function "printf" commonly used in C programming. The printf function is available in the standard input/output library that is added to this program by the statement #include <stdio.h> on the third line. The function "main", which is expected in a typical C or C++ program, is declared with no input arguments, as indicated by the "(void)" on the right, and no returned values, as indicated by the "void" on the left. On the lines that follow, the curly brackets contain the code for main( ) with its single statement calling on the printf function. In the printf argument, the initial control command \n advances to a new line, producing a blank line before printing "Hello World!". The two additional \n commands move to a new line after printing the text and then produce a blank line as the cursor advances to a second new line.

If you are more familiar with input and output using the C++ iostream, the code below attaches the appropriate C++ functions and namespace. The code will also produce an executable "Hello World" program after compiling and linking with Visual C++.

```
/* Hello World Example - Uses the "iostream" operators
Writes "Hello World" to the screen*/
#include <iostream>
using namespace std;
void main(void)
{
cout << "\nHello World ! \n\n";
}
```

We will now use the program coding shown above to create an operating "Hello World" program using Visual C++ and the development environment. We start by executing Visual Studio. You should see the screen of Figure 1.1 after Visual Studio starts and you close its Start Page. From the initial screen, we need to create a project to contain the program and its associated files. A program file is then created within the project. We will start this process by clicking on **File** to produce the drop down menu list shown in Figure 1.3. Then click on

New and then **Project** (**File > New > Project**) to pop up the New Project window of Figure 1.4 (clicking on the toolbar button toward the left provides a shortcut to the New Project window).

In the standard installation of Visual Studio, you can expect to see additional options available under "Project Types" in addition to Visual C++. In any case, click on and highlight the Visual C++ Projects option. Then look through the available project templates on the right side of the window. We want an empty template so the C++ Empty Project icon should be selected as shown in Figure 1.4. At this point, the project needs a name. As you can see, we have entered "HelloProject" in the Name box of Figure 1.4. A folder with this name will automatically be created to store the project at the disk location shown in the Location box in the New Project window. If you would like to use a different location for your project, you can change the Location box entry as you like. We have used "C:\" to create the project folder directly on the hard drive. At

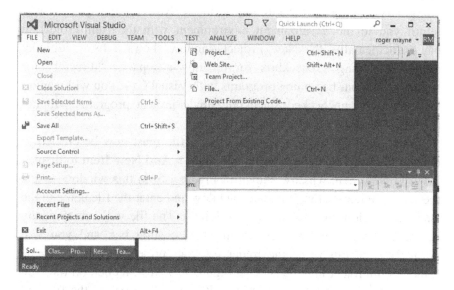

Figure 1.3 Select "New" Under "File" to Begin a New Project

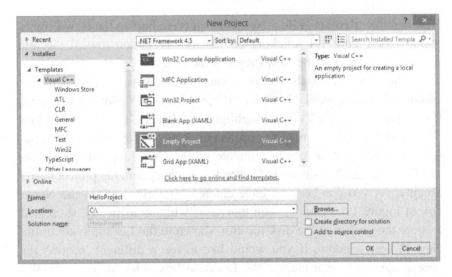

Figure 1.4 In the "New Project" Window, Select the Empty C++ Project

this point, clicking on the OK button in the New Project window will return you to the development environment with the HelloProject in place. Incidentally, the New Project window shows a few additional options including a checkbox for creating a separate "directory for solution". For our beginning programs with Visual C++, you will want to leave this box unchecked since our single project programs will not require this extra level of directories.

Since an empty project was selected, a file must now be created to contain the program code. Click on **Project > Add New Item** to display the Add New Item window shown in Figure 1.5. In this window, select the C++ File icon in the Templates window and enter the file name in the Name box below (we have entered "Hello"). The file will automatically be placed in the folder indicated in the Location box and you will normally want this to be the folder for your project. In this case, the folder HelloProject may be seen in Figure 1.5. Now, a click on the Add button at the bottom of the Add New Item window creates the file and returns to the HelloProject development environment as shown in Figure 1.6.

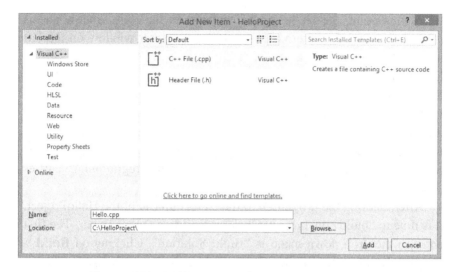

Figure 1.5 The Add New Item Window for the HelloProject

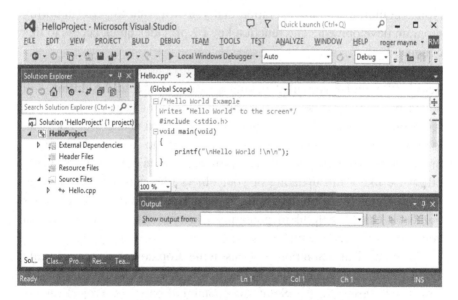

Figure 1.6 The HelloProject with Code Entered in Hello.cpp

At this point, the Hello.cpp file appears in the Edit window and is ready for code to be entered. The Solution Explorer window on the left now indicates the presence of Hello.cpp as a Source File in the HelloProject. To continue this example, we have entered the "Hello World" code into the Edit window. You may enter either of the program forms shown above (we're using the printf form). Notice that the development environment color codes the entered text for easy recognition, indicating commented text (green), reserved words to be recognized by the compiler (blue), and other programming entries (black).

After entering the program into the Hello.cpp file of the HelloProject, it is time to "build" the project. Click on **Build** on the menu bar. The first entry in the drop down menu is "Build Solution". Clicking on **Build > Build Solution** will compile all project files that have changed since the last build and will then carry out all linking of the compiled files and appropriate libraries so that an executable file is constructed and ready for execution. This **Build > Build Solution** command provides the typical compiling/linking operation that you will want to perform during program development. The function key F7 provides quick access to this command.

The next option in the drop down menu list under the Build menu bar item is "Rebuild Solution". Clicking on **Build > Rebuild Solution** will delete previous intermediate and output files from your project folder, recompile all source files (whether there have been changes or not), and then link the resulting files. You may want to follow this rebuild procedure if you have moved your project between computers or would otherwise like a full updating of your object files and links. A click on **Build > Clean Solution** deletes intermediate and output files of previous builds. It can be helpful in preparing a project file to move between computers or to share with others.

After the "Build Solution" options in the drop down menu, the "Build Project" options appear using the name of your current project (in this case "HelloProject"). For Solutions containing only one Project (as we will be considering), the Build Solution options and the Build Project options are equivalent. In the next item of the drop down menu, the Batch Build... entry allows multiple builds to be conducted (not something you need to worry about now). The Configuration Manager item in the drop down menu allows switching from a "Debug" mode to a "Release" mode when building projects. The release mode is intended to produce a finished and portable executable (more about this in a later section). The "Compile" entry at the bottom of the drop down menu list allows the compiling of files to be performed without a full build. This action compiles a file, revealing any coding or typing errors, but no linking with libraries or other compiled files will take place. The compile option provides a quick way to check syntax errors, for example.

After we selected **Build > Build Solution** for a test of our HelloProject, the result shown in Figure 1.7 was obtained from the development environment. The Output window shows a compiling error (in this case, "Printf" was entered instead of "printf" for the print function). By double clicking on the error listing in the Output window (or in the Task List), the actual error line is indicated in the Edit window as may be seen in Figure 1.7. After changing the "Printf" to "printf", the HelloProject builds successfully and creates an executable. The

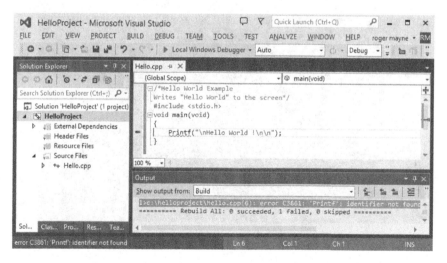

Figure 1.7 Display of a Compiler Error in the HelloProject

executable may be run from within the development environment by clicking on the small arrow to the left of the Local Debugger box on the toolbar (it can be seen in Figure 1.7).

If you watch very carefully as HelloProject executes, you will see the display of Figure 1.8. A window appears containing HelloProject.exe in its title bar and displaying the line "Hello World!" with a blank line before it and a blank line afterward. You do have to watch carefully, however, because we have not yet provided a means to stop the window and hold it on the screen. After showing the window, and displaying "HelloWorld!", the program simply ends by closing the window and returning to the development environment. We will learn how to hold the window on the screen in Section 1.5. At this point you can exit from the development environment by closing its window at the X in the upper right hand corner. The files of your latest programming efforts are automatically saved and if there are any doubts, you will be asked about saving the updated project files.

Figure 1.8 Watch Carefully to See this Result from HelloProject

You have, of course, noticed that the HelloProject runs in a simplified window in the old style "DOS" format. This window is the standard format for a "Console Application" and is the default appearance for the project structure selected as we started the creation of HelloProject. We will use this console window format during our introductory discussions throughout Chapters 1, 2, and 3 while we explore the world of Visual C++ programming. We will discuss programming concepts and object-oriented programming in this format. When we begin graphics programming in Chapter 4, you will see the traditional Windows format that you normally expect for a program running on a personal computer.

1.4 Exploring the Project Folder

At this point, if you have followed the steps above successfully, the HelloProject has been created with its executable HelloProject.exe. All of your work resides in the folder *C:\HelloProject* on the hard drive. Close the Visual C++ development environment and look over the contents of *C:\HelloProject* through "File Explorer". The top of Figure 1.9 shows *C:\HelloProject* with the "content" option selected by clicking on **View > Content**. The only file that you have directly created by entering your own text is Hello.cpp. All of the other files in this folder were automatically created by Visual C++. In addition, during the compiling and linking process, Visual C++ also created the folder called "Debug" and the files it contains. The file HelloProject.sln is the "Solution File" which stores all of the information about your recent work on HelloProject for the development environment. Clicking on HelloProject.sln in "File Explorer" will start the development environment and will load HelloProject so that you can continue working on it. Also, if you are working in the development environment and click on **File > Open Solution**, you will be able to access folders of your previous work through their .sln files. Projects that have been recently edited with Visual C++ are also accessible through the Visual C++ Start Page or by clicking on **File > Recent Projects** within the development environment.

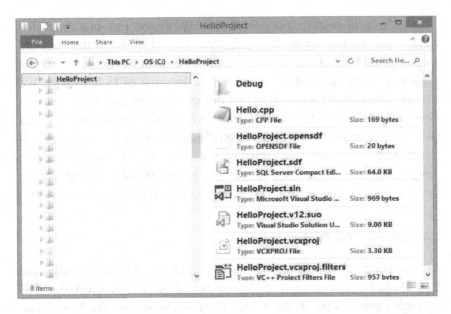

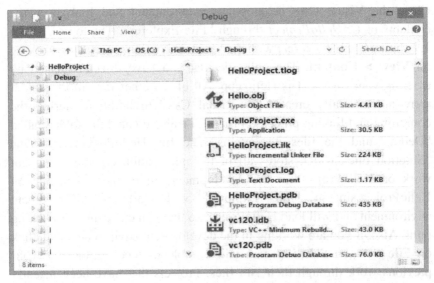

Figure 1.9 The HelloProject and Debug Folders

In the folder *C:\HelloProject\Debug*, displayed at the bottom of Figure 1.9, the HelloProject.exe file is the executable file for the HelloProject. It is the end result of your programming effort after compiling and linking. If you double click on it in "File Explorer", it will execute. But, again, watch carefully. We have still not provided any code to hold the program window on the screen after it executes. It will simply flash on the screen and then disappear as soon as it writes "Hello World!" because it has completed executing.

For a Visual C++ project, the Debug folder is expendable. If you completely delete the Debug folder for a project, the entire project is still described within the remaining files of the project folder. In this case, the HelloProject folder itself contains the full project information. When you open your project into the development environment by clicking on the HelloProject.sln file and then click on **Build > Build Solution** or **Build > Rebuild Solution**, Visual C++ will carry out compiling and linking and will recreate the Debug folder along with the executable HelloProject.exe. The Debug folder can become very large. During a programming session with Visual C++, it is useful to have it available since the files it contains speed compiling and linking. However, in terms of storage space for your work and portability (e.g. for storage on a flash disk), it is much easier to handle the project folder by excluding the Debug folder. Visual C++ will rebuild it when you need it again or after you have transferred the project to a different computer.

In addition to the .sln and .exe files created by Visual C++, several other file types are created. Fortunately, you can write many very interesting programs and never have to learn the details of these other files. But, just to mention a few of the file types, the .vcxproj file contains project specific information such as where project source files are located and how to build the project. These files are now in XML format. In earlier versions of Visual C++, the extension .vcproj was used. The .suo file describes the configuration of the development environment that has been used for the solution including, for example, the window arrangements. When you reenter the development environment for a project, it will appear essentially the same as when you last left the project. The .suo file is normally a "hidden" file and will appear in the project folder only if you are displaying hidden files. The .sdf file contains program details including the information used by Class View. As you can see in Figure 1.9, it can be a very large file and may make file transfer inconvenient. It is important to note that the .sdf file may be deleted if necessary. Visual C++ will automatically regenerate it when needed. The .idl file specifically retains linking information. The .vcxproj.filters file contains the file management information for the solution and files added to the solution.

Other files in the Debug folder in addition to the .exe file include the .obj files generated by the compiling process and the .ilk file for linking information. The .log files maintain a record of compiling and linking while the .pdb file contains information used by the program debugging tool.

1.5 Modifying the HelloProject

Let's now return to the HelloProject and fix it so that its display will remain on the screen after execution. Return to the HelloProject by finding the file HelloProject.sln in the *C:\HelloProject* folder and then double clicking on it. Once Visual C++ has started, you should see HelloProject just as you left it. The workspace area is where you can see the structure of a project at a glance. Display the Solution Explorer by clicking on the "Solution Explorer" tab at the bottom of the workspace area or by clicking on **View > Solution Explorer** from the menu bar. The Solution Explorer window reveals the various files which have been created and which you may want to view or edit (see Figure 1.10). In this simple project, only the Hello.cpp file that we created as a source file can be seen. If you double click the file name, it is displayed in the Edit window and the cursor appears in the file, ready to allow text editing. If you now click on the "Class View" tab or on **View > Class View** from the menu bar, you can display the Class View window and see the classes, functions and variables associated with the project (on the right in Figure 1.10). In this simple project when you click on the expand icon (>) for HelloProject, "Global Functions and Variables" appears. Clicking on "Global Functions and Variables" then allows the function "main" to be shown below the dividing bar. Double click on "main" below the

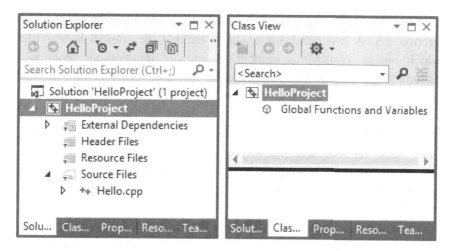

Figure 1.10 The Workspace Window for Solution Explorer and Class View

dividing bar and the cursor will move to main() in the file Hello.cpp displaying the code. This feature is very helpful as projects and programs become more complicated and include many functions and classes.

Let's now fix the HelloProject so that it operates easily as a standalone executable. We will do this by arranging to have "Hello World!" remain on the screen until you are ready to terminate the program. The lines of code below (in printf form) will provide that capability:

```
/*  Hello World Example - Writes "Hello World" to the screen
And waits for a keystroke to terminate*/
#include <stdio.h>
#include <conio.h>
void main (void)
{
printf ("\n\n Hello World!\n\n");
printf ("\n\n\n\n\nFinished reading?  Strike any key...\n");
_getch();
}
```

Only three changes have been made from the original program in Section 1.3. A line has been added to include the conio.h header file which makes available a number of console input/output functions, including _getch(). A line is also added that uses the function printf to skip several lines and then outputs the text "Finished reading? Strike any key...". The last new line added only contains the Visual C++ function _getch(). This "get character" function waits for a single keystroke entry to be made. As used here, the line containing the _getch() function is the last instruction in the program and the program will simply terminate after a keystroke is received. Use the Edit window to modify your code to this form and build the modified project.

If you have been using the C++ iostream form, the code below includes the "Finished reading, strike any key" prompt and the use of _getch() to wait for a keystroke:

```
/*  Hello World Example - Uses the "iostream" operators
Writes "Hello World" to the screen
And waits for a keystroke to terminate*/
#include <iostream>
using namespace std;
#include <conio.h>
void main(void)
{
cout << "\nHello World ! \n\n";
cout << "\n\n\n\nFinished reading? Strike any key...\n";
_getch();
}
```

When you execute the modified HelloProject within the Visual C++ development environment, you should see the display of "Hello World!" along with the statement to strike any key. A keystroke will then terminate the modified HelloProject. Figure 1.11 shows the modified HelloProject running within the development environment and waiting for the final keystroke.

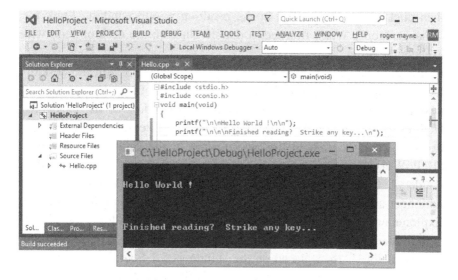

Figure 1.11 The Modified HelloProject Running in Visual C++

When you are satisfied with your program, exit Visual C++ and we'll now look at running the executable on its own. Use File Explorer to open the *C:\HelloProject\Debug* folder. Double click on HelloProject.exe to execute the program. Execution of the program opens a "HelloProject" window, writes "Hello World!", and displays the finished reading prompt. It then waits for a keystroke. With your keystroke, the HelloProject executable will terminate and the window will close. In addition to being executed from its own folder, the HelloProject.exe file can be used like any other executable program in Windows. For example, if you right click on the file, a popup window will appear that offers you several options. If you click on the "Create Shortcut" menu item, a shortcut to HelloProject.exe will appear in the Debug folder. You can now click on and drag this shortcut from its folder to the desktop and drop it there, where it will appear with a default icon. The caption name can then be edited by clicking on the name itself to highlight it and then clicking again. You can edit it as you like perhaps simply calling it "HelloWorld!". The icon can also be edited by right clicking on it and then clicking on **Properties** in the resulting popup window. Look for "Change Icon". When finished, a double click on the desktop icon will execute the program.

Figure 1.12 shows the lower corner of the desktop with the desktop icon we selected for "Hello World!" (comprising of a globe and screen, next to the icon for the File Explorer). The window of the executing HelloProject is also shown, waiting for its final keystroke. Notice that executing the program in this way results in the simple window title "HelloWorld!" (the edited name for the icon label or shortcut) and that the detailed folder information shown in the window title of Figure 1.11 no longer appears. In Windows 8.1, returning to the Debug folder in File Explorer and right clicking on HelloProject.exe also allows the option "Pin to Start" to be selected. By clicking on "Pin to Start", the shortcut to the executable is then placed on the Windows 8.1 Start Screen where it becomes a tile and can be executed directly like any Windows "app".

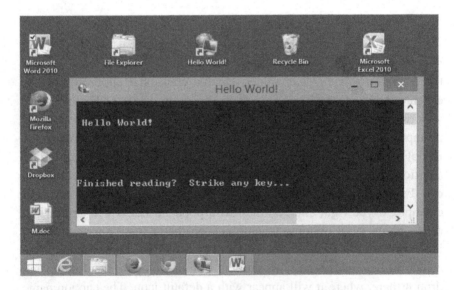

Figure 1.12 Part of the Desktop with the "Hello World!" Icon and
the HelloWorld! Window Waiting for Its Final Keystroke

1.6 Creating a "Release" Version

The HelloProject executable created and discussed above was compiled and linked by Visual C++ in the "Debug" configuration which is the default setting for the "Configuration Manager". This means that the executable program produced in building a project is prepared to run in conjunction with the debug support that is part of Visual C++. This debug support can be very helpful in finding errors during program execution (Visual C++ "Help" provides considerable information on the debugging capabilities of the development environment, look for "Debugging in Visual Studio" and "MFC Debugging Techniques"). The Debug configuration is automatically selected by Visual C++ to make these tools available. However, the executable file created by a build in the Debug configuration has the disadvantage that it is often larger than necessary and somewhat more cumbersome and inefficient for your PC to load and execute. Depending on the complexity of your program, the Debug executable may not execute on a PC that does not contain all of the library files that are part of your Visual C++ installation.

A Release version of your program will be more compact and can run more reliably on a PC without an installation of Visual C++. To set the "Release" configuration, click on **Build > Configuration Manager** and then use the resulting window (Figure 1.13) to select the Release configuration rather than the Debug configuration for both the Solution and Project (recall that, in general, a Solution can contain more than one Project). In the Release configuration, building or rebuilding HelloProject will create a "Release" folder, which contains a "HelloProject.exe" file in Release form. Of course, this version of the HelloProject.exe can be executed directly from the folder *C:\HelloProject\Release*. It can also be placed on the desktop as before and can be more easily transported to other PCs (for the most portability, look for the use of Static Libraries under the project's Properties). The Release folder is expendable just like the Debug folder. You can delete the Release folder (along with HelloProject.exe). When a build or rebuild of the HelloProject is performed from within the Release configuration, Visual C++ will automatically reconstruct the Release folder including the executable.

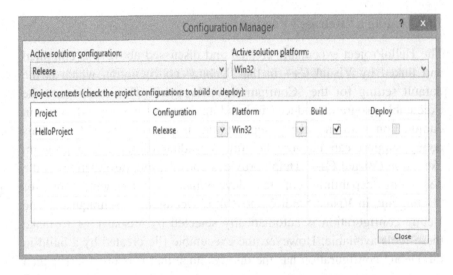

Figure 1.13 Setting the Active Project Configuration to "Release"

1.7 Exploring the "Media Pack" and Example Programs

The HelloProject described in the sections above is intended to guide you through an initial programming experience with Visual C++ and to help you become familiar with the development environment. In the next sequence of simple projects, we expand on the "Hello World" idea to carry out a review of several basic C/C++ programming concepts. In the next sections we will consider simple examples to illustrate: (1) the use of a while loop for repetitive operations, (2) the definition and use of a function within a program, and (3) the handling of keyboard inputs. However, instead of asking you to write your own code at each step, we have provided a full set of sample files for your use in the book's Companion Media Pack available for download from World Scientific's website. Instructions for downloading the Companion Media Pack are presented in detail in the Appendix.

Throughout this book, and at each stage of our discussion, we will use the sequence of example programs contained in the media pack to progress toward our programming goals. Having the example files available will relieve you of the need to enter every keystroke to study an example. Of course, we will explain all of the details needed to understand the examples and we will discuss the code on a line-by-line basis as necessary.

After you have downloaded the Companion Media Pack and reviewed the discussion in the Appendix, we suggest having a "working copy" of the sample projects readily available while studying and exploring the tutorial chapters. This should be separated from your more permanent copy of the sample projects which should be considered as a "master copy" ready for use in restoration when needed. Typically, the sample project files after downloading and extraction will be in "Read-only" form. Before using the project folders, you will need to remove the Read-only attribute. As an example, to remove the Read-only attribute for the sample projects of Chapter 1, right click on the folder *Chap1* in a Microsoft File Explorer display to expose an options menu and then click on **Properties**. In the resulting dialog, remove the check mark on the Read-only attribute and apply the change to the "folder, subfolders and files".

Figure 1.14 now focuses on the projects of Chapter 1 where our example project subfolders have all been located in a working folder titled "ExamplePrograms". The figure provides a view of the file structure of the book's sample projects. The File Explorer view to the left in Figure 1.14 shows the *Chap1* folder opened to a subfolder named *Printf*. In *Printf*, each of the example projects for Chapter 1 is shown in its own project folder. There are nine example projects in Chapter 1 and each project folder has been slightly renamed to add a number in front of the original project name. These numbers keep the projects in the proper sequence. For example, *1_Hello* is the first example project and it was originally developed with the name "Hello". This is the very first introductory project that we have previously discussed as "HelloProject". The second project named *2_HelloPlus* is the modification of the original HelloProject discussed in Section 1.5. This modification added the call to the function _getch() in order to hold "Hello World!" on the screen.

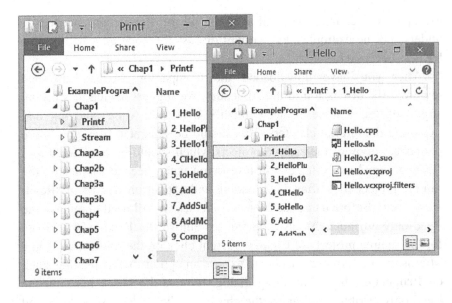

Figure 1.14 Folders for the Chapter 1 Example Files

We'll now continue to discuss the first set of examples in the folder labeled *Chap1*. The window on the left in Figure 1.14 shows that there are two subfolders *Printf* and *Stream* which contain two sets of projects for the Chapter 1 examples. The *Printf* folder contains the Chapter 1 example programs using the printf function for output. The *Stream* folder contains exactly the same Chapter 1 programs using the C++ iostream. The iostream projects have been provided for your reference here in Chapter 1. In the chapters to follow we will focus on projects using only the printf form since formatting for the output of text in Windows programming (beginning in Chapter 4) follows much the same pattern.

The series of example projects in printf form is shown by name in the window to the right in Figure 1.14. The folder *1_Hello* contains the project files for the simple Hello World program described in Section 1.1. You can view it and edit it from the Visual Studio development environment by double clicking on the Hello.sln file as it appears on the right in Figure 1.14. All of the necessary files for the HelloProject are included in the folder *1_Hello*, although the automatically replaceable .sdf file has been excluded. We have also removed the Debug folder. After clicking on the .sln file to enter Visual C++ the .sdf file is automatically regenerated. Then, if you build or rebuild the project with Visual C++, the Debug folder (or Release folder — depending on the active configuration selected) will be created along with the executable file Hello.exe.

The project folder *2_HelloPlus* is exactly the second form of the HelloProject described above in Section 1.5. It uses the _getch() function and the finished reading prompt to obtain a keystroke before ending the program and closing its window. If you have had any difficulty creating and executing either form of the HelloProject, you should review *1_Hello* and *2_HelloPlus* carefully before continuing. At this point, choose from the *Printf* or *Stream* folders depending on your preference. However, as we move toward graphics programming in Windows, you will find the printf output format to be useful. If you have not used it before, you will have more opportunity to become familiar with it in the next several sections.

1.7.1 The Hello10 program

The project in the *3_Hello10* folder is an extension of the Hello World program. It has been modified to write "Hello World" ten times using a "while" loop. The program code is shown in Table 1.1 with added line numbers for reference. Note, as mentioned, that we are using the printf output format. From our set of sample projects, you can access this code in the folder *Chap1\Printf\3_Hello10*. Double clicking on Hello10.sln in the folder will load the project into Visual C++. After Visual C++ starts, you can bring the source code shown in Table 1.1 into the Edit window by clicking on Hello10.cpp in the Solution Explorer window.

The program uses the integer variable inc (declared in line 06 and initialized to zero) for control of a while loop. As execution begins, the function _getch() in line 07 holds a blank screen until a keystroke is received. After a keystroke is received, the printf function at line 08 uses the control command "\a" to activate an "alarm" (you may want to turn

Table 1.1 Listing of Hello10.cpp

```
01        /* A Hello World example with multiple lines of output (Hello10)*/
02        #include <stdio.h>
03        #include <conio.h>
04        void main (void)
05        {
06            int inc = 0;
07            _getch();
08            printf("\a");
09            while  (inc < 10)
10            {
11                    printf ("\n  Hello World !  \n");
12                    inc++;
13            }
14            _getch();
15        }
```

your volume up, it's typically a small "beep"). The while loop (lines 09–13) then executes ten times (until inc = 10). Each time through it uses the printf function of line 11 to display Hello World and increments inc at line 12. After the loop is completed, a second _getch() at line 14 is used to hold the Hello World output lines on the screen until a final keystroke is received. Give it a try — build and execute Hello10 and compare its operation to the code. Edit and rebuild the program a few times, move the alarm to different locations or copy it to multiple locations, print Hello World 5 times (or 25 times) instead of 10.

1.7.2 Adding a clear screen function

In the folder *4_ClHello* we show a program which defines and uses a "function" to perform a screen clearing operation. Of course, functions are an important part of C/C++. They allow access to standard library resources and are the natural way to develop a section of program code that you may want to use at several points in your program or in several different programs. The purpose of this simple demonstration function is to clear the console window of previous interactions before proceeding to the next set of dialog. The code for this project is in the set of sample files in the folder *Chap1\Printf\4_ClHello*. You can double click on

ClHello.sln to load the project into Visual C++ and in the file ClHello.cpp you will find the coding in Table 1.2.

The "clear" function does not require any input and so its input argument list is shown as "(void)" in line 04. It also is not generating a return value and thus its overall declaration is "void clear (void)". This declaration takes place before the description of the "main" function beginning on line 05 so that the statement clear() within main() can be recognized. For convenience, we have placed the definition of the function clear at the end of main(). The function clear is re-declared at

Table 1.2 Listing of ClHello.cpp

```
01      /*A Hello World example with a screen clearing function*/
02      #include <stdio.h>
03      #include <conio.h>
04      void clear (void);
05      void main (void)
06      {
07              int inc = 0;
08              _getch();
09              printf ("\a");
10              while  (inc < 10)
11              {
12                      printf ("\n  Hello World !  \n");
13                      inc++;
14              }
15              printf ("\n\n\nStrike any key to clear...\n");
16              _getch();
17              printf ("\a");
18              clear();
19              printf ("Strike any key to end...\n");
20              _getch();
21      }
22      void clear (void)
23      {
24              int i = 0;
25              for (i; i < 25; i++)
26              {
27                      printf ("\n");
28              }
29      }
```

line 22 in Table 1.2 and its prototype or definition presents the function statements in lines 23–29. First, the integer i, declared and initialized as zero in line 24, is used as a counter for the "for" loop of lines 25–28. The printf statement on line 27 uses the "\n" command to produce a new line with each execution of the for loop. After 25 new lines, the console window is considered cleared and the function ends.

Now, looking through main() in Table 1.2, lines 07–14 will accept a keystroke, sound the alarm and use a while loop to print Hello World ten times just as in the Hello10 program. After that, line 15 displays a "Strike any key to clear..." prompt. After a keystroke, an alarm sounds and on line 18, the clear function is called to clear the screen followed by a "Strike any key to end..." prompt. Finally, line 20 waits for the closing keystroke.

1.7.3 Accepting input into the Hello example

This final example in the series of "Hello" programs can be found in the folder *Chap1\Printf\5_ioHello*. The program ioHello.cpp in Table 1.3 begins by writing ten lines of Hello World but then makes use of keyboard input to change the Hello message. The clear function of the previous section is used to remove old dialog. The first several lines of this program (up to line 14) are much the same as the ClHello program of the previous section. However, line 08 declares an array of character variables (i.e. a "character string") called cstring which is used

Table 1.3 Listing of ioHello.cpp

```
01      /*A Hello World example with keyboard input*/
02      #include <stdio.h>
03      #include <conio.h>
04      void clear(void);
05      void main (void)
06      {
07              int inc = 0;
08              char cstring[7];
09              _getch();
10              while  (inc < 10)
11                      {
```

Table 1.3 (*Continued*)

```
12                          printf ("\nHELLO WORLD ! \n");
13                          inc++;
14                  }
15                  printf ("\n\n\nCare to say \"HELLO\" to someone else? ");
16                  printf(" Strike any key...");
17                  _getch();
18                  clear();
19                  printf ("\nEnter a name (6 characters max)\n\n");
20                  scanf_s ("%6s", cstring,7);
21                  clear();
22                  printf("\a");
23                  for (inc = 0; inc < 10; inc++)
24                  {
25                          printf ("\nHELLO %6s ! \n", cstring);
26                  }
27                  printf ("\n\n\nStrike any key to end...\n");
28                  _getch();
29          }
30  void clear (void)
31  {
32          int i = 0;
33          for (i; i < 25; i++)
34          {
35                  printf ("\n");
36          }
37  }
```

in the program to handle input from the keyboard. At line 15, the prompt to change the Hello message is printed to the screen and at line 17 we are waiting for a keystroke. After a keystroke, line 18 clears the screen and then a prompt for a new name is shown. At line 20, the "scanf_s" function is to obtain the character string that we have called cstring. It uses a string format defined by %6s for the character array and a maximum input width of seven. After the new name has been entered into cstring from the keyboard, the screen is cleared (line 21), the alarm is sounded, and the new hello statement is printed ten times using a for loop (which starts by resetting the variable "inc" to zero). Here, the printf function is used in line 25 with a %6s format to output the cstring array. Finally, line 27 prompts for the keystroke to close the program. A typical final display for ioHello is shown in Figure 1.15.

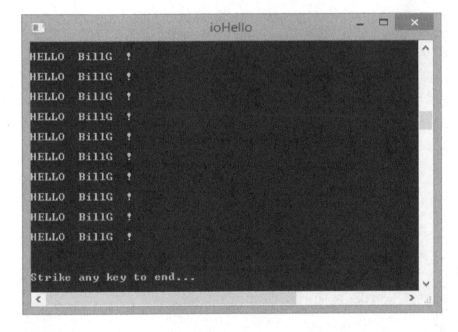

Figure 1.15 Hello to BillG from ioHello

1.8 Performing Simple Calculations

In the previous sections we have introduced the Visual C++ environment and we have begun writing console application programs in a series of "Hello World" examples. In this section, the next step is to provide a set of example programs for simple calculations that illustrate the use of numerical inputs and outputs and screen dialog for calculation purposes. Although we use only very simple arithmetic operations in the selected examples, it is easy to extend these ideas to more complicated calculations. Along with our other introductory examples, the set of simple calculation examples is in the folder *Chap1* which should now be located on your hard drive. Display the contents of the folder *Chap1\Printf\6_Add*. Then, by double clicking on Add.sln, Visual C++ will start with the Add project loaded.

1.8.1 Simply adding

The example program of *Chap1\Printf\6_Add* obtains two numbers by console input and adds them together. It then outputs the result to the screen. The Add.cpp program file is shown in Table 1.4. Operation of the program begins in main() at line 07 with the declaration of the floating point variables a and b (the numbers to be added) and then the variable c which will be the result of the summation. Line 09 prompts the user to input the first variable and line 10 uses the scanf_s function to obtain the keyboard input. The format is defined by %f to indicate that a floating point variable will be the input while the argument of & a for the scanf_s function actually defines the memory address where the variable "a" is located. The operator "&" can be read as "address of". With this information, scanf_s directly places the results of the keyboard input into the contents of "a". Incidentally, the input of "a" ends when the "enter" key is struck. If a decimal point has been included, it will be properly positioned in "a". If a decimal point has not been included, when the enter key is struck it will be positioned by default at the end of the

Table 1.4 Listing of Add.cpp

```
01      /*Calculation Example - Requests the input of two numbers
02      Adds them and outputs the sum*/
03      #include <stdio.h>
04      #include <conio.h>
05      void main(void)
06      {
07              float a,b;
08              float c;
09              printf ("\nEnter first number: ");
10              scanf_s ("%f",&a);
11              printf ("\nEnter second number: ");
12              scanf_s ("%f",&b);
13              c=a+b;
14              printf ("\nThe sum is: ");
15              printf (" %8.2f",c);
16              printf ("\n\n\nStrike any key to end...\n");
17              _getch();
18      }
```

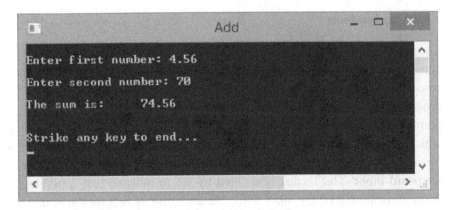

Figure 1.16 Results from the Add Program

input digits. Lines 11 and 12 similarly obtain the input of b from the keyboard. Lines 13–15 carry out the summation and then output c. The output format used for c is defined as %8.2f and provides a total of eight spaces for the output with 2 digits after the decimal point. The _getch() at line 17 waits for the closing keystroke. Figure 1.16 shows a typical output from the program Add.

1.8.2 Including an Add subroutine

For a calculation as simple as an addition, placing the calculation code directly in main() is convenient. However, for more complex calculations, this is usually not appropriate and an individual function to carry out the calculation is desired. This procedure allows a calculation to be placed at several points in a program without having to repeat the code. The program in the folder *Chap1\Printf\7_AddSub* and shown in Table 1.5 provides an example of using a function for a calculation and returning the result.

In this program, the function Sum is declared in line 04 where two floating point variables are specified as input arguments and a floating point result is also specified. The function Sum is defined in lines 19–24. The re-declaration in line 19 identifies Num1 and Num2 to be used as variable names within the function for the two floating point inputs.

Table 1.5 Listing of AddSub.cpp

```
01      /*Calculation Example - With a function to carry out the summation*/
02      #include <stdio.h>
03      #include <conio.h>
04      float Sum(float, float);
05      void main(void)
06      {
07              float a,b;
08              float c;
09              printf ("\nEnter first number: ");
10              scanf_s("%f",&a);
11              printf ("\nEnter second number: ");
12              scanf_s("%f",&b);
13              c = Sum (a,b);
14              printf ("\nThe sum is: ");
15              printf (" %8.2f",c);
16              printf ("\n\n\nStrike any key to end...\n");
17              _getch();
18      }
19      float Sum (float Num1, float Num2)
20      {
21              float Num3;
22              Num3 = Num1 + Num2;
23              return (Num3);
24      }
```

Num3 is declared in line 21 and calculated in line 22 by adding Num1 and Num2. It is specified as the return variable from Sum in line 23. The function main() here is very similar to main() in the Add example. It obtains the two inputs in lines 09–12. It then makes use of the function Sum in line 13 where c is set equal to the value returned by calling on the function Sum. In the same way, of course, functions can be used for calculations that are much more complicated than simple addition.

1.8.3 Running repeated additions

The AddSub project described in the previous section carries out only a single calculation. The project contained in the folder *Chap1\ Printf\8_AddMore* includes additional coding to allow multiple additions to be performed as desired by the user. As shown in Table 1.6 for the file

Table 1.6 Listing of AddMore.cpp

```
01    /*Calculation Example - Allows repeated summations*/
02    #include <stdio.h>
03    #include <conio.h>
04    void Addition (void);
05    void main(void)
06    {
07            char KeyStruck = 'y';
08            while (KeyStruck == 'y')
09            {
10                    Addition();
11                    printf ("\n\n\nAnother sum? (y or n) ");
12                    KeyStruck = _getche();
13            }
14    }
15    void Addition (void)
16    {
17            float a,b,c;
18            printf ("\n\nEnter first number: ");
19            scanf_s("%f",&a);
20            printf ("\nEnter second number: ");
21            scanf_s("%f",&b);
22            c=a+b;
23            printf ("\nThe sum is: %8.2", c);
24    }
```

AddMore.cpp, the function used for summing has been upgraded and is now called the Addition function. This function prompts for and accepts keyboard inputs, performs the summation, and then displays the result. By calling this function as needed, further additions can be performed when desired.

The Addition function is declared in line 04 without any input arguments and without a returned value. In the re-declaration and prototype of lines 15–24, it can be seen that the function is self-contained. Line 17 declares variables a, b and c. Lines 18–21 contain the prompts for input and use scanf_s to obtain the values of a and b from the keyboard. The addition of a and b then takes place to determine the sum as c which is printed to the screen with an appropriate label in line 23. The function main() manages the use of the Addition function. In main(), the character variable KeyStruck is declared and initialized as "y"

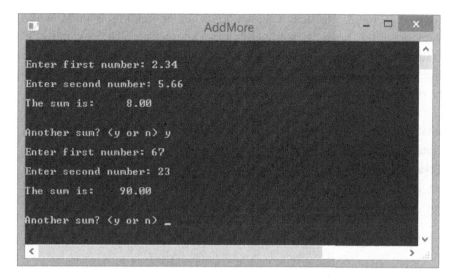

Figure 1.17 Execution of the AddMore Program

(for "yes", of course) in line 07. The while loop of lines 08–13 then executes as long as KeyStruck is equal to "y". The Addition function is called in line 10 to carry out a full summation. The prompt in line 11 asks the user if another addition is desired. Then line 12 obtains the response by setting the value of KeyStruck using a version of the "get character" function available in conio.h. The function _getche waits for a key stroke and then returns the "value" for the key. It also "echoes" the character by showing it on the screen. If the new value of KeyStruck is still "y", the while loop will execute again and perform another summation. If the updated KeyStruck is no longer "y", the while loop does not execute and the program terminates. Figure 1.17 shows two sample calculations performed with AddMore.

1.8.4 Compounding interest

The previous examples in this section have dealt with a simple adding program to review some of the basic principles of programming and interacting with the user. This last example is intended to present the somewhat more practical calculation of compounding interest while demonstrating another mode of user interaction. The example is contained in the folder *Chap1\Printf\9_Compound*. Double clicking on the file Compound.sln will bring the project into the Visual C++ environment. The program is shown below in Table 1.7.

The calculations performed in this example program are in double precision and accordingly, the variables Principal, NewPrincipal and Rate are declared as "double" in line 07. In lines 10–13, we define the Principal and Rate as $1000 and 7% respectively with EndYear set to 1 and the character variable KeyStroke set to "0". At the top of the program window, line 14 prints an opening message to strike

Table 1.7 Listing of Compound.cpp

```
01      /*Calculation Example - Based on a given principal and interest rate
02      Calculates new principals, entering "s" ends the program*/
03      #include <stdio.h>
04      #include <conio.h>
05      void main(void)
06      {
07              double Principal, NewPrincipal, Rate;
08              int EndYear;
09              char KeyStroke;
10              Principal = 1000.0;
11              Rate = 0.07;
12              EndYear = 1;
13              KeyStroke = '0';
14              printf ("Strike any key for one more year. Strike\"s\" to stop...\n\n\n\n");
15              printf (" Year   Starting Principal   Ending Principal\n\n\n");
16              while (KeyStroke != 's')
17              {
18                      NewPrincipal = (1.0 + Rate)*Principal;
19                      printf ("%4d       %8.2f          %8.2f \n\n",EndYear, Principal,
20                      NewPrincipal);
21                      Principal = NewPrincipal;
22                      EndYear++;
23                      KeyStroke = _getch();
24              }
25      }
```

any key to continue and to "Strike "s" to stop...". The next line prints column headings for the program output. Then the while loop of lines 16–24 executes. It calculates NewPrincipal and prints it along with the present values of EndYear and Principal in the carefully arranged format statement of lines 19 and 20 which line up the numbers and columns appropriately. Line 22 increments EndYear and line 23 waits for a keystroke. This time, the statement KeyStroke = _getch() is used to record the actual keystroke received (without echoing it) and the variable KeyStroke takes on that value. At the top of the while loop, KeyStroke is tested. If KeyStroke = s, the while loop will not execute and the program will terminate. Of course, striking any other key will allow the while loop to execute again to re-compute NewPrincipal and the other variables and display another line of output. Figure 1.18 shows the program output in the Compound window after several lines of calculations.

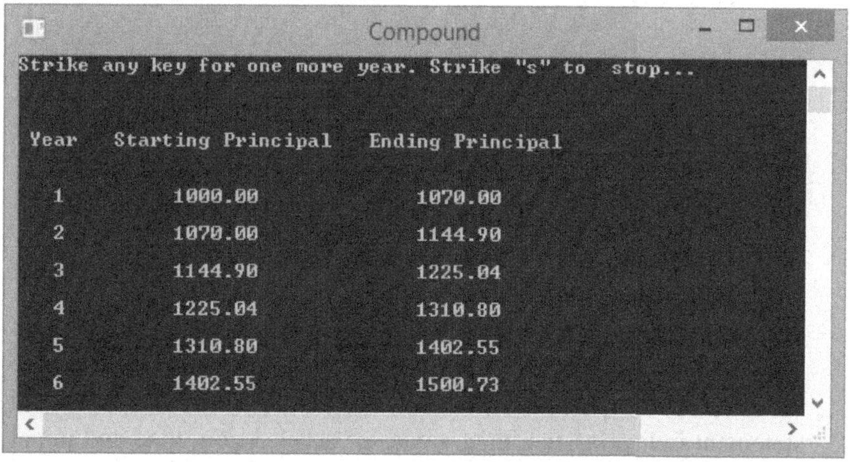

```
Compound                                      _  □  ✕

Strike any key for one more year. Strike "s" to  stop...


Year    Starting Principal    Ending Principal

  1          1000.00              1070.00

  2          1070.00              1144.90

  3          1144.90              1225.04

  4          1225.04              1310.80

  5          1310.80              1402.55

  6          1402.55              1500.73
```

Figure 1.18 Output from the Compound Program after Several Keystrokes

1.9 Exercises

1. The series of "HELLO" programs uses the screen clearing function clear() which executes printf("\n") in a "loop" 25 times. Write a similar function (perhaps named "Print10") to carry out the printing of "Hello World" ten times. Install your new function in Hello10, ClHello and ioHello. In each case replace the original lines of code in main() with a call to this function.

2. Modify the AddMore program of Section 1.8.3 to become a DivideMore program. Ask the user to input a number and its divisor. Then display the quotient. Ask the user if he/she would like to perform another division and repeat or terminate as appropriate.

3. Write a small program based on the simple physics problem of calculating the velocity of a body moving with a constant acceleration. The equation you will need is:

$$v = v_o + at$$

   where
$$a = \text{constant acceleration level}$$
$$t = \text{time of interest}$$
$$v_o = \text{initial velocity}$$
$$v = \text{velocity at time } t$$

   Using the model of the "Addition" programs, prompt the user for an input of initial velocity, a value of constant acceleration and the time of interest. Output the result by displaying a nicely formatted statement indicating the input values of acceleration, time and initial velocity along with the calculated velocity at time t. Be sure you use a set of consistent units. For example, meters/second for velocity and meters/second^2 for acceleration.

4. Modify the program of Exercise 3 above to calculate the position of a body moving from rest with constant acceleration. The new equation is:

$$p = p_o + \tfrac{1}{2}at^2$$

where

p_o = initial position
p = current position

Prompt the user for an input of initial position, a value of constant acceleration and the time of interest. Output the result by displaying a nicely formatted statement indicating the input values and the calculated position. Consistent units here could be meters for position and meters/second^2 for acceleration.

5. The program Compound of Section 1.8.4 has the initial account balance and percentage rate specified within the program.

(a) Modify Compound so that a user can input the initial balance and the interest rate before the year by year calculations begin. In this way, compounding with different initial balances and different interest rates can be explored.

(b) A further modification to consider is the adjustment of the program so that interest rate can be changed by the user each year before the annual calculation is completed and displayed. Notice that the format of "%lf" may be used to input variables of type double.

Chapter 2

Arrays, Pointers and Structures

The world of Windows programming with Visual C++ is fully imbedded in the object-oriented capability of the C++ programming language. In this chapter we will continue to use the console application format of Visual C++ to move further into PC programming and especially to prepare for the discussion of C++ classes and objects presented in Chapter 3. Along the way, we will quite naturally encounter additional features of the Visual C++ environment and we will discuss them as necessary.

Our discussion begins with the important concept of "arrays" for handling data. We will start with vectors as one-dimensional arrays and then matrices as two-dimensional arrays. The use of pointers is then discussed which allows access to arrays when data in array form is transferred between functions. "Structures" are introduced as practical tools for conveniently packaging data for storage and manipulation. We indicate that pointers can be used to manipulate structures and then we show how structures themselves can be manipulated as arrays. This leads very naturally to the object-oriented capability of C++ which is the subject of Chapter 3.

As in Chapter 1, the focus of our discussion is on concepts in C/C++ programming and not on detailed language issues. We present the basic concepts in a series of programming examples, which allow your skills to grow in a step-by-step fashion. In the examples, we show the important lines of code complete with line numbers and we explain the details of each of our example programs by discussing individual lines of code. This chapter continues to apply the console application format. When we get to Chapter 4, you'll begin to see programming in the Windows environment that you are familiar with as a PC user.

2.1 Working with a One-Dimensional Array

When handling significant amounts of data it is frequently necessary to group the data into a manageable form by using arrays. These arrays permit data clusters to be easily handled in a sequential manner, moving one step at a time through the array containing the data. The first of the examples for this chapter is found in the example folder *Chap2\1_VectorG* (only printf formatting is now being considered). In the VectorG project, clicking on VectorG.sln will bring the project into the Visual Studio environment. The file VectorG.cpp contains the code shown in Table 2.1. It defines and operates on a one-dimensional array of five values. As discussed below, the array is defined globally and as a "global array" it is directly available for use by any of the functions in the program file.

Line 04 in the code of Table 2.1 is the statement "float Vector [5]". This declares the floating point array named Vector and reserves space in memory for five values. Declaring the array before the declaration of the function main() makes the array called Vector a "global array". For the listing in Table 2.1, this means that the array Vector is available for use directly within main() and also from within the function named VecFunction which is declared on line 05 and described in prototype form in lines 23–32.

In main(), the program begins by assigning values to each entry in the array Vector. This assignment is done within the for loop of lines 10–14. The loop executes with the integer loop counter i incrementing from zero to four. In the loop, line 12 of the example simply sets each entry in the array to the current value of i so that Vector[0] = 0, Vector[1] = 1, Vector[2] = 2, etc. In C/C++ nomenclature, notice that the first entry in the array is entry number zero and not entry number one. Notice also that line 12 uses the "float" operator to appropriately convert the integer value of i to a floating point number (watch for compiler "warnings" if you neglect to do this). Line 09, before the for loop, prints a heading indicating that the initial values of the array Vector will be displayed. Then line 13, within the for loop, prints out the individual entries in the array Vector each time that the for loop executes.

Table 2. 1 Listing of VectorG.cpp

```
01   /*One-Dimensional Array Example*/
02   #include <stdio.h>
03   #include <conio.h>
04   float Vector [5];
05   void VecFunction (void);
06   void main (void)
07   {
08       int i;
09       printf("\nThese are the initial values of the array \"Vector\"");
10       for (i = 0; i < 5; i++)
11       {
12           Vector[i] = float(i);
13           printf( "\n %8.2f ", Vector[i] );
14       }
15       _getch();
16       VecFunction();
17       _getch();
18       printf ("\n\n\nBack in main now - here are final values for Vector");
19       for (i = 0; i < 5; i++)  { Vector[i] += 2; printf( " \n %8.2f ", Vector[i]); }
20       printf("\n");
21       _getch();
22   }
23   void VecFunction(void)
24   {
25       int i;
26       printf (" \n\nNow in VecFunction - here are new values for Vector ");
27       for (i = 0; i < 5; i++)
28       {
29           Vector[i] = Vector[i] + 2;
30           printf( " \n %8.2f ", Vector[i] );
31       }
32   }
```

At this point you should be sure to have copied the folder of example programs for Chapter 2 (called *Chap2*) to a convenient location on your hard drive. Load the VectorG project into Visual C++ by moving to *Chap2\1_VectorG* and double clicking on VectorG.sln. Use **Build > Rebuild Solution** to create an executable and then execute it. You should then see the initial values of the array Vector displayed in the program window as indicated in Figure 2.1.

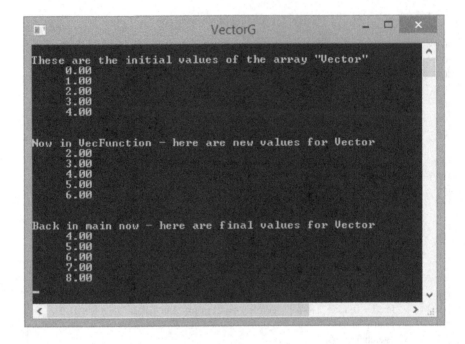

Figure 2.1 Output from the VectorG Program

The _getch() function on line 15 of Table 2.1 holds the initial Vector on the screen waiting for a key stroke. When a keystroke is received, the function VecFunction is called in line 16 and it manipulates the array Vector. VecFunction has access to Vector because it is a global array. In the for loop of lines 27–31, each entry in Vector is incremented by two and the new value is printed in line 30. After VecFunction executes, the call to the function _getch() on line 17 waits for a keystroke. After a keystroke is received, line 18 prints a header for the final output of Vector and the for loop compacted into line 19 increments each entry in Vector by two before printing it out. Figure 2.1 shows the full output of the VectorG program.

2.2 Using a Pointer for a One-Dimensional Array

In the VectorG example of the previous section, we worked with a simple one-dimensional array called Vector. By defining Vector as a global array, it was available to main() and also to the function named VecFunction in the project above. In C and C++ it is very common to use pointers to pass variable and array addresses between functions rather than to make global declarations. The use of pointers avoids the need for a global declaration and does not require additional memory to be used for variables or arrays. Using an "address" allows direct access to the original memory location. Compared to the global variable approach, pointers also make the contents of a variable or array available to a function without having to refer specifically by name to that array or variable within the function and a local name can be used conveniently.

2.2.1 The basic pointer concept

When a variable is declared in a program statement, a space in computer memory is reserved for it. The variable name itself refers to the value stored in that memory location. The address of the variable is represented by the variable name preceded by an ampersand (&). For example, the declaration statement "int i" reserves 32 bits (ones and zeros) in memory for "i" and the address of its location in memory can be represented as "&i". Variable types called "pointers" are provided to refer directly to memory addresses by name. Pointers are declared by using the name of the appropriate variable type followed by an asterisk. For example, int* PointerName1 declares a pointer called PointerName1 for an integer variable, float* PointerName2 declares a pointer for a floating point variable, double* PointerName3 declares a pointer for a double precision variable, etc. After a pointer has been declared with its variable name, that pointer name can be used to refer directly to an address in memory. Notice, however, that the "*" in these declarations can be used just after the variable type as we have done or just before the name of the pointer. For example, the statement int *PointerName is exactly equivalent to int* PointerName. Let's consider the following three statements:

```
int i;
int* intPointer;
intPointer = &i;
```

The first of these statements declares the integer variable called i, the second declares the integer pointer called intPointer and the last statement sets the value of intPointer to the address of i as it is positioned in memory. While writing program code, the value of i may, of course, always be represented by "i". But, after the sequence of statements above, the value of i may also be represented by "*intPointer" where the asterisk now preceding intPointer should be read as "contents of". In this way, intPointer refers to the memory location of i within the computer. And *intPointer gives direct access to the contents of intPointer, which is the value of i itself.

The example project *Chap2\2_SimpPointer* illustrates these ideas. You can see it in the listing of Table 2.2 and you can access it by double clicking on SimpPointer.sln in its project folder. In the code of Table 2.2, lines 06 and 07 declare i and intPointer, line 08 sets intPointer to the address of i, and line 09 sets i to 15 (just an arbitrary value for this

Table 2.2 Listing of the file SimpPointer.cpp

```
01   /*Basic Pointer Example*/
02   #include <stdio.h>
03   #include <conio.h>
04   void main(void)
05   {
06       int i;
07       int* intPointer;
08       intPointer = &i;
09       i = 15;
10       printf ("\n\n\nThis is the value of i:  %d\n\n", i);
11       printf ("This is the value of *intPointer:  %d \n\n", *intPointer);
12       printf ("This is the value of &i:  %p \n\n", &i);
13       printf ("This is the value of intPointer:  %p \n\n", intPointer);
14       printf ("\nStrike any key to end...\n");
15       _getch();
16   }
```

example). Then line 10 displays the value of i and line 11 displays the contents of intPointer, using the decimal integer format %d and referring to the contents as *intPointer. Of course, these results are the same. Line 12 displays the address of i and line 13 displays intPointer which, of course, also contains the address of i (notice the use of the pointer format %p to show memory location in hexadecimal format). The results from SimpPointer are shown in Figure 2.2. For any given execution of the program, the specific memory address for i will not typically be the same as shown here.

2.2.2 The pointer concept for a one-dimensional array

In Section 2.1 we worked with a simple one-dimensional array and in Section 2.2.1 we discussed the "pointer" concept. In this section we will bring the two ideas together and use a pointer to allow a function to have direct access to an array. Consider the statements below:

```
float Vector[5];
float* PtVector;
PtVector = Vector;
```

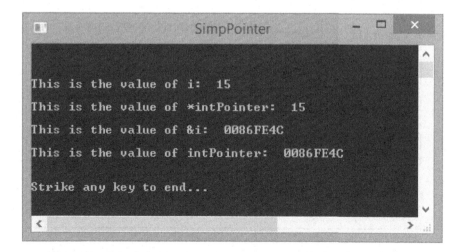

Figure 2.2 Display of Integer and Pointer Values from SimpPointer

The first of these statements declares the floating point array Vector[5]. The second declares a floating point pointer PtVector and the third statement sets PtVector to represent the starting address of the array. The use of the name of a one-dimensional array without subscript represents the address of the first entry in the array so that "Vector" is equivalent to "&Vector[0]". Figure 2.3 shows a representation of the array Vector[5] as it resides in memory. A cell is shown for each of the floating point entries in the array from Vector[0] to Vector[4]. The figure shows the pointer PtVector identifying the location of Vector[0] (where the value of PtVector is the address of Vector[0]). Incrementing PtVector to PtVector +1 automatically moves to the address of the next entry in the array, Vector[1]. This is shown in Figure 2.3 with increments in PtVector referring to the next entry in the array until PtVector + 4 corresponds to &Vector[4].

In reality, like all variables of type float, the entries in Vector[5] each occupy four bytes in memory (where a "byte" contains eight "bits", i.e. ones and zeros) with two bytes used for the number itself and two bytes

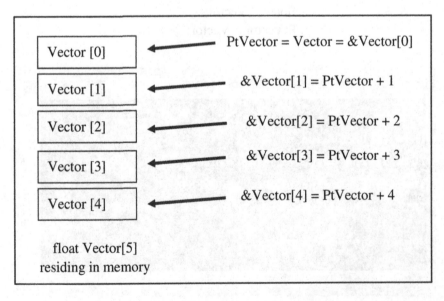

Figure 2.3 "Pointing" to Locations in Memory for Entries in the Array Vector[5]

used for its mantissa. One special feature of using pointers to specify addresses in memory is that incrementing a pointer will automatically move within memory from one variable in an array to the next. It is not necessary to worry about the byte-to-byte details. This is true regardless of the variable type (integer, float, double, etc.) as well for structures and objects which will be discussed shortly. This is also the reason why pointers are always declared in association with a particular type of variable, structure or object.

2.2.3 Using a pointer with a one-dimensional array

In Section 2.1 we worked with a simple one-dimensional array and in Section 2.2.2 we discussed the "pointer" concept for addressing the entries in an array. In this section we will bring the two ideas together in a simple program and use a pointer to allow a function to have direct access to an array. The program below is from the example project VecPointer that you can find in the folder *Chap2\3_VecPointer*. Double clicking on VecPointer.sln will make the file VecPointer.cpp available to you. The listing of the file is shown in Table 2.3. The VecPointer example performs the same operations as the VectorG example of Section 2.1. However, in this case, the array Vector is not declared globally. Instead, it is declared locally in main() and passed to the function now called PtVecFunction by use of a pointer to the array.

In looking through the listing of VecPointer.cpp in Table 2.3, we see that the floating point array Vector[5] is only declared locally in main() at line 08. Line 09 declares the floating point pointer PtVector. In line 10 the pointer PtVector is set to the address of the first entry in the array. In summary, after lines 08–10, the pointer PtVector contains the address of the array entry Vector[0].

The function PtVecFunction is initially declared at line 04 and is shown in prototype form in lines 25–35. It has been prepared to manipulate the one-dimensional array by having access to it through a pointer. The input argument "float*" shown for PtVecFunction in line 04 means that a floating point pointer is expected as an input to PtVecFunction. In the redeclaration of PtVecFunction in line 25, the pointer is given the variable name Ptr for use within the function. The for loop of lines 30–34 then manipulates the contents of the array Vector[5] in line 32 using Ptr. It addresses each entry using the expression *(Ptr + i) and adds two to its contents. In this expression, the "*" should be read as "contents of" according to the discussion of Section 2.2.1.

Table 2.3 Listing of VecPointer.cpp

```
01    /*Pointer Example for a One-Dimensional Array*/
02    #include <stdio.h>
03    #include <conio.h>
04    void PtVecFunction(float*);
05    void main(void)
06    {
07        int i;
08        float Vector[5];
09        float* PtVector;
10        PtVector = Vector;
11        printf("\nThese are the initial values in the array \"Vector\"");
12        for (i=0;i<5;i++)
13        {
14            Vector[i] = float(i);
15            printf("\n%8.2f",Vector[i]);
16        }
17        _getch();
18        PtVecFunction(PtVector);
19        _getch();
20        printf("\n\n\nBack in main now - here are final values for Vector");
21        for (i=0;i<5;i++){Vector[i] += 2;printf("\n%8.2f",Vector[i]);}
22        printf("\n");
23        _getch();
24    }
25    void PtVecFunction(float* Ptr)
26    {
27        int i;
28        printf("\n\n\nNow in PtVecFunction – Vector accessed by pointer.");
29        printf("\nThese are incremented values for Vector");
30        for (i=0;i<5;i++)
31        {
32            *(Ptr+i) = *(Ptr+i) + 2;
33            printf("\n%8.2f",*(Ptr+i));
34        }
35    }
```

The expression "Ptr + i" serves to move from one entry in the array to the next as i is incremented by the for loop. The next line in the for loop (line 33) prints out each array entry after it has been incremented.

Returning to main(), line 11 provides the header line for the output of the initial vector values. The for loop of lines 12–16 initializes the array Vector[5] and its initial values are printed at line 15. After a keystroke (line 17), the function PtVecFunction is called at line 18 and its argument passes the pointer PtVector to it. Of course, PtVecFunction then increments the entries of the array by two and displays the values. After another keystroke at line 19, each of the entries in Vector[5] are again incremented by two and Vector[5] is displayed a final time by lines 20–22.

The overall result is equivalent to the VectorG example of Section 2.1 and the program window after execution looks much the same as Figure 2.1. The important change in the VecPointer example from the VectorG example of Section 2.1 is that the array is now locally declared instead of globally. In this format, a pointer is then used to pass the array address to PtVecFunction.

2.2.4 A vector summing function with pointers

As a second example of the use of pointers for one-dimensional arrays, consider the VectorSum project located in *Chap2\4_VectorSum*. The file VectorSum.cpp is as shown in Table 2.4. This program adds the contents of two vectors (one-dimensional arrays) by passing pointer values to a function which actually performs the summation of the vectors. The function VectorSum is declared in line 04 of the code with an input argument list consisting of three double precision pointers to "float" variables. These are intended to provide access to three vectors. The first two of the vectors are to be added together and the third is the results vector. Lines 07–09 of main() contain the local declarations and initializations of Vector1[5], Vector2[5] and SumVector[5]. Line 07 takes advantage of the C/C++ capability to initialize an array during its declaration and sets the five Vector1 entries to 0, 1, 2, 3, and 4 respectively. Lines 08 and 09 then use C/C++ syntax which initializes the full contents of the Vector2 and SumVector arrays to zero.

Table 2.4 Listing of VectorSum.cpp

```
01    /*An Example Passing Pointers to a Vector Summing Function*/
02    #include <stdio.h>
03    #include <conio.h>
04    void VectorSum(double*, double*, double*);
05    void main(void)
06    {
07        double Vector1 [5] = {0, 1, 2, 3, 4};
08        double Vector2 [5] = {0};
09        double SumVector [5] = {0};
10        int i;
11        printf("\nThese are the initial values of Vector1 and Vector2");
12        for (i=0;i<5;i++)
13        {
14            Vector2[i] = 2. * double(i);
15            printf("\n%8.2f %8.2f",Vector1[i], Vector2[i]);
16        }
17        VectorSum(Vector1, Vector2, SumVector);
18        _getch();
19        printf("\n\n\nBack from the VectorSum function - this is the sum\n");
20        for (i=0;i<5;i++)
21        {
22            printf("%8.2f\n", SumVector[i]);
23        }
24        _getch();
25    }
26    void VectorSum(double* Ptr1, double* Ptr2, double* Ptr3)
27    {
28        int i;
29        for (i=0;i<5;i++)
30        {
31            *(Ptr3+i) = *(Ptr2+i) + *(Ptr1+i);
32        }
33    }
```

The initialization of vectors as above is often good practice since, without initializing the array values, the array contents begin with completely arbitrary values. The entries in Vector2 are set to new values in the for loop of lines 12–16 and the values for Vector1 and Vector2 are displayed by line 15. Line 17 calls the function VectorSum to

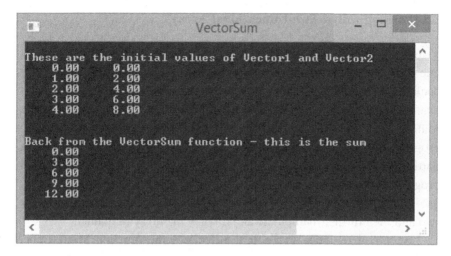

Figure 2.4 Final Display for VectorSum

perform the addition and the array names Vector1, Vector2 and SumVector are the arguments passed to the function. These array names serve as pointers to the first entry in each of the arrays. The function VectorSum is defined in lines 26–33 of Table 2.4. The redeclaration of the function identifies Ptr1, Ptr2 and Ptr3 as names to be used within the function for the pointers to the three vectors (in this case, the original Vector1, Vector2 and SumVector respectively). The for loop of lines 29–32 carries out the vector addition for each of the five vector entries. Line 31 uses pointer notation to move through the vectors starting at Ptr1, Ptr2 and Ptr3 and as i increments from 0 to 4 each of the summations is performed. In each case, use of the pointer Ptr3 allows the initial values of SumVector to be replaced by the summation results. Finally, after the keystroke required by line 18, the summation results are displayed by the for loop in lines 20–23 of main(). This outputs each entry in SumVector so that the final display of the program VectorSum appears as in Figure 2.4.

2.3 Working with a Two-Dimensional Array[a]

Two-dimensional arrays are somewhat more complicated to handle than one-dimensional arrays. We will begin by considering a globally declared two-dimensional array to review matrix manipulations. This example program is in the folder *Chap2\5_MatrixG* and the listing of the MatrixG.cpp file appears in Table 2.5. As with most of our example programs up to this point, this example is not designed to serve a particularly useful purpose but it is designed to illustrate a useful programming concept. In this case, we initialize a two-dimensional array, use a specially defined function to multiply each entry in the array by two and then further manipulate and display the array in main().

Line 04 of the code in Table 2.5 declares the function MatrixFunc. Line 05 declares the floating point two-dimensional array aMatrix[3][2]. This is a global declaration since it takes place before the declaration of main(). MatrixFunc is intended to access the global array directly and thus "void" appears for its input arguments and output. In main(), lines 10–17 contain a nested pair of for loops which set the initial values of the array entries. Specifically, line 13 sets the value of each entry to the sum of its row and column number and then line 14 displays the value. After the inner for loop, line 16 provides a fresh line at the end of each row. Following a keystroke at line 18, the function MatrixFunc is called in line 19. It is described in lines 32–44. MatrixFunc operates on aMatrix in the nested for loops of lines 36–43, with line 39 explicitly doubling each entry in the global array. Line 40 then outputs the entry's value. After returning to main() and following a keystroke, lines 22–29 repeat the doubling process and display the resulting aMatrix. Figure 2.5 shows the window for MatrixG after execution.

---

[a]This discussion of two-dimensional arrays is presented here for completeness. After Sections 2.3 and 2.4, we do not use two-dimensional arrays for programming applications again until Chapter 9. You may want to postpone reading of these sections until then.

Table 2.5 Listing of MatrixG.cpp

```
01    /*An Example with a Global Matrix*/
02    #include <stdio.h>
03    #include <conio.h>
04    void MatrixFunc(void);
05    float aMatrix[3][2];
06    void main(void)
07    {
08        int i,j;
09        printf("\nThe initial set of values in aMatrix - (i+j):\n");
10    for (i=0;i<3;i++) {
11        for(j=0;j<2;j++)
12            {
13            aMatrix[i][j] = float(i) + float(j);
14            printf("%8.2f ", aMatrix[i][j]);
15            }
16        printf("\n");
17        }
18        _getch();
19        MatrixFunc();
20        _getch();
21        printf("\n\n\nReturning to \"main\", aMatrix is doubled again:\n");
22    for (i=0;i<3;i++) {
23        for (j=0;j<2;j++)
24            {
25            aMatrix[i][j] = 2 * aMatrix[i][j];
26            printf("%8.2f ",aMatrix[i][j]);
27            }
28        printf("\n");
29        }
30        _getch();
31    }
32    void MatrixFunc(void)
33    {
34        int i,j;
35        printf("\n\n\nFrom MatrixFunc with aMatrix doubled :\n");
36    for (i=0;i<3;i++) {
37        for(j=0;j<2;j++)
38            {
39            aMatrix[i][j] = 2 * aMatrix[i][j];
40            printf("%8.2f ",aMatrix[i][j]);
41            }
42        printf("\n");
43        }
44    }
```

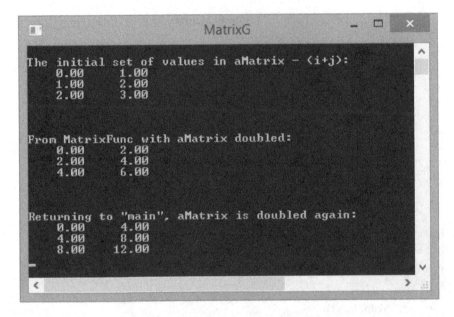

Figure 2.5 Output Window for MatrixG

2.4 Pointing to a Two-Dimensional Array

The first step in using pointers to pass and manipulate two-dimensional arrays is to visualize the two-dimensional array stretched out row-by-row into a one-dimensional array the way it appears in memory. This is shown in Figure 2.6 where the array aMatrix[3][2] is shown on the left similar to the way it would be stored in computer memory. In this case, the first two entries are the first row of the array, the next two entries are the second row and finally the last two entries are the third row. A pointer to this array will define the address of the first entry in the array and incrementing from this pointer value will move down through the array, in effect moving across each row of the two-dimensional array before moving down to the next row. In Figure 2.6 we use MatrixPntr to point to the array. Setting it equal to aMatrix[0] defines the pointer to be the address of the first entry in the first row of the matrix. This could also

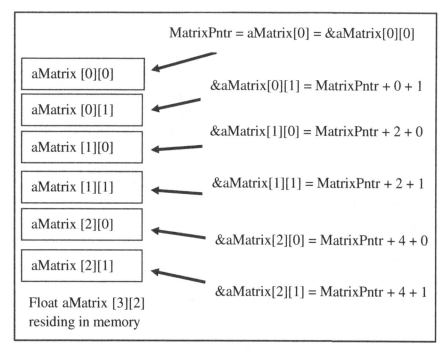

MatrixPntr = aMatrix[0] = &aMatrix[0][0]

aMatrix [0][0]

&aMatrix[0][1] = MatrixPntr + 0 + 1

aMatrix [0][1]

&aMatrix[1][0] = MatrixPntr + 2 + 0

aMatrix [1][0]

aMatrix [1][1]   &aMatrix[1][1] = MatrixPntr + 2 + 1

aMatrix [2][0]

&aMatrix[2][0] = MatrixPntr + 4 + 0

aMatrix [2][1]

&aMatrix[2][1] = MatrixPntr + 4 + 1

Float aMatrix [3][2]
residing in memory

Figure 2.6 "Pointing" to Locations in Memory for the Array aMatrix[3][2]

be specified equivalently by setting MatrixPntr to &aMatrix[0][0]. On the right side of Figure 2.6 are the pointers to each of the entries in aMatrix. Notice that the addresses can be defined conveniently by:

$$\&aMatrix[i][j] = MatrixPntr + NumCols*i + j$$

Here NumCols is the number of columns with the value of NumCols = 2 for Figure 2.6.

2.4.1 A matrix pointer program

The example found in *Chap2\6_MatPointer* uses pointers for addressing a two-dimensional array. It performs the same matrix manipulations as the MatrixG project of Section 2.3 but follows a pointer approach corresponding to Figure 2.6. The MatPointer.cpp file is listed below in Table 2.6. Notice that the function MatPointerFunc is declared in line 04 with a floating point pointer as its argument and that the two-dimensional array aMatrix[3][2] is now declared as a local array in main() at line 08. At line 09, the floating point pointer MatrixPntr is declared. And at line 10 it is assigned the address of the first entry of the array aMatrix. The nested for loops of lines 12–19 then define and display the initial values of the aMatrix entries as the sum of row and column position.

Line 21 invokes the function MatPointerFunc supplying MatrixPntr as its argument so that it can access aMatrix. The function MatPointerFunc is re-declared and prototyped in lines 34–46. As indicated in line 34, the pointer is called Ptr within the function. The nested for loops of lines 38–45 double the values of the array entries and print out the new values. Line 41 has been carefully arranged to make use of the pointer format and to have the row indicator i and the column indicator j refer to the correct array entry. The "*" should still be

Table 2.6 Listing of MatPointer.cpp

```
01    /*Pointer Example for a Two-Dimensional Array*/
02    #include <stdio.h>
03    #include <conio.h>
04    void MatPointerFunc (float*);
05    void main(void)
06    {
07        int i,j;
08        float aMatrix[3][2];
09        float* MatrixPntr;
10        MatrixPntr = aMatrix[0];
11        printf("\nThe initial set of values in aMatrix - (i+j):\n");
12    for (i=0;i<3;i++) {
13        for(j=0;j<2;j++)
14            {
15            aMatrix[i][j]=float(i) + float(j);
16            printf("%8.2f ", aMatrix[i][j]);
17            }
18        printf("\n");
19        }
20        _getch();
21        MatPointerFunc(MatrixPntr);
```

Table 2.6 (*Continued*)

```
22       _getch();
23       printf("\n\n\nReturning to \"main\", aMatrix is doubled again:\n");
24   for (i=0;i<3;i++) {
25       for (j=0;j<2;j++)
26           {
27               aMatrix[i][j]*=2;
28               printf("%8.2f ",aMatrix[i][j]);
29           }
30       printf("\n");
31   }
32   _getch();
33   }
34   void MatPointerFunc(float* Ptr)
35   {
36       int i,j;
37       printf("\n\n\nFrom MatrixFunc with aMatrix doubled:\n");
38   for (i=0;i<3;i++) {
39       for(j=0;j<2;j++)
40           {
41               *(Ptr + 2*i + j) = *(Ptr + 2*i + j) * 2;
42               printf("%8.2f ",*(Ptr + 2*i + j));
43           }
44       printf("\n");
45       }
46   }
```

read here as "contents of" but in line 41 it is also used to perform a multiplication by two. After execution of the function, lines 24–31 in main() again double the entries in the array and print them out. Of course, since MatPointerFunc was working directly with the aMatrix array by using pointers, its changed values are still present upon return to main() and the new doubling in line 27 reflects those values. When you compile and run the MatPointer project, you will find that the display window for MatPointer is essentially identical to Figure 2.5 for the MatrixG program.

2.4.2 Matrix multiplication with pointers

Our final example for arrays and pointers carries out the multiplication of a matrix times a vector using pointers. This mathematical operation is often used in computer graphics programs. If we consider the vector as a one-dimensional array with m rows, it can be multiplied by a matrix with n rows and m columns. The resulting product vector will be a vector with n rows. Multiplying the n x m matrix aMatrix times the vector aVector with m rows yields a product vector called bVector with each of its n entries defined as:

$$bVector[i] = \sum_{j=1}^{m} aMatrix[i][j] \times aVector[j]$$

In our example of *Chap2\7_Multiply* a 4x4 matrix is multiplied times a 4x1 vector. With a click on Multiply.sln, you can bring it into Visual C++. Build it and execute it to see its operation. The matrix-vector multiplication that it performs is often used in three-dimensional graphics operations including the rotation and translation of objects.

The file Multiply.cpp is shown in Table 2.7. The matrix multiplying function MatrixMult is declared in line 04 with three double precision floating point pointers as arguments. In main(), from lines 08–10,

Table 2.7 Listing of Multiply.cpp

```
01    /*A Matrix Multiplication Example Using Pointers*/
02    #include <stdio.h>
03    #include <conio.h>
04    void MatrixMult (double*, double*, double*);
05    void main(void)
06    {
07        int i,j;
08        double aMatrix[4][4];
09        double aVector[4];
10        double bVector[4];
11        printf("\nThe initial set of values in aMatrix \n");
12    for (i=0;i<4;i++) {
13        for(j=0;j<4;j++)
14            {
15            aMatrix[i][j]=1. + double(i);
16            printf("%8.2f ", aMatrix[i][j]);
17            }
18        printf("\n");
19        }
20        printf("\nThese are the values for aVector");
```

Table 2.7 (*Continued*)

```
21    for (i=0;i<4;i++)
22        {
23            aVector[i] = 1. + double(i);
24            printf("\n%8.2f",aVector[i]);
25        }
26        printf("\n");
27        MatrixMult (aMatrix[0], aVector, bVector);
28        _getch();
29        printf("\nThese are the multiplication results in bVector");
30    for (i=0;i<4;i++)
31        {
32            printf("\n%8.2f",bVector[i]);
33        }
34        printf("\n");
35        _getch();
36    }
37    void MatrixMult(double* MPtr, double* aVecPtr, double* bVecPtr)
38    {
39        int i,j;
40        double RunSum;
41    for (i=0;i<4;i++) {
42        RunSum = 0;
43        for(j=0;j<4;j++)
44            {
45            RunSum = RunSum + (*(MPtr + 4*i + j))*(*(aVecPtr + j));
46            }
47        *(bVecPtr+i) = RunSum;
48        }
49    }
```

aMatrix[4][4], aVector[4], and bVector[4] are all declared as double precision local variables. We want to multiply aVector by aMatrix using the equation above to obtain the product called bVector.

Lines 12–19 contain the nested for loops which set initial values for the aMatrix entries with values of one plus the row number. The output statement of line 16 displays each of the aMatrix values with line 18 creating a new line for each matrix row. Lines 21–25 similarly set initial values for the aVector and display them. Line 27 calls the MatrixMult function and supplies aMatrix[0] as the matrix pointer along with the names aVector and bVector which serve as pointers to the two

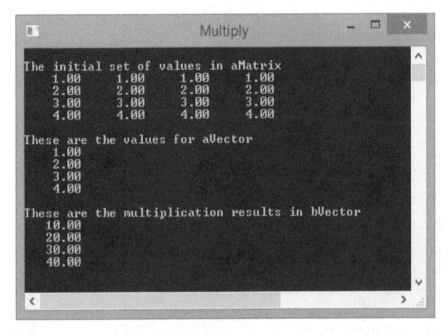

Figure 2.7 Output Window for Multiply

vectors. The results of the multiplication are loaded into bVector by MatrixMult during the calculations. This can be seen in the prototype of MatrixMult shown in lines 37–49. In line 37, MPtr is declared as the matrix pointer, and aVecPtr and bVecPtr are declared as the vector pointers for use in the function. The double precision variable RunSum is set to zero in line 42 and serves as a running summation variable while the nested for loops of lines 41–48 carry out the multiplication. Line 45 is critical and creates the running sum for each row using pointers to the entries in the matrix and vector. Line 47 then uses the pointer to the bVector to store each result value from RunSum. Before another running sum is made, RunSum is reset to zero in line 42. After MatrixMult has executed and a keystroke is received, main() outputs the resulting product in bVector using the for loop of lines 30–33. The final display window after the matrix multiplication is shown in Figure 2.7.

2.5 Structures

It is very common in programming applications for data to occur in natural combinations which describe items of interest for computation. This is true for the widest range of applications ranging from bank accounts (where a person's name, balance, and interest rate might form a natural data combination), to pixel color (where red, green and blue proportions are natural data), to primitive shapes (where dimensions, material density and volume are typical data). In order to be able to handle clusters of data, the C/C++ language provides the ability to form and manipulate data structures. A data structure can be declared in a program by defining the variables or "structure members" which form the structure, including the names and data types of the variables. Any valid C++ data type can be used as a structure member including arrays and other structures. For the bank account example, mentioned above, a declaration of the structure type BankAccount might appear as:

```
struct BankAccount
{
char PersonName[20];
int AccountNumber;
double Balance;
double InterestRate;
}
```

In this case, the type of structure is BankAccount and the structure members are the character string for the name, the integer variable for account number, and the double precision variables for balance and interest rate.

This capability of declaring data structures was originally included in the C language and continues to be used in C++ with only modest modification. The very important notion of "objects" and object-oriented programming is a direct outgrowth of the data structure concept. We will discuss objects in more detail in Chapter 3 after we have become familiar with the idea of forming and manipulating packages of data using the structure concept. The sections below present a series of "struct" examples starting with simple addition and then moving on to deal with pointers for structures and arrays of structures.

2.5.1 A first example of a data structure

We begin looking at data structures with the programming example shown in *Chap2\8_StructOne*. In this example we deal with a group of numbers which are to be added together and we use a simple data structure to describe them within the structure type AddData. The structure type AddData is then used in a function prepared to add the numbers it contains. The listing in Table 2.8 below is from the file StructOne.cpp in the StructOne project. Lines 04–07 declare the structure type AddData containing the three double precision variables called Add1, Add2 and Add3. Notice that the syntax for the struct declaration includes the name of the structure followed by curly brackets that enclose the declarations of the variables that are the structure members.

Table 2.8 Listing of StructOne.cpp

```
01    /*Use of the structure AddData*/
02    #include <stdio.h>
03    #include <conio.h>
04    struct AddData
05    {
06        double Add1, Add2, Add3;
07    };
08    double Sum(struct AddData);
09    void main(void)
10    {
11        double Total;
12        struct AddData Set1;
13        Set1.Add1 = 1.;
14        Set1.Add2 = 2.;
15        Set1.Add3 = 3.;
16        printf ("These are the numbers initialized in \"main\":");
17        printf ("\n%8.2f %8.2f %8.2f", Set1.Add1, Set1.Add2, Set1.Add3);
18        _getch();
```

Table 2.8 (*Continued*)

```
19      Total = Sum (Set1);
20      _getch();
21      printf ("\n\nThis is the result of the summation:");
22      printf ("\n%8.2f\n", Total);
23      _getch();
24    }
25    double Sum(struct AddData Numbers)
26    {
27      double Result;
28      printf ("\n\nThese are the numbers added in the function \"Sum\":");
29      printf ("\n%8.2f %8.2f %8.2f ", Numbers.Add1, Numbers.Add2,
30              Numbers.Add3);
31      Result = Numbers.Add1 + Numbers.Add2 + Numbers.Add3;
32      return (Result);
33    }
```

Line 08 declares the function Sum which is designed to add the set of three variables together. The input argument for Sum is shown as the structure type AddData and the returned variable from Sum, after a summation is performed, is of type double. We will discuss Sum shortly. Line 12 declares Set1 as the name of a structure of type AddData. Also notice that lines 13–15 set initial values for each of the three variables which are the structure members of Set1. The syntax used to address one of the variables in the structure is to use the name of the structure followed by a dot or period (referred to as the "member access operator") and then the name of the structure member. Line 14, for example, is setting the Add2 variable in Set1 to two. Line 17 of the program above displays the initialized values of the Set1 variables. In the printf statement of line 17, each variable is referred to by the structure name followed by a period and then the name of the structure member. Line 19 passes Set1 on to the function Sum and the returned value becomes the Total, which is finally displayed in line 22.

Looking now at the function prototype of Sum, we see in line 25 that the AddData structure passed into Sum is given the local name Numbers. Lines 29 and 30 display Add1, Add2 and Add3 again by using the syntax: structure name, period, variable name. The summation is performed in line 31 and, of course, Result is returned in line 32. Figure 2.8 shows the display of the StructOne window after execution.

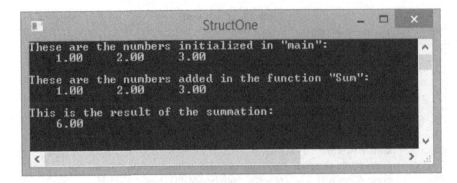

Figure 2.8 Display Window for StructOne

2.5.2 Further exploring the structure AddData

The StructOne example in the previous section introduced the data structure concept and used a simple structure called AddData to carry out a summation operation. This section continues the theme and works with the StructTwo project available in the folder *Chap2\9_StructTwo*. The StructTwo.cpp file is shown in Table 2.9. It begins again by declaring the

Table 2.9 Listing of StructTwo.cpp

```
01    /*A Second Example with the Structure AddData*/
02    #include <stdio.h>
03    #include <conio.h>
04    struct AddData
05    {
06        double Add1, Add2, Add3;
07    };
08    double Sum(AddData);
09    void main(void)
10    {
11        double Total;
12        AddData Set1, Set2;
13        Set1.Add1 = 1.;
14        Set1.Add2 = 2.;
15        Set1.Add3 = 3.;
16        printf ("This is the first set of numbers initialized in \"main\":");
```

Table 2.9 (*Continued*)

```
17        printf ("\n%8.2f %8.2f %8.2f", Set1.Add1, Set1.Add2, Set1.Add3);
18        _getch();
19        Total = Sum (Set1);
20        printf ("\n\nThis is the result of the first summation:");
21        printf ("\n%8.2f\n", Total);
22        _getch();
23        Set2 = Set1;
24        Set2.Add1*=2;
25        Set2.Add2*=2;
26        Set2.Add3*=2;
27        printf ("\nThese are the Set2 numbers from \"main\":");
28        printf ("\n%8.2f %8.2f %8.2f", Set2.Add1, Set2.Add2, Set2.Add3);
29        _getch();
30        Total = Sum (Set2);
31        printf ("\n\nThis is the result of the Set2 summation:");
32        printf ("\n%8.2f\n", Total);
33        _getch();
34    }
35    double Sum(AddData Numbers)
36    {
37        double Result;
38        Result = Numbers.Add1 + Numbers.Add2 + Numbers.Add3;
39        return(Result);
40    }
```

structure of type AddData in lines 04–07. In line 08 we see the new declaration of the function Sum. Here we take advantage of the C++ capability to reference a data structure without using the "struct" prefix once the structure has been declared.

The input argument for Sum in line 08 now appears only as "AddData". Also, in main() at line 12 Set1 and Set2 are declared as structures of type AddData. As in line 08, we are again able to dispense with the struct prefix in this statement. Lines 13–21 initialize Set1, carry out the summation and display the result. Line 23 takes advantage of the ability to equate two data structures of the same type. In this case, the individual Set2 variables are all set equal to their corresponding Set1 values by line 23. Afterward, the Set2 values can still be addressed and manipulated separately as we see in lines 24–26 where each of the values is multiplied by two. The Set2 variables are displayed in line 28.

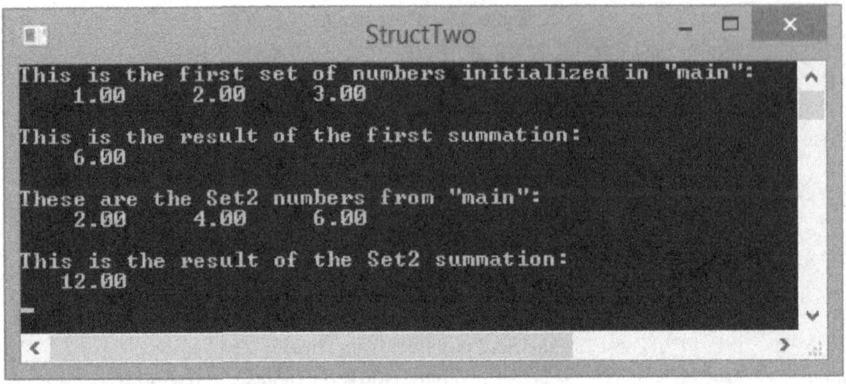

Figure 2.9 Final Display from StructTwo

A summation is performed by passing Set2 on to the function Sum in line 30 and then the Total is displayed by line 32. The resulting final display is shown in Figure 2.9.

2.5.3 Pointing to a structure

Pointers can be used to represent the memory locations of structures in much the same way as they are used for variables and arrays. Once a pointer has been defined for a particular structure, each variable which is a structure member can be addressed by using the pointer name in conjunction with the variable name. This is illustrated in the listing of StructPointer.cpp in Table 2.10 from the folder *Chap2\10_StructPointer*. The first indication of the use of a pointer in this listing is at line 08 where the function Sum is declared with the argument AddData*. This means that, in its revised form, Sum is expecting to receive a pointer input providing the address of the particular AddData structure on which it should operate. At line 12 in main(), the AddData structure Set1 is declared and the AddData pointer PtrSet1 is declared on line 13. Line 14 assigns PtrSet1 to represent the memory location of Set1 (denoted as &Set1).

Lines 15–19 assign values to the variables of Set1 and display them. Line 21 passes the pointer PtrSet1 into the function Sum to give access to Set1 (incidentally, the notation &Set1 could have been used directly in calling Sum since &Set1 can also serve as a pointer). Looking now at the Sum prototype in lines 27–35, we can see in the re-declaration

Table 2.10 Listing of StructPointer.cpp

```
01    /*Using a Pointer to Refer to a Structure*/
02    #include <stdio.h>
03    #include <conio.h>
04    struct AddData
05    {
06        double Add1, Add2, Add3;
07    };
08    double Sum(AddData*);
09    void main(void)
10    {
11        double Total;
12        AddData Set1;
13        AddData* PtrSet1;
14        PtrSet1 = &Set1;
15        Set1.Add1 = 2.;
16        Set1.Add2 = 4.;
17        Set1.Add3 = 6.;
18        printf ("These are the numbers initialized in \"main\":");
19        printf ("\n%8.2f %8.2f %8.2f", Set1.Add1, Set1.Add2, Set1.Add3);
20        _getch();
21        Total = Sum (PtrSet1);
22        _getch();
23        printf ("\n\nThis is the result of the summation:");
24        printf ("\n%8.2f\n", Total);
25        _getch();
26    }
27    double Sum(AddData* aPointer)
28    {
29        double Result;
30        printf ("\n\nThese are accessed by pointer in the function \"Sum\":");
31        printf ("\n%8.2f %8.2f %8.2f ", aPointer->Add1, aPointer->Add2,
32                aPointer->Add3);
33        Result = aPointer->Add1 + aPointer->Add2 + aPointer->Add3;
34        return(Result);
35    }
```

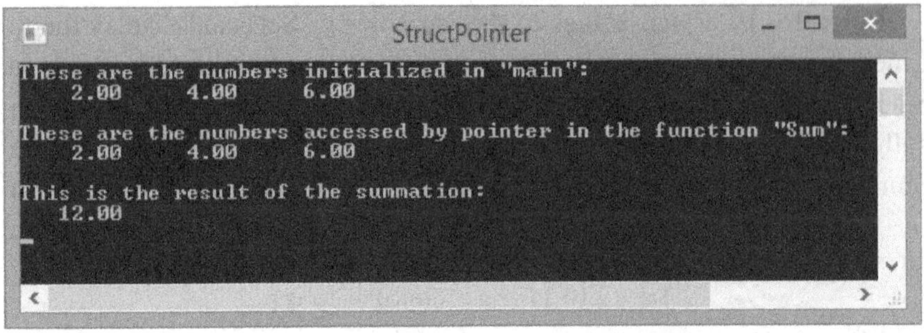

Figure 2.10 StructPointer Results

of line 27 that the pointer argument received by the function is given the name aPointer to be used within the function. Each of the variables within the data structure can be addressed by using an expression with the name of the pointer and an "arrow" (formed by a minus sign and a greater than sign) followed by the name of the variable of interest. For example, aPointer->Add1 refers to the first variable of the structure. This notation is used directly in lines 31 and 32 where the variable values are displayed and in line 33 where the summation takes place. It should also be mentioned that the form *aPointer.Add1 would be an equivalent use of the pointer format that is seen less commonly than the arrow format. After returning from the Sum function, the program concludes by displaying the summation result in line 24. The output displayed by StructPointer is shown in Figure 2.10.

2.5.4 An array of structures

The use of the data structure concept can be extended to develop arrays of data structures. This means that once a structure type has been established (as for "AddData" in the previous sections) it is possible to declare an array corresponding to a particular structure type. The example StructArray can be found in the folder *Chap2\11_StructArray*.

This example illustrates the process of developing and using a data structure array. Table 2.11 contains the file StructArray.cpp. It extends our discussion of the data structure type AddData by first incorporating the "Total" into AddData and then showing how an array of AddData structures can capture a series of summation data and results. Lines 04–08 declare the modified structure AddData including the three numbers to be added as well as the resulting Total. Line 09 then declares the Sum function without a return value and with a pointer to AddData as its input argument. Line 12 in main() declares Set[4] as an array of structures of type AddData. Then lines 14–17 assign values to each of the variables in Set[0] including an initial value of zero for Total.

The for loop in lines 18–31 manipulates the full Set array. Lines 22–25 within the for loop assign values for Set[1], Set[2] and Set[3] based on the initial values used for Set[0] (notice that each set of values is successively doubled). The remainder of the for loop then calculates the sums for each of the data sets and displays the results. Line 27 calls the

Table 2.11 Listing of StructArray.cpp

```
01    /*Forming an Array of the AddData Structures*/
02    #include <stdio.h>
03    #include <conio.h>
04    struct AddData
05    {
06         double Add1, Add2, Add3;
07         double Total;
08    };
09    void Sum (AddData*);
10    void main(void)
11    {
12         AddData Set[4];
13         int i;
14         Set[0].Add1 = 1.;
15         Set[0].Add2 = 2.;
16         Set[0].Add3 = 3.;
17         Set[0].Total = 0;
18    for (i = 0; i < 4; i++)
19         {
20         if (i>0)
21             {
```

Table 2.11 (*Continued*)

```
22              Set[i] = Set[i-1];
23              Set[i].Add1 = Set[i].Add1*=2;
24              Set[i].Add2 = Set[i].Add2*=2;
25              Set[i].Add3 = Set[i].Add3*=2;
26              }
27          Sum (&Set[i]);
28          printf ("\n\nFor data Set[%d],", i);
29          printf (" the resulting sum is:%8.2f\n",Set [i].Total);
30          _getch();
31          }
32      }
33      void Sum(AddData* aPointer)
34      {
35          printf ("\nThese are the numbers added in the function \"Sum\":");
36          printf ("\n%8.2f %8.2f %8.2f ", aPointer->Add1, aPointer-> Add2,
37                      aPointer->Add3);
38          aPointer->Total=aPointer->Add1+aPointer->Add2+aPointer->Add3;
39      }
```

function Sum and passes the pointer for an AddData structure to it so that the summation can be carried out for that structure and a value can be determined for Total. Looking at the prototype of the function Sum in lines 33–39, note that the local name for the AddData pointer within the function is aPointer (as indicated in line 33).

The values of the Add1, Add2 and Add3 variables are displayed in lines 36 and 37 by using the "arrow" notation. Then the summation to obtain Total takes place at line 38, again with the arrow notation. There is no return statement needed in the function because the summation result is retained in Total, which has now been included as a member of the structure AddData. Lines 28 and 29, back in the for loop after the call to Sum, display a label appropriate for Set[i] and also display the result of the summation with the notation Set[i].Total. Line 30 requires that keystrokes be entered at each cycle of the for loop to move through the data sets. Figure 2.11 shows the final display from the StructArray program.

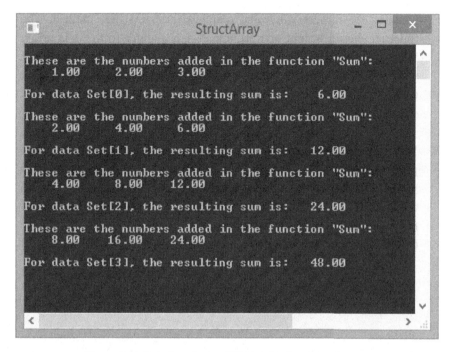

These are the numbers added in the function "Sum":
   1.00   2.00   3.00

For data Set[0], the resulting sum is: 6.00

These are the numbers added in the function "Sum":
   2.00   4.00   6.00

For data Set[1], the resulting sum is: 12.00

These are the numbers added in the function "Sum":
   4.00   8.00   12.00

For data Set[2], the resulting sum is: 24.00

These are the numbers added in the function "Sum":
   8.00   16.00   24.00

For data Set[3], the resulting sum is: 48.00

Figure 2.11 Complete Output Window for StructArray

2.6 Exercises

1. Write a program that uses a function to multiply a constant value times a 1-D array of five values. The initial entries in the vector array should be equal to twice the value of their array position i. The program should allow the user to input the value of the constant from the keyboard. Your function should accept two arguments, the value of the constant and a pointer to the array. In the function, each array value should be replaced by its new value after the multiplication. As output from main(), display the array before multiplication, the input value of the constant and the resulting array after multiplication.

2. In this program, you should allow the user to input five values from the keyboard which are read into the 1-D array Value[5]. Create a function that will sort the values in this array so that Value[0]

contains the largest value and Value[4] contains the smallest. The function should accept one argument — a pointer to the 1-D array. When the function concludes, it should replace the original array values with the ordered values. Display the values in the array after it is entered by the user. Display the array again after it has been put in order by the function.

3. Write a program which uses a function to perform the scalar or "dot" product of two 4x1 vectors. The function arguments should be pointers to each of the two vector arrays. The function should return the scalar product. Initialize the vector values as they are declared in main(). Display the two vectors and display the results of the calculation in neatly labeled form. The scalar product S of vectors V1 and V2 is given by:

$$S = \sum_{i=0}^{3} V1[i] \times V2[i]$$

4. Write a program that creates a 4x4 matrix and allows you to input a 4x1 vector. Your program should use a function to multiply the matrix times the vector and pass the result back to the main() function. Print out the input vector, the matrix and the output vector. Use only "pointers" for passing the matrix and vectors between functions.

5. Write a program to multiply a row vector times a matrix. The matrix should be 4x4 with entries equal to twice the product of the row i and column j values. You should be able to input the entries into the 1x4 row vector from the keyboard. Your program should use a function to multiply the row vector times the matrix and pass the result back to main(). After the calculation, display the input row vector, the matrix and the resulting output row vector. Use only "pointers" for passing the matrix and row vectors between functions.

Chapter 3

Introducing Classes and Objects

The most significant difference between C and C++ is the inclusion of classes and objects as part of the language. Since this object-oriented capability is an "increment" in capability from the original "C" programming language, the name "C++" was a natural name (at least in the minds of programmers) to indicate that the new language was an "increment of C".

The use of classes is a direct extension of the concept of data structures, as introduced in Section 2.5. However, in addition to providing convenient organization of data in the same manner as allowed by a structure declaration, classes offer the possibility of creating specialized functions called "member functions" or "methods" to handle the data. While this may seem to be a relatively modest extension, it actually creates a philosophical shift in the nature of computer programming. With an object-oriented philosophy, the emphasis in programming takes a step away from developing the intricacies of programming logic. Instead, the emphasis moves toward understanding the nature of the application data and the development of the organization and the functional tools to manipulate it. With this object-oriented approach, you will see that the function main() in a completed C++ program almost contains a specialized language developed for the application at hand.

3.1 A First Example of C++ Classes

As a first example of classes, let's consider the file Rectangles.cpp from the project found in the folder *Chap3\1_Rectangles*. This "Rectangles" project was initially created as an "empty" project and the Rectangles.cpp file was added to it as a "new item". The code shown in Table 3.1 was then inserted into the Rectangles.cpp file. This follows exactly the spirit of our process originally used for creating the Hello Project back in Chapter 1, Section 1.3.

In Table 3.1, the general structure of a class declaration is illustrated in lines 04–19 where we define the class called "CRectangles". The purpose of this class is to handle data describing simple rectangular shapes. Line 07 in the code declares the variables m_length and m_width which may be referred to as "data members", as "instance variables", or also as "member variables". The term "member variables" is quite commonly used in Windows programming and we will use it here. In general, the member variables are intended to define the nature of the objects which can be described by the class. In the case of this rectangles class, the member variables m_length and m_width provide a sufficient description for the purpose of our example program. They, of course, represent the length and width of a rectangle. The conventions of starting the class name with a "C" and using an "m_" as a prefix for member variables is a common practice which immediately identifies class names and member variables in a program code. This convention can be helpful in dealing with large programs. We will follow it in this chapter and throughout most of this book.

Lines 09–18 declare the "member functions" for the CRectangles class as being CRectangles, ShowSpecs and ShowArea. These are also referred to as "methods", but mostly in other object-oriented languages. We will use the term "functions" in our discussion throughout this book. The prototype for each of these member functions is also included in Table 3.1. These member functions have been specifically designed for the class. The first member function, CRectangles in lines 09–11, is referred to as a "constructor function". Every class must have a function with the same name as the class. Nominally, this function serves to construct the object[a], that is, to define the values for the object's member

---

[a] Correspondingly a "destructor function" serves to destroy objects so that they may be removed from memory when desired. A destructor function for our CRectangles class would be given the name ~CRectangles.

variables based on the argument values it receives. Lines 10 and 11, of course, are defining the rectangle member variables. However, the constructor function need not actually specify any of the member variable values and may, in fact, not have any input arguments at all. In this case it would be called an "empty" constructor function. The other member functions for the CRectangles class are declared and defined in lines 12–18. These functions are intended to perform specific operations related to the class and typically make use of the member variables. For

Table 3.1 Listing of Rectangles.cpp

```
01   /* This is the file Rectangles.cpp */
02   #include <stdio.h>
03   #include <conio.h>
04   class CRectangles
05   {
06       private:
07       double m_length, m_width;
08       public:
09       CRectangles (double l, double w) {
10       m_length = l;
11       m_width = w;                    }
12       void ShowSpecs(void) {
13       printf("\n\n\n This Rectangle has length = %8.2f", m_length);
14       printf("\n and width = %8.2f\n", m_width);               }
15       void ShowArea(void) {
16       double area;
17       area = m_length*m_width;
18       printf("\n Rectangle Area = %8.2f \n",area);               }
19   };
20   void main (void)
21   {
22       double length = 300;
23       double width = 150;
24       CRectangles Rectang1 (length, width);
25       CRectangles Rectang2 (length/2, width/2);
26       Rectang1.ShowSpecs();
27       Rectang1.ShowArea();
28       _getch();
29       Rectang2.ShowSpecs();
30       Rectang2.ShowArea();
31       _getch();
32   }
```

example, the ShowSpecs function simply displays the length and width of a rectangle. The ShowArea function carries out a calculation using the member variables and displays the rectangle area.

The terms "private" on line 06 and "public" on line 08 refer to the accessibility of the member variables and/or member functions. Public member variables or member functions are accessible from any point in a program. Private variables or functions are not accessible from outside the class. A "protected" status may also be declared which does not allow general access but does permit access from derived classes (a bit more on this in Section 3.5). The private status is the default status and is automatically in effect if a status declaration is not made.

In the constructor function CRectangles, of lines 09–11, the two double precision input variables are given the local names "l" and "w" in the argument list. Then, in lines 10 and 11 of Table 3.1, these variables are directly used to set the values of the two member variables m_length and m_width for the rectangle object being defined. ShowSpecs and ShowArea are member functions designed to work on objects of the CRectangles class and use member variable values to carry out calculations and operations on objects of the CRectangles class. The ShowSpecs function defined in lines 12–14 has access to the CRectangles member variables because it is a member function of the class. It simply displays the values of the m_length and m_width variables with appropriate labels. The ShowArea function of lines 15–18 uses the member variables m_length and m_width to calculate and then display the rectangle area. Notice that each of the functions is defined within its own set of brackets and that the overall CRectangles class is declared within brackets (at line 05 and line 19) followed by a semicolon (line 19).

The function main() for the rectangles program is shown in lines 20–32 of Table 3.1. It declares and sets particular values for variables of length and width as 300 and 150 respectively in lines 22 and 23. Lines 24 and 25 use C++ syntax to declare two different rectangle objects by calling the CRectangles constructor function using the object name and the desired argument values. Line 24 defines the object Rectang1 as having dimensions 300 by 150. Line 25 defines the object Rectang2 as being 150 by 75. Lines 26 and 27 activate member functions for the

Rectang1 object using the name of the object, the "member access operator" (which is a period) and then the name of the function. In line 26 the function ShowSpecs is called and uses the member variables for Rectang1 to display its specifications. Similarly, line 27 calls the function ShowArea to calculate and display the area of Rectang1. After a keystroke (line 28), lines 29 and 30 apply the same member functions to Rectang2. The display resulting after full execution of the Rectangles program is shown in Figure 3.1.

3.2 Variations on the Rectangles Program

The project in the folder *Chap3\2_RectanglesEC* contains a version of the rectangles program with a few significant variations. As you look over the file RectanglesEC.cpp shown in Table 3.2, the first thing that you should notice is that the class declaration is made in lines 04 to 13 without immediately including function prototypes. This is a common way to define classes particularly for more complicated programs. In this form, the nature of the class and its various functions can be seen compactly in the class declaration. Then, following the class

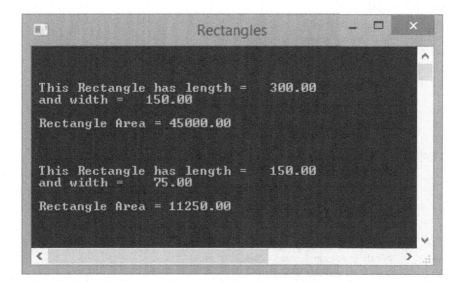

Figure 3.1 Display of the Rectangles Window after Execution

declaration, the function prototypes are presented. In this case, the prototypes are in lines 14–28. Notice that this format uses both the class name and the function name for the re-declaration of the functions at the beginning of each prototype. The class name is used with a double colon between it and the function name as can be seen on lines 14, 15, 18, 21 and 25 of Table 3.2.

This program also introduces the notion of the empty constructor function. With the empty constructor shown in line 14, no input arguments are required, the constructor function itself does not contain any actions and the member variables for the class are not initialized. In this program the constructor is declared in line 08 without arguments and is prototyped in line 14 where nothing appears between the two curly

Table 3.2 Listing of RectanglesEC.cpp

```
01    /* This is the file RectanglesEC.cpp */
02    #include <stdio.h>
03    #include <conio.h>
04    class CRectangles
05    {
06         double m_length, m_width;
07         public:
08         CRectangles(void);
09         void DefineRectangle (double,double);
10         void ShowSpecs(void);
11         void ShowArea(void);
12         void ShowPerim(void);
13    };
14    CRectangles::CRectangles(){}
15    void CRectangles::DefineRectangle (double l, double w)  {
16    m_length = l;
17    m_width = w;                            }
18    void CRectangles::ShowSpecs()  {
19    printf("\n\n\n This Rectangle has length = %8.2f", m_length);
20    printf("\n and width = %8.2f\n", m_width);              }
21    void CRectangles::ShowArea()  {
22    double area;
23    area = m_length*m_width;
24    printf("\n Rectangle Area = %8.2f \n",area);           }
25    void CRectangles::ShowPerim()  {
26    double perim;
```

Table 3.2 (*Continued*)

```
27        perim = 2*m_length+2*m_width;
28        printf(" Rectangle Perimeter = %8.2f \n",perim);  }
29   void main (void)
30   {
31        CRectangles Rectang1;
32        CRectangles Rectang2;
33        double length = 300;
34        double width = 150;
35        Rectang1.DefineRectangle (length, width);
36        Rectang2.DefineRectangle (length/2, width/2);
37        Rectang1.ShowSpecs();
38        Rectang1.ShowArea();
39        Rectang1.ShowPerim();
40        _getch();
41        Rectang2.ShowSpecs();
42        Rectang2.ShowArea();
43        Rectang2.ShowPerim();
44        _getch();
45   }
```

brackets that normally enclose the function statements (clearly it's "empty"). The empty constructor function is convenient because its use permits objects to be declared in a simple line of code and without arguments in the same way that ordinary variables are declared. It is possible to use multiple constructor functions in an "overloaded" form. With this approach, the same function name may be used with different argument lists. When a function call is made, the appropriate function form is chosen based on the argument list used in the function call. For clarity, we will not be using overloaded functions in our example programs.

Table 3.2 shows the use of the function DefineRectangle to serve as an unofficial constructor function and to define our rectangle objects as they are needed in the rest of the program. The DefineRectangle function is declared on line 09 and prototyped in lines 15–17 where it simply sets the member variables m_length and m_width to the values of the input arguments, just like the original constructor function in the previous example.

The operation of the program RectanglesEC can be seen in main() on lines 29–45 of Table 3.2. The declarations of Rectang1 and Rectang2 now appear just like variable declarations in lines 31 and 32. In lines 35 and 36 these objects are specifically defined by using the DefineRectangle function. The rest of the program displays the specifications for each rectangle, the area and also the perimeter. The new function called ShowPerim has been declared in line 12. It is prototyped in lines 25–28 and calculates and displays rectangle perimeters. It is applied in lines 39 and 43 of main(). Notice that the declaration of the member variables at line 06 makes use of the default private status for data members and does not specifically define their status. Finally, note that all of the member functions have been declared as public. Since we have planned to access each of these functions from main(), this can only be done if they are public.

As you enter the folder *Chap3\2_RectanglesEC* and build and execute this project, you should expect the results to appear very much as in Figure 3.1 with the addition of the perimeter information.

3.3 Using Separate Files

In developing larger programs it is common to use separate files to provide a modular organization of the program code. One way of facilitating this with C++ classes is to move the class declarations and member function prototypes to a separate file. To illustrate this, we take our current rectangles example program and rearrange it to have separate files. This new arrangement is now contained in the folder *Chap3\3_RectanglesSF*, where the header file RectanglesSF.h has been used for the class CRectangles. Header files such as this may be created within a Visual C++ project by clicking on **File > Add New Item**. When the Add New Item window appears (similar to Figure 1.5), "Visual C++" should be highlighted on the left side of the window and "Header File (.h)" on the right side. The desired file name (in this case, RectanglesSF) may then be entered without an extension (since ".h" is assumed) followed by clicking on the Add button. The Add New Item window then closes, and space for the new file appears in the Edit window of Visual Studio so text can then be typed into the file (or cut and pasted).

Table 3.3 Listing of RectanglesSF.h

```
01   /* This is the header file RectanglesSF.h */
02   #include <stdio.h>
03   #include <conio.h>
04   class CRectangles
05   {
06       double m_length, m_width;
07       public:
08       CRectangles(){}
09       DefineRectangle (double l, double w)  {
10       m_length = l;
11       m_width = w;                         }
12       ShowSpecs()  {
13       printf("\n\n\n\n This Rectangle has length = %8.2f", m_length);
14       printf("\n and width = %8.2f\n", m_width);              }
15       ShowArea()  {
16       double area;
17       area = m_length*m_width;
18       printf("\n Rectangle Area = %8.2f \n",area);            }
19       ShowPerim()  {
20       double perim;
21       perim = 2*m_length+2*m_width;
22       printf(" Rectangle Perimeter = %8.2f \n",perim);        }
23   };
```

Our RectanglesSF.h file is shown in Table 3.3. Notice that it begins with the "includes" for stdio.h and conio.h at lines 02 and 03. The full class declaration including function prototypes is then made in lines 04–23. The final bracket and the concluding semicolon for the class declaration are on line 23.

The program file RectanglesSF.cpp is shown in Table 3.4 and now contains only the most significant program code using primarily the member functions of the Rectangles class. Note that it begins with an "include" statement at line 02 to associate the header file with the program file. The function main() is then contained within lines 03–17 and is very much the same as main() in Section 3.2 above.

We'll now use this RectanglesSF project to consider a few features of the Visual C++ development environment for exploring and

Table 3.4 Listing of RectanglesSF.cpp

```
01    /* This is the program file RectanglesSF.cpp*/
02    #include "RectanglesSF.h"
03    void main (void)
04    {
05        double l = 30;
06        double w = 15;
07        CRectangles Rectang1, Rectang2;
08        Rectang1.DefineRectangle (l,w);
09        Rectang2.DefineRectangle (l/2,w/2);
10        Rectang1.ShowSpecs();
11        Rectang1.ShowArea();
12        Rectang1.ShowPerim();
13        Rectang2.ShowSpecs();
14        Rectang2.ShowArea();
15        Rectang2.ShowPerim();
16        _getch();
17    }
```

manipulating project coding. Load the project contained in *Chap3\3_RectanglesSF* into Visual C++ by double clicking on the file RectanglesSF.sln. After it is loaded, click on the Solution Explorer tab or **View > Solution Explorer** to place the Solution Explorer in the workspace area. You should see a folder symbol with the label "RectanglesSF" and a ">" symbol in front of it. Clicking on the ">" allows you to see the available files, including source files, header files and resource files. You should also see ">" symbols on the folders. Clicking on each of the ">" symbols exposes a label for the RectanglesSF.cpp file under Source and RectanglesSF.h under Header. No files will be found under Resource for this program. Files under "External Dependencies" have been automatically included by the development environment. For each of files shown, double clicking on a specific file label will bring the individual file into the Edit window ready for viewing and editing. The Solution Explorer window is shown to the left of Figure 3.2 in undocked form.

If you now click on the "Class View" tab or **View > Class View** you will find the Class View window in the workspace area. You should see

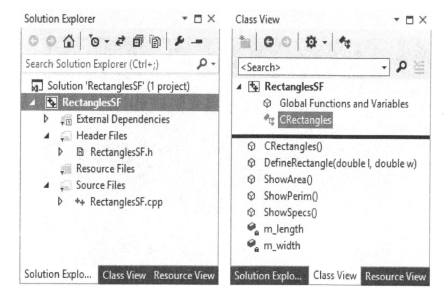

Figure 3.2 Solution Explorer and ClassView Windows for RectanglesSF

a "RectanglesSF" label as well as the standard label for "Global Functions and Variables" — click on that label to see what appears. Now, if you click on the label for CRectangles you should see all of the class members, both member variables and member functions appear in the lower portion of the Class View window as you can see on the right of Figure 3.2. Notice that "lock symbols" appear on the private member variables to indicate their status. Also note that double clicking on any of the member functions or variables will move the cursor in the Edit window to the line of code displaying the declaration of the data member or the definition of the member function that you clicked. If necessary, a change of file will also be made in the Edit window to bring up the appropriate program line. Clicking on member functions and variables in the Class View window provides a very convenient tool to view and edit code in more complex projects.

When you build and execute RectanglesSF, the resulting display window should appear as in Figure 3.3.

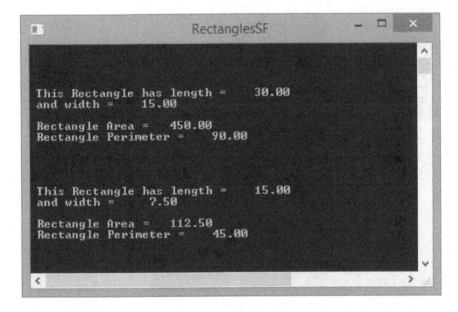

Figure 3.3 The RectanglesSF Display after Execution

3.3.1 Another arrangement with separate files

The project RectanglesSF discussed above showed the use of a header file to help organize an object-oriented program by separating class definitions and member functions from the file containing the program's function main(). The project contained in *Chap3\4_RectanglesSF2* takes this idea one step further. Instead of using two files, three are used. The file RectanglesSF2.h contains the declaration of the class Rectangles without the member function prototypes. The function prototypes are described in Functions.cpp and only the function main() appears in the file RectanglesSF2.cpp.

Figure 3.4 shows the files contained in the RectanglesSF2 project. Notice that the files RectanglesSF2.h, Functions.cpp, and RectanglesSF2.cpp now appear in the project folder. Also note that the .sdf is clearly the largest and recall that it can be deleted if file space is

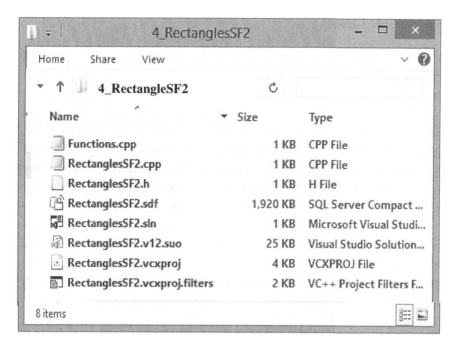

Figure 3.4 Files in the Project RectanglesSF2

an issue. It will be recreated when the project is opened again by Visual Studio. Of course, to explore the individual project files on your own, click on the RectanglesSF2.sln file to bring the project into the Visual Studio environment. Use the Solution Explorer window to look at the individual files. Use the Class View window to move through the class members — both the member functions and variables. Notice that right clicking on the member functions in Class View allows you to move either to the function declaration or the function definition. After you have compiled and executed this program, you should find that it operates much the same as the RectanglesSF program described above and that it has an output window nearly identical to Figure 3.3.

3.4 Multiple Classes

It is very natural to develop programs that include a large number of classes especially in Windows applications. This next example is a first step toward understanding projects with multiple classes. You will find it in the folder *Chap3\5_TwoDobjects* and you can bring it into Visual Studio by clicking on the solution file TwoDobjects.sln. It contains the project TwoDobjects with two independent classes for two different types of geometric objects. The classes here are defined independently and are used independently. The listing in Table 3.5 is for the header file TwoDobjects.h which contains the declarations for the two classes — our original rectangles class called CRectangles and an additional class for circles called CCircles. CRectangles is declared in lines 04–12. The new CCircles class is declared in lines 13–21. It has only one data member, m_diameter which is private by default. It also has member

Table 3.5 Listing of TwoDobjects.h

```
01    /* This is the file TwoDobjects.h */
02    #include <stdio.h>
03    #include <conio.h>
04    class CRectangles
05    {
06         double m_length, m_width;
07         public:
08         CRectangles (double l, double w);
09         void ShowSpecs();
10         void ShowArea();
11         void ShowPerim();
12    };
13    class CCircles
14    {
15         double m_diameter;
16         public:
17         CCircles (double d);
18         void ShowSpecs();
19         void ShowArea();
20         void ShowPerim();
21    };
```

Table 3.6 Listing of Functions.cpp

```
01    /* This is the file Functions.cpp */
02    #include "TwoDobjects.h"
03        CRectangles::CRectangles (double l, double w) {
04        m_length = l;
05        m_width = w;                        }
06        void CRectangles::ShowSpecs() {
07        printf("\n\n This Rectangle has length = %8.2f", m_length);
08        printf("\n and width = %8.2f\n", m_width);                        }
09        void CRectangles::ShowArea() {
10        double area;
11        area = m_length*m_width;
12        printf(" Rectangle Area = %8.2f \n",area);                        }
13        void CRectangles::ShowPerim() {
14        double perim;
15        perim = 2*m_length+2*m_width;
16        printf(" Rectangle Perimeter = %8.2f \n",perim);                        }
17        CCircles::CCircles (double d) {
18        m_diameter = d;                        }
19        void CCircles::ShowSpecs() {
20        printf("\n\n This Circle has diameter = %8.2f \n",m_diameter);                        }
21        void CCircles::ShowArea() {
22        double area;
23        area = 3.14158*(m_diameter*m_diameter)/4.;
24        printf(" Circle Area = %8.2f \n",area);                        }
25        void CCircles::ShowPerim() {
26        double perim;
27        perim = 3.14158*m_diameter;
28        printf(" Circle Circumference = %8.2f \n",perim);                        }
```

functions to display the object specifications (line 18), and to calculate and display area (line 19) and perimeter (line 20). Although these member functions may have the same names as the functions for CRectangles, they are clearly different functions. You can see this easily in the function prototypes for CRectangles and CCircles shown in the file Functions.cpp (Table 3.6).

The Functions.cpp file for the TwoDobjects project contains the CRectangles constructor function (lines 03–05) as we have seen it previously in Section 3.1. The other member functions in lines 06–16 for CRectangles are also in the same form that we have seen earlier. The

Table 3.7 Listing of TwoDobjects.cpp

```
01    /* This is the file TwoDobjects.cpp */
02    #include "TwoDobjects.h"
03    void main (void)
04    {
05        double l = 300;
06        double w = 150;
07        double d = 200;
08        CRectangles Rectang1 (l,w);
09        Rectang1.ShowSpecs();
10        Rectang1.ShowArea();
11        Rectang1.ShowPerim();
12        CCircles Circ1 (d);
13        Circ1.ShowSpecs();
14        Circ1.ShowArea();
15        Circ1.ShowPerim();
16        _getch();
17    }
```

CCircles member functions are intended to handle the circle geometry. The CCircle constructor in lines 17 and 18 simply sets the m_diameter value to the input argument d. The CCircles::ShowSpecs function in lines 19 and 20 outputs the circle's diameter. The ShowArea function of lines 21–24 calculates the area and displays it. The ShowPerim function of lines 25–28 computes the circumference and displays it. Notice that the function prototypes in the file of Table 3.6 each use the class name in re-declaring the function so that each of the functions is uniquely identified.

The file TwoDobjects.cpp containing main() is in the TwoDobjects project folder and is shown in Table 3.7. An include statement for the header file appears at line 02. The remainder of the file contains the function main() which primarily consists of calls to the CRectangles and CCircles member functions. At line 08, Rectang1 is declared as an object of the CRectangles class and given a length and width. At line 12, Circ1 is declared as an object of the CCircles class and given a diameter. In lines 09–11, the Rectang1 specifications, area and perimeter are displayed. In lines 13–15, the same information is displayed for Circ1.

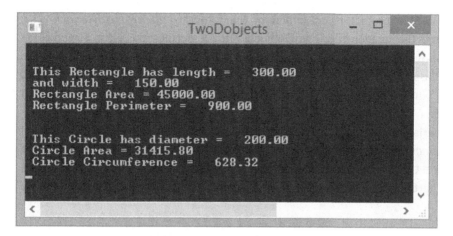

Figure 3.5 The TwoDobjects Display

Of course, the functions of the same name act differently because they are applied to objects of the two different classes. Objects of the CRectangles class invoke the CRectangles member functions and objects of the CCircles class invoke its member functions. Figure 3.5 shows the TwoDobjects window after execution of the program.

3.5 An Example of Derived Classes

Interrelated classes offer great flexibility and advantages in organizing computer programs and permitting the sharing and coordination of member variables and member functions between classes. When we begin to develop Windows programs in Chapter 4, you will see many examples of these ideas. For the moment, let's consider an initial example which uses a base class and derived classes and illustrates the concept of the "virtual function". In this case, we return to our rectangles and circles recognizing that they are two different geometric objects of two dimensions. This example demonstrates a program organization that allows them to be treated either independently as rectangle objects and circle objects or in a unified way as "TwoDobjects".

This project is contained in the folder *Chap3\6_TwoDobjectsVIRT* and the header file TwoDobjectsVIRT.h defines the class structure as shown in Table 3.8. The file begins with the class declarations for a base class called CTwoDobjects in lines 04–10. The classes CRectangles and CCircles are treated as classes derived from the CTwoDobjects class. In this case, the CTwoDobjects class does not in itself have member variables. But it has member functions which are declared as "virtual functions" in lines 07–09 and defined to be "empty". The declaration of the CRectangles class is in lines 11–19. The syntax of line 11 states that the CRectangles class is derived from the CTwoDobjects class and the

Table 3.8 Listing of TwoDobjectsVIRT.h

```
01     /* This is the file TwoDobjectsVIRT.h */
02     #include <stdio.h>
03     #include <conio.h>
04     class CTwoDobjects
05     {
06         public:
07         virtual void ShowSpecs(void){ }
08         virtual void ShowArea(void){ }
09         virtual void ShowPerim(void){ }
10     };
11     class CRectangles:public CTwoDobjects
12     {
13         double m_length, m_width;
14         public:
15         CRectangles (double l, double w);
16         virtual void ShowSpecs();
17         virtual void ShowArea();
18         virtual void ShowPerim();
19     };
20     class CCircles:public CTwoDobjects
21     {
22         double m_diameter;
23         public:
24         CCircles (double d);
25         virtual void ShowSpecs();
26         virtual void ShowArea();
27         virtual void ShowPerim();
28     };
```

term "public" in line 11 indicates that the relationship between the classes allows mutual access to member functions and member variables. The member variables for the rectangles are on line 13. The declaration of the CCircles class appears quite similarly in lines 20–28. Line 20 indicates that CCircles is derived from CTwoDobjects. Line 22 declares its member variable.

The member functions for CRectangles and CCircles are declared in lines 15–18 and lines 24–27 respectively. They use the same names as the member functions for the class CTwoDobjects and the functions are again declared as "virtual". The use of virtual functions allows special

Table 3.9 Listing of TwoDobjectsVIRT.cpp

```
01    /* This is the file TwoDobjectsVIRT.cpp */
02    #include "TwoDobjectsVIRT.h"
03    void main (void)
04    {
05        double l = 300;
06        double w = 150;
07        double d = 200;
08        CRectangles Rectang1 (l,w);
09        CCircles Circ1 (d);
10        Rectang1.ShowSpecs();
11        Rectang1.ShowArea();
12        Rectang1.ShowPerim();
13        Circ1.ShowSpecs();
14        Circ1.ShowArea();
15        Circ1.ShowPerim();
16        _getch();
17        CTwoDobjects* PtObj1;
18        CTwoDobjects* PtObj2;
19        PtObj1 = &Rectang1;
20        PtObj2 = &Circ1;
21        PtObj1->ShowSpecs();
22        PtObj1->ShowArea();
23        PtObj1->ShowPerim();
24        PtObj2->ShowSpecs();
25        PtObj2->ShowArea();
26        PtObj2->ShowPerim();
27        _getch();
28    }
```

treatment of objects from derived classes. In this case, when an object derived from the CTwoDobjects base class is processed, it can automatically be directed to the proper member function depending on whether it is a rectangle or a circle. This behavior is referred to as "polymorphism" and is a key feature of derived classes.

The Functions.cpp file for this TwoDobjectsVIRT project is identical to the functions file in the TwoDobjects project as shown in Table 3.6 of the previous section. The file which contains the main() for this project is TwoDobjectsVIRT.cpp. It is shown in Table 3.9 beginning with the include statement for the header file at line 02. Lines 05–07 set values for the dimensions. As in the previous examples, lines 08 and 09 use the normal constructor functions to describe the objects Rectang1 and Circ1 with their dimensions. Lines 10–15 then display the Rectang1 and Circ1 objects with their characteristics indicating that the derived class member functions can be used directly in the normal way.

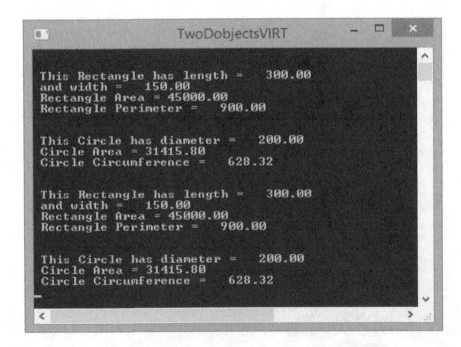

Figure 3.6 The Window for TwoDobjectsVIRT after Full Execution

The added capability offered by virtual functions is indicated by the coding in lines 17–26 of Table 3.9. After the _getch() in line 16, the lines 17 and 18 declare the pointers PtObj1 and PtObj2 for use with objects of the class CTwoDobjects. On the next lines (19 and 20) these pointers are set to the addresses of Rectang1 and Circ1 respectively. Lines 21–23 then use the pointer PtObj1 to call on the ShowSpecs, ShowArea and ShowPerim functions for the first object (Rectang1). The virtual function allows the proper version of each of these functions to be invoked. In this case, the characteristics of Rectang1 are properly displayed as can be seen in Figure 3.6. Lines 24–26 use the pointer PtObj2 to call on ShowSpecs, ShowArea and ShowPerim for its object. This time the CCircle class member functions are automatically applied and the values for Circ1 are displayed (again, see Figure 3.6).

3.5.1 Using a pointer array with derived classes

Section 3.5 above provides an indication of the way that a family of related objects can be processed with special treatment for each type of object. The use of pointer arrays helps to automate this process and the project contained in the folder *Chap3\7_TwoDobjectsPTR* provides an example of the use of pointers for this purpose. Click on the TwoDobjectsPTR.sln file and explore the project. You should notice that

Table 3.10 Listing of TwoDobjectsPTR.cpp

```
01    /* This is the file TwoDobjectsPTR.cpp */
02    #include "TwoDobjectsPTR.h"
03    void main (void)
04    {
05        double l = 300;
06        double w = 150;
07        double d = 200;
08        CTwoDobjects* ObjPointer[4];
09        CRectangles Rectang1 (l,w);
10        CRectangles Rectang2 (l/2,w/2);
11        CCircles Circ1 (d);
12        CCircles SmCirc(d/3);
13        ObjPointer[0] = &Rectang1;
```

Table 3.10 (*Continued*)

```
14        ObjPointer[1] = &Circ1;
15        ObjPointer[2] = &Rectang2;
16        ObjPointer[3] = &SmCirc;
17   for (int i = 0; i < 4; i++)  {
18        ObjPointer[i]->ShowSpecs();
19        ObjPointer[i]->ShowArea();
20        ObjPointer[i]->ShowPerim();
21        }
22        _getch();
23   }
```

the header file TwoDobjectsPTR.h is identical to the header file for the project TwoDobjectsVIRT just discussed in Section 3.5. Similarly the Functions.cpp file is also equivalent to the functions file of Sections 3.4 and 3.5 except for minor labeling changes.

The TwoDobjectsPTR.cpp file has changed considerably from the previous example as can be seen in Table 3.10. In the function main(), after initializing the dimension variables, line 08 declares ObjPointer as an array of pointers for class CTwoDobjects. Lines 09–12 create the objects Rectang1, Rectang2, Circ1 and SmCirc. Then, lines 13–16 set the ObjPointer entries to the addresses of the individual objects. Finally, the for loop of lines 17–21 cycles through each of the four objects showing the specifications, area and perimeter. The appropriate rectangle or circle functions are applied for each of the 2-D objects. After execution, the display window appears as in Figure 3.7.

The virtual function concept is very useful in a number of advanced programming applications. In Windows programming with MFC Applications, you may frequently see virtual functions automatically generated in the programming process. It may not be necessary for you to write such functions yourself, but you should be familiar with the concept. Virtual functions particularly come into play in Chapters 10 and 11 when we consider touch screen programming and gesture functions.

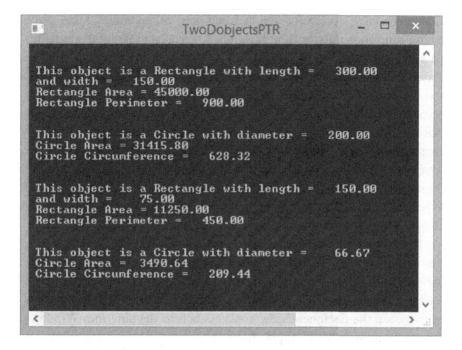

Figure 3.7 The Display for TwoDobjectsPTR

3.6 Simulating the Document/View Architecture

In Chapter 4 we will begin programming for Windows applications with Visual C++. An impressive amount of detail is involved in Windows programming. Much of this detail involves the use of functions and organization built into the Visual Studio development environment and often managed and programmed within the Microsoft Foundation Classes by "Application Wizards". The programming skills required for program creation depend on an understanding of the environment and how to work within it.

Programming for Windows in an MFC Application is a most realistic way to develop complex Windows programs and to harness the wide range of capabilities provided by Visual C++. As we begin to use MFC Applications in the next chapter, you will find that much of the program is automatically written for you and that your programming takes place by inserting code into the right locations to create a program that satisfies your needs. The most fundamental part of this process is an understanding of the basic organization provided in MFC Applications and referred to as the document/view architecture. A key feature of this organization is that the data is considered to be part of a "document" and that the storage and manipulation of the data within the document is considered to be separate from the display of the document. A "document" class is provided for storing and manipulating the data in the document. While a "view" class is provided to display the document and to handle interactions with the user while the program is running. Most of your Windows programming will take place within these two classes.

The rest of this section contains a series of simple simulations to illustrate the basic ideas of the document/view architecture. We will use the same C++ programming techniques and the console application format of Visual C++ as in previous sections. But we will use them now to introduce the document/view concepts before stepping into Windows programming with MFC Applications.

3.6.1 The DocView project

"DocView" is the first of our simulation projects and is contained in the folder *Chap3\8_DocView*. Its header file DocView.h is shown in Table 3.11 and declares each of the classes. The document class here is CDocStore and is intended to handle "document" objects which contain program data. This class is declared in lines 04–12 and has been designed for the simple physics problem of a body accelerating at constant acceleration for a certain total time. The values of the constant acceleration and total time variables are the "given" items in this problem. We also consider ourselves to be interested in certain results — the final velocity and the final position of the body at the end of the time period.

In Table 3.11, the given acceleration level and the given total time are represented as member variables created in CDocStore as the "inputs" to this document. The calculated results are also represented as member

Table 3.11 Listing of DocView.h

```
01    /* This is the file DocView.h */
02    #include <stdio.h>
03    #include <conio.h>
04    class CDocStore
05    {
06        public:
07        double m_Acceleration, m_TotalTime;
08        double m_FinalVelocity, m_FinalPosition;
09        public:
10        CDocStore ();
11        void UpDateDoc(double, double);
12    };
13    class CDocView
14    {
15        public:
16        CDocView ();
17        void DisplayDoc(CDocStore);
18    };
```

variables in CDocStore corresponding to the final velocity and the final position. In this form, each document declared as an object will be given the input member variables and the results member variables will be calculated. Notice that all of the member variables have been declared to be public. In this case, this arrangement is useful because display operations will be carried out by functions in a separate viewing class which requires access to the CDocStore member variables.

The constructor function for the CDocStore class is declared in line 10 of Table 3.11 without input arguments. In addition, another member function called UpDateDoc is declared in line 11. As you will see, the UpDateDoc function serves as a constructor function where the given problem variables are defined and stored as member variables. They are then used to compute member variables for the results to complete the document. The viewing class in this project is declared in lines 13–18 and is called CDocView. It does not require any member variables since its purpose in this project is to display and not to store. Its member function DisplayDoc, which is declared in line 17 will display the data from the document for the user. Notice that DisplayDoc expects to

Table 3.12 Listing of Functions.cpp

```
01    /* This is the file Functions.cpp */
02    #include "DocView.h"
03        CDocStore::CDocStore() {
04        m_Acceleration = 0.;
05        m_TotalTime = 0.;
06        m_FinalVelocity = 0.;
07        m_FinalPosition = 0.;                    }
08        void CDocStore::UpDateDoc(double a, double t) {
09        m_Acceleration = a;
10        m_TotalTime = t;
11        m_FinalVelocity = m_Acceleration*m_TotalTime;
12        m_FinalPosition=m_Acceleration*m_TotalTime*m_TotalTime/2.;        }
13        CDocView::CDocView (){};
14        void CDocView::DisplayDoc(CDocStore DocName) {
15        double Out1 = DocName.m_Acceleration;
16        double Out2 = DocName.m_TotalTime;
17        double Out3 = DocName.m_FinalVelocity;
18        double Out4 = DocName.m_FinalPosition;
19        printf("\nStarting with zero initial velocity and position");
20        printf("\nConstant acceleration level = %6.2f \n",Out1);
21        printf("Total acceleration time = %6.2f\n",Out2);
22        printf("\nFinal velocity = %6.2f",Out3);
23        printf("\nFinal position = %6.2f \n\n\n\n",Out4);                }
```

receive an argument that is an object of the class CDocStore — so that it knows the name of the document containing the data which it is expected to display and it will be able to have access to the data.

Let's look at the function prototypes for the DocView project contained in the file Functions.cpp and shown in Table 3.12. The document constructor function is shown in lines 03–07. It has an empty input argument list as you can see in line 03. However, it does initialize all of the member variables to zero. This may be desirable so that storage space for these variables is not filled with arbitrary values. The UpdateDoc member function is re-declared and prototyped in lines 08–12. As you can see, this function receives the given acceleration level and the total time. It sets the member variables for acceleration and total time to equal the function input values. Then, it also calculates the final velocity and the final position member variables according to the well-known physics equations shown in lines 11 and 12.

Now consider the CDocView viewing class. Notice first, in line 13, that its constructor function is empty and that there are no member variables to set. The function DisplayDoc is re-declared and prototyped in lines 14–23. This is the function that actually "displays" the CDocStore member variables. In this function, lines 15–18 obtain the values of the four output variables by addressing the document. Each of these output variables represents one of the member variables stored in the document object of the CDocStore class. As indicated in the re-declaration of line 14, DocName is used to refer to the document object within the DisplayDoc function. You can see this in lines 15–18 where each of the member variables is addressed. The output, along with some simple labeling, is displayed by the printf statements in lines 19–23 of the DisplayDoc function.

In Tables 3.11 and 3.12 we have described our simulated document and view classes called CDocStore and CDocView, respectively. A project based on these classes replies on the file DocView.cpp from the folder *Chap3\8_DocView*. This file contains the function main() for the project and is shown in Table 3.13. It makes use of the classes CDocStore and CDocView to carry out the program operations. In the simple declaration statement of line 07, "aDocument" is declared as an object of the CDocStore class. This simple declaration can be made because the CDocStore constructor function does not require any input arguments. Similarly, an object called "aDisplay" of the CDocView class is declared on line 08. In line 09, the UpDateDoc function sets the values of the aDocument member variables using particular input values for acceleration and total time. Of course, UpDateDoc computes the resulting final velocity and position to set values for the remaining member variables of aDocument. With the document completed, line 10 displays the contents of aDocument. After a keystroke (line 11), line 12 calls the UpDateDoc function to redefine the contents of aDocument. Line 13 then displays the updated version of the document. Figure 3.8 shows the display window for the DocView project after execution is completed.

We have very much simplified the document and view concepts in the discussion above. However, as you begin using the MFC

Table 3.13 Listing of DocView.cpp

```
01    /* This is the file DocView.cpp */
02    #include "DocView.h"
03    void main (void)
04    {
05        double acc = 10;
06        double time = 10;
07        CDocStore aDocument;
08        CDocView aDisplay;
09        aDocument.UpDateDoc(acc,time);
10        aDisplay.DisplayDoc(aDocument);
11        _getch();
12        aDocument.UpDateDoc(acc/2,2*time);
13        aDisplay.DisplayDoc(aDocument);
14        _getch();
15    }
```

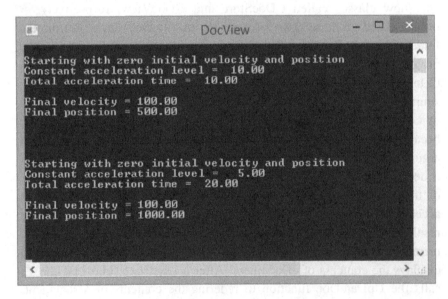

Figure 3.8 The DocView Display

Application format, you will see that the basic organizational idea we have described forms the kernel of the document/view architecture. The program's data is considered to make up a "document" and a special document class is available to store and manipulate the data in the document. The second special class is developed to "view" the document. It also handles general interactions with the user to allow manipulation of the display. The MFC Application Wizard will automatically name, declare and begin prototyping many of the classes and functions that you need. Your programming will consist of "filling in the blanks" as needed for your application. The Application Wizard also eliminates the function main() — think of it as having "main" hidden away somewhere in the Windows operating system. You must provide arrangements for your program to initialize or calculate document member variables during program execution and also provide for the member variables to be updated as user interactions make it necessary. Display operations are automatically initiated whenever a window is resized, restored or maximized. As long as you have provided the right coding, the display process will maintain a view of the document in the window on your screen or even place it on your printer.

3.6.2 The document pointer

There are a few more items to be addressed to help complete your picture of the document and view concepts. This section deals with the DocViewPTR project in the folder *Chap3\9_DocViewPTR*. This project is identical to the DocView project of Section 3.6.1. But, instead of using the document name as an argument for the viewing function, a pointer to the document is used. This is the most common approach in MFC Applications and requires only a minimal change in programming from the DocView project in Section 3.6.1 above. The most significant modification is to the Functions.cpp file. The new functions file for the DocViewPTR project is shown in Table 3.14. The revised DisplayDoc function is re-declared and prototyped in lines 14–23 where the argument for the DisplayDoc function has now become DocPtr — a pointer to objects of the CDocStore class. Notice that lines 15–18 now set the DisplayDoc outputs by using the pointer to access the document's member variables.

Table 3.14 Listing of Functions.cpp (for DocViewPTR)

```
01    /* This is the file Functions.cpp */
02    #include "DocViewPTR.h"
03        CDocStore::CDocStore() {
04        m_Acceleration = 0.;
05        m_TotalTime = 0.;
06        m_FinalVelocity = 0.;
07        m_FinalPosition = 0.;                              }
08        void CDocStore::UpDateDoc(double a, double t) {
09        m_Acceleration = a;
10        m_TotalTime = t;
11        m_FinalVelocity = m_Acceleration * m_TotalTime;
12        m_FinalPosition=m_Acceleration*m_TotalTime*m_TotalTime/2.;        }
13        CDocView::CDocView (){};
14        void CDocView::DisplayDoc(CDocStore* DocPtr) {
15        double Out1 = DocPtr->m_Acceleration;
16        double Out2 = DocPtr->m_TotalTime;
17        double Out3 = DocPtr->m_FinalVelocity;
18        double Out4 = DocPtr->m_FinalPosition;
19        printf("\nStarting with zero initial velocity and position");
20        printf("\nConstant acceleration level = %6.2f \n",Out1);
21        printf("Total acceleration time = %6.2f\n",Out2);
22        printf("\nFinal velocity = %6.2f",Out3);
23        printf("\nFinal position = %6.2f \n\n\n\n",Out4);                  }
```

The files for DocViewPTR.h and DocViewPTR.cpp are nearly unchanged from the original DocView project of the previous section and their full text will not be presented here. The two very simple changes made are: (1) to declare the DisplayDoc function in DocViewPTR.h using the pointer argument in the form:

void DisplayDoc(CDocStore*)

and (2) to call the DisplayDoc function in DocViewPTR.cpp by passing the document address instead of the document name as indicated below:

aDisplay.DisplayDoc(&aDocument)

If you build and execute the DocViewPTR project in the folder *Chap3\9_DocViewPTR*, you should find the display identical to that shown in Figure 3.8 of the previous section.

3.6.3 Using "Get" functions

In the previous two examples we have demonstrated the MFC Application process of using a view class for display and a document class for storage. In both of the examples we declared the document member variables (i.e. the member variables of the class CDocStore) as public so that they could be directly accessed by the display function of the class CDocView. One alternative to using public member variables in the document class (CDocStore) is to allow the member variables to be private and then provide public functions which allow their values to be

Table 3.15 Listing of DocViewGET.h

```
01    /* This is the file DocViewGET.h */
02    #include <stdio.h>
03    #include <conio.h>
04    class CDocStore
05    {
06        private:
07        double m_Acceleration, m_TotalTime;
08        double m_FinalVelocity, m_FinalPosition;
09        public:
10        CDocStore ();
11        void UpDateDoc(double, double);
12        double GetAcc();
13        double GetTTime();
14        double GetFVel();
15        double GetFPos();
16    };
17    class CDocView
18    {
19        public:
20        CDocView ();
21        void DisplayDoc(CDocStore*);
22    };
```

obtained as needed. Each of these functions simply returns the value of a particular member variable when it is called. By the use of such "Get" functions, the values of the member variables can become publicly accessible while the private variables themselves cannot be changed from outside their class.

The example project DocViewGET in the folder *Chap3\ 10_DocViewGET* illustrates this approach. The header file DocViewGET.h is shown in Table 3.15. You can see in lines 06–08 that all of the member variables of the CDocStore class are now private. The added member functions for the CDocStore class have been declared in lines 12–15. These are the "Get" functions and each of them has been prepared to return a double precision member variable. The declaration for the CDocView class in lines 17–22 is unchanged.

The listing for the Functions.cpp file of the CDocViewGET project is shown in Table 3.16. The Get functions are re-declared and prototyped in lines 13–16 where each of them is a single line function returning a value for the appropriate member variable. With this arrangement, it is necessary to change the DisplayDoc member functions to be able to obtain the CDocStore member variables through the new functions. This can be seen in lines 19–22 where the output variable values are being

Table 3.16 Listing of Functions.cpp (CDocViewGET)

```
01    /* This is the file Functions.cpp */
02    #include "DocViewGET.h"
03        CDocStore::CDocStore() {
04        m_Acceleration = 0.;
05        m_TotalTime = 0.;
06        m_FinalVelocity = 0.;
07        m_FinalPosition = 0.;                          }
08        void CDocStore::UpDateDoc(double a, double t) {
09        m_Acceleration = a;
10        m_TotalTime = t;
11        m_FinalVelocity = m_Acceleration * m_TotalTime;
12        m_FinalPosition=m_Acceleration*m_TotalTime*m_TotalTime/2.;          }
13        double CDocStore::GetAcc() {return (m_Acceleration);}
14        double CDocStore::GetTTime() {return (m_TotalTime);}
15        double CDocStore::GetFVel() {return (m_FinalVelocity);}
16        double CDocStore::GetFPos() {return (m_FinalPosition);}
```

Table 3.16 (*Continued*)

```
17        CDocView::CDocView(){};
18        void CDocView::DisplayDoc(CDocStore* DocPtr) {
19          double Out1 = DocPtr->GetAcc();
20          double Out2 = DocPtr->GetTTime();
21          double Out3 = DocPtr->GetFVel();
22          double Out4 = DocPtr->GetFPos();
23          printf("\nStarting with zero initial velocity and position");
24          printf("\nConstant acceleration level = %6.2f \n",Out1);
25          printf("Total acceleration time = %6.2f\n",Out2);
26          printf("\nFinal velocity = %6.2f",Out3);
27          printf("\nFinal position = %6.2f \n\n\n\n",Out4);              }
```

set by using the document pointer DocPtr to access the appropriate Get functions. The function main() in the file DocViewGET.cpp is unchanged from the previous example. If you compile and execute the project, you will obtain the same result as in the previous two sections, with the display as shown in Figure 3.8.

3.6.4 Using objects as member variables in a document

This is our concluding project for the simulation of MFC Applications. It continues with the document storage and viewing concepts of the previous Section 3.6 projects. However, in this case, we introduce the use of objects as member variables within the document storage class. The objects that we use are from the CRectangles class which we described in Section 3.1. The project name is DocViewOBJ and it can be found in the folder *Chap3\11_DocViewOBJ*. The file DocViewOBJ.h is shown in Table 3.17 and includes both the class declarations and the function prototypes.

The declaration and prototypes for the CRectangles class are shown in lines 04–21. Just as in Section 3.5, the member variables represent the length and width and we have the member functions ShowSpecs and ShowArea. By declaring the CRectangles class before the CDocStore class, CRectangles objects can be recognized as member variables in the class CDocStore. The declaration and prototypes for CDocStore are shown in lines 22–30. Notice that line 24 declares two objects of the

Table 3.17 Listing of DocView.h

```
01    /* This is the file DocView.h */
02    #include <stdio.h>
03    #include <conio.h>
04    class CRectangles
05    {
06         double m_length, m_width;
07         public:
08         CRectangles () {
09         m_length = 0.;
10         m_width = 0.;                        }
11         void DefineRectangle (double l, double w)  {
12         m_length = l;
13         m_width = w;                          }
14         void ShowSpecs () {
15         printf("\n\n This Rectangle has length = %8.2f", m_length);
16         printf("\n and width = %8.2f\n", m_width);                  }
17         void ShowArea () {
18         double area;
19         area = m_length*m_width;
20         printf(" Rectangle Area = %8.2f \n",area);                  }
21    };
22    class CDocStore {
23         public:
24         CRectangles m_Rect1, m_Rect2;
25         public:
26         CDocStore (){}
27         void UpDateDoc (CRectangles Rect1, CRectangles Rect2) {
28         m_Rect1 = Rect1;
29         m_Rect2 = Rect2;                        }
30    };
31    class CDocView {
32         public:
33         CDocView (){}
34         void DisplayDoc (CDocStore* DocPtr) {
35         DocPtr->m_Rect1.ShowSpecs();  DocPtr->m_Rect1.ShowArea();
36         DocPtr->m_Rect2.ShowSpecs();  DocPtr->m_Rect2.ShowArea();          }
37    };
```

CRectangles class as public member variables for CDocStore. This simple declaration is facilitated by the empty constructor function for the CRectangles class. Line 26 shows the empty constructor function for CDocstore. The function UpDateDoc is declared and prototyped in lines

27–29. Notice that the input arguments for UpDateDoc are two objects of the CRectangles class which directly become the member variables for the CDocStore document object as indicated in lines 28 and 29.

The CDocView class is declared in lines 31–37 and, as previously, CDocView is intended for displaying "documents" from the CDocStore class. In this case, the documents will contain two CRectangles objects. The DisplayDoc member function is declared and prototyped in lines 34–36. DisplayDoc receives a pointer to a CDocStore object (a document). Lines 35 and 36 then call on the ShowSpecs and ShowArea functions to display the information in the document.

The function main() controls the document definition and display. It's in the file DocViewOBJ.cpp as listed in Table 3.18. Two rectangle objects, aRect and bRect, are declared in line 07 and are specifically defined in lines 10 and 11. Document1 is declared in line 08 and aRect

Table 3.18 Listing of DocViewOBJ.cpp

```
01    /* This is the file DocViewOBJ.cpp */
02    #include "DocViewOBJ.h"
03    void main (void)
04    {
05        double rL = 250;
06        double rW = 125;
07        CRectangles aRect, bRect;
08        CDocStore Document1, Document2;
09        CDocView Screen;
10        aRect.DefineRectangle (rL, rW);
11        bRect.DefineRectangle (2*rL, 2*rW);
12        Document1.UpDateDoc(aRect, bRect);
13        Screen.DisplayDoc(&Document1);
14        _getch();
15        rL = 25;
16        rW = 12.5;
17        aRect.DefineRectangle (rL, rW);
18        bRect.DefineRectangle (2*rL, 2*rW);
19        Document2.UpDateDoc(aRect, bRect);
20        Screen.DisplayDoc(&Document2);
21        _getch();
22    }
```

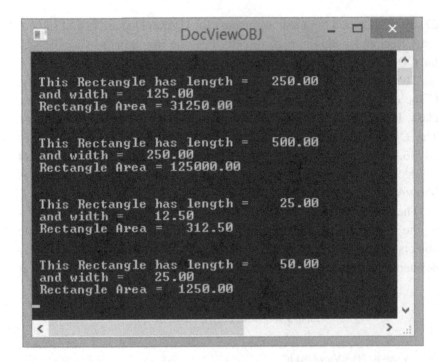

Figure 3.9 Display Window for DocViewOBJ after Execution

and bRect are used to define its member variables in line 12. Line 09 declares a CDocView object called "Screen". In line 13, DisplayDoc is called for the Screen object and given a pointer to Document1 so that it may display the Document1 information.

The function main() also contains a second document which is declared as Document2 in line 08. After Document1 is displayed by line 13, the program pauses until a keystroke is received (line 14). Then a second set of rectangles is defined in lines 15–18 and used in defining Document2 through the UpDateDoc function in line 19. Information on this second document is displayed by calling the DisplayDoc function in line 20.

You can enter the folder *Chap3\11_DocViewOBJ* and click on the file DocViewOBJ.sln to bring it into the Visual Studio environment. When you build and execute it, you should see the display results of Figure 3.9.

While you have the project in the development environment, click on the ClassView tab in the workspace area and explore the class structure for the project.

The purpose of our simulation of the MFC Application structure has been to introduce the idea of separating the storage and display operations in a computer program. The "document" concept provides the basis for storing application information. The "viewing" concept relies on functions specialized for presenting the application information and these functions obtain that information by having direct access to individual documents. In each of our simulations, the CDocStore class was used to store document objects and the CDocView class was used to house the programming for viewing documents. This last document/view example (DocViewOBJ) has shown that documents can contain objects as well as simple variables and that a given program can manipulate more than one document. In the next section, we will begin using the MFC Application format of Visual C++ and its Application Wizard. As we move along, you will find that main() is no longer used and that most of your programming will be carried out by managing and creating code in the document class and viewing class templates provided by the MFC Application format.

3.7 Exercises

1. Modify the project RectanglesEC (*Chap3\2_RectanglesEC*) by adding a function to the CRectangles class. The function name should be ShowBigD and it should identify the bigger of the rectangle dimensions and print it out neatly formatted. The output should look similar to the output for the functions ShowArea and ShowPerim. Exercise your new function by inserting it into main() so that it is applied to Rectang1 and Rectang2.

2. For the TwoDobjects project (*Chap3\5_TwoDobjects*), provide an additional class for right triangle objects and call it CRtTriangles. This new class should use member variables "m_Base" and "m_Height" to describe right triangles and should also contain

appropriate functions for ShowSpecs, ShowArea and ShowPerim. Modify the function main to include creation of a CRtTriangles object called Triang1 of comparable dimensions to the other objects. After outputting details for the Rectang1 and Circ1 objects, use your CRtTriangles member functions to output the specs, area and perimeter of the Triang1 object.

3. For the TwoDobjectsPTR project add a CRtTriangles class (similar to Exercise 2) as another class derived from CTwoDobjects. Work with the project located in *Chap3\7_TwoDobjectsPTR* and use virtual functions as seen for the CRectangles and CCircles classes. In the function main(), define two objects of your CRtTriangles class (perhaps calling them BigTri and LittleTri). Also increase the array size for ObjPointer to "6". Have ObjPointer[4] represent BigTri and ObjPointer[5] represent LittleTri. Finally modify the "for" loop outputting the TwoDobject information so that the BigTri and LittleTri objects are described after the rectangles and circles.

Chapter 4

Beginning Windows Programming

In this chapter we begin programming for Windows applications with Visual C++. The Visual C++ package provides capabilities for programming across the widest possible range of interests from writing game programs to management applications. Engineering and technical programming fall somewhere in between — potentially involving complex calculations, data manipulation, graphics, and animation. Visual C++, like many Microsoft products, provides a large number of tools for handling programming tasks. In fact, there is such an abundance of tools that it can often be hard to find the things that may be of most interest to you. In the next few chapters we provide an introduction to these tools. We have placed a focus on graphics programming because graphics are often an inherent part of technical applications and because the skills required for basic graphics are at a level appropriate for introducing Windows concepts. We aim at developing a familiarity with Windows operations and at using the available Visual C++ tools to store, manipulate and graphically display data generated during program execution. We have tried to take a direct approach and to not consider the many details, options or capabilities that could prove distracting.

The Visual C++ MFC Applications format is a very convenient environment for Windows programming. Using the organization of an MFC Application is a very realistic way to develop programming skills which access the wide range of capabilities offered by Visual C++ and the personal computer Windows environment. As we begin our discussion of Windows programming, it may seem at times that we are getting mired in details. Just keep in mind that there are far more details out there. We avoid many of them by using the organization of the MFC Application and its "Application Wizards" which provide programming structure and templates. Our work with MFC Applications will use the document/view architecture. This is the convenient approach to storing and displaying data which we began discussing at the end of Chapter 3. If you are looking for a quick start to Windows programming but have not read Section 3.6, you should look it over before proceeding. Object-oriented programming is an important aspect of MFC Applications and Windows. If you have experience with C programming but have little exposure to the classes and objects of C++, you should start at the beginning of Chapter 3.

4.1 A Blank Project

In many ways, programming for Windows is more like writing a part of someone else's program rather than completely writing your own. For example, your C++ Windows program will not have a function main(). In the most direct form of Windows programming a WinMain function is used instead with a structure and functions that interact directly with the operating system. The MFC Application form of Windows programming used here provides a well-organized program structure. In an MFC application, a great deal of prewritten code is supplied which includes a built in WinMain function. Programming with MFC Applications then becomes a matter of inserting just the right amount of additional program code in the just the right places. We will begin this introduction to Windows programming by creating a very simple program that is "blank" in that it contains no added code, only the standard coding of an MFC Application. You will see, however, that it produces an executable program which opens a perfectly normal (but empty) active window showing standard Windows features and capabilities.

Begin this initial exercise by launching Visual Studio from the desktop. From the opening screen, click on **File > New > Project** (or the "New Project" toolbar button towards the left) in order to obtain the New Project window shown in Figure 4.1. There you should click on the installed Visual C++ templates and select "MFC Application". In Figure 4.1 we have edited the "Location" space to show only "C:\". The title "BlankProject" has been entered into the space for "Name". As with the

Console Applications of earlier chapters, the created project will reside in a folder with the same name. We have also chosen not to create a "solution" directory since we will be dealing only with a single project at a time. In this case, the folder for BlankProject will be created directly on the C:\ drive.

With a click on OK, the window for the MFC Application Wizard will appear as shown in Figure 4.2. This window describes a default project format which could be accepted by just clicking on Finish. However, along the left side of the Wizard window are the entry points which allow changes to the project structure. We will change this project to have a "Single document interface". To do so, we click on the "Application Type" item on the left side of the window to see the basic Application Wizard options in Figure 4.3. In this window, click the radio button for "Single document" as shown to replace the default "Multiple documents". As we start Windows programming, a single document will keep us plenty busy. Also in Figure 4.3, leave in place the default support for the document/view architecture and select the project style "MFC

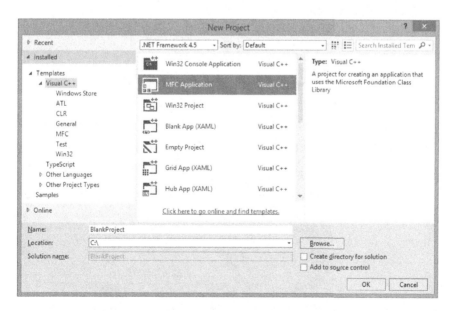

Figure 4.1 Creating a New MFC Application Project

Figure 4.2 The First MFC Application Window

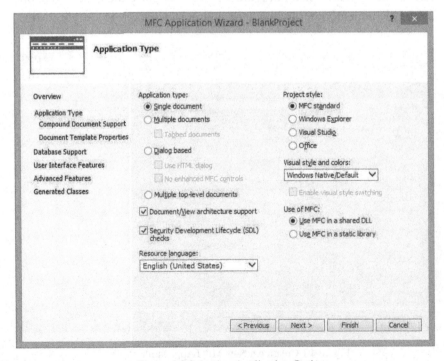

Figure 4.3 Selecting Application Options

Standard". Also set the "Visual style..." to "Windows Native/Default" to obtain a standard Windows look for your program. The "Use of MFC" item at the right side of the window governs the structure of executable files built during compiling and linking. Selecting the default "Use MFC in a shared DLL" leads to an executable which is compact in size but requires a set of ".dll" library files in order to execute. These files are automatically present if Visual C++ is installed on your computer. Choosing "Use MFC in a static library" leads to a larger executable file. This executable form, when created under the "Release configuration", is intended to run on other computers without a Visual C++ installation and without separately providing the .dll files. For now, we will accept the default "Use MFC in a shared DLL". However, for any project this can be changed by selection at the time of creation or by an adjustment at a later time to change the project's "Properties".

In general we will be accepting the Application Wizard defaults for our programming projects (except for the single document interface) and, if you're in a hurry at this point, you can just click on Finish to conclude the set up process. However, you should take a few moments to click on some of the other items at the left of the Application Wizard window to explore other possible options. Click on the "Document Template Strings" entry to see the variety of labeling options which have been filled out for you in default form based on the name of your project — in this case "BlankProject". You can edit these if you like, including the "Main frame caption" which is the title that appears in your program window while it is executing. If the program is expected to create output files, you can create a customized file extension in the "File extension" box. Notice that if you specify a file extension, a default filter name will also be suggested to identify your program's files. The suggested name can then be edited as desired.

The "Database Support" item on the left of the window provides the capability to link with a variety of data base packages. The "User Interface Features" item allows you to adjust window appearance and functionality for your program. We are using the defaults which lead to a classic Windows appearance. The "Advanced Features" item allows you to add or remove several features. For example, "Windows Sockets" would be important for network communication. Notice that support for printing and print preview is included as a default. We will leave this capability in place for our projects since we will do some printing in a few later examples.

The "Generated Classes" item indicates the various classes that are to be automatically created by the Application Wizard. Notice, for example, that the name for the view class is created by placing a "C" in front of the project name "BlankProject" and then adding "View" to create "CBlankProjectView" as the name to be used for the view class. By clicking on this name in the "Class name" box, you have the opportunity to edit it. The other default class names are created similarly including the document class name of CBlankProjectDoc. Each of these names can be edited if desired. You can also edit the file names associated with each of the classes.

One of the more significant options under "Generated Classes" is the possibility of changing the base class for the view class. In the structure furnished by the Application Wizard, the class CBlankProjectView is actually derived from a base class and the selection of a particular base class makes different capabilities available. We will be using the default base class called CView which is a compromise between graphics and text capabilities. Another option is the base class CEditView which is designed for text processing with convenient scrolling and editing capability. At this point, clicking on Finish will conclude the set up process and return to the development environment with BlankProject fully loaded into the Visual Studio environment and ready for editing.

4.1.1 Exploring BlankProject

We won't be editing or adding code to BlankProject, but we do want to look it over carefully to see what has been done for us by the choice of a Visual C++ MFC Application. In the Visual Studio environment for the BlankProject, notice that the build options are just as they were for the Console Application projects of previous chapters. Clicking on **Build > Rebuild Solution** assures a full compiling and linking of files. Clicking on **Build > Build Solution** only compiles and links as needed to accommodate changes since the last build. The Output window will keep

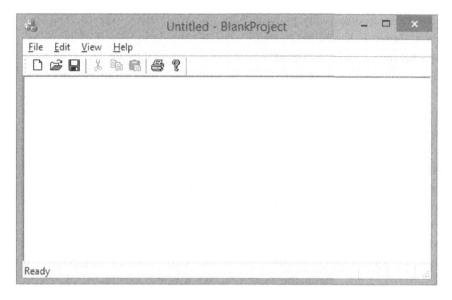

Figure 4.4 The Window for BlankProject

you informed of the compiling/linking process. After a successful compile and linking of BlankProject, you will see "Build: 1 succeeded, 0 failed, 0 up-to-date, 0 skipped" or "Rebuild All: 1 succeeded, 0 failed, 0 skipped" depending on your choice of Build Solution or Rebuild Solution. The resulting executable file for BlankProject can then be run by clicking on the arrow next to the Debug box on the toolbar. This should result in the window of Figure 4.4. Although BlankProject has not been coded to do anything, its display window has standard Windows capability. You can maximize it, minimize it, click and drag its title bar to move it, or click and drag its edges to resize it. You can also click on menu bar items (even though they're not functional). Finally, click on the "X" in the upper right hand corner to close BlankProject. This will terminate its execution and return to the Visual Studio development environment. There, we can look at all of the code and organization that has been provided by the Application Wizard.

Figure 4.5 shows two views of the Class View window for BlankProject. The smaller window on the left shows the five classes that have been automatically generated by the Application Wizard. The first class shown is CAboutDlg which services the dialog window activated by clicking on **Help > About** on the menu bar of BlankProject. The third and fourth classes shown are CBlankProjectDoc and CBlankProjectView which are the document and view classes. These two classes will receive most of our attention in programming with the MFC Application format in Section 4.2 and also in the following chapters.

To get a general idea of the execution of a Windows program in the Application Wizard format, consider the Class View window on the right of Figure 4.5 where CBlankProjectApp has been expanded to show its member functions in the lower portion of the Class View window. As execution of BlankProject begins, it triggers the function WinMain which is built into the MFC Application. WinMain then calls on the member function InitInstance from the class CBlankProjectApp. It activates the document, the view and the window for the BlankProject

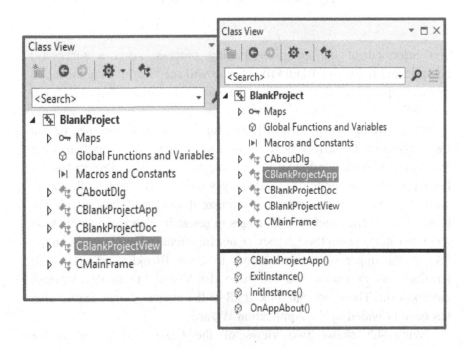

Figure 4.5 The Class Structure of BlankProject

program. You can have a look at InitInstance by clicking on it as a member function of the class CBlankProjectApp. The function WinMain also calls on the member function Run of the class CWinApp. The CWinApp class is the base class for CBlankProjectApp and can be seen with a click on the ">" to expand CBlankProjectApp and then a click on the ">" for Base Types. The function Run starts the display of BlankProject in an active window ready to be serviced by the operating system. As inputs of mouse clicks or keystrokes are received for BlankProject, the function Run passes these "Windows messages" into the program for processing by the appropriate functions. Of course, BlankProject is "blank" and does not, in itself, carry out any operations. Finally, when the BlankProject window is closed, the program terminates and Run stops operating.

The start of the overall execution process begins with the declaration of an object called "theApp" of the class CBlankProjectApp. The object theApp can be seen in the Class View window by clicking on "Global Functions and Variables". You can also see the code where it is declared by clicking on theApp when it appears in the Class View window. This click places the file BlankProjectView.cpp in the Edit window positioned for you to see the declaration of theApp as an object.

The whole execution process is intricate to say the least. But fortunately, you can manage quite well without mastering all of the details. The trick in programming for MFC Applications rests primarily on creating functions and entering code in just the right places within the document and view classes. In Section 4.2 we will begin this programming process.

4.1.2 The BlankProject files

Creation of our BlankProject program simply used the default programming furnished by the MFC Application Wizard and we did not prepare any additional C++ coding. The Application Wizard automatically created a number of files during its set up process. Those files are shown listed in Figure 4.6. The folder BlankProject contains nineteen files and three sub-folders. Just as we have seen in projects of

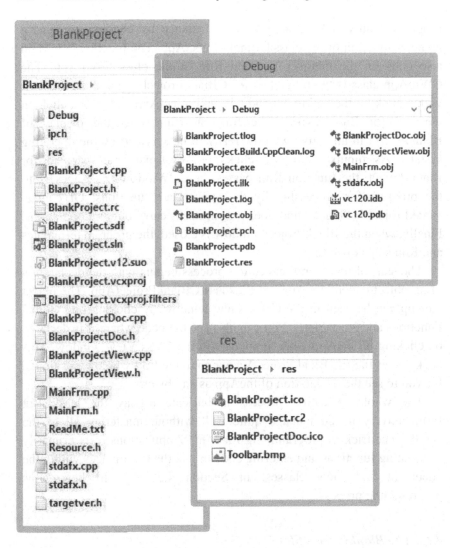

Figure 4.6 Files for the Project "BlankProject"

the first three chapters, the file BlankProject.sln is the "solution file" which stores the latest information about your work on a current project for the development system. Clicking on it will load the project into the Visual C++ environment ready for editing. Also shown in the folder BlankProject is the file ReadMe.txt. We won't reproduce it here but it contains a brief description of the files that the Application Wizard created and you should read it over.

The files in the folder *BlankProject\res* of Figure 4.6 were also created by the Application Wizard and they contain the basic resource information necessary to support the menu bars, tool bars, etc. which are part of the project window. You can obtain an idea of their contents by returning to BlankProject in the Visual C++ development environment. In the development environment, from the menu bar you can click on the Resource View tab at the bottom of the workspace area. A click on **View > Resource View** from the menu bar will also display the Resource View window. Once you have displayed the Resource View window, click on the expand sign ">" next to BlankProject to show the BlankProject resource folder. Clicking on the next expand symbol will show the individual resource folders. As an example, click on the ">" sign next to the item Menu then click on IDR_MAINFRAME. The menu bar contents will appear in the Edit window ready for editing. We will consider menu bar editing later, for now just close Visual C++.

The folder *BlankProject\Debug* also appears in Figure 4.6. It contains fourteen files and a folder containing a build log. These were created by Visual C++ during compiling and linking. The BlankProject.exe file is in the Debug folder and is the executable file for the project. Of course, you can execute it by clicking on it through Windows Explorer. You can also make a shortcut to it, place it on your desktop, etc. as discussed earlier. Just as discussed in Section 1.5, setting the active configuration to "Release" under **Build > Configuration Manager** will produce a Release folder similar to the Debug folder but with an executable in release form which can be more readily run on other PCs. As with the Console Application projects, the Application Wizard Debug and Release folders contain the bulkiest files of the project. Precompiled header files in particular (.pch) are useful for speeding repeated build operations during program development but are very large in size. This also applies to the folder ipch which contains additional precompiled information.

To make project files more compact for transporting or to save space on your computer hard drive, you can delete the Debug (or Release) folder in your project as mentioned previously in Sections 1.3 and 1.5.

The .sdf file also remains expendable and can be deleted if desired as well as the ipch folder. The rest of the project can then be transported easily, occupying minimal file space. When the project is loaded into Visual C++ a new .sdf file and ipch folder will be created as necessary. Then, when you carry out a build or rebuild operation, the Debug (or Release) folder will also be regenerated.

4.2 A First Windows Project

The first example Windows project in which we have inserted our own "homemade" C++ coding is called FirstWin. It can be found in the folder *Chap4\1_FirstWin*. Just as in the example programs for Console Applications of Chapters 1–3, we have grouped the project folders for examples together under a folder for the chapters. In this case, our first group of Windows projects is in the folder *Chap4*. We've also tried to provide orderly names for the individual example folders by adding a number before the original project name. In this case, our initial project FirstWin is located in the folder named *1_FirstWin*.

Now, let's consider the example. Go to the folder *Chap4\1_FirstWin* and open the FirstWin project by double clicking on the file FirstWin.sln. You can explore the project in the Visual C++ environment by looking at the Solution Explorer, Class View and Resource View windows and then clicking on member functions, member variables, resources, file names, etc. You should see that the project looks quite similar to the BlankProject that we discussed in Section 4.1. A small amount of code has been added to this project, however, so that it actually does a little something. Click on **Build > Rebuild Solution** to compile and link the project and create an executable. Then execute the program. You should see the window shown in Figure 4.7.

We have obtained this display by programming several lines of code within the class CFirstWinView which is the view class for our FirstWin project. In particular, code has been inserted only in the OnDraw member function of CFirstWinView. This function is automatically created by the MFC Application Wizard. It is called as the FirstWin

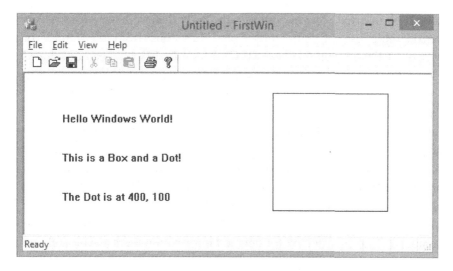

Figure 4.7 Display of the Project FirstWin

program begins execution and the project window is first initialized. It is also automatically called whenever the window must be redrawn after being maximized or being moved, etc.

You can find the inserted code by going to the Class View window of the Visual Studio development environment. In the Class View window, expand the FirstWin project to expose its classes and then click on the CFirstWinView class. You will then see its member functions appear in the lower half of the Class View window. These have been automatically generated by the Application Wizard. Some of these are used for printing. Others are related to initializing the project window. For example, GetDocument associates the given window with the document that contains program data. For now, simply double click on the OnDraw function. The code for this function will appear in your Edit window and you can scroll through it. The OnDraw listing is also shown in Table 4.1.

The coding that we have inserted follows the Application Wizard's "TODO" comment line which appears on line 06 of Table 4.1. The Application Wizard itself wrote everything else and also wrote the "TODO" comment indicating where the "draw code for native data" should be inserted. As you will see, the code that we have added makes considerable use of both classes and functions from the library of Microsoft Foundation Classes (MFC). These tools have been developed especially for use in Windows programming and make it possible to carry out a wide range of programming tasks without programming all the details. They form a complex web of classes and functions — but fully understanding them before beginning to write programs is simply not realistic. Our approach here is to summarize MFC features only as necessary and to discuss specific functions when we use them in programs. Visual C++ Help contains very complete information on these classes and functions and is easy to use. You can access Help through the Microsoft Development Network (MSDN) or as downloaded to your computer. You should look for detailed information there as you feel you need it.

Let's begin discussing the OnDraw function of FirstWin by considering line 02 in Table 4.1 where the function redeclaration is made at the top of the prototype. The original declaration of the OnDraw member function is in the definition of the CFirstWinView class. It can be found by right clicking on OnDraw in the Class View window and then clicking on "Go To Declaration" in the resulting options menu. In Table 4.1, line 02 of OnDraw shows the input argument (CDC* pDC) for the function. The CDC refers to the class CDC which is a class of device context objects provided by the Microsoft Foundation Classes.

As we have mentioned earlier, the first "C" in CDC is the standard indicator of a class name. The "DC" represents "device context". For us, the device context simply refers to the window on the computer screen but it may also represent other devices including printers, for example. As the OnDraw function is called, it receives the pointer pDC so that it can write or draw to the correct device (typically the program's window). Please note that the pointer name pDC was suggested in the default coding of OnDraw by showing the function argument as (CDC* /*pDC*/) in the originally prepared code for line 02. We accepted the suggested pointer name pDC by deleting the comment indicators.

Line 04 in Table 4.1 has been provided by the Application Wizard to obtain a pointer to the current active document by calling the

Table 4.1 Listing of the OnDraw function from FirstWinView.cpp

```
01    /* This is the OnDraw function for FirstWin */
02    void CFirstWinView::OnDraw(CDC* pDC)
03    {
04        CFirstWinDoc* pDoc = GetDocument();
05        ASSERT_VALID(pDoc);   if (!pDoc) return;
06        // TODO: add draw code for native data here
07        int CenterX, CenterY, BoxW, BoxH;
08        CenterX = 400;
09        CenterY = 100;
10        BoxW = 150;
11        BoxH = 150;
12        pDC->MoveTo(CenterX - BoxW/2, CenterY - BoxH/2);
13        pDC->LineTo(CenterX + BoxW/2, CenterY - BoxH/2);
14        pDC->LineTo(CenterX + BoxW/2, CenterY + BoxH/2);
15        pDC->LineTo(CenterX - BoxW/2, CenterY + BoxH/2);
16        pDC->LineTo(CenterX - BoxW/2, CenterY - BoxH/2);
17        pDC->SetPixel(CenterX,CenterY,0);
18        int StartTextX, StartTextY;
19        StartTextX = 50;
20        StartTextY = 50;
21        CString Buffer;
22        Buffer.Format(L"Hello Windows World!");
23        pDC->TextOut(StartTextX,StartTextY,Buffer);
24        Buffer.Format(L"This is a Box and a Dot!");
25        pDC->TextOut(StartTextX,StartTextY + 50,Buffer);
26        Buffer.Format(L"The Dot is at %d, %d",CenterX, CenterY);
27        pDC->TextOut(StartTextX,StartTextY + 100,Buffer);
28    }
```

GetDocument function, OnDraw can then access data for its operations by using the document pointer. In this example, we are not yet using a document for data storage and so line 04 is not a necessity although it is automatically furnished. The statements in line 05 are present to confirm that a document has been appropriately associated with the window.

The homemade code in OnDraw that draws the picture and writes the text into the program window begins by declaring and initializing several integer variables in lines 07–11. These variables represent the center location and the height and width of the box to be drawn into the window. The coordinate system used is the default Windows graphics coordinate system where the values are in pixel units and the origin of the x-y coordinate system is at the upper-left hand corner of the window. The x coordinate is positive to the right, the y coordinate is positive downward. Our box is centered at x = 400 and y = 100 with width BoxW and height BoxH of 150 pixels.

Lines 12–16 actually draw the box. Line 12 calls a function MoveTo which is a CDC member function intended to operate on objects of the CDC class (working with "help" in the development environment, you can find a full description of the function CDC::MoveTo). The program window is a CDC object. The pointer pDC is a pointer identifying the program window which is passed into OnDraw when it is called by the system. Think of the MoveTo in line 12 as moving a pencil in the window (but without drawing) to a pixel position located at the upper-left hand corner of the box to be drawn. Line 13 then calls the LineTo member function of the CDC class (CDC::LineTo). Again the pointer pDC is used to indicate the current window. This LineTo function call draws a line from the upper-left hand box corner to the upper-right. Similarly, lines 14–16 draw down the right side, across the bottom and up the left side of the box. Line 17 then activates a single pixel at the center of the box with the CDC function SetPixel. The SetPixel arguments CenterX and CenterY locate the pixel position. The last item in its argument list controls color and produces a black pixel when set to zero.

Now, let's look at the code in Table 4.1 for displaying text in the window. Lines 18–20 declare and initialize the variables used for text positioning. Line 21 declares an object of the CString class called Buffer. You can explore the details of CString with Visual C++ help. It has many member functions designed to facilitate the manipulation of character strings. We use the Format member function in line 22. The Format function accepts an input argument equivalent to the argument for the familiar printf function that we used in Console Applications. Note that an "L" (for literal) is added to printf formatting to adjust for the Unicode characters required in MFC Applications. After line 22, the Buffer object contains the formatted text in a character string that can be displayed in our window. Line 23 uses the pointer pDC and the CDC function TextOut to display the contents of Buffer (Hello Windows World!) in our window. Lines 24 and 25 use the same approach to reload

Buffer and write the next line of text into the window. Finally, line 26 uses the decimal integer format (%d) to place the box center coordinate values into Buffer and line 27 displays them. In each use of TextOut, the first two arguments are the x-y coordinates in pixels where writing of the text begins and the last item is the CString object to be displayed. By looking at lines 23, 25 and 27, you can see that the three lines of text each begin at the same x coordinate value while the y coordinates of each line are separated by 50 pixels to comfortably separate the lines.

Before leaving this section, you should be able to look at the code of Table 4.1 and understand the way each item is displayed in the program window of Figure 4.7.

4.3 Receiving Keyboard Inputs

Windows programs including computation or animation typically receive inputs with user clicks on menu items and toolbar buttons and by numbers entered into open dialog boxes. We will certainly discuss these topics in later chapters, however, basic inputs from the keyboard can also be a convenient way to interact with an operating program. Keyboard input is also relatively simple and suitable as a first step to understanding interactions with a Windows program.

We will use basic keyboard inputs as provided within the Windows messaging system. Our example project for this purpose is called KeyStrike and it's located in the folder *Chap4\2_KeyStrike*. You should load it into Visual C++ and build and execute it. You will be prompted to "Strike a key" and after a keystroke, the display should appear similar to Figure 4.8. The program writes the character symbol for the key input along with its corresponding ASCII code (more explanation shortly). As you keep striking keys, the display is updated. If you strike an "A" or a "C", a special message is displayed.

We'll now look at the coding for this program. The initial prompt from KeyStrike is displayed by the OnDraw function of the view class CKeyStrikeView which you should be able to find in Visual Studio by

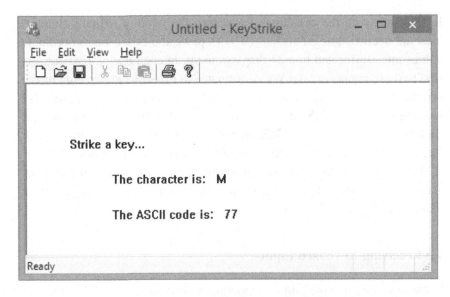

Figure 4.8 The KeyStrike Display after Striking M

expanding the class CKeyStrikeView in the Class View window. Clicking on the OnDraw function will then bring it into the Edit window. The OnDraw listing is shown in Table 4.2. You can see that it declares the CString object Buffer at line 07 of Table 4.2 and the member function Format is used at line 08 to fill Buffer with the prompt message. In line 09, the pointer pDC is used to indicate the current window and the member function TextOut writes the prompt beginning 50 pixels from the left of the window and 60 pixels down from the top.

The only other homemade code written for this project is in the function OnKeyDown of the class CKeyStrikeView. This function was created as a message handler for the KeyStrike program. It is called whenever a keystroke is received while the window "has focus" (this means that the window is the currently active window on the computer desktop). This type of function is referred to as a "Windows message handler" because the keystroke is actually received by the Windows operating system and information about it is then sent to the KeyStrike

Table 4.2 Listing of OnDraw from KeyStrikeView.cpp

```
01   /* Listing of the OnDraw function */
02   void CKeyStrikeView::OnDraw(CDC* pDC)
03   {
04        CKeyStrikeDoc* pDoc = GetDocument();
05        ASSERT_VALID(pDoc);   if (!pDoc) return;
06        // TODO: add draw code for native data here
07        CString Buffer;
08        Buffer.Format(L"Strike a key...");
09        pDC->TextOut(50,60,Buffer);
10   }
```

program in the form of a "Windows message". The OnKeyDown function is intended to "handle" the message. You can take a look at the coding of the OnKeyDown function by clicking on it in the Class View window. We will discuss it thoroughly below in Section 4.3.2. But before discussing the code for OnKeyDown, let's consider the process used to create the OnKeyDown function ready for coding.

4.3.1 Creating the OnKeyDown message handler

As you look at the procedure below, the creation of a function like the OnKeyDown message handler may seem tedious but the Application Wizard actually does most of the work for you. When you have become familiar with the process, only a few "points and clicks" are required to establish the function.

We will look at creation of the OnKeyDown message handler by starting a new Visual C++ project. Close KeyStrike by clicking on **File > Close Solution** (or just close the development environment and restart it). To begin the new project click on **File > New > Project**. When the New Project window appears, click on Visual C++ Projects and highlight MFC Application. Use the project name DemoKeyStrike and click OK. When the MFC Application Wizard window appears, click "Application Type". Then select the single document application and the MFC standard style. Click Finish. You should now have the new project DemoKeyStrike in place containing only its Application Wizard coding.

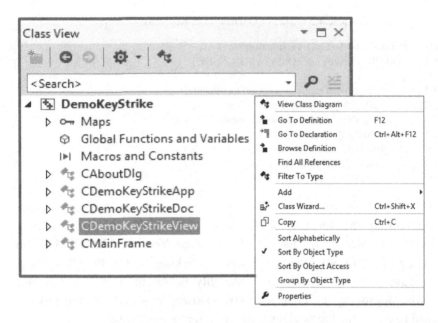

Figure 4.9 Selecting "Properties" for the View Class

We have created this project to demonstrate the preparation of a function to handle a Windows message. In this case, we want the handler to be an OnKeyDown function in the class CDemoKeyStrikeView. To begin creating the function, click the Class View tab on the workspace to show the Class View window. Then click the DemoKeyStrike ">" sign to see the project classes as in the Class View window of Figure 4.9. A right click on the class CDemoKeyStrikeView will pop up the options window to the right in Figure 4.9. Then, clicking on **Properties** leads to the display of the Properties window in a form similar to that shown in Figure 4.10.

Explore the Properties window toolbar with the mouse cursor to find the "Messages" button (usually the button to the right of the lightning bolt) and click on it. This will display the list of Windows messages ("WM_") as shown in Figure 4.10. Scroll through the messages to find WM_KEYDOWN, the message sent out when a key is pressed. Click on

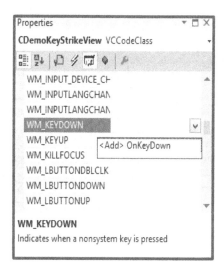

Figure 4.10 Properties Window of the View Class

WM_KEYDOWN to highlight it and activate its neighboring drop down item. A click on the drop down arrow will display "<Add> OnKeyDown" and clicking on this item will add the function OnKeyDown to the class CDemoKeyStrikeView. The Properties window can then be closed.

Now, if you click on CDemoKeyStrikeView in the Class View window, the list of members of the class CDemoKeyStrikeView will be displayed. The function OnKeyDown in this list is a newly added member function. Clicking on OnKeyDown displays the empty OnKeyDown function in the Edit window ready for you to add code, just as shown in Figure 4.11. At this point, the function OnKeyDown is ready to be edited. If you were to provide the correct code in OnKeyDown and also enter the appropriate OnDraw code into the OnDraw function, the program DemoKeyStrike could be compiled and executed. It would operate just like our KeyStrike example program.

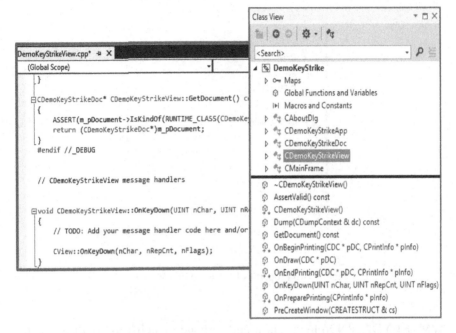

Figure 4.11 OnKeyDown as a Member Function of the View Class

4.3.2 Code for the OnKeyDown function

In the section above we showed the process of using the view class Properties window to create a member function for Windows message processing. We'll now continue our discussion by returning to the original KeyStrike program located in the folder *Chap4\2_KeyStrike*. Bring this program back into the Visual Studio development environment by clicking on KeyStrike.sln so that we can continue our discussion of the program code. Keep in mind that we have written code into only two functions. The first is the OnDraw function (shown in Table 4.2). This function executes as the program starts and displays the "Strike a key" prompt. The second place where we have entered code is in the OnKeyDown function which is the message handler and is discussed below.

You will find the OnKeyDown function easily from the Class View window by clicking on the expand sign next to the class CKeyStrikeView and then clicking on the OnKeyDown member function. This will take you directly to the function definition. Notice that if you right click on OnKeyDown, you'll have a choice of going to the function definition or declaration or several other options. As we just discussed in Section 4.3.1, the OnKeyDown function has been set up as a member function of the view class CKeyStrikeView. It is activated as a "key down" Windows message is received by the program and will execute its code as shown completely in Table 4.3. Line 02 is the redeclaration of the OnKeyDown function (the Wizard placed the original declaration of OnKeyDown into in the file KeyStrikeView.h for the class CKeyStrikeView).

The standard OnKeyDown arguments provided are shown in line 02 of the table and include nChar, which represents the key that has been pressed, a variable nRepCnt which counts repetitions if the key is held down and nFlags, which encodes several pieces of keystroke information (Help can be used to explore further details). We will be dealing only with the keystroke variable nChar in this simple program. Incidentally, the keystrokes discussed here are "non-system keystrokes" i.e. keystrokes received without depression of the Alt or Ctrl keys. Line 04 contains the Wizard's "TODO" statement and line 05 is the first line of code which we have actually written. Line 05 simply declares a character variable with the descriptive name KeyStruck and sets it to the nChar input received in the Windows message.

Line 06 is more complicated. There is an MFC class for directly outputting to an open window without using the OnDraw function. The class name is CClientDC, which represents a "client device context" and line 06 declares the object aDC of the CClientDC class. The argument "this" in line 06 refers to the current window so that aDC is defined by line 06 as an object of the CClientDC class. It represents this current window. Line 07 declares Buffer and BufferSpaces as two CString objects and line 08 uses the Format function to fill BufferSpaces with spaces. Lines 09–11 then use the TextOut function to place three

Table 4.3 Listing of OnKeyDown from KeyStrikeView.cpp

```
01    /* Listing of the OnKeyDown function */
02    void CKeyStrikeView::OnKeyDown(UINT nChar, UINT nRepCnt, UINT nFlags)
03    {
04         // TODO: Add your message handler code here and/or call default
05         char KeyStruck = nChar;
06         CClientDC aDC(this);
07         CString Buffer, BufferSpaces;
08         BufferSpaces.Format(L"                              ");
09         aDC.TextOut(100,100,BufferSpaces);
10         aDC.TextOut(100,140,BufferSpaces);
11         aDC.TextOut(100,180,BufferSpaces);
12         Buffer.Format(L"The character is:  %c",KeyStruck);
13         aDC.TextOut(100,100,Buffer);
14         Buffer.Format(L"The ASCII code is:  %d",KeyStruck);
15         aDC.TextOut(100,140,Buffer);
16    if (KeyStruck == 'A') {
17         Buffer.Format (L"HEY! - you've entered an \"A\"");
18         aDC.TextOut(100,180,Buffer);
19         }
20    if (KeyStruck == 67) {
21         Buffer.Format (L"GEE! - you've entered a \"C\"");
22         AfxMessageBox(Buffer, MB_OK);
23         }
24         CView::OnKeyDown(nChar, nRepCnt, nFlags);
25    }
```

lines of spaces into the current window (as represented by the object aDC). When new keystrokes are received, these lines of spaces erase anything that has been previously written on the lines. In this way, with repeated keystrokes, the text to be written by lines 13, 15 and 18 of Table 4.3 will appear against a blank background and will not contain any fragments of text from previous outputs.

Line 12 fills the CString object Buffer with an appropriate label and the character KeyStruck. The Buffer is then printed by line 13. Line 14 again fills Buffer with KeyStruck and a label but this time the %d format is used to write the decimal integer number that represents the character. This is the well-known ASCII code (American Society for Computer and Information Interchange) for representing keyboard characters. Line 15 displays the ASCII code for the character struck. As you strike characters in the running program you can see their ASCII equivalents displayed. Notice that the character set used here is rather limited. For example, only uppercase letters are considered.

Lines 16–19 provide a special line of output if the character A is struck and lines 20–23 provide a special output for striking a C. The C output information appears in an official Windows message box and line 22 indicates the standard format to create such an output. Notice that the if statement in line 20 uses the ASCII representation of "67" to test for a C. We have shown these special outputs for "A" and "C" just to indicate that keystroke inputs can easily trigger particular actions with the right code in the OnKeyDown function. The final line of the function at line 24 is the default code provided by the Application Wizard and ends the function by calling the base class (CView) version of OnKeyDown.

4.4 Revision of the KeyStrike Program

You may have noticed that the KeyStrike program of the previous section does not fully function as a Windows program. There is a difficulty with this version of KeyStrike that will be discussed thoroughly in this section. To see the difficulty, execute the KeyStrike program and strike a key. You should see the corresponding character and ASCII code neatly displayed. Now try to maximize the program window. Is something missing? When the window is redrawn, you can still see the "Strike a key" prompt. But, the previous display of the input character and its ASCII code has disappeared. The reason for this is that the OnDraw function of the view class is the only function automatically called by the Windows operating system after the user performs a maximize, a resize, or a restore operation on the program window. In the KeyStrike program, the prompt "Strike a key" is written by the OnDraw function. But the character and the ASCII outputs are only written by the OnKeyDown function, which is only executed when a key is pressed. After maximizing the KeyStrike window, strike a key and notice that new keystrokes are still handled properly.

There are a few ways to fix the KeyStrike display problem. But the basic issue is that OnDraw is the only function automatically called by

Windows when a redisplay is needed. To maintain a consistent display, OnDraw must be able to access the most recent keystroke information and contain the code to fully redisplay that information. This means first, that the KeyStruck variable for the last keystroke cannot simply be local within the OnKeyDown function but must also be available to OnDraw. And second, that a display operation similar to the one in the OnKeyDown function of KeyStrike must be performed by the OnDraw function to provide a full renewal of the display when needed.

We have made the necessary changes to KeyStrike in a new project called KeyStrikeMv (where the "Mv" indicates that a member variable of the view class has been introduced and is critical to program operation). The project KeyStrikeMv is located in the folder *Chap4\3_KeyStrikeMv*. You should bring this project into the Visual C++ development environment and build and execute it. Notice that the program has full Windows functionality — redrawing the display after window resizing maximizing, etc. We will show the coding required for these changes in listings below. However, it is also necessary to carry out a few new operations in the development environment. Specifically, a new member variable will be added to the view class (we're calling it m_KeyStruck) and also a new member function (WriteToScreen) will be added. You can see these in the current KeyStrikeMv project by exploring its Class View window.

We will now consider a demonstration sample project to show how these members are added. Let's start by executing Visual Studio and creating a new Visual C++ single document project with MFC standard style. We'll call it DemoKeyStrikeMv (you can review the creation details by referring to Section 4.1). Once the project is ready, open the Class View window and expand the classes, focusing on the view class CDemoKeyStrikeMvView as shown to the left of Figure 4.12. Right click on this class to pop up the option window in the middle of Figure 4.12. Then click on Add to see the option to add a variable or a function as shown on the right in Figure 4.12. At this point, click on Add Variable to reveal the Add Member Variable Wizard of Figure 4.13. Entries are required in only a few of the boxes to make the "char" variable named m_KeyStruck a member of the view class as shown. Click Finish when the form is complete.

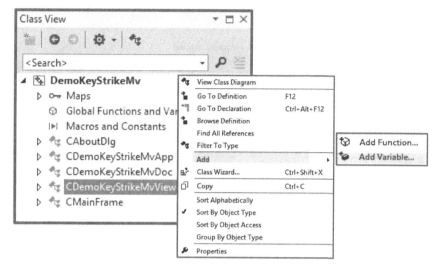

Figure 4.12 Adding a Member Variable to the View Class

Next, right click again on CDemoKeyStrikeMvView and click again on Add. This time, in Figure 4.12, click on Add Function and you will see the Add Member Function Wizard of Figure 4.14. Place "void" in the Return type and enter the name WriteToScreen for the function which will be used to display text outputs. Since we will use the member variable m_KeyStruck for the keystroke data, no input argument is needed for WriteToScreen. No entry in Parameter name is required and the remaining boxes can also be left empty. Click Finish to conclude. In addition to m_KeyStruck and WriteToScreen, an OnKeyDown message handler function is also needed by DemoKeyStrikeMv. You can add this exactly as described for DemoKeyStrike in Section 4.3.1.

When you have finished adding the new members to the class CDemoKeyStrikeMvView, use the Class View window to review the members of the view class. The member variable m_KeyStruck, the member function WriteToScreen, and the member function OnKeyDown should all be present. As a member variable of the view class, m_KeyStruck is available for use by all of its member functions including, for our purposes: OnDraw, OnKeyDown and WriteToScreen.

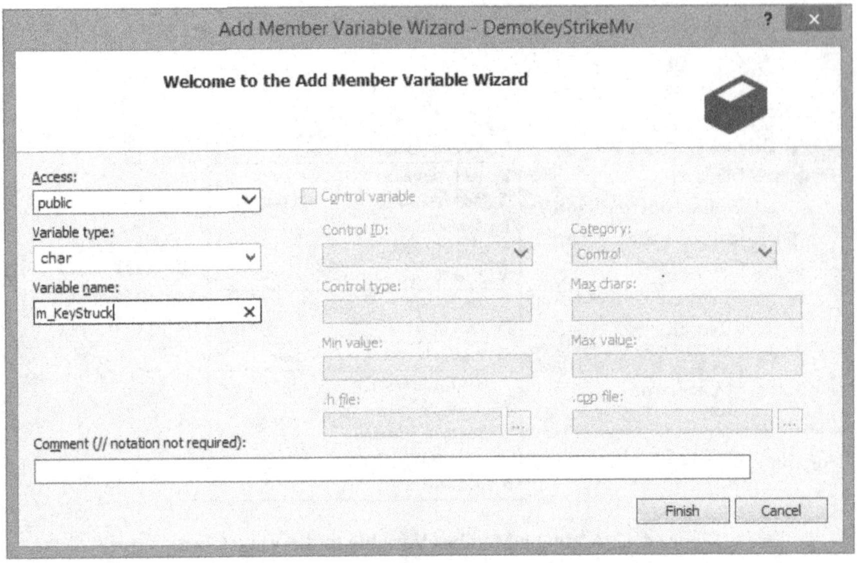

Figure 4.13 The Add Member Variable Wizard

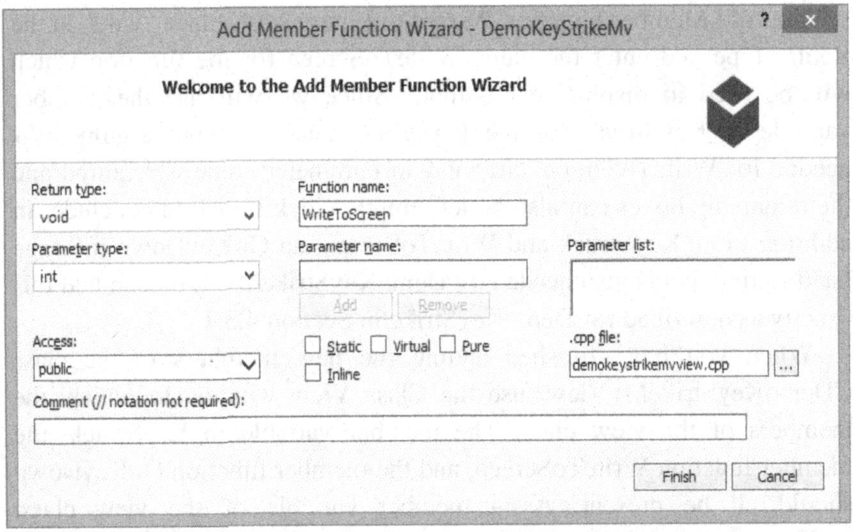

Figure 4.14 Dialog for Adding a Member Function

In this project, the OnKeyDown function serves to update m_KeyStruck whenever a key is pressed. The latest value of m_KeyStruck is then displayed by WriteToScreen when needed. The coding required to make this demonstration project work can be explored in the KeyStrikeMv example of Chap4\3_KeyStrikeMv. The code is described in detail in the section below.

4.4.1 Coding for KeyStrikeMv

Load the project KeyStrikeMv into Visual C++ from the folder *Chap4\3_KeyStrikeMv* so that we can explore the coding necessary to take advantage of the view class member variable m_KeyStruck. The first step is to consider the initialization of m_KeyStruck as the program starts to execute. This initialization is performed in the view class constructor function CKeyStrikeMvView located in the file KeyStrikeMvView.cpp. You can find it easily by clicking on the constructor function CKeyStrikeMvView in the Class View window. The listing is shown in Table 4.4 below. Line 03 is the initialization statement automatically inserted by the Add Member Variable Wizard as the member variable m_KeyStruck is added to the view class. The default initialization to "0" provided by the Wizard may be seen at line 03. When an override of this initialization is desired, it can be easily done by adding code immediately after the "TODO..." instruction in line 05 of Table 4.4. In this case, an initial value of "0" ASCII will not be overridden since it corresponds to a null (i.e. empty) character and is satisfactory for our application.

The next coding to consider is in the OnDraw function of Table 4.5. For this project, only Line 07 has been added to the Application Wizard

Table 4.4 Listing of CKeyStrikeMvView from KeyStrikeMvView.cpp

```
01   /* This is the CKeyStrikeMvView function */
02   CKeyStrikeMvView::CKeyStrikeMvView()
03   : m_KeyStruck(0)
04   {
05        // TODO: add construction code here
06   }
```

Table 4.5 Listing of OnDraw from KeyStrikeMvView.cpp

```
01    /* This is the OnDraw function */
02    void CKeyStrikeMvView::OnDraw(CDC* pDC)
03    {
04        CKeyStrikeMvDoc* pDoc = GetDocument();
05        ASSERT_VALID(pDoc); if (!pDoc) return;
06        // TODO: add draw code for native data here
07        WriteToScreen();
08    }
```

template. It calls the WriteToScreen function which will handle all of the display output. The full OnKeyDown function is shown in Table 4.6. It now contains only two inserted lines of code at lines 05 and 06. In line 05, m_KeyStruck is set to the value of the newly input keystroke. In line 06 the WriteToScreen function is called. The WriteToScreen function is now expected to do all of the hard work in the program as it is called from both On Draw and OnKeyDown.

The WriteToScreen listing is presented in Table 4.7 where you can see the similarity of its code to the OnKeyDown function of the original KeyStrike project. Line 04 identifies the client device context for the current window. Lines 05–07 set up the buffers for the text display and write "Strike a key". The if statement of line 08 is not satisfied as the window first opens since m_KeyStruck was initialized as "0" (null character). But, as keys are pressed, m_KeyStruck is no longer null and the if statement is satisfied. Then, with each keystroke, lines 10–24 output m_KeyStruck in both character and ASCII form including the special information for the input of an "A" or "C".

Table 4.6 Listing of OnKeyDown from KeyStrikeMvView.cpp

```
01    /* This is the OnKeyDown function */
02    void CKeyStrikeMvView::OnKeyDown(UINT nChar,UINT nRepCnt,UINT nFlags)
03    {
04        // TODO: Add your message handler code here and/or call default
05        m_KeyStruck = nChar;
06        WriteToScreen();
07        CView::OnKeyDown(nChar, nRepCnt, nFlags);
08    }
```

Table 4.7 Listing of WriteToScreen from KeyStrikeMvView.cpp

```
01   /* This is the WriteToScreen function */
02   void CKeyStrikeMvView::WriteToScreen()
03   {
04        CClientDC aDC(this);
05        CString Buffer, BufferSpaces;
06        Buffer.Format(L"Strike a key...");
07        aDC.TextOut(50,60,Buffer);
08   if (m_KeyStruck != 0)
09        {
10        BufferSpaces.Format(L"                    ");
11        aDC.TextOut(100,100,BufferSpaces);
12        aDC.TextOut(100,140,BufferSpaces);
13        aDC.TextOut(100,180,BufferSpaces);
14        Buffer.Format(L"The character is:  %c",m_KeyStruck);
15        aDC.TextOut(100,100,Buffer);
16        Buffer.Format(L"The ASCII code is:  %d",m_KeyStruck);
17        aDC.TextOut(100,140,Buffer);
18   if (m_KeyStruck == 'A') {
19        Buffer.Format (L"HEY! - you've entered an \"A\"");
20        aDC.TextOut(100,180,Buffer);
21        }
22   if (m_KeyStruck == 67) {
23        Buffer.Format (L"GEE! - you've entered a \"C\"");
24        AfxMessageBox(Buffer, MB_OK);
25        }
26        }
27   }
```

4.5 Using the Document Class for Storing the "Key"

In Section 4.3 we used the example program KeyStrike to take in keystrokes and output both their character and ASCII representations. In Section 4.4 we discussed a windowing display problem with KeyStrike that required better storage of our KeyStruck variable. We then introduced the example program KeyStrikeMv and made m_KeyStruck a member variable of the view class. This change made m_KeyStruck available to be updated or used anywhere in the view class and provided a solution for the windowing display problem. The m_KeyStruck variable is just a single piece of data that we have been using only for user interaction and display. It is perfectly reasonable to make it a view class member variable and to use it only within the view class for display purposes. However, most real data used by computer programs come in much larger quantities and must be manipulated by computational methods of many different types. In the document/view organization of an MFC Application, the appropriate way to keep the data separate from viewing operations is to store it within member variables of the document class.

To illustrate this document storage process, we will now take our KeyStrike project to the next level, storing the keystroke variable in the document class. The example KeyStrikeDMv may be found in the folder *Chap4\4_KeyStrikeDMv*. Load it into Visual C Studio and compile and execute it. You should see that it behaves exactly as the KeyStrikeMv program with proper windowing operations and proper display of each key as it is pressed. The organization, however, of KeyStrikeDMv is considerably different than KeyStrikeMv. Use the Class View window to look over the class structure. Notice that the document class CKeyStrikeDMvDoc now contains m_Savekey as a member variable which is used to save the last keystroke entered. The view class no longer contains m_KeyStruck as a member variable.

The document class member variable m_Savekey was added with the Add New Variable Wizard (right click on CKeyStrikeDMvDoc, click on Add, click on Variable). Its declaration was created by the Wizard within the declaration of the class CKeyStrikeDMvDoc in the file KeyStrikeDMvDoc.h. It is initialized by default in the constructor function CKeyStrikeDMvDoc (shown in Table 4.8) and set to "0" ASCII at line 03. If desired, this can be overridden by adding code after line 05 in Table 4.8. The function OnNewDocument in the document class can also be useful for overriding the initialization. The OnNewDocument function is automatically called at the beginning of program execution and before the OnDraw function is called. It is also called when **File > New** is clicked from the menu bar or the "New" toolbar item is clicked. We will begin to look more thoroughly at the OnNewDocument function in Chapter 5. However, since keystrokes are now being stored through m_Savekey in the document class, some changes in the view class

Table 4.8 Listing of CKeyStrikeDMvDoc from KeyStrikeDMvDoc.cpp

```
01    /*Listing of the CKeyStrikeDMvDoc function*/
02    CKeyStrikeDMvDoc::CKeyStrikeDMvDoc()
03    : m_ SaveKey (0)
04    {
05        // TODO: add one-time construction code here
06    }
```

functions are required to access m_Savekey as needed. The revised OnDraw function is shown in Table 4.9. Here, we make use of the document pointer operations automatically included by the Application Wizard. In this case, line 04 identifies a pointer to the current document and line 05 performs a debugging check. The only line of code that we have entered in this OnDraw function is at line 07. You can see that it calls a modified form of the WriteToScreen function which receives the stored keystroke as an argument. The keystroke is stored as m_Savekey in the document and accessed through the document pointer pDoc.

You can, of course, look at the WriteToScreen function for KeyStrikeDMv in detail by clicking on it in the Class View window. However, it is nearly unchanged from the previous KeyStrikeMv version of Table 4.7. The major change can be noted directly in its redeclaration:

void CKeyStrikeDMvView::WriteToScreen(char KeyStruck)

This redeclaration was generated automatically by the Add Member Function Wizard in response to a right click on the view class and the selection of the option Add Member Function. We completed the Add

Table 4.9 Listing of OnDraw from KeyStrikeDMvView.cpp

```
01    /* Listing of the OnDraw Function */
02    void CKeyStrikeDMvView::OnDraw(CDC* pDC)
03    {
04        CKeyStrikeDMvDoc* pDoc = GetDocument();
05        ASSERT_VALID(pDoc);  if (!pDoc) return;
06        // TODO: add draw code for native data here
07        WriteToScreen (pDoc->m_ SaveKey);
08    }
```

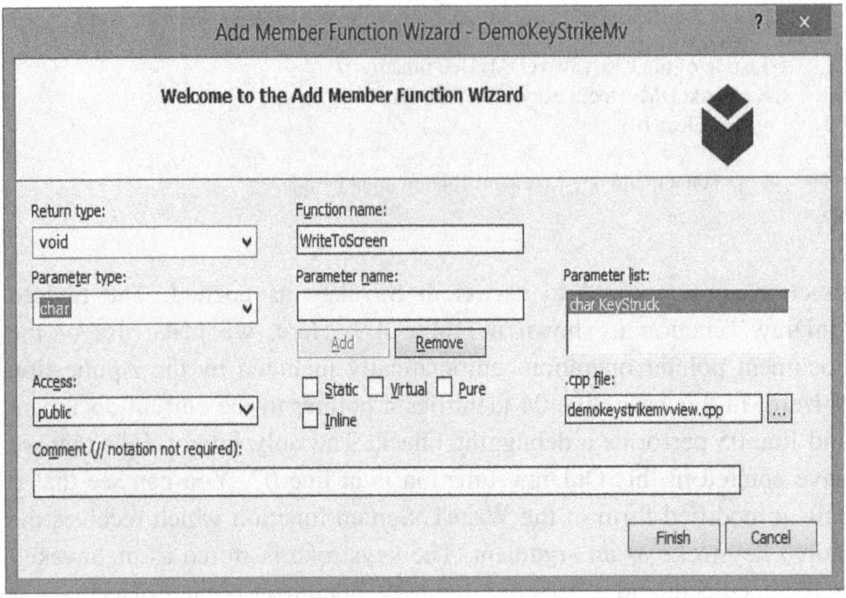

Figure 4.15 Adding WriteToScreen with the KeyStruck Argument

Member Function window as shown in Figure 4.15. Notice that the character variable added to the parameter list has been given the local name KeyStruck. From this information and from Table 4.9 you can see that the WriteToScreen function now obtains its keystroke information from the newly established document class member variable. This happens as the pDoc->m_Savekey variable is passed into WriteToScreen as an argument. Other than this, WriteToScreen performs the same display operations as before.

The last piece of program revision needed to adapt to the use of document class storage can be seen in the listing of the OnKeyDown function shown in Table 4.10. The homemade code added to the function begins by identifying the active document in line 05. Line 06 then uses the document pointer to set the document variable m_Savekey to the value of the key pressed. Line 07 uses an MFC CDocument class

Table 4.10 Listing of OnKeyDown from KeyStrikeDMvView.cpp

```
01  /* This is the listing of the OnKeyDown function */
02  void CKeyStrikeDMvView::OnKeyDown(UINT nChar,UINT nRepCnt,UINT nFlags)
03  {
04        // TODO: Add your message handler code here and/or call default
05        CKeyStrikeDMvDoc* pDoc = GetDocument();
06        pDoc->m_ SaveKey = nChar;
07        pDoc->UpdateAllViews(NULL);
08        CView::OnKeyDown(nChar, nRepCnt, nFlags);
09  }
```

function called UpdateAllViews which updates the view of the window document. You can find the function details for UpdateAllViews with Visual C++ Help. However, when executed with the NULL argument, it results in execution of the OnDraw function to redraw the display using the current document data (in this case, a keystroke sets a new value for m_Savekey and represents a change in the document).

The use of document storage for m_Savekey in this program is only an example. It is not strictly necessary for this simple application. However, the strategy for document storage used here for m_Savekey is the same as in more complex programs containing much more data. In general, you will want your Application Wizard programs to use the view class to handle the display and interactions with the user. The document class should contain member variables to store data for the application and should have the member functions necessary to manipulate it. In the next chapter, we will start performing graphics operations with more data and a wide variety of manipulations. The usefulness of the document/view organization will then become quite apparent.

4.6 Exercises

1. Using the FirstWin project of Section 4.2 as an example, create a program that draws an equilateral triangle with a side length of 150 pixels. Locate the triangle center at x = 100 and y = 400. Change the

output text appropriately for this new drawing and place it at a convenient location.

2. Modify the FirstWin project of Section 4.2 so that the program displays an empty window when it begins execution. When the user strikes an "R" on the keyboard, the program should display the rectangle and its associated text. When the user strikes any other key, the window should refresh and display an empty window.

3. Combining Exercises 1 and 2, develop a program that will display an empty window when it starts. Striking an "R" should refresh the window and display the rectangle and its text. Striking a "T" should refresh the window and display the triangle and its text. Striking any other key should display an empty window.

Chapter 5

Basic Graphics

This chapter continues the discussion of programming in the Windows environment. We go beyond the simple graphics operations introduced in Chapter 4 and we also extend the document storage ideas that were initially presented in Chapter 4 for the storage of individual keystrokes. A series of new graphics concepts are described in this chapter. The concepts are all presented in example programs and the individual functions are described in full detail. The line numbered listings of the important coding should allow you to follow the logic at each step and to see how the code segments fit into the MFC Application template.

The chapter begins by introducing line drawing operations using mouse inputs in Section 5.1. In Section 5.2 the document/view structure is used to store mouse drawing data and to provide full Windows functionality while making simple drawings. "Rubber-banding" during line drawing operations is described in Section 5.3 and from there we go on to look at a basic animation process in Section 5.4. In Section 5.5, the drawing of circles is added to our programming repertoire. Grid drawing is described in Section 5.6 which illustrates the use of snap-to-grid operations to provide a drawing guide and to allow accurate drawings. Also in Section 5.6, we demonstrate a strategy for saving drawings to files and recovering them based on the serialize function provided by the MFC Application Wizard. Finally, in Section 5.7, the printer output of graphic displays is discussed.

5.1 Drawing with the Mouse

The use of mouse clicks and mouse movements for computer drawing operations is a common part of many computer programs. Features are readily available in the Application Wizard to facilitate these types of drawing operations and we will explore them in the next few sections. The most basic mouse functions are shown in the project MouseDraw which is contained in *Chap5\1_MouseDraw*. In that folder, a click on MouseDraw.sln will load the project into Visual C++ so that you can inspect it. MouseDraw was created as a single document project with MFC Standard style using all of the set up defaults. When you build and execute the program, notice that each left click of the mouse draws a line to the cursor position and that each right click starts a new line at the cursor position. If your first click is a left mouse click, the first line begins at the upper left corner of the window.

In MouseDraw, only the view class CMouseDrawView contains homemade coding and that coding is confined to three functions: the class constructor function CMouseDrawView, and the two message handling functions, OnLButtonDown and OnRButtonDown. The variable m_CurrentPoint is used to identify the starting position of each line and it has been made a member variable of the view class CMouseDrawView. You should notice that m_CurrentPoint is an object of the MFC class CPoint. The CPoint class contains two member variables (the integers x and y) which can conveniently define the coordinates of a point on the display screen in units of pixels.

The member variable m_CurrentPoint has been added to the view class CMouseDrawView by right clicking in the ClassView window on the class name CMouseDrawView and using the procedure which was followed in Section 4.4 (for making m_KeyStruck a view class member variable in the KeyStrikeMv project). Figure 5.1 shows m_CurrentPoint as an object of the CPoint class being added as a member variable to the view class. If you now expand the class CMouseDrawView in the Class View window of the MouseDraw project, m_CurrentPoint is seen as its only member variable. The initial coordinate values of m_CurrentPoint are set in the view class constructor function CMouseDrawView as you can see in the listing of Table 5.1. The function CMouseDrawView is in effect as the program starts and is the appropriate place to initialize view class member variables. In Table 5.1, line 03 contains a default initialization of m_CurrentPoint coded by the Member Variable Wizard.

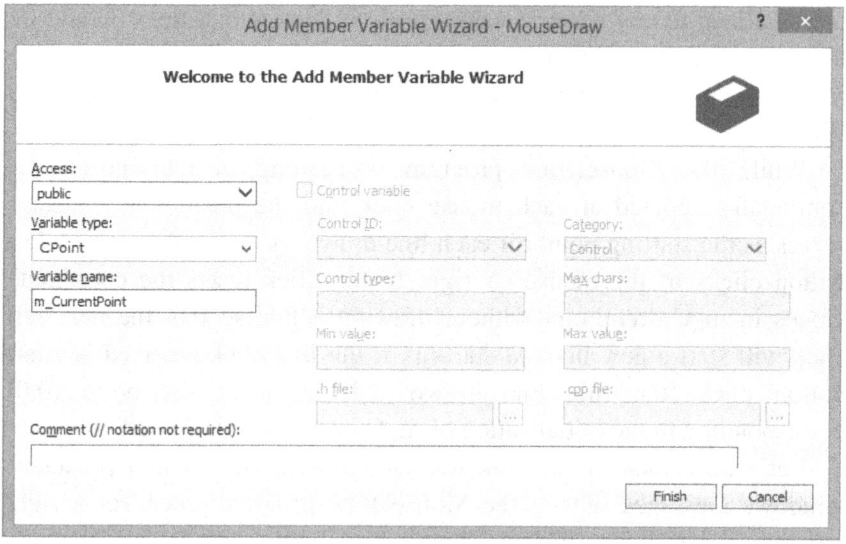

Figure 5.1 Adding m_CurrentPoint as a Member Variable

Table 5.1 Listing of CMouseDrawView from MouseDrawView.cpp

```
01    /* This is the listing of CMouseDrawView */
02    CMouseDrawView::CMouseDrawView()
03    //: m_CurrentPoint(0)
04    {
05        // TODO: add construction code here
06        m_CurrentPoint.x = 0;
07        m_CurrentPoint.y = 0;
08    }
```

We have deactivated line 03 by turning it into a comment line so that we can take control of the initialization process ourselves using the inserted lines 06 and 07.

The member variable m_CurrentPoint is an object of the CPoint class and has its own two data members for the point's x and y coordinate values. Line 06 of the code shown sets the initial value of the x coordinate of m_CurrentPoint to zero and line 07 sets its y coordinate to zero. Of course, the insertion of lines 06 and 07 allows the coordinates to be initialized to any specific values desired. Notice that lines 06 and 07 follow the "TODO" instruction and are the only lines we inserted. The rest of the function code in Table 5.1 was created by the Application Wizard.

While the MouseDraw program is running, m_CurrentPoint is continually updated at each mouse click and the position it indicates serves as the starting point for each line drawn. A line is drawn with left button clicks of the mouse. A right button click resets the coordinate values in m_CurrentPoint without drawing a line so that the next left click will start a new line. At start-up, if the first click received is a left button click, the first line drawn will begin at the point (0,0) corresponding to the initialization of m_CurrentPoint discussed above.

Let's now look at the function OnRButtonDown which processes windows messages sent to the MouseDraw program whenever a right mouse button is clicked (generating the windows message WM_RBUTTONDOWN). This message handler function was introduced into the project by using the Properties window of the view class as we discussed in Section 4.3 (where the OnKeyDown function was inserted into the KeyStrike project). The function listing is shown in Table 5.2. When a right mouse button click occurs, the arguments provided by the MFC Application are nFlags and "point" which are received as arguments by the function as shown in line 02.

The unsigned integer nFlags can be decoded to determine the state of various virtual keys including the control and shift key as well as the mouse buttons (see Help for details). For this program we'll only use the CPoint object called "point" which contains the x and y coordinates in pixels of the mouse cursor location when the button is clicked. As previously mentioned for pixel coordinates, x is the horizontal axis and y is the vertical axis (positive downward). The origin is at the upper left corner of the window. Line 05 is the only line of inserted code written in Table 5.2. It simply sets m_CurrentPoint to the present mouse position ready to define the start of the next line to be drawn. The Application Wizard provided the function call of line 06.

When mouse clicks occur while MouseDraw is running, windows messages for left button down are handled by the OnLButtonDown

Table 5.2 Listing of OnRButtonDown from MouseDrawView.cpp

```
01    /* This is the listing of OnRButtonDown */
02    void CMouseDrawView::OnRButtonDown(UINT nFlags, CPoint point)
03    {
04        // TODO: Add your message handler code here and/or call default
05        m_CurrentPoint = point;
06        CView::OnRButtonDown(nFlags, point);
07    }
```

function (added to the project by right clicking on the view class, selecting Properties, etc.). The function is listed in Table 5.3. This function actually places lines on the screen corresponding to the left button clicks. However, before the lines can be drawn, the "pen" used for drawing must be specified. Line 05 in Table 5.3 declares the object called BluePen of the class CPen. CPen is an MFC class designed to hold the information necessary to describe pens used to draw lines into a window. The properties of BluePen are defined in line 06 of OnLButtonDown with a call to the CreatePen member function of CPen (full details are available in Visual C++ Help). In the argument list in line 06, the entry PS_SOLID indicates that a solid line is to be drawn. Then a pen width of two pixels is indicated and finally the color blue is specified. The MFC function RGB is used to define the pen color in the

Table 5.3 Listing of OnLButtonDown from MouseDrawView.cpp

```
01    /* This is the listing of OnLButtonDown */
02    void CMouseDrawView::OnLButtonDown(UINT nFlags, CPoint point)
03    {
04        // TODO: Add your message handler code here and/or call default
05        CPen BluePen;
06        BluePen.CreatePen(PS_SOLID,2,RGB(0,0,255));
07        CClientDC aDC(this);
08        aDC.SelectObject(&BluePen);
09        aDC.MoveTo(m_CurrentPoint);
10        aDC.LineTo(point);
11        m_CurrentPoint = point;
12        CView::OnLButtonDown(nFlags, point);
13    }
```

argument list of line 06. It defines the red, green and blue color components of the pen. Each RGB component may range from 0 to 255. In line 06, the values of 0 for red, 0 for green and 255 for blue, correspond to a bright blue pen. If this color system is not familiar to you, it can be explored easily, for example in MicroSoft Paint (by clicking on **Home > EditColors**) you can study the effect of various RGB choices.

After the pen is defined in Table 5.3, line 07 of OnLButtonDown identifies the current window as the client device context aDC. Line 08 then assigns BluePen to be the drawing object for aDC using the member function SelectObject. Finally, the MoveTo of line 09 moves the pen to the line starting point indicated by m_CurrentPoint and the LineTo of line 10 draws a line to the present cursor position given by "point" as received in the argument list of line 02. After the line is drawn, line 11 updates m_CurrentPoint to the point specified by this mouse click so that the next left mouse click will start a line at this point. Line 12 was furnished by the Application Wizard.

As you exercise the MouseDraw program, notice that if your first mouse click is with the left button, the first line drawn originates at the

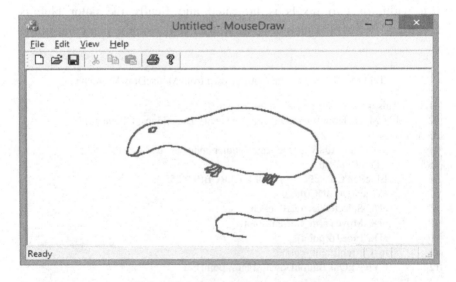

Figure 5.2 A Drawing Made with MouseDraw

point (0,0) which is the upper left window corner. This corresponds to the initial setting of m_CurrentPoint in CMouseDrawView. However, if the first click is with the right button, the line starting position is updated and a following left button click draws a line beginning at the updated starting position.

The MouseDraw program was used to create the image shown in Figure 5.2. As you work with this program, notice that if you resize, minimize or maximize the window while you have a drawing in it, the drawing will disappear. In the next section we arrange to store the drawing data so that it can be redrawn as needed for window operations.

5.2 Saving the Drawn Image

The storage and redisplay of data, as we demonstrated in Sections 4.4 and 4.5 of the previous chapter, provide the key to having full Windows functionality for resizing, restoring and maximizing the windows of an operating program. The most general strategy for storing data to be used and reused during program operation is to store that data within member variables of the document class. We introduced that approach in a very simple way in the KeyStrikeDMv project of Section 4.5 where we stored keystroke information. In the project of this section, called SimpleDraw, we extend the strategy for storing drawing data so that it can be easily redisplayed by the OnDraw function when needed for resizing, restoring, etc.

SimpleDraw is a single document project set-up with MFC Standard style using Application Wizard defaults. It is in the folder *Chap5\2_SimpleDraw* and, of course, you can load it into Visual C++ by clicking on the file SimpleDraw.sln. Building and executing the program you should find that it allows drawing with clicks of the mouse buttons just like MouseDraw of the previous section. But when you now make window adjustments by moving, restoring, maximizing, etc., the drawing in the window redisplays normally and maintains your drawing status. In this program you might also notice that if the first click at start-up is a left mouse click, the first line begins near the window center instead of at the upper left corner of the window as it did in MouseDraw.

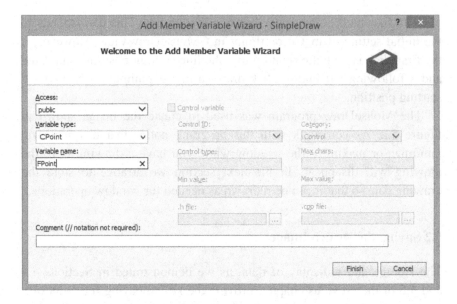

Figure 5.3 Adding FPoint in the Wizard Window

5.2.1 Creating member variables for SimpleDraw

SimpleDraw has the ability to store a line drawn image and redisplay it as necessary for normal Windows functionality. We will now discuss the procedure that can be used to provide that ability. The first step is to add the necessary member variables to the document class CSimpleDrawDoc. These member variables are added by right clicking on CSimpleDrawDoc and then clicking on **Add > Add Variable** to display the Add Member Variable Wizard. The Wizard window of Figure 5.3 shows the array name of FPoint and its variable type of CPoint as entered. LPoint was similarly entered as a document class member variable along with NumLines as an integer variable.

With these variables added to CSimpleDrawDoc, the class CSimpleDrawDoc can be expanded in the Class View window to see NumLines, FPoint and LPoint all as member variables. A double click on one of the variable names (e.g. FPoint) in the Class View window then moves the Edit window to the line of code where the variable is declared as shown in Figure 5.4. Notice that all three of the variable declarations appear together in the declaration of the class CSimpleDrawDoc. The Wizard automatically inserted them into the CSimpleDrawDoc declaration which is located in the header file SimpleDrawDoc.h. At this point, the declarations of the names FPoint and LPoint are in place. For our purposes, these data members must be converted to arrays by adding [100] to the two CPoint declarations created by the Wizard. The new lines of code thus become CPoint FPoint[100] and CPoint LPoint[100]. Of course, the default declaration of the integer NumLines does not require any adjustment. Incidentally, when it is convenient, the Add Member Variable Wizard can be by-passed and a member variable can be directly inserted into a class declaration (either the document class or view class) by writing the code for the variable declaration at the appropriate location.

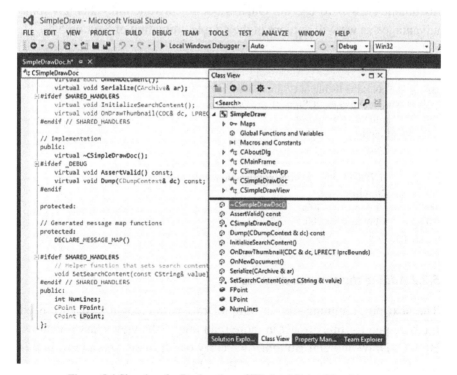

Figure 5.4 Showing the Declaration of FPoint, LPoint, NumLines

Table 5.4 shows a listing of the constructor function for the document class CSimpleDrawDoc. The Wizard inserted the default initializations of the variables shown in lines 03–05 of the function. We have inserted the comment symbols into lines 03–05 which serve to deactivate the default initializations (note, in any case, that the default FPoint and LPoint initializations would not be effective for arrays). To take control of the initialization, we have added lines 08–10 into the constructor function. Lines 09 and 10 define the x and y coordinates of the first point of the first line. With the values shown in Table 5.4, starting SimpleDraw with an initial left mouse click without a right click will result in a line beginning at (400,200) near the center of the SimpleDraw window.

Except for the first entry in the FPoint array, the rest of the array entries still remain undefined. If it were necessary to initialize them, we could easily add a loop to Table 5.4 to set all of the entries to zero or some other specific value. A second option for initialization in the document class is to use the OnNewDocument function. This has some advantages as we will explore in the simple animation of Section 5.4.

Table 5.4 Listing of CSimpleDrawDoc from SimpleDrawDoc.cpp

```
01     /* This is the listing of CSimpleDrawDoc */
02     CSimpleDrawDoc::CSimpleDrawDoc()
03     //: NumLines(0)
04     //, FPoint(0)
05     //, LPoint(0)
06     {
07          // TODO: add one-time construction code here
08          NumLines =0;
09          FPoint[0].x= 400;
10          FPoint[0].y= 200;
11     }
```

5.2.2 Adding the pen and drawing

The next programming step in SimpleDraw is to recognize that we need the blue pen for this project in more than one of the view class functions. Both OnDraw and OnLButtonDown carry out drawing operations. In this situation, it is best to make the CPen object a member variable of the view class CSimpleDrawView. You can do this by right clicking on CSimpleDrawView in the Class View window, activating the Add Member Variable Wizard, and declaring the CPen object m_BluePen. You can see that this has been completed by expanding the view class in the Class View window and seeing m_BluePen listed as a member variable. The Add Member Variable Wizard does not create an initialization statement for the CPen object. We initialize m_BluePen in the view class constructor function CSimpleDrawView shown in Table 5.5 by directly adding line 05 to the function. As in the previous project, the CPen member function CreatePen is used to set up a solid blue pen two pixels wide. With m_BluePen declared and initialized as a member variable, it is available to any function in the view class and need not be defined again.

The OnDraw function of CSimpleDrawView appears in Table 5.6 and is the code executed when the program window first opens and every time the window needs to be redrawn after resizing, etc. The first line of added code at line 07 uses the device context pointer pDC (in the argument list) to select m_BluePen for drawing. Note that if other pens were available at this point, they could have been selected instead. The for loop of lines 08–11 draws any stored lines on the screen. It uses the document pointer pDoc to access NumLines from the document and for each line, the statement in line 09 moves to the first point on the line and the statement of line 10 draws a line to the second point on the line. Notice that the first time this program executes, NumLines will be zero, the for loop will not execute, and nothing will be drawn. You will see below that as lines are drawn with mouse clicks, the mouse functions

Table 5.5 Listing of CSimpleDrawView from SimpleDrawView.cpp

```
01    /* This is the listing of CSimpleDrawView */
02    CSimpleDrawView::CSimpleDrawView()
03    {
04          // TODO: add construction code here
05          m_BluePen.CreatePen(PS_SOLID,2,RGB(0,0,255));
06    }
```

Table 5.6 Listing of OnDraw from SimpleDrawView.cpp

```
01    /* This is the listing of OnDraw */
02    void CSimpleDrawView::OnDraw(CDC* pDC)
03    {
04         · CSimpleDrawDoc* pDoc = GetDocument();
05          ASSERT_VALID(pDoc);     if (!pDoc)return;
06          // TODO: add draw code for native data here
07          pDC->SelectObject(&m_BluePen);
08    for (int i=0; i < pDoc->NumLines; i++) {
09          pDC->MoveTo(pDoc->FPoint[i]);
10          pDC->LineTo(pDoc->LPoint[i]);
11          }
12    }
```

have been coded to increment NumLines and add points to the FPoint and LPoint arrays. Whenever the window is adjusted and must be redrawn, OnDraw executes and redraws the image stored in the document by NumLines and the arrays FPoint and LPoint.

The message handling functions for mouse clicks OnRButtonDown and OnLButtonDown were added to the view class CSimpleDrawView by using the Properties window of the CSimpleDrawView class. The right button function is listed in Table 5.7 and only serves to start a fresh line. It must, however, have access to the document and line 05 obtains the document pointer pDoc for that purpose. Line 06 is the only other line of homemade code. It uses the document pointer to directly set the coordinates of the first point of the current line to "point" which is the present cursor position as received in the argument list of line 02. Notice

Table 5.7 Listing of OnRButtonDown from SimpleDrawView.cpp

```
01    /* This is the listing of OnRButtonDown */
02    void CSimpleDrawView::OnRButtonDown(UINT Nflags, CPoint point)
03    {
04         // TODO: Add your message handler code here and/or call default
05         CSimpleDrawDoc* pDoc = GetDocument();
06         pDoc->FPoint[pDoc->NumLines] = point;
07         CView::OnRButtonDown(nFlags, point);
08    }
```

that NumLines is not incremented here. Also note that if the user's first input when the program starts is a right click, FPoint[0] will be set to the cursor coordinates and line drawing will begin at that point. Repeated right clicks simply reset the first point of the line and it is not until a left click is received that NumLines will be incremented.

The left button down function is listed below in Table 5.8 and does the most work of our functions in SimpleDraw. A line drawing operation is completed with each left button click. NumLines is incremented and the current LPoint and the next FPoint coordinates are set to the present cursor position. Line 05 of OnLButtonDown obtains the pointer pDoc to allow document access. Line 06 obtains the client device context aDC to represent the current window, line 07 selects m_BluePen for drawing (it's available since it is a view class member variable). Line 08 obtains the current NumLines value from the document and line 09 moves to the coordinates of the first point on the current line. Line 10 actually draws the blue line to the mouse cursor position and line 11 saves the cursor position as the last point on the line. Line 12 then saves the first point on the next line as this cursor position — anticipating the drawing of

Table 5.8 Listing of OnLButtonDown from SimpleDrawView.cpp

```
01    /* This is the listing of OnLButtonDown */
02    void CSimpleDrawView::OnLButtonDown(UINT nFlags, CPoint point)
03    {
04        // TODO: Add your message handler code here and/or call default
05        CSimpleDrawDoc* pDoc = GetDocument();
06        CClientDC aDC(this);
07        aDC.SelectObject(&m_BluePen);
08        int i = pDoc->NumLines;
09        aDC.MoveTo(pDoc->FPoint[i]);
10        aDC.LineTo(point);
11        pDoc->LPoint[i] = point;
12        pDoc->FPoint[i+1] = point;
13        pDoc->NumLines++;
14        CView::OnLButtonDown(nFlags, point);
15    }
```

successive lines. Finally, line 13 increments NumLines in the document. Please recall that a right button click will override the FPoint coordinates if a fresh line is desired. Line 14 is provided by the Application Wizard.

The end result of the SimpleDraw project is a program that will store the image created by mouse clicks within document class member variables. Those member variables are available to be used in redrawing operations as window refreshing is required. The OnDraw function of CSimpleDrawView obtains access to the document variables and redraws the image whenever it is called upon by the windows operating system in response to user commands to maximize, restore, resize, etc. You may have noticed that the document member variables NumLines, FPoint and LPoint depart from our member variable naming convention. These variables were specifically defined to share information between the document class and the view class and are quite obviously member variables of the document class. For simplicity in this situation, we have dispensed with the standard "m_" prefix for the member variable names. But we will continue to use the prefix to identify member variables being passed only between functions of the same class — either within the view class or the document class. And we will certainly insert the "m_" prefix whenever it seems helpful for clarity.

5.3 Drawing with Rubber-Banding

We continue this discussion of programming approaches for basic mouse drawing operations by enhancing our simple drawing program with the addition of rubber-banding to the drawing process. Rubber-banding is the familiar strategy for drawing a line while holding down the mouse button and watching the line extend or retract as the mouse cursor is moved. Our rubber-banding project is SimpleDrawRBnd. It is a single document project with MFC Standard style and set-up defaults. It is available in *Chap5\3_SimpleDrawRBnd*. If you build and execute this program you will find that it behaves very much as SimpleDraw but with a rubber-banding feature. A right click will start a fresh line. Clicking and holding the left button will allow you to see the line as you are moving the mouse. Lifting the left mouse button leaves the line drawn on the screen.

The document member variables NumLines, FPoint and LPoint are again used here as previously and the structure of the OnDraw function will redraw the window contents when necessary.

In the SimpleDrawRBnd project, the document class is unchanged from SimpleDraw. The functions OnDraw and OnRightButtonDown of the view class are also exactly the same as in the previous SimpleDraw project (Tables 5.6 and 5.7) and will not be discussed further. The variables m_BluePen of the CPen class, m_OldPoint of the CPoint class and the CString variable m_LeftDown have all been made member variables of the view class CSimpleDrawRBndView. These variables are initialized in the view class constructor function of Table 5.9. We have commented out the default initializations in lines 03 and 04 and replaced them with our own initializations in lines 07–10. The member variable m_OldPoint is used in the rubber-banding operations and we have initially set its coordinates to (0,0) in lines 07 and 08. Line 09 initializes m_LeftDown to "No". This variable is used to keep track of the left mouse button status. Of course, line 10 defines the blue pen.

The function OnLButtonDown of Table 5.10 is the handler for the Windows message WM_LBUTTONDOWN. As previously, it was added to the view class using its Properties window. The code shown in Table 5.10 was entered into the Visual C++ Edit window. When a left mouse click is received, line 05 of OnLButtonDown calls on the GetDocument function to identify the document associated with the window. Line 06

Table 5.9 Listing of CSimpleDrawRBndView from SimpleDrawRBndView.cpp

```
01   /* This is the listing of CSimpleDrawRBndView */
02   CSimpleDrawRBndView::CSimpleDrawRBndView()
03   //: m_OldPoint(0)
04   //, m_LeftDown(_T(""))
05   {
06       // TODO: add construction code here
07       m_OldPoint .x=0;
08       m_OldPoint.y=0;
09       m_LeftDown = "No";
10       m_BluePen.CreatePen(PS_SOLID,2,RGB(0,0,255));
11   }
```

Table 5.10 Listing of OnLButtonDown from SimpleDrawRBndView.cpp

```
01    /* This is the listing of OnLButtonDown */
02    void CSimpleDrawRBndView::OnLButtonDown(UINT nFlags, CPoint point)
03    {
04        // TODO: Add your message handler code here and/or call default
05        CSimpleDrawRBndDoc* pDoc = GetDocument();
06        m_LeftDown = "Yes";
07        CClientDC aDC(this);
08        aDC.SelectObject(&m_BluePen);
09        int i = pDoc->NumLines;
10        aDC.MoveTo(pDoc->FPoint[i]);
11        aDC.LineTo(point);
12        m_OldPoint = point;
13        CView::OnLButtonDown(nFlags, point);
14    }
```

records that the left button is down by setting the member variable m_LeftDown to "Yes". Lines 07 and 08, identify the object aDC to represent the window and select m_BluePen for drawing in it. In line 09, the current value of NumLines is retrieved using the document pointer and line 10 moves to the first point on this line ready to draw. Line 11 draws an initial line to the current cursor position. Notice, however, that this current point immediately becomes m_OldPoint in line 12, in anticipation of possible rubber-banding operations.

When a movement of the mouse is noticed in the program window, the function OnMouseMove (added to the view class through the Properties window) is called to process the Windows message WM_MOUSEMOVE. This function appears in the listing of Table 5.11. In lines 05–07 the document pointer is identified and m_BluePen is readied for drawing. The basic strategy in carrying out rubber-banding operations is to draw a background color line to erase the line at the previous mouse cursor position and then draw in a new line at the new cursor position using the proper color. This could be done by having two defined pens and swapping them between operations (a WhitePen with RGB (255,255,255) would be useful for erasing in this case). However, an alternative to pen swapping is to make use of a CDC member function

Table 5.11 Listing of OnMouseMove from SimpleDrawRBndView.cpp

```
01    /* This is the listing of OnMouseMove */
02    void CSimpleDrawRBndView::OnMouseMove(UINT nFlags, CPoint point)
03    {
04        // TODO: Add your message handler code here and/or call default
05        CSimpleDrawRBndDoc* pDoc = GetDocument();
06        CClientDC aDC(this);
07        aDC.SelectObject(&m_BluePen);
08        aDC.SetROP2(R2_NOTXORPEN);
09    if (m_LeftDown == "Yes") {
10        aDC.MoveTo(pDoc->FPoint[pDoc->NumLines]);
11        aDC.LineTo(m_OldPoint);
12        aDC.MoveTo(pDoc->FPoint[pDoc->NumLines]);
13        aDC.LineTo(point);
14        m_OldPoint = point;
15        }
16        CView::OnMouseMove(nFlags, point);
17    }
```

intended to facilitate such operations. The SetROP2 function controls "raster operations", i.e. drawing to the screen. You can see all of its details in Visual C++ Help. By default, drawing operations are performed in the raster operation mode R2_COPYPEN. This means that when a pen color has been selected for drawing, it will be used directly for drawing operations. We use line 08 to override the default for our rubber-banding needs and specify R2_NOTXORPEN as the operation mode. This means that an "exclusive or" logic operation will be performed whenever drawing takes place at a pixel. For the blue pen we've selected, this means that if a pixel is white, it will be colored blue. If the pixel is already blue, it will be colored white to erase it. In this way, existing lines are automatically erased and new lines are automatically drawn.

The drawing operations of lines 10–13 are protected by the if statement of line 09 and will only be carried out if the left button is down during mouse movement. In line 10, the pen is moved to the first point on the current line. Line 11 then draws a line to m_OldPoint and because

Table 5.12 Listing of OnLButtonUp from SimpleDrawRBndView.cpp

```
01      /* This is the listing of OnLButtonUp */
02      void CSimpleDrawRBndView::OnLButtonUp(UINT nFlags, CPoint point)
03      {
04              // TODO: Add your message handler code here and/or call default
05              CSimpleDrawRBndDoc* pDoc = GetDocument();
06              m_LeftDown = "No";
07              pDoc->LPoint[pDoc->NumLines] = point;
08              pDoc->NumLines++;
09              pDoc->FPoint[pDoc->NumLines] = point;
10              CView::OnLButtonUp(nFlags, point);
11      }
```

of the "exclusive or" operation, this erases any existing line. Line 12 moves the pen back to the line's first point. Line 13 then draws in a fresh blue line to the present cursor position "point" as received from the function argument. Line 14 resets m_OldPoint in preparation for the next erasing operation. While the mouse is being moved, new lines are being drawn, erased and redrawn many times. The process seems quite continuous to a user creating a drawing with the rubber-banding line.

The rubber-banding process stops when the left mouse button is raised. This results in a Windows message which is processed by the view class function OnLButtonUp shown in Table 5.12 (and created, of course, through the Properties window). Once again, this function obtains a document pointer in line 05. Line 06 sets m_LeftDown to "No" so that the mouse move function stops operating and leaves the last rubber-banded line displayed on the screen. Line 07 records the last point on the current line, setting the current LPoint to the present mouse position. Line 08 increments NumLines, ready for the next line. And line 09 sets the first point in the next line to the present mouse position. Finally, OnRButtonDown remains as in Table 5.7, so that a click of the right mouse button will reset FPoint in OnRButtonDown to start a fresh line.

5.4 Moving an Image — Simple Forms of Animation

In Section 5.2 we presented a strategy for storing a line drawing. In that section we defined document class member variables to store a drawing generated by mouse clicks. We used that document information in the OnDraw function as part of providing Windows functionality. This strategy for storing and retrieving drawings has a wide range of applications and in this section we will demonstrate a few approaches to using drawing storage for some simple animation purposes.

The example project that we have assembled is called SimpleAnimate and you'll find it in the folder *Chap5\4_SimpleAnimate*. After you have built and executed SimpleAnimate, you should see the drawing shown in Figure 5.5. But the interesting part of this program requires a few inputs from the user, for example, try a click of the left mouse button in the program window and move the mouse. Before we discuss how the resulting image motion takes place, let's take a look at the OnNewDocument function for the SimpleAnimate project as shown in Table 5.13. This function is a standard part of the document class and is

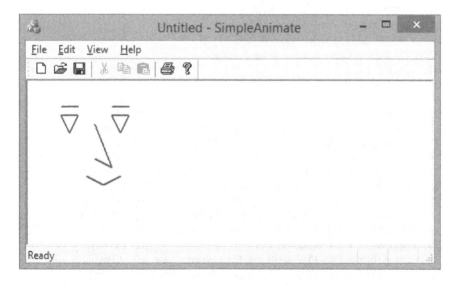

Figure 5.5 The Start-Up Drawing from SimpleAnimate

called by Windows when a program is initially executed and also when a "new" document is requested (by clicking on **File > New** or the corresponding toolbar button while the program is running).

The code we have inserted into OnNewDocument initializes the document for our needs. We use it to provide initial values for the document member variables NumLines, FPoint and LPoint as you can see in Table 5.13. Accordingly, no member variable initialization is performed in the constructor function CSimpleAnimateDoc. A CPoint object called NoseTip has been created as a member variable of the document class and is used to position our simple face. It is also initialized in OnNewDocument at lines 08 and 09 where its x and y coordinates are set to (100,100). NumLines = 12 is set in line 10 corresponding to the twelve lines that make up the face image. The FPoint and LPoint coordinates for each of the lines are shown in lines

Table 5.13 Listing of OnNewDocument from SimpleAnimateDoc.cpp

```
01  /* This is the listing of OnNewDocument */
02  BOOL CSimpleAnimateDoc::OnNewDocument()
03  {
04    if (!CDocument::OnNewDocument())
05    return FALSE;
06    // TODO: add reinitialization code here
07    // (SDI documents will reuse this document)
08    NoseTip.x = 100;
09    NoseTip.y = 100;
10    NumLines = 12;
11    FPoint[0].x  =   0; FPoint[0].y  =   0;  LPoint[0].x  = -20; LPoint[0].y  = -10;
12    FPoint[1].x  =   0; FPoint[1].y  =   0;  LPoint[1].x  = -20; LPoint[1].y  = -50;
13    FPoint[2].x  = -50; FPoint[2].y  = -40;  LPoint[2].x  = -40; LPoint[2].y  = -60;
14    FPoint[3].x  = -40; FPoint[3].y  = -60;  LPoint[3].x  = -60; LPoint[3].y  = -60;
15    FPoint[4].x  = -60; FPoint[4].y  = -60;  LPoint[4].x  = -50; LPoint[4].y  = -40;
16    FPoint[5].x  =  10; FPoint[5].y  = -40;  LPoint[5].x  =  20; LPoint[5].y  = -60;
17    FPoint[6].x  =  20; FPoint[6].y  = -60;  LPoint[6].x  =   0; LPoint[6].y  = -60;
18    FPoint[7].x  =   0; FPoint[7].y  = -60;  LPoint[7].x  =  10; LPoint[7].y  = -40;
19    FPoint[8].x  = -60; FPoint[8].y  = -70;  LPoint[8].x  = -40; LPoint[8].y  = -70;
20    FPoint[9].x  =   0; FPoint[9].y  = -70;  LPoint[9].x  =  20; LPoint[9].y  = -70;
21    FPoint[10].x = -30; FPoint[10].y =  10;  LPoint[10].x = -10; LPoint[10].y =  20;
22    FPoint[11].x = -10; FPoint[11].y =  20;  LPoint[11].x =  10; LPoint[11].y =  10;
23    return TRUE;
24  }
```

11–22. You can study these point coordinates with pencil and paper if you like (that's the way they were generated). The lines describe the simple face that we see in Figure 5.5 based on a coordinate system where the "nose tip" is at (0,0). Line 23 is part of the default programming provided by the Application Wizard.

The listing of the OnDraw function for the SimpleAnimate project is shown in Table 5.14. The function is only slightly modified from the form used in Sections 5.2 and 5.3. The for loop of lines 08–14 displays the drawing stored in the FPoint and LPoint arrays of the document class. The key difference in this new version of OnDraw is in the addition of the NoseTip coordinates to each of the stored drawing points contained in FPoint and LPoint. Lines 09–12 contain a summation which translates the stored points in the FPoint and LPoint arrays so that they will be displayed relative to the NoseTip coordinates. The MoveTo and LineTo operations of lines 13 and 14 then draw each of the lines in the image. In the initial drawing of our simple face, the nose tip is at the (100,100) position specified in OnNewDocument and shown in Figure 5.5. Movement of the image can be created by changing the coordinate values of NoseTip to change the position of the image as drawn by the

Table 5.14 Listing of OnDraw from SimpleAnimateView.cpp

```
01    This is the listing of OnDraw */
02    void CSimpleAnimateView::OnDraw(CDC* pDC)
03    {
04        CSimpleAnimateDoc* pDoc = GetDocument();
05        ASSERT_VALID(pDoc); if (!pDoc)return;
06        // TODO: add draw code for native data here
07        pDC->SelectObject(&m_BluePen);
08    for (int i=0; i < pDoc->NumLines; i++) {
09        int Fx = pDoc->FPoint[i].x + pDoc->NoseTip.x;
10        int Fy = pDoc->FPoint[i].y + pDoc->NoseTip.y;
11        int Lx = pDoc->LPoint[i].x + pDoc->NoseTip.x;
12        int Ly = pDoc->LPoint[i].y + pDoc->NoseTip.y;
13        pDC->MoveTo(Fx,Fy);
14        pDC->LineTo(Lx,Ly);
15        }
16    }
```

OnDraw function. In this SimpleAnimate program, NoseTip can be changed by various mouse or keyboard interactions as we will discuss in the following sections.

5.4.1 Movement by mouse inputs

When the user clicks the left mouse button in the SimpleAnimate program, the OnLButtonDown function listed in Table 5.15 is activated. This function sets the NoseTip coordinates to the mouse cursor position and immediately moves the drawing to that location. Specifically, line 05 obtains a pointer to the active document and line 06 uses the pointer to change the coordinate values of NoseTip. Line 07 sets the view class member variable m_LeftDown to "Yes" to record that the left button is being held down and preparing for possible mouse movements. On line 08, the function UpdateAllViews is called for the document. This MFC function (mentioned previously in Section 4.5) is provided within the document base class CDocument. With the argument NULL, it updates all of the device contexts carrying a view of the document. In our case, this means that the open window is erased and that the OnDraw function is called to redraw our face using the new NoseTip coordinates. Note that the initial value of m_LeftDown was set to "No" in the constructor function CSimpleAnimateView. When the left button is released again, the OnLButtonUp function (not listed here) simply sets m_LeftDown back to "No".

Table 5.15 Listing of OnLButtonDown from SimpleAnimateView.cpp

```
01    /* This is the listing of OnLButtonDown */
02    void CSimpleAnimateView::OnLButtonDown(UINT nFlags, CPoint point)
03    {
04        // TODO: Add your message handler code here and/or call default
05        CSimpleAnimateDoc* pDoc = GetDocument();
06        pDoc->NoseTip = point;
07        m_LeftDown = "Yes";
08        pDoc->UpdateAllViews(NULL);
09        CView::OnLButtonDown(nFlags, point);
10    }
```

Table 5.16 Listing of OnMouseMove from SimpleAnimateView.cpp

```
01    /* This is the listing of OnMouseMove */
02    void CSimpleAnimateView::OnMouseMove(UINT nFlags, CPoint point)
03    {
04         // TODO: Add your message handler code here and/or call default
05         CSimpleAnimateDoc* pDoc = GetDocument();
06    if (m_LeftDown == "Yes") {
07         pDoc->NoseTip = point;
08         pDoc->UpdateAllViews(NULL);
09         }
10         CView::OnMouseMove(nFlags, point);
11    }
```

The next mouse interaction feature is provided through the OnMouseMove function listed in Table 5.16. This function was brought into the SimpleAnimate project to process "mouse move" Windows messages. Line 05 of the function identifies the current document and line 06 checks to see if the left button is down. If it is, line 07 sets the NoseTip coordinates to the present mouse position, represented by "point" as received in the argument list of line 02. Then line 08 calls the UpdateAllViews function for the document. This results in clearing the window and the OnDraw function redrawing the face at the new NoseTip position. With the left button down, mouse motions result in movement of our simple face with the nose tip following the cursor. You can execute the program and use the mouse to move the image around the screen. Notice that window resizing, maximizing, etc. result in redrawing of the image by OnDraw so that the image remains at the appropriate position in the window.

5.4.2 Movement by keyboard input

The adjustments of the NoseTip coordinates have also been linked to keyboard inputs in this program by using the capabilities of the familiar OnKeyDown function. For the SimpleAnimate project, the OnKeyDown listing is shown in Table 5.17. As expected, the initial statement in line 05 obtains a pointer to the active document. Line 06 sets KeyStruck to

Table 5.17 Listing of OnKeyDown from SimpleAnimateView.cpp

```
01  /* This is the listing of OnKeyDown */
02  void CSimpleAnimateView::OnKeyDown(UINT nChar,UINTnRepCnt,UINTnFlags)
03  {
04       // TODO: Add your message handler code here and/or call default
05       CSimpleAnimateDoc* pDoc = GetDocument();
06       char KeyStruck = nChar;
07       if (KeyStruck == 37) { pDoc->NoseTip.x-=20; }
08       if (KeyStruck == 38) { pDoc->NoseTip.y-=20; }
09       if (KeyStruck == 39) { pDoc->NoseTip.x+=20; }
10       if (KeyStruck == 40) { pDoc->NoseTip.y+=20; }
11       if (KeyStruck == 'T') { SetTimer(1,500,NULL); }
12  if (KeyStruck == 'S') {
13       KillTimer(1);
14       pDoc->NoseTip.x = 100;
15       pDoc->NoseTip.y = 100;
16       }
17       pDoc->UpdateAllViews(NULL);
18       CView::OnKeyDown(nChar, nRepCnt, nFlags);
19       }
```

the keyboard input nChar received as an argument in line 02. KeyStruck is then processed by the series of if statements in lines 07–16. The up, down, right, and left arrow keys are represented by the ASCII codes 37–40. Lines 07–10 change the NoseTip coordinates by 20 pixels in the appropriate direction if an arrow key is struck. The call to UpdateAllViews in line 17 redraws the image in its new position.

Line 11 of the OnKeyDown Function provides another option for moving the image. If the keystroke received is a "T", a Windows timer is initialized by calling the MFC SetTimer function. The arguments of SetTimer in line 11 set timer number "1" to send a timer message every 500 milliseconds. The final NULL argument of the SetTimer function activates standard default timer options. For more details see Visual C++ Help. For a keystroke input of "S", the if statement of line 12 calls the MFC function KillTimer (with an argument of "1") to turn off timer number one. Lines 14 and 15 then reset NoseTip to its original (100,100) coordinate values. After the S key has been struck, UpdateAllViews in line 17 will redisplay our simple face at its original position.

Table 5.18 Listing of OnTimer from SimpleAnimateView.cpp

```
01    /* This is the listing of OnTimer */
02    void CSimpleAnimateView::OnTimer(UINT nIDEvent)
03    {
04          // TODO: Add your message handler code here and/or call default
05          CSimpleAnimateDoc* pDoc = GetDocument();
06          pDoc->NoseTip.x+=20;
07          pDoc->NoseTip.y+=10;
08          pDoc->UpdateAllViews(NULL);
09          CView::OnTimer(nIDEvent);
10    }
```

The OnTimer function listed in Table 5.18 makes changes in the NoseTip coordinate values as the timer ticks. The OnTimer function responds to the Windows timer message (WM_TIMER) at each tick. It was created by using the Properties window to add the message handler function to the view class. Whenever a timer message is received, the timer number is received as the single OnTimer argument shown in line 02. Here we only have a single timer active so we do not have to test the event (i.e. timer) number. With multiple timing operations, checking the timer number would be necessary. As usual, line 05 identifies the document of interest, then lines 06 and 07 create an animation movement by incrementing the NoseTip x and y coordinates by 20 pixels and 10 pixels respectively. Line 08 calls on the UpdateAllViews function to redraw the newly positioned image with each tick of the timer.

With the keyboard controls described above, striking the arrow keys allows the face to be moved back and forth and up and down the screen as desired. If you strike a T, the timer activation causes the drawing to move across and down the screen in increments occurring at half-second intervals. This principle of moving the image at timed intervals is the basis of animation and quality animation revolves around generating good images at a sufficiently fast rate to appear realistic. Just as striking a T starts our simple animation, striking an S stops the timer and returns the drawing to its original position. Notice, by the way, that the mouse movement options remain active with the keyboard controls in place and, in fact, you'll find you can use either mode of control independently.

5.5 Including Circles

Up to this point, the examples of this chapter have focused on drawing with simple straight lines using the MFC functions MoveTo and LineTo. Certainly, more general drawing operations are routinely performed in computer graphics programs and the purpose of this section is to provide some insight into more complicated drawing procedures and the program organization that can handle different shapes.

Our example project is SimpleDrawCirc. To develop it, we returned to our original SimpleDraw program of Section 5.2 and then added circle drawing capability. You'll find this example in the folder *Chap5\5_SimpleDrawCirc*. It was created as a single document project in the MFC Standard style with the Application Wizard. If you build and execute the program, you will be able to draw lines just as in our original SimpleDraw program (left click to draw a line, right click to start a fresh line). But, striking a C on the keyboard now enters a "circle mode" where you are prompted to draw a circle using a right click to define its center and a left click to specify the radius and carry out the circle drawing. A simple error test rejects any left clicks made before a right click has located the center. You can return to "line mode" by striking an L on the keyboard. Both the lines and the circles are stored in the document class so that OnDraw can refresh the program window as needed.

5.5.1 Drawing and storing the circles

The basis of this program is a homemade function for drawing circles called DrawCirc. It draws circles with the input arguments of center position and radius. DrawCirc was created as a member function of the view class with a right click on CSimpleDrawCircView in the Class View window and then by using the Add Member Function Wizard.

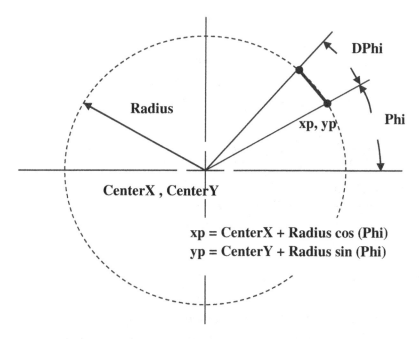

Figure 5.6 Drawing a Segment of a Circle

DrawCirc can be directly called for circle drawing operations from anywhere in the view class. Incidentally, the MFC drawing functions Ellipse and Arc are provided in the CDC class and are readily available for drawing circles. We have used our own DrawCirc function in this example to show the details of a process for drawing curved shapes based on small individual line segments. The geometry of the circle drawing operation is shown in Figure 5.6 and the listing of the function is shown in Table 5.19. The drawing approach used is referred to as "parametric drawing" since we use the circle angle Phi as a parameter to generate the coordinates of points on the circle. For each value of Phi we determine the corresponding pixel coordinate values for both xp and yp and the circle is drawn as a series of small straight lines while incrementing Phi from 0 to 2π radians (0 to 360 degrees).

In Table 5.19, the argument list of line 02 shows the circle center position as the CPoint object Center along with the circle Radius. Line 04 obtains the device context aDC and line 05 selects the blue pen. Phi is

Table 5.19 Listing of DrawCirc from SimpleDrawCircView.cpp

```
01    /* This is the listing of DrawCirc */
02    void CSimpleDrawCircView::DrawCirc(CPoint Center, double Radius)
03    {
04        CClientDC aDC(this);
05        aDC.SelectObject(&m_BluePen);
06        double Phi = 0.;
07        int nseg = 50;
08        double DPhi=(2.*3.14158)/nseg;
09        aDC.MoveTo(int(Center.x+Radius),Center.y);
10    for (int i = 1; i<=nseg; i++) {
11        Phi+=DPhi;
12        int xp = int(Center.x + Radius * cos(Phi));
13        int yp = int(Center.y + Radius * sin(Phi));
14        aDC.LineTo(xp, yp);
15        }
16    }
```

initialized at zero in line 06 and the number of straight-line segments to be used in the circle is set to fifty in line 07. The angular increment DPhi is set in line 08 based on the number of segments (2π/nseg).

Line 09 carries out a move to the Phi = 0 position on the circle. Then the for loop of lines 10–15 moves around the circle, drawing with small straight line segments. Line 11 increments Phi at each step. Lines 12 and 13 set the pixel coordinates xp and yp in accordance with the trigonometric equations in Figure 5.6 while line 14 draws the individual line segments using the LineTo function. Notice that Figure 5.6 is presented in the traditional format with the y axis vertically upward. Of course, the Windows y axis is downward so that actual drawing of the circle by the DrawCirc function proceeds in a clockwise direction in the display window rather than the counter clockwise direction of Figure 5.6.

The organization of data storage for our lines and circles is quite apparent in the listing of the OnDraw function shown in Table 5.20. In the document class CSimpleDrawCircDoc for this project, we have added the member variables NumCircs, CircCenter and CircRadius to store the number of circles along with the center and radius of each circle. These items are in addition to the member variables for the

Table 5.20 Listing of OnDraw from SimpleDrawCircView.cpp

```
01    /* This is the listing of OnDraw */
02    void CSimpleDrawCircView::OnDraw(CDC* pDC)
03    {
04        CSimpleDrawCircDoc* pDoc = GetDocument();
05        ASSERT_VALID(pDoc); if (!pDoc)return;
06        // TODO: add draw code for native data here
07        pDC->SelectObject(&m_BluePen);
08    for (int i=0; i < pDoc->NumLines; I++) {
09        pDC->MoveTo(pDoc->FPoint[i]);
10        pDC->LineTo(pDoc->LPoint[i]);
11        }
12    for (i=0; i < pDoc->NumCircs; i++) {
13        DrawCirc(pDoc->CircCenter[i], pDoc->CircRadius[i]);
14        }
15    }
```

straight line data that we have previously used. We have moved the initialization of all of the required member variables to OnNewDocument so that clicking on **File > New** in the executing program clears the screen and starts a new drawing. The OnDraw function draws straight lines in lines 08–11 of the code in Table 5.20. It obtains NumLines from the document in line 08 and then draws each line with the MoveTo and LineTo functions in lines 09 and 10. The for loop of lines 12–14 handles circles in a similar way. NumCircs is obtained from the document in line 12 to control the for loop. The circle center and radius are retrieved from the document and placed in the DrawCirc argument list in line 13. Each circle is drawn by the DrawCirc function in line 13 using the process described above and shown in Table 5.19.

5.5.2 Controlling the drawing mode

Let's now look at switching between drawing modes and the process of storing the circle and line data as drawing takes place. At this point, we are using keystrokes to switch between drawing modes. The OnKeyDown function of Table 5.21 contains the significant code. The view class member variable m_DrawMode identifies the current drawing

Table 5.21 Listing of OnKeyDown from SimpleDrawCircView.cpp

```
01   /* This is the listing of OnKeyDown */
02   void CSimpleDrawCircView::OnKeyDown(UINT nChar,
03                        UINTnRepCnt,UINTnFlags)
03   {
04       // TODO: Add your message handler code here and/or call default
05       CSimpleDrawCircDoc* pDoc = GetDocument();
06       CClientDC aDC(this);
07       char KeyStruck = nChar;
08   if (KeyStruck == 'C') {
09       m_DrawMode = "Circles";
10       aDC.TextOut(10,5,L"Circles...");
11       aDC.TextOut(10,25,L"right click for circle center,");
12       aDC.TextOut(10,45,L"left click for radius.");
13       }
14   if (KeyStruck == 'L') {
15       m_DrawMode = "Lines";
16       pDoc->UpdateAllViews(NULL);
17       }
18       CView::OnKeyDown(nChar, nRepCnt, nFlags);
19   }
```

mode. It is initialized as "Lines" in the constructor function CSimpleDrawCircView so that the program begins execution ready to draw lines. When a C has been pressed, the if statement in line 08 of Table 5.21 is satisfied and the code of lines 09–13 executes. In line 09 the draw mode is set to "Circles" and then lines 10–12 place the three lines of text for the circle drawing prompt at the upper left corner of the display. Note that we have not used the Format function here as we did in Chapter 4. If a simple line of text without formatting is being displayed, it can be defined directly as a character string in the TextOut function. When L is pressed on the keyboard, the if statement of line 14 is satisfied, the draw mode is set to "Lines" by line 15 and then the UpdateAllViews function is called at line 16. This results in the execution of the OnDraw function which clears the window and redraws the present drawing. In the redrawing process, the circle drawing prompt disappears. Line 18 is provided by the Application Wizard.

Table 5.22 Listing of OnRButtonDown from SimpleDrawCircView.cpp

```
01    /* This is the listing of OnRButtonDown */
02    void CSimpleDrawCircView::OnRButtonDown(UINT nFlags, CPoint point)
03    {
04        // TODO: Add your message handler code here and/or call default
05        CSimpleDrawCircDoc* pDoc = GetDocument();
06        if (m_DrawMode == "Lines") { pDoc->FPoint[pDoc->NumLines] = point; }
07    if (m_DrawMode == "Circles") {
08        pDoc->CircCenter[pDoc->NumCircs] = point;
09        m_CenterSet = "Yes";
10        }
11        CView::OnRButtonDown(nFlags, point);
12    }
```

With the drawing mode given by m_DrawMode, clicks of the right and left mouse buttons develop the individual lines or circles and store the data describing them. The function OnRButtonDown is listed in Table 5.22. If the drawing mode is "Lines", the statement of line 06 is executed to set FPoint, the starting point of a new line, to the current mouse position. If the drawing mode is "Circles", line 08 sets the coordinates in CircCenter to the mouse position. Line 09 then sets the variable m_CenterSet to "Yes" indicating that the center coordinates have been set for this circle. If successive right mouse clicks are received in the line mode, the statement at line 06 simply resets the first point of the next line to be drawn to the mouse position at the new right click. A line is not drawn until a left click is received. Similarly for the circle mode, line 08 allows successive right clicks to repeatedly reset the center of the next circle to the new mouse position. A circle will not be drawn until a left click is received.

The OnLButtonDown function processes left mouse clicks as shown in the listing of Table 5.23. Lines 09–14 apply when the draw mode is set to "Lines". Line 09 recovers NumLines from the document and lines 10 and 11 draw the line into the window from the line start point to the mouse position when the left click was received. Lines 12–14 then store LPoint, the next FPoint and the incremented NumLines in the document class member variables. If the drawing mode is "Circles" and the circle

Table 5.23 Listing of OnLButtonDown from SimpleDrawCircView.cpp

```
01    /* This is the listing of OnLButtonDown */
02    void CSimpleDrawCircView::OnLButtonDown(UINT nFlags, CPoint point)
03    {
04        // TODO: Add your message handler code here and/or call default
05        CSimpleDrawCircDoc* pDoc = GetDocument();
06        CClientDC aDC(this);
07        aDC.SelectObject(&m_BluePen);
08    if (m_DrawMode == "Lines") {
09        int i = pDoc->NumLines;
10        aDC.MoveTo(pDoc->FPoint[i]);
11        aDC.LineTo(point);
12        pDoc->LPoint[i] = point;
13        pDoc->FPoint[i+1] = point;
14        pDoc->NumLines++;
15        }
16    if ((m_DrawMode == "Circles") && (m_CenterSet == "Yes")) {
17        int j = pDoc->NumCircs;
18        int dx = point.x - pDoc->CircCenter[j].x;
19        int dy = point.y - pDoc->CircCenter[j].y;
20        double RadSq = dx*dx+dy*dy;
21        pDoc->CircRadius[j] = sqrt(RadSq);
22        DrawCirc(pDoc->CircCenter[j], pDoc->CircRadius[j]);
23        pDoc->NumCircs++;
24        m_CenterSet = "No";
25        }
26        CView::OnLButtonDown(nFlags, point);
27    }
```

center has been set by a right click, lines 17–22 compute and store the circle data and draw the circle. Line 17 obtains NumCircs from the document. Line 18 obtains the x position of the mouse click point relative to the circle center x coordinate and line 19 obtains the y coordinate of the mouse click point relative to the circle center y coordinate. Lines 20 and 21 then compute the circle radius and store it in the document. Line 22 calls the DrawCirc function to draw the circle with the specified center coordinates and radius. Finally, line 23 increments NumCircs to prepare for a new circle and line 24 resets m_CenterSet to "No" so that a right click will have to be received before

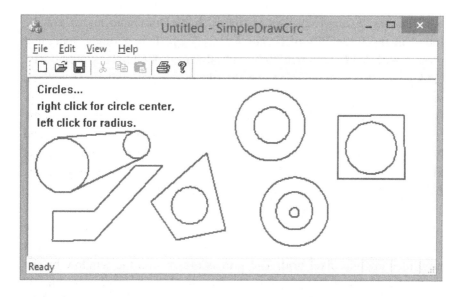

Figure 5.7 Circle Mode Drawing in SimpleDrawCirc

another left click will be processed in circle mode. Figure 5.7 shows the window for SimpleDrawCirc in circle mode and includes an example line and circle drawing. From the appearance of the figure, it's quite clear that a snap-to-grid option would be useful here to make an accurate drawing. We will discuss snap-to-grid in the next section.

5.6 Snap-to-Grid and Saving Data to Files

In Sections 5.1 and 5.2 of this chapter, we presented the most basic ideas for making line drawings in the Windows environment. Section 5.1 showed how to use mouse clicks for drawing and Section 5.2 showed how to use document class member variables to store the drawing and make it available for OnDraw to redraw it as needed for Windows updates. We now return to the original SimpleDraw program of Section 5.2 and extend it to illustrate programming concepts for two other important features of interactive programming: using snap-to-grid to make accurate drawings and saving a drawing to a file.

This next example project is titled SimpleDrawSnap and it can be found in the folder *Chap5\6_SimpleDrawSnap*. It is a single document project with MFC Standard style and all set-up defaults. As previously, clicking on the SimpleDrawSnap.sln file in *Chap5\6_SimpleDrawSnap* will load the project into Visual C++ and you can build and execute it. Notice that a pixel grid is part of the display. Also note that if you draw lines with left and right mouse clicks (there's no rubber-banding included here), you'll see that the lines begin and end at positions on the pixel grid. You can also store and retrieve drawings by using **File > Save As, File > Open**, etc. We'll discuss this all in more detail below.

Let's begin studying SimpleDrawSnap by looking at its OnDraw function which is listed in Table 5.24. Its form is quite the same as the OnDraw function of our original SimpleDraw project of Section 5.2 but now includes the pixel grid. The grid is drawn into the window by the nested for loops of lines 07–09. The first for loop beginning on line 07 moves the pixel coordinate xp from 0 to 1000 in increments of 10, The next for loop of line 08 moves the pixel coordinate yp from 0 to 800 in increments of 10. The SetPixel statement in line 08 then places pixels on the screen column by column until the screen is filled with a grid of pixels at 10 unit intervals. The grid density and range of pixel values can

Table 5.24 Listing of OnDraw from SimpleDrawSnapView.cpp

```
01    /* This is the listing of OnDraw */
02    void CSimpleDrawSnapView::OnDraw(CDC* pDC)
03    {
04        CSimpleDrawSnapDoc* pDoc = GetDocument();
05        ASSERT_VALID(pDoc); if (!pDoc)return;
06        // TODO: add draw code for native data here
07    for (int xp=0;xp<1000;xp+=10) {
08        for (int yp=0;yp<800;yp+=10) {pDC->SetPixel(xp,yp,0); }
09        }
10        pDC->SelectObject(&m_BluePen);
11    for (int i=0; i < pDoc->NumLines; i++) {
12        pDC->MoveTo(pDoc->FPoint[i]);
13        pDC->LineTo(pDoc->LPoint[i]);
14        }
15    }
```

Table 5.25 Listing of OnRButtonDown from SimpleDrawSnapView.cpp

```
01    /* This is the listing of OnRButtonDown */
02    void CSimpleDrawSnapView::OnRButtonDown(UINT nFlags, CPoint point)
03    {
04        // TODO: Add your message handler code here and/or call default
05        CSimpleDrawSnapDoc* pDoc = GetDocument();
06        NearestGridPoint(&point);
07        pDoc->FPoint[pDoc->NumLines] = point;
08        CView::OnRButtonDown(nFlags, point);
09    }
```

be adjusted to fill your window or screen as desired. The remainder of OnDraw deals with regenerating the line drawing using the now familiar document member variables NumLines, FPoint and LPoint. Line 04 gets the document pointer and line 10 selects m_BluePen (the view class member variable) for drawing so that the for loop of lines 11–14 can draw the stored lines.

The next step in programming SimpleDrawSnap requires a strategy for establishing the nearest grid point to the mouse cursor position as a mouse click occurs. With such a strategy in place, each mouse click during drawing can be redirected to the nearest grid point and drawings can be made to accurately placed points. In fact, except for calling the nearest grid point function, the mouse button message functions OnRButtonDown and OnLButtonDown of SimpleDrawSnap are quite the same as the originals of SimpleDraw. The nearest grid point function carries out the "snap-to-grid". This can be seen in our listing of OnRButtonDown as shown in Table 5.25. Line 06 of OnRButtonDown carries out the shift to the nearest grid point with a call to the prepared function NearestGridPoint. This function receives a pointer (CPoint*) to the cursor object "point" and evaluates the mouse position relative to the pixel grid points. It then replaces the coordinates of "point" with the nearest grid point to the mouse cursor. A similar statement has been inserted into the message handler function OnLButtonDown.

The NearestGridPoint function was created by right clicking in the ClassView window on the class name CSimpleDrawSnapView and then adding NearestGridPoint with the Add Member Function Wizard. The

Table 5.26 Listing of NearestGridPoint from SimpleDrawSnapView.cpp

```
01    /* This is the listing of NearestGridPoint */
02    void CSimpleDrawSnapView::NearestGridPoint(CPoint* PtClickedPoint)
03    {
04         double SavSqDis = 1.0E06;
05         int SavX, SavY, dx, dy;
06         int PointX = PtClickedPoint->x;
07         int PointY = PtClickedPoint->y;
08    for (int xp=0;xp<1000;xp=xp+10) {
09    for(int yp=0;yp<800;yp=yp+10) {
10         dx = abs(xp - PointX);
11         dy = abs(yp - PointY);
12    if(dx<10 && dy<10) {
13         double SqDis = dx*dx + dy*dy;
14    if (SqDis < SavSqDis) {
15         SavSqDis = SqDis;
16         SavX = xp;
17         SavY = yp;
18    }
19    }
20    }
21    }
22         PtClickedPoint->x = SavX;
23         PtClickedPoint->y = SavY;
24    }
```

process was first discussed in Section 4.4 for the WriteToScreen function. In this case, however, CPoint* is entered as a Parameter type, PtClickedPoint (pointer to the clicked point) is entered as a Parameter name for the NearestGridPoint function and a click of the Add button includes it as a parameter.

The function created by the Wizard for NearestGridPoint is, of course, only a blank template ready for coding. After programming, it appears as in Table 5.26. The input argument (CPoint* PtClickedPoint) is shown in line 02 and provides access to the mouse cursor position. In lines 06 and 07, PointX and PointY are set to the coordinate values of the cursor position. Then the nested for loops of lines 08–21 cycle through the pixels to find the one nearest to the cursor. The strategy is a simple sorting process with the if statement of line 12 making sure that only the closest pixels are given a careful test. For those closest pixels, line 13 computes the square of the distance from the cursor position to the pixel. The if statement block of lines 14–18 checks for the smallest squared distance so that the variables SavX and SavY retain the coordinates of the closest pixel when the for loops have cycled through all the pixels. Finally, the pointer PtClickedPoint is used in lines 22 and 23 to replace the coordinates of the clicked mouse point with the coordinates of its nearest grid point. Of course, the efficiency of this sort process could be much improved but we leave that as an exercise for the interested reader.

5.6.1 Saving drawing data in a file

If you have built and executed the SimpleDrawSnap program, you have found that the snap-to-grid feature makes it relatively easy to create accurate drawings with parallel and perpendicular lines. The next step in managing the drawing process is to be able to save generated drawings. The MFC function "Serialize" is furnished within the MFC Application as a standard function of the document class and provides a very convenient tool for saving data in files. Most of the required effort was already completed in providing the document class member variables needed for window updating by the OnDraw function. For the case of our simple line drawings, saving a drawing to disk is just a matter of sending the document member variables off to a file. We have modified the template Serialize function to both write data to files and read data from files as can be seen in Table 5.27.

In the function redeclaration of line 02 in Table 5.27, Serialize receives the argument "ar" referring to an object of the class CArchive provided in the MFC. This archive object connects to the Windows file system so that data can be written to files or read from files by using insertion (<<) or extraction (>>) operators in conjunction with the archive object. This process is completely integrated with the Windows file system and is activated by clicking on **File > Save** or **File > Save As** in executing program. Files stored with this process make use of the storage dialog that you expect with Windows programs. After storage, when you click on **File**, your files are listed as "recent files". You can even receive reminders to save files before exiting your program.

Table 5.27 Listing of Serialize from SimpleDrawSnapDoc.cpp

```
01    /* This is the listing of Serialize */
02    void CSimpleDrawSnapDoc::Serialize(CArchive& ar)
03    {
04    if (ar.IsStoring()) {
05         // TODO: add storing code here
06         ar<<NumLines;
07    for (int i = 0; i<=NumLines; I++) {
08         ar<<FPoint[i]<<LPoint[i];
09         }
10         }
11         else {
12         // TODO: add loading code here
13         ar>>NumLines;
14    for (int i = 0; i<=NumLines; I++) {
15         ar>>FPoint[i]>>LPoint[i];
16         }
17         }
18    }
```

The code for writing to a file appears in lines 06–09 under the TODO instruction of line 05 in Table 5.27. Line 06 sends the NumLines variable to the archive to indicate how many entries will appear in the file. The for loop of lines 07–09 then writes the FPoint and LPoint array entries for each line to the archive. Notice that the CPoint class is supported by the archiving process so that only the point objects and not the individual coordinate values need to be written at each stage. After the TODO instruction of line 12, the process of reading from a file is described by lines 13–16. The first item written to the file was NumLines, so line 13 reads it back first. This value of NumLines is then used in the for loop of lines 14–16 to read back the FPoint and LPoint coordinates for each line. After the Serialize function executes, the document view is automatically redrawn.

You should exercise this program now, make a few drawings, save them as files and place them in various directories. Retrieve the files, add more to the drawings and save them again. In Figure 5.8 you can see an example drawing of "Widgets" made with SimpleDrawSnap. Notice that the program's window title now automatically includes the file name.

Incidentally, if you would like to see a "reminder to save" message when exiting SimpleDrawSnap, enter the single line of code:

pDoc->SetModifiedFlag();

somewhere in your function OnLButtonDown. With this addition, whenever you make a left button mouse click in your program, the SetModifiedFlag will remember that a modification was made and if you attempt to exit the program without saving, a reminder to save the file will appear.

5.7 Printing a Full Size Drawing

Up to this point we have not been concerned with printing a document and have worked in "pixel" units for all of our graphics operations. These are the default graphics units in Windows programming and refer

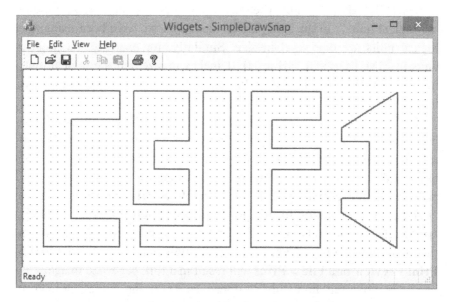

Figure 5.8 Display of the Widgets File by SimpleDrawSnap

directly to the resolution of the drawing or plotting device carrying out the display operations. Typically this is either a computer monitor or a printer. If you have tried to make a printout of one of our graphics programs or have simply tried to carry out a **File > Print Preview** for one of our programs you have seen a very small image on your graphics screen. This is because the pixel spacing of a printer is at high resolution and many "pixels per inch" are drawn compared to a standard computer monitor. Of course, you can always make useful printouts of a standard window display by using **Alt+PrintScreen** on a typical keyboard to copy the window image to the clipboard and then paste the image into a document. These "Print Screen" images are very versatile, print quite nicely, and provide a simple and practical way of capturing your graphics efforts (most of the figures in this book have been inserted in this way).

The key, however, to making accurate and full size printouts directly from graphics programs is to utilize the alternative "mapping modes" available in Windows. The default mapping mode that we have been working with is MM_TEXT and the alternatives include MM_LOENGLISH, MM_HIENGLISH, MM_LOMETRIC and MM_HIMETRIC. The units used in these mapping modes are referred to as "logical units". In the MM_TEXT mode that we have been using, the logical units are one pixel in size. Similarly, for example, the logical units in MM_LOENGLISH are 0.01 inches in size and the logical units in MM_LOMETRIC are 0.10 millimeters. The "device units" are always in pixels.

Our example program for this section is SimpleDrawPrint and it can be found in the folder *Chap5\7_SimpleDrawPrint*. Before you start following the programming strategy in this section you may want to build and execute SimpleDrawPrint. Note that the program has scroll bars and a coarse pixel grid. If you use **File > Print Setup** to select a "Landscape" orientation for the program, you'll notice that the scrolling arrangement reasonably covers the grid range displayed. Lines drawn in this figure with right and left mouse clicks will snap-to-grid and a **File > Print Preview** or a **File > Print** will result in a full, page size image.

Let's now see how this is done. To start, the SimpleDrawPrint program is nearly a duplicate of the SimpleDrawSnap program described

Table 5.28 Listing of OnInitialUpdate from SimpleDrawPrintView.cpp

```
01    /* This is the listing of OnInitialUpdate*/
02    void CSimpleDrawPrintView::OnInitialUpdate()
03    {
04         CScrollView::OnInitialUpdate();
05         // TODO: calculate the total size of this view
06         CSize TotalSize;
07         TotalSize.cx = 1100;
08         TotalSize.cy = 850;
09         int XBorder = 0;    int YBorder = 25;
10         int Reduction = 100;
11         m_UpperLeft.x = XBorder;
12         m_UpperLeft.y = -YBorder;
13         m_LowerRight.x = XBorder + TotalSize.cx - Reduction;
14         m_LowerRight.y = -YBorder - (TotalSize.cy - Reduction);
15         SetScrollSizes(MM_LOENGLISH, TotalSize);
16    }
```

in Section 5.6 but it was created to utilize scrolling and the MM_LOENGLISH mapping mode. When SimpleDrawPrint was formed as a new project, it was set up as a Single Document application with MFC Standard style and all defaults except for an adjustment under Generated Classes. Here the Base class for the Generated class CSimpleDrawPrintView was set to CScrollView rather than the default CView. This change activates scrolling in the program window. It also automatically inserts a view class function called OnInitialUpdate. This function is called when a view is first activated. In our case it is used to set the scrolling parameters for the view and we also use it as a convenient location to set the pixel range for our snap-to-grid display.

The listing of the OnInitialUpdate function for SimpleDrawPrint is shown in Table 5.28. The key statement in this function is at line 15 where the function SetScrollsizes of the CScrollView class is used to set the scrolling conditions for the program window. The first input parameter in line 15 sets the mapping mode and the second input, TotalSize, sets the size of the scrolling view. TotalSize is declared in line 06 as an object of the class CSize provided by the MFC. The CSize class is very similar to the CPoint class but its member variables cx and cy are intended to define a size in two dimensions. The cx and cy values for

TotalSize are set in lines 07 and 08 at 1100 (for 11 inches) and 850 (for 8.5 inches). In this way, TotalSize represents an (American) standard size page positioned in the landscape orientation when it is used in line 15. The two view class member variables m_UpperLeft and m_LowerRight are CPoint objects which are defined in lines 11–14 (note that the y convention is now positive "up"). They position and adjust the range for snap-to-grid operations of the program so that it can cover the page appropriately. The integer variables XBorder, YBorder and Reduction (set in lines 09 and 10) are used to control the range adjustment so that a pixel grid ranging from the point m_UpperLeft to the point m_LowerRight fits reasonably on the page.

5.7.1 Carrying out the coordinate changes

The coordinate convention has changed with the change of the mapping mode from MM_TEXT to MM_LOENGLISH. The original coordinate convention of MM_TEXT (origin at the window upper left, x axis positive to the right, y axis positive down) moves to the

Table 5.29 Listing of OnDraw from SimpleDrawPrintView.cpp

```
01    /* This is the listing of OnDraw*/
02    void CSimpleDrawPrintView::OnDraw(CDC* pDC)
03    {
04        CSimpleDrawPrintDoc* pDoc = GetDocument();
05        ASSERT_VALID(pDoc); if (!pDoc)return;
06        // TODO: add draw code for native data here
07    for (int xp = m_UpperLeft.x; xp <= m_LowerRight.x; xp += 50) {
08    for (int yp = m_UpperLeft.y; yp >= m_LowerRight.y; yp -= 50 {
09        pDC->SetPixel(xp,yp,0);
10        }
11    }
12        pDC->SelectObject(&m_BluePen);
13    for (int i=0; i < pDoc->NumLines; i++) {
14        pDC->MoveTo(pDoc->FPoint[i]);
15        pDC->LineTo(pDoc->LPoint[i]);
16        }
17    }
```

MM_LOENGLISH convention (origin at the window upper left, x axis positive to the right, y axis positive up). The most obvious result of this change is that the y coordinate values are negative for all points in the window.

The OnDraw file for SimpleDrawPoint is shown in Table 5.29. The coding is very much the same as we used in the original SimpleDrawSnap project of Section 5.6. However, the grid plotting statements of lines 07–11 have been adjusted to show the pixel grid over the range of coordinate values beginning at m_UpperLeft and extending to m_LowerRight (these are the view class member variables set in OnInitialUpdate). Notice that the grid size has been changed to 50 and that line 08 moves through the grid by taking negative steps in yp until LowerRight.y is reached.

The last portion of the OnDraw function in lines 12–16 draws the existing lines of the figure by accessing the arrays FPoint and LPoint in the document class. These statements are the familiar ones from SimpleDrawSnap. But, in order to function properly, the coordinate values in the FPoint and LPoint arrays must be expressed in MM_LOENGLISH units (e.g. the y coordinate values must be negative).

The values for the FPoint and LPoint arrays result from mouse clicks handled as usual by the view class functions OnLButtonDown and OnRButtonDown. The complicating factor in the mouse click process is that the coordinate values passed into OnLButtonDown and OnRButtonDown through the CPoint object "point" are in pixel units (recall that these are referred to as device units) which are the units of the computer screen. But, fortunately, there is a convenient set of functions which can convert from the device units of the screen to the logical units of MM_LOENGLISH. The listing of the OnRButtonDown function is shown in Table 5.30. Line 06 in this code identifies the current device context as the CClientDC object aDC. Line 07 then calls the MFC function OnPrepareDC as the interface between the device context and the scrolled view, particularly adjusting the origin for the present scroll position. Line 08 calls the coordinate conversion function DPtoLP which converts from "device points" (the mouse click's pixel coordinates) to

Table 5.30 Listing of OnRButtonDown from SimpleDrawPrintView.cpp

```
01    /* This is the listing of OnRButtonDown */
02    void CSimpleDrawPrintView::OnRButtonDown(UINT nFlags, CPoint point)
03        {
04        // TODO: Add your message handler code here and/or call default
05        CSimpleDrawPrintDoc* pDoc = GetDocument();
06        CClientDC aDC(this);
07        OnPrepareDC(&aDC);
08        aDC.DPtoLP(&point);
09        NearestGridPoint(&point);
10        pDoc->FPoint[pDoc->NumLines] = point;
11        CScrollView::OnRButtonDown(nFlags, point);
12        }
```

"logical points" (the current MM_LOENGLISH mapping mode). Since the address of the object "point" is passed to the function DPtoLP, the conversion directly changes "point" to the MM_LOENGLISH coordinate values. Line 09 then passes the coordinate corrected "point" on to our function NearestGridPoint.

In this project, the function NearestGridPoint is modified from its Section 5.6 description (Table 5.26) in much the same way as OnDraw was modified in Table 5.29. The grid search is now performed over the range from m_UpperLeft to m_LowerRight and the grid size is changed to 50. After execution of line 09 is completed in Table 5.30, "point" contains the coordinates of the nearest pixel in MM_LOENGLISH units and line 10 then stores the coordinates in the document class array FPoint. The coding adjustments made to handle left button mouse clicks in the function OnLButtonDown are quite identical to those shown in Table 5.30. The overall result of these changes is that mouse cursor positions are transformed into appropriate coordinates with the correct origin and that the FPoint and LPoint arrays reflect these coordinate values. Now, when the OnDraw function of Table 5.29 is executed, it will draw the correct lines. Selecting **File > Print** or **File > Print Preview** results in an appropriate full page image. The print preview shown in Figure 5.9 is in landscape mode and shows a test drawing on a normal 8.5 x 11 inch page. The printed copy will contain the figure shown, drawn to accurate dimensions.

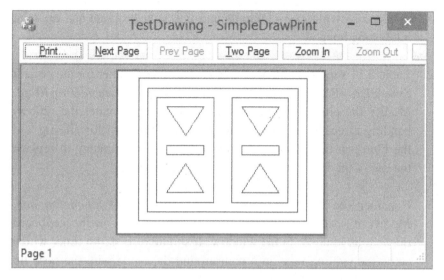

Figure 5.9 A Print Preview Display from SimpleDrawPrint

The use of SetScrollSizes is convenient for scaling and full size printing capabilities. However, a number of functions and strategies may also be considered for particular applications. For example, the mapping mode of MM_ANISOTROPIC allows different scales on the x and y axes. MM_ISOTROPIC forces both axes to have the same scale. The CDC class functions SetWindowOrg, SetWindowExt, SetViewPortOrg and SetViewPortExt permit adjustments of document size and origin location and also allow custom scaling. SetMapMode allows more control of the mapping mode without entering into a scrolling mode.

5.8 Exercises

1. Starting with the project SimpleDraw in *Chap5\2_SimpleDraw*, experiment with the pen definition using the CreatePen function shown in Table 5.5. Change the pen to red, to magenta, etc. Increase its width to several pixels. Use a dashed pen. Initially, experiment without changing the pen name (keep it at m_BluePen). When you find a pen that you like, change the pen name appropriately in all of

the necessary places — compile and link your program and draw an interesting image.

2. Table 5.11 shows the OnMouseMove message handler for the project SimpleDrawRBnd from the folder *Chap5\3_SimpleDrawRBnd*. Modify the project so that this message handler creates the rubber-banding effect by using a white pen (m_WhitePen) for erasing and the blue pen (m_BluePen) for drawing. Use this strategy to replace the use of the function SetROP2 in OnMouseMove.

3. Consider the SimpleAnimate project in *Chap5\4_SimpleAnimate*. Modify it so that the response to striking a "C" on the keyboard draws a large circle in the window. It should also start a timer which starts the smiling face on a path around the circle with the nose tip touching it. You may wish to make use of the DrawCirc function in Table 5.19, of course, making modifications as necessary.

4. Modify the SimpleDrawCirc project so that both circles and lines are drawn by rubber-banding. The SimpleDrawCirc project is located in the folder *Chap5\5_SimpleDrawCirc*.

5. Modify the SimpleDrawCirc project in the folder *Chap5\ 5_SimpleDrawCirc* to include the drawing of rectangles. When the user presses an "R", a prompt with rectangle drawing instructions should appear. The first mouse click should define the upper left corner of the rectangle, the second mouse click should define the lower right. Create your own rectangle drawing function similar to DrawCirc or use the MFC function "Rectangle".

6. Consider the project SimpleDrawSnap located in *Chap5\ 6_SimpleDrawSnap*. Modify this project to include drawing lines, circles and rectangles. Follow the pattern suggested in Exercise 5 above but include snap-to-grid for each drawing operation. Also, make provisions to save drawings containing lines, circles and rectangles in a file and be able to recover a drawing by reading its file.

Chapter 6

Introducing Windows Tools

We have been working steadily toward the development of programs with the look and feel of the Windows software that is familiar to you on the PC desktop. Chapter 4 presented our first Windows programs and introduced the document/view organization. Chapter 5 presented drawing operations with a mouse and the creation of simple graphics images. It also emphasized data storage in the document class. This chapter and the next make use of the basic Windows tools that are provided in the Microsoft Foundation Classes to facilitate the creation of menu bar items, drop down menus, dialog boxes, toolbars, etc. When you conclude these chapters, you should feel quite comfortable with Windows programming and be ready to go on to a few applications which contain animations, graph plotting and representative technical calculations.

The examples in this chapter are based on revisiting one of our projects from Chapter 5 — the SimpleDraw project of Section 5.2. We begin by renaming the project MenuDraw to emphasize our interest in working with menus in this chapter. We then proceed to "clean up" the menu items and the toolbar of the project to display only those options which are available in the program. In the process we edit the "About" box so that it displays an appropriate version number along with some useful information about the current version. Additional features are then developed including the modification of the drop down "Edit" menu to perform a simple delete operation on a line drawing. As we move through this chapter we will create our own menu bar items, drop down menus, toolbar items, dialog boxes, etc. and we'll carefully describe the process of creating them on a click-by-click basis.

6.1 A First Look at Resource Editing

The example project called MenuDraw Version 0.0 can be found in the folder *Chap6\0_MenuDraw*. This project is essentially identical to the SimpleDraw project of Section 5.2 but the project has been renamed as MenuDraw along with its files. In our first use of Windows Resources we will take MenuDraw 0.0 and revise it so it takes on the form of the new version MenuDraw 1.0. You can find the new version in its completed form in the folder *Chap6\1_MenuDraw*. Before you start following the revision process below, you may want to build and execute both the 0.0 and 1.0 versions of MenuDraw to notice the difference in the appearance of the project windows. You should also explore the drop down menus to see how they change between versions. Notice that if you draw a few lines with MenuDraw 1.0, you can click on **Edit > Delete Line** to remove the last line drawn.

6.1.1 Cleaning up the drop down menus

We'll now begin the revision process to demonstrate the development of MenuDraw 1.0 starting with MenuDraw 0.0. Begin by making your own practice copy of the folder *Chap6\0_MenuDraw*. Then bring the project MenuDraw 0.0 into the Visual Studio development environment by double clicking on MenuDraw.sln in your practice folder. In the development environment, display the Resource View window in the workspace area. You can click on **View > Resource View** from the menu bar or look for the resource tab at the bottom of the workspace area. When you have displayed the Resource View window in the workspace, you should see the item MenuDraw with a ">" sign. Click on the ">" to display MenuDraw.rc as shown to the left in Figure 6.1. Click on the ">" sign for MenuDraw.rc to see the full list of resource items for the MenuDraw project beginning with "Accelerator". Next, expand the Menu resource by clicking on its ">" and you should then see IDR_MAINFRAME (the resource ID representing the main menu bar) as shown to the right in Figure 6.1. Now a double click on IDR_MAINFRAME should bring the main menu bar into the Edit window of the development environment as shown in Figure 6.2.

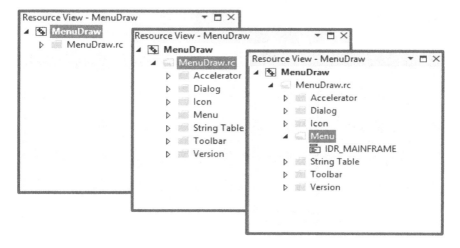

Figure 6.1 Exploring the Resource View Window

We'll begin our clean-up process by recognizing that our simple MenuDraw program is not intended to save files to disk or print output. Since we won't be using these items, we would like to delete them from the "File" menu bar item in the program window. If you click on **File** on the menu bar displayed in the Edit window, the drop down File menu appears as in Figure 6.2 and you can edit it very easily. We want to retain the "New" item and the "Exit" item in the drop down menu but remove everything else. Click on the "Open" item to highlight it and strike the **Delete** key. You'll see "Open" disappear and the "Save" item becomes highlighted. Strike the **Delete** key repeatedly until only "New" and "Exit" remain. The "Type Here" entry also continues to show. If you build and execute the project at this time, you'll find in the project window that when you click on **File** on the menu bar, the drop down menu will only contain "New" and "Exit". Of course, a click on **Exit** will terminate the program and close the window. Clicking on **New** discards the current document and begins another by executing the OnNewDocument function. If you draw a few lines, you'll find that clicking on **New** erases them so you can start again. You should notice that the menu entry for "New" indicates that "Ctrl+N" provides an

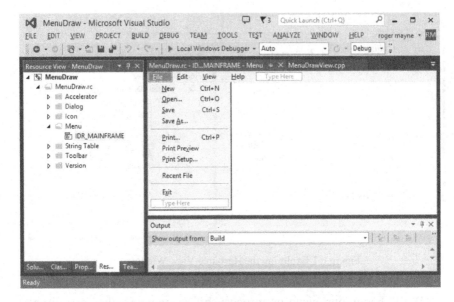

Figure 6.2 Showing the Menu Bar in the Edit Window

accelerator key for "New". This means that striking "N" while pressing the control key has the same effect as clicking on **New**.

The drop down "Edit" menu for MenuDraw 0.0 contains more items than we need. We would like to retain the "Undo" item but all of the others should be deleted. To do this, we return to the menu bar in the resource Edit window (Figure 6.2) and click on "Edit" to see its drop down list. This time we click on the small separator line under "Undo" to highlight it. Striking the Delete key deletes it and moves the highlight to "Cut". Delete "Cut" and all of the items below it. If you now build and execute the program, a click on **Edit** will show only the "Undo" item and since we have not yet provided a function for the Undo command, it will appear grayed out. In this process, if you find that a "Build" operation leaves you with a compiler or linker error related to the resource files, switch to "Rebuild" to perform a full recompile and relink.

Returning to the menu bar in the resource Edit window, the "View" and "Help" items remain. The drop down "View" menu contains "Toolbar" and "Status Bar" items. These are both useful to control the presence of the toolbar and the status bar in the window and we can leave them in place in the "View" menu. The "Help" menu only contains the "About" item. Clicking on **About** pops up a dialog window containing the program version number and any additional information that may be included to describe the character of the program. We will be making use of this "About" dialog so we want to leave the "Help" menu item in place. Incidentally, if you did want to delete the "Help" item from the menu bar, you could click on it to highlight it and then press delete to remove it.

6.1.2 Cleaning up the toolbar

Let's now turn our attention to the toolbar in the program window. The resource editor can be used to edit the toolbar. Return to the Resource View window in the workspace and click on the Toolbar ">" sign to reveal IDR_MAINFRAME. Double click on this and the Edit window will fill with the toolbar editor. Your development environment should now look something like Figure 6.3. This figure shows the toolbar in the Edit window with the button for File > Open ready for editing. It is also ready to help you create customized icons for individual buttons but we will not be doing that at this time.

For now, we would like to keep the File > New button (the first one) and the information button (the last one) on the toolbar but we would like to remove all of the others for our simple program. This is done by clicking on and dragging each button off of the toolbar. For example, the file open button shown in Figure 6.3 should be clicked on and dragged into white space on the Edit window. Don't use the delete key, you'll find that it deletes the icon graphics so that new graphics can be drawn into it but the button itself will not be removed. When you finish deleting buttons, build and execute MenuDraw so that you can see the window shown in Figure 6.4 with a nice, tidy toolbar. If you would like to remove the separator line between the "New" button and the "About" button (as in Figure 6.4), return to the toolbar in the Edit window and click and drag the "About" button over to the "New" button. After another build and execute, the buttons should not show a separation line.

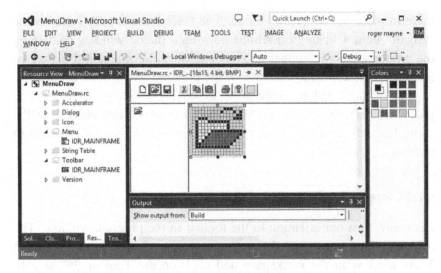

Figure 6.3 Editing the Toolbar

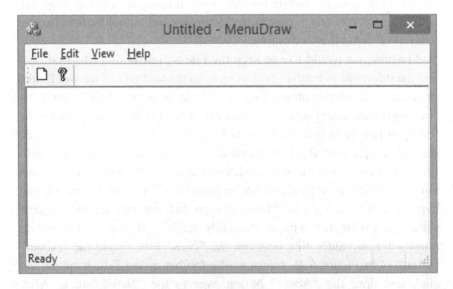

Figure 6.4 The MenuDraw Window with a Reduced Toolbar

6.1.3 Editing the "About" dialog

In an operating Windows program, when **Help > About** is clicked on the menu bar or when the "?" button is clicked on the toolbar, a dialog window opens on the screen that presents some detailed information about the program you are using including the version number and copyright date. We will now look into the process of editing that dialog window and inserting appropriate information into it.

Assuming that you are following along in our revision of MenuDraw Version 0.0 to create MenuDraw Version 1.0, you should display the Resource View window in the workspace area. Then click on the ">" next to Dialog. If you follow with a double click on IDD_ABOUTBOX, the development environment should appear similar to Figure 6.5. The "About" dialog is ready for editing. All of the items in the box including the dialog title itself can be edited and adjusted. A right click on the title bar of the dialog window pops up a menu of options. If you left click on **Properties** in the options menu, the Properties window appears, as shown in Figure 6.6.

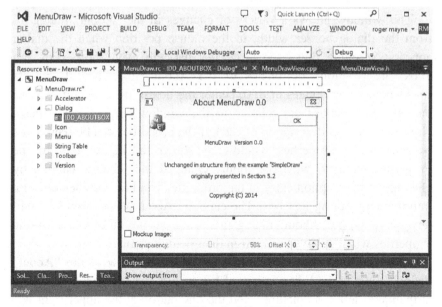

Figure 6.5 Editing the "About" Dialog

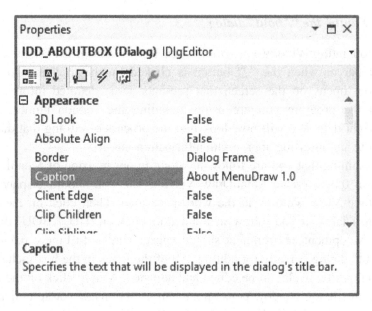

Figure 6.6 Properties Window for the "About" Dialog

This window allows a variety of changes in the "About" dialog — from the dialog border width, to the mouse position when the dialog appears. Scrolling down the properties list will even show xPos and yPos, the position coordinates of the About Box when it appears (incidentally, coordinates of (0,0) center the box in the program window but any other values are relative to the window's upper left corner). Notice that a brief description of each of the properties can be seen at the bottom of the Properties window as shown in Figure 6.6. In the Properties window, we have simply changed the window caption by clicking on the Caption entry in the properties window and then clicking into the neighboring text box. The caption "About MenuDraw 1.0" will now serve as the "About" dialog title while all the other entries in the Properties window have been left in their default status.

Close the Properties window to return to the view of the "About" dialog shown in the Edit window of Figure 6.5, the MFC icon appearing at the upper left is a "picture", and the OK button at the upper right is a "push button". The version information and the copyright date are in

"Static Text" boxes. As you will see in the following sections, these are items that can be added to any dialog window but the "About" dialog window automatically contains a specific set of items along with a set of default entries in each of the boxes. Clicking and dragging any of the various items allows their repositioning in the "About" dialog window as desired. The Format menu bar item provides some centering and spacing tools that you should try out. Clicking to highlight a text box and then clicking and pulling the box edges or corners allows resizing (but not for the icon). Clicking to highlight and then pressing the delete key will remove the item. Clicking to highlight and right clicking pops up a menu of options and then clicking on **Properties** pops up an appropriate Properties window for the item. If you would like to change the program's icon from the default MFC icon, you can edit the icon itself by returning to the Resource View window and clicking on the ">" next to Icon. A click on IDR_MAINFRAME then opens the MFC icon to allow direct editing of the icon image. The other route to icon editing is to directly replace the project's .ico file included in its resource ("res") folder with a .ico file of your choice.

For now, we will just focus on editing the text box which includes the version statement for the "About" dialog. Return to the view of the "About" dialog in the Edit window shown in Figure 6.5. Click in the middle of the version statement to highlight it, right click to pop up the options menu and then click on **Properties** to bring up the Properties window shown in Figure 6.7. This window contains many options which you can explore. We have used all of the default settings except for changing "Align Text" to "Center". The Caption entry in Figure 6.7 contains the text displayed in the text box. It can be edited to display an appropriate Version 1.0 message by simply clicking in the Caption box and then editing or pasting in the desired text. Notice that "\n" yields a new line just as in printf formatting. Figure 6.8 shows our final "About" dialog for MenuDraw 1.0.

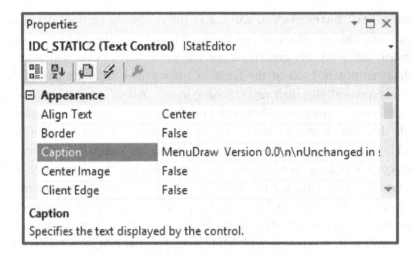

Figure 6.7 Properties Window for a "Text Box"

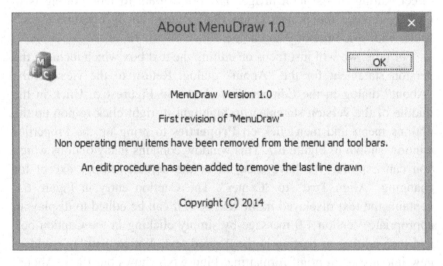

Figure 6.8 The About Dialog for MenuDraw 1.0

6.1.4 Installing Delete Line as an edit command

In addition to having a neater menu bar and a neater toolbar, Version 1.0 of MenuDraw contains an added functional feature that extends the original SimpleDraw program. We have provided the ability to delete the last line in our drawing operations with the menu bar command Edit > Delete Line. To demonstrate the procedure for editing menu items and linking them to program code, let's return to the Resource View window in the workspace area and click on IDR_MAINFRAME to insert the menu bar into the Edit window. Click on the "Edit" item on the menu bar and then click on the "Undo" item to highlight it as shown in Figure 6.9. A right click on "Undo" will pop up the options menu and clicking on **Properties** will bring up the Properties window shown in Figure 6.10. Of course, several options are made available in the Properties window. The Popup item, for example, will pop-up another menu list if it is set to True.

We have mostly accepted the defaults in the Properties window. This includes leaving the ID text box unchanged to allow the name "ID_EDIT_UNDO" to serve as the event handler ID for the Delete Line

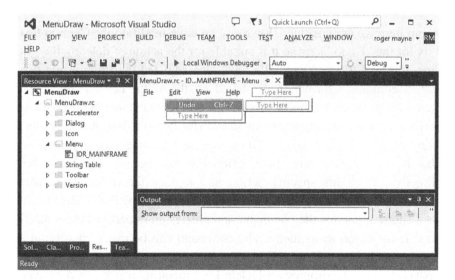

Figure 6.9 Preparing to Edit the "Undo" Command

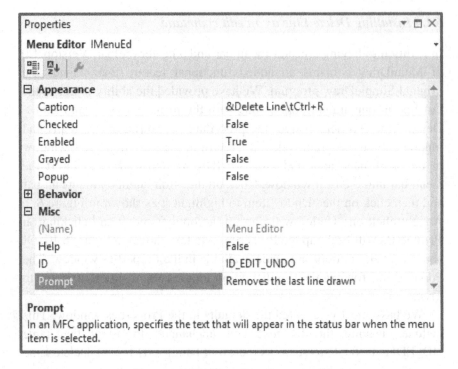

Figure 6.10 The Menu Item Properties Window

menu item we are creating. However, we have modified the Caption text box for the "Undo" item so it is suitable for the action of deleting the last line drawn by the program. We have also adjusted the Prompt text box which contains information displayed on the status bar for this menu item. The Caption box in the Properties window contains the text that is written as the drop down menu item. The current default text in this window is "&Undo\tCtrl+Z". Since we are adjusting this command so that it will delete a line, the Caption box has been changed to more directly reflect this specific action and replace the default text with "&Delete Line\tCtrl+R". The ampersand (&) preceding the D identifies it as a shortcut key for the command and creates an underline below the D as it is displayed in its menu. The command can be executed without a mouse click by striking a D with the alternate character key pressed (Alt+D) while the drop down Delete Line menu item is being displayed

(Alt+E does this). With our editing of the Caption text, the drop down menu item will now read "<u>D</u>elete Line" and "Ctrl+R" will be displayed on the same line. The "Ctrl+R" indicates that R will be used as an accelerator key for this command. It will execute the Delete Line command at any time (not just when the drop down item is displayed) by striking R while pressing the control key (Ctrl+R).

At the bottom of the Properties window shown in Figure 6.10 is the "Prompt" text box which contains information displayed on the status bar for this menu item. Delete the default text in the Prompt box and enter a phrase similar to "Removes the last line drawn". The Menu Item Properties window can now be closed and you can build and execute your program in its present form. If you do, you should see a display very much like Figure 6.11 when you click on **Edit** and move your mouse cursor to the Delete Line item. An expected difference is that your Delete Line item will still be grayed out (indicating that it is not available) since coding has not yet been provided to execute the Delete Line command.

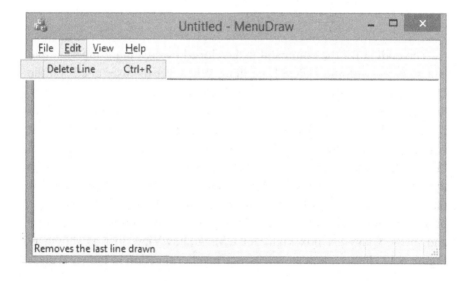

Figure 6.11 Delete Line Menu Item in the MenuDraw Window

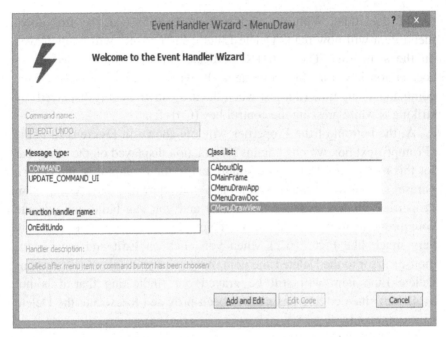

Figure 6.12 Using the Event Handler Wizard

The coding for the command is developed by creating a function that is associated with the Delete Line item. Whenever the user clicks on the Delete Line command (or inputs the shortcut or accelerator key strokes), the function will execute. We create the function by using the Event Handler Wizard. To activate it, display the menu bar resource in the Edit window (Figure 6.9) and click on the "Edit" menu item. Then click on "Delete Line" to highlight it and right click on "Delete Line" to pop-up the options menu. A click on **Add Event Handler** should then display the Event Handler Wizard window of Figure 6.12 with the Command name ID_EDIT_UNDO. In the Message type box, highlight Command and in the Class list box highlight CMenuDrawView just as shown in Figure 6.12. This will create a message handler function in the view class to be called whenever the Delete Line menu item is clicked. In Figure 6.12, we have selected CMenuDrawView to keep this user interaction function in the view class (placing it in the document class is an alternative). The Function handler name box displays the default name OnEditUndo which can be changed if desired. We will accept the default name and the other settings by clicking the Add and Edit button. This closes the Event Handler Wizard window and moves directly to the new OnEditUndo function which has become a member function of the class CMenuDrawView. If you return to the Class View window, you can see that OnEditUndo has indeed been added to the class CMenuDrawView.

A click on the OnEditUndo member function in Class View will return you to the Edit window where you can see the simple template for the function as provided by the Wizard and ready for the insertion of your coding. Only three lines have been added to OnEditUndo as shown in Table 6.1. Line 05 obtains the current document pointer. Line 06 decrements the NumLines variable (and thus removes the last line in the drawing). Line 07 calls on UpdateAllViews so that the image is redrawn without the last line. Notice that repeatedly using the command **Edit > Delete Line** will remove the lines of the drawing one at a time and that the if statement in Line 06 prevents NumLines from falling below zero.

Table 6.1 Listing of OnEditUndo from MenuDrawView.cpp (Ver. 1.0)

```
01    /* This is the listing of OnEditUndo */
02    void CMenuDrawView::OnEditUndo()
03    {
04        // TODO: Add your command handler code here
05        CMenuDrawDoc* pDoc = GetDocument();
06        if (pDoc->NumLines!=0) { pDoc->NumLines--; }
07        pDoc->UpdateAllViews(NULL);
08    }
```

6.1.5 Including accelerator keys

You can build and execute the MenuDraw program including the revisions through Section 6.1.4 above and the code of Table 6.1. When you execute the program you will find that it allows you to draw lines with left and right clicks of the mouse button and when you want to delete the most recent line, clicking on **Edit > Delete Line** will remove it. If you use the shortcut keys Alt +E +D, you will also be able to remove a line without a mouse click. However, the Ctrl+R command advertised in the drop down menu item "Delete Line" will not yet work because we still have to insert it.

To insert this accelerator key, return to the Resource View window. Click on the accelerator "+" sign to expand it and then double click on IDR_MAINFRAME to see the display of the accelerator keys. As shown in Figure 6.13, the object IDs for various commands appear in the Edit window along with the accelerator keys provided by default. Notice that the familiar Ctrl+X for cut and Ctrl+V for paste are among those which appear. Also notice that ID_EDIT_UNDO appears with Ctrl+Z as a default accelerator. You can click on this line to highlight it and double click on the "Z" entry to pop-up a small edit box (as shown in Figure 6.13) where you can change the Z to R. There are a few options here including, for example, the use of the Alt key instead of the Ctrl key. However, simply changing the Z to an R is all that is necessary to provide our desired accelerator key of Ctrl+R (where "R" represents "Remove").

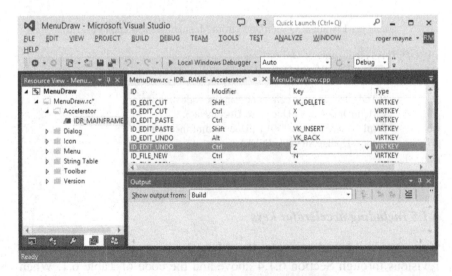

Figure 6.13 Editing the Accelerator Keys

The accelerator key table in the Edit window of Figure 6.13 also includes another entry for ID_EDIT_UNDO showing the unadvertised accelerator key of Alt+Backspace. Any of the accelerator key lines can be easily edited by clicking on the individual lines and entries and making desired changes to the "Modifier" or the "key". To illustrate this and to provide another convenient Delete Line accelerator we will edit the second entry for ID_EDIT_UNDO. Click on the accelerator table line ID_EDIT_UNDO indicating Alt+Backspace. On that line, click on the Alt and in the resulting box, replace the Alt by clicking on the empty line. Now click on VK_Back and in its box, scroll down to VK_Left and click on it. This second ID_EDIT_UNDO line should now show "none" and "VK_Left" (this is the left arrow key) as the entries.

At this point, a build and execute of MenuDraw should produce a completed program with a tidy menu bar and toolbar. When you operate the program you should be able to draw lines with right and left mouse clicks as before. You should also be able to delete lines by clicking on **Edit > Delete Line**, or by using the shortcut Alt+E+D, or by using the accelerator key Ctrl+R indicated in the menu, or by using the unadvertised left arrow key which also serves as an accelerator. The MenuDraw Version 1.0 project in the folder *Chap6\1_MenuDraw* contains all of the changes we have made here in Section 6.1. Notice that the only changes in actual C++ programming were in adding the OnEditUndo function of Table 6.1 to the view class and providing just three additional lines of code. The resource editing process is very powerful. It plays an important role in programming and achieving the look and feel of a Windows program with Visual C++.

6.2 Adding an Item to the Menu Bar (Version 2.0)

Our next exercise in exploring the standard Windows tool set is to add a new menu bar item. We will call this item Line Style and its purpose will be to change the style of the lines used in displaying the current drawing from solid lines to dashed lines. The menu item will operate as a "toggle", switching between solid lines and dashed lines and vice versa.

Table 6.2 Listing of CMenuDrawView from MenuDrawView.cpp (Ver. 2.0)

```
01   /* This is the listing of CMenuDrawView */
02   CMenuDrawView::CMenuDrawView()
03   //: m_LineStyle(_T(""))
04   {
05       // TODO: add construction code here
06       m_LineStyle = "Solid";
07       m_SolidPen.CreatePen (PS_SOLID, 2, RGB(0,0,255));
08       m_DashedPen.CreatePen (PS_DASH, 1, RGB(0,0,255));
09   }
```

The project MenuDraw Version 2.0 contains this change and you will find it in the folder *Chap6\2_MenuDraw*. You can build and execute it to become familiar with Version 2. Draw several lines and then click on Line Style to see what it does. In the rest of this section we will start with the previous program MenuDraw 1.0 and revise it into MenuDraw 2.0.

The first step in revising Version 1 is to provide a dashed pen and a solid pen in the view class. To do this we create the CPen objects m_DashedPen and m_SolidPen as member variables of CMenuDrawView. We do it by right clicking on CMenuDrawView in the Class View window and selecting **Add > Add Variable**. The class name CPen is used for the variable type in both cases. Since we won't need m_BluePen any longer, it can be deleted. To do so, double click on m_BluePen in the Workspace window. This will take you to the line in the declaration of the class CMenuDrawView where m_BluePen is declared as a member variable. You can simply delete this line or use "//" to comment it out. When you finish, notice that m_BluePen no longer appears as a member variable in the view class. You will also want to remove the statement initializing m_BluePen from the constructor function CMenuDrawView. In addition to adding the new pen objects, we will need to add one more member variable to the view class. This will define whether we are in dashed mode or solid mode. Let's call the new variable m_LineStyle and declare it as a CString variable type.

We initialize m_LineStyle, m_SolidPen and m_DashedPen in the view class constructor function CMenuDrawView as shown in Table 6.2. Here you can see that at line 03 we have commented out the default

Table 6.3 Listing of OnDraw from MenuDrawView.cpp (Ver. 2.0)

```
01    /* This is the listing of OnDraw */
02    void CMenuDrawView::OnDraw(CDC* pDC)
03    {
04        CMenuDrawDoc* pDoc = GetDocument();
05        ASSERT_VALID(pDoc); if(!pDoc)return;
06        // TODO: add draw code for native data here
07        if (m_LineStyle == "Solid"){pDC->SelectObject(&m_SolidPen);}
08        if (m_LineStyle == "Dashed"){pDC->SelectObject(&m_DashedPen);}
09    for (int i=0; i < pDoc->NumLines; i++) {
10        pDC->MoveTo(pDoc->FPoint[i]);
11        pDC->LineTo(pDoc->LPoint[i]);
12        }
13    }
```

initialization of m_LineStyle and that line 06 defines the initial line style as "Solid". Line 07 creates a solid blue pen two pixels wide and line 08 creates a blue pen for dashed lines. Note, incidentally, that the dashed pen style only permits a width of one pixel.

With the solid and dashed pens both defined, we need to select the correct pen for drawing operations based on the status of m_LineStyle. Table 6.3 shows a listing of the revised OnDraw function where lines 07 and 08 select m_SolidPen or m_DashedPen for drawing based on m_LineStyle. The for loop of lines 09–12 then draws the stored line drawing in the normal way. Similarly, drawing also takes place in the mouse drawing function OnLButtonDown and the solid or dashed pen must be selected there based on m_LineStyle. Two lines equivalent to lines 07 and 08 of OnDraw (Table 6.3) have been inserted into OnLButtonDown to perform the selection. These can be seen in Table 6.4 for OnLButtonDown, once again at lines 07 and 08.

If you have been following along in this revision to create MenuDraw Version 2.0, you now have a program that will build and execute. However, it will only draw solid lines since we have not as yet made a provision to change line style by changing the value of m_LineStyle. We now introduce a function to toggle m_LineStyle which is activated by the menu bar item Line Style. First, we add Line Style to the menu bar by

Table 6.4 Listing of OnLButtonDown from MenuDrawView.cpp (Ver. 2.0)

```
01     /* This is the listing of OnLButtonDown */
02     void CMenuDrawView::OnLButtonDown(UINT nFlags, CPoint point)
03     {
04         // TODO: Add your message handler code here and/or call default
05         CMenuDrawDoc* pDoc = GetDocument();
06         CClientDC aDC(this);
07         if (m_LineStyle == "Solid") { aDC.SelectObject(&m_SolidPen); }
08         if (m_LineStyle == "Dashed") { aDC.SelectObject(&m_DashedPen); }
09         int i = pDoc->NumLines;
10         aDC.MoveTo(pDoc->FPoint[i]);
11         aDC.LineTo(point);
12         pDoc->LPoint[i] = point;
13         pDoc->FPoint[i+1] = point;
14         pDoc->NumLines++;
15         CView::OnLButtonDown(nFlags, point);
16     }
```

moving to the Resource View window in the workspace area and expanding the Menu item to find IDR_MAINFRAME. Double click on this to place the menu bar in the Edit window. Now click on and highlight the small rectangle "Type Here" next to Help on the menu bar in the Edit window. Type in "&Line Style" to provide Alt+L as a shortcut. Then right click on this new button to pop-up the options window and select **Properties**. The Properties window should now be displayed in the form of Figure 6.14. Since we do not want the Line Style menu bar to produce its own pop-up menu, we look for the Popup line and change the True entry to False. Notice that the Caption line contains the text for the menu bar item as we entered it. Also notice that the Prompt entry contains the text that will appear on the status bar during program operation. We have entered the phrase "Toggles between solid and dashed lines" for the prompt. You can now close the Properties window.

The event handler function for the Line Style menu bar item is created by a right click on the Line Style item on the menu bar as shown in the Edit window. This is followed by a click on **Add Event Handler** in the resulting options menu. The Event Handler Wizard window

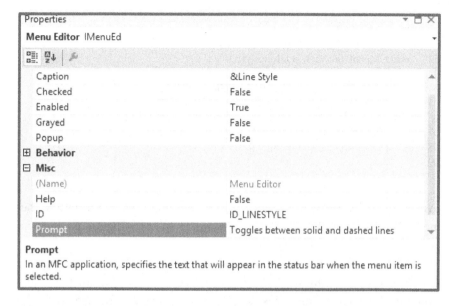

Figure 6.14   The "Line Style" Properties Window

appears similar to Figure 6.12 shown earlier. We should see the Command name ID_LINESTYLE and we want a Message type of "Command" with CMenuDrawView highlighted in the Class list. We then accept the default event handler name of OnLinestyle by clicking on the Add and Edit button. The member function OnLinestyle has now been added to CMenuDrawView and is ready for editing.

In the Class View window of the workspace area, expand the view class CMenuDrawView to find OnLineStyle as a new member function. Click on it and it will appear in the Edit window ready for you to add code to the function. The coding is relatively simple, as you can see in Table 6.5, with four lines added to the default function. Lines 06 and 07 change m_LineStyle by toggling to the new mode and line 08 then updates the view (using UpdateAllViews for the document) in order to redraw the window with the changed line style. To put the menu bar in final order, return to Resource View in the Workspace window and bring the main menu bar into the Edit window. Click and drag the "Help" item

Table 6.5 Listing of OnLineStyle from MenuDrawView.cpp (Ver. 2.0)

```
01    /* This is the listing of OnLineStyle */
02    void CMenuDrawView::OnLinestyle()
03    {
04        // TODO: Add your command handler code here
05        CMenuDrawDoc* pDoc = GetDocument();
06    if (m_LineStyle == "Solid")  { m_LineStyle = "Dashed"; }
07        else { m_LineStyle = "Solid"; }
08        pDoc->UpdateAllViews(NULL);
09    }
```

over to the right of the Line Style item. When you lift the left button, the menu bar items will be reordered with "Help" moving to its normal position at the end of the menu bar list.

You can now build and execute your revised program or go directly to the project in *Chap6\2_MenuDraw* to study its operation. Our new function OnLineStyle provides the ability to change the member variable m_LineStyle so that we can switch between a solid line presentation and a dashed line presentation with a click of the Line Style menu item. Notice that since this menu item does not produce a drop down menu, the shortcut key Alt+L directly produces a change in line style. Also, notice that the prompt appears in the status bar as soon as the Line Style menu item is clicked.

6.3 A Drop Down Menu for Color Selection (Version 3.0)

The next step in our tour of Windows tools is to add a Line Color item to the menu bar to be used for color selection. This new menu item is to produce a drop down menu in which the user can select the desired color for display of the line drawn image. The project MenuDraw 3.0 contains the completed coding and resource additions necessary for the added menu capability. It is located in the folder *Chap6\3_MenuDraw* and you can build and execute the program to try it out. For example, clicking on **Line Color > Green** will change the color of the lines in the display to green. In the discussion below, we will start with MenuDraw Version 2.0

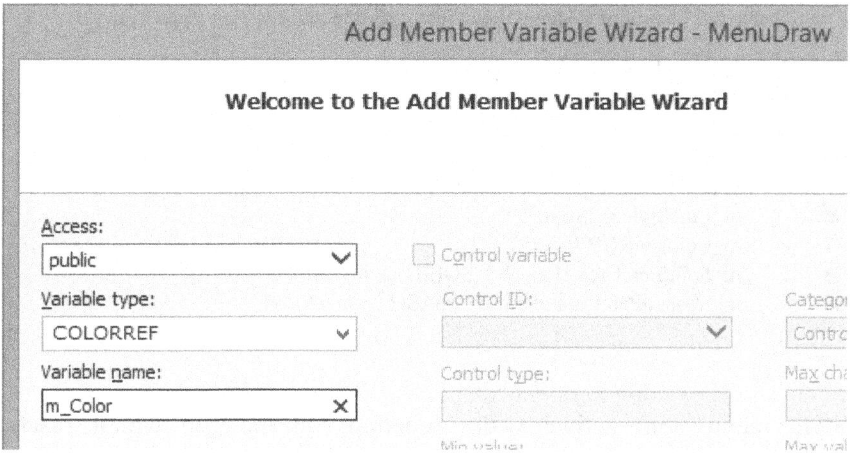

Figure 6.15 Adding the COLORREF Variable to the View Class

and describe the process of revising it to include the Line Color menu bar item and the drop down menu of MenuDraw Version 3.0.

The first step in the revision process is to consider the change required in the view class member variables to be able to store the pen color information. The variable m_Color should be added to the class CMenuDrawView for this purpose and is of type COLORREF as shown in Figure 6.15. COLORREF is an MFC data type in a 32 bit format which contains red, green and blue color information. The MFC function RGB is available to conveniently specify color and when RGB is executed, it returns a result of type COLORREF. In order to initialize m_Color, we make use of the constructor function CMenuDrawView. The revised listing of CMenuDrawView is shown in Table 6.6. Line 06 sets the initial line style to solid (note that line 03 deactivates the default initialization). Line 07 initializes m_Color to blue by using the function RGB and then lines 08 and 09 initialize both the dashed pen and the solid pen by using m_Color as the color argument in the CreatePen function.

As in the previous version, this program uses the m_LineStyle variable to switch between solid and dashed lines. Clicking on the Line

Table 6.6 Listing of CMenuDrawView from MenuDrawView.cpp (Ver. 3.0)

```
01    /* This is the listing of CMenuDraw */
02    CMenuDrawView::CMenuDrawView()
03    //: m_LineStyle(_T(""))
04    {
05         // TODO: add construction code here
06         m_LineStyle = "Solid";
07         m_Color = RGB(0,0,255);
08         m_SolidPen.CreatePen (PS_SOLID, 2, m_Color);
09         m_DashedPen.CreatePen (PS_DASH, 1, m_Color);
10    }
```

Style menu item activates the function OnLineStyle which resets m_LineStyle. We will provide similar functions in a drop down color selection menu to reset m_Color and to define pens as necessary to change the drawing color. We begin by displaying Resource View in the workspace area (you can always find it by clicking on **View > Resource View** on the Visual Studio menu bar). Then, expand Menu and double click on IDR_MAINFRAME to place the project menu bar in the Edit window. Now click on the small "Type Here" rectangle at the right end of the menu bar to highlight it and enter Line &Color as seen in Figure 6.16. The ampersand is entered before the C in this case so that Alt+C will provide a shortcut (the L shortcut key has already been used for Line Style).

At this point, we will create the first of the drop down menu items. In Figure 6.16, the beginning of the drop down menu is indicated by the small "Type Here" rectangle below the Line Color menu item in the Edit window. Click on the small rectangle to highlight it, then enter &Red so that Alt+C+R furnishes a shortcut sequence. Now let's take a look at the Properties windows. Open the Line Color Properties window by right clicking on Line Color and then selecting Properties in the options menu or by simply double clicking the Line Color box. In the Properties window, note the Caption entry of Line &Color which could be edited if desired. Also note that the command ID is not accessible since this menu bar item generates a drop down menu list. In this case, the command IDs

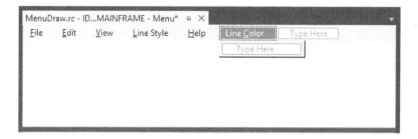

Figure 6.16 Adding the Line Color Menu Item

are associated with the drop down menu items. Close this Properties window and click on the Red menu item to display its Properties window. Notice that the default command ID is ID_LINECOLOR_RED to reflect the two menu item entries. We'll keep this ID but we do want to enter a Prompt (for the status bar) to reflect the action corresponding to clicking Red. We've entered "Change line color to red".

You can now enter additional drop down menu items for other colors. We have used &Green, &Blue and Blac&k. After you have entered all of these items, return to the Properties window for each of them to confirm the command ID and to provide a suitable entry for the Prompt. When you finish the drop down menu items, building and executing the program will allow you to see that the drop down menu list is actually in place (although grayed out) and ready to have functions and coding attached.

6.3.1 Providing a functional connection to the menu items

We have now completed the addition of the menu bar item Line Color and its drop down menu items to MenuDraw Version 3.0. However, we have not yet made any functional connection between these items and the program. The next step is to add event handler functions for each menu item. For the sequence Line Color > Red, an event handler can be provided by right clicking on Red to bring up the options window and selecting **Add Event Handler**. The window for the Event Handler

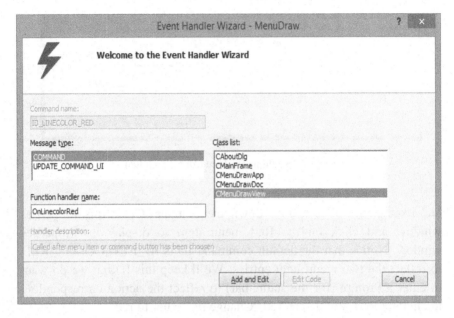

Figure 6.17 Creating the Event Handler Function

Wizard will then appear. It contains the default Command name: ID_LINECOLOR_RED and the highlighted Message type: Command along with the default Function handler name: OnLinecolorRed (which can be edited). Since we want this handler function to be in our view class, the CMenuDrawView class should be highlighted in the Class list. With these settings in place, as shown in Figure 6.17, clicking the Add and Edit button in the wizard window will create the OnLinecolorRed function in the view class. Repeat this process for the green, blue and black menu items to create their individual handler functions. When you are finished, explore the CMenuDrawView member functions to be sure your event handlers are all in place. Also, before we go on from here to add function coding, you should click and drag the "Help" menu item down to the right end of the menu bar items so that the menu bar appears in its standard form.

We can now edit the color functions beginning with the drop down menu item Red. From the Class View window in the workspace area and

Table 6.7 Listing of OnLinecolorRed from MenuDrawView.cpp (Ver. 3.0)

```
01    /* This is the listing of OnLineColorRed */
02    void CMenuDrawView::OnLinecolorRed()
03    {
04        // TODO: Add your command handler code here
05        CMenuDrawDoc* pDoc = GetDocument();
06        m_Color = RGB(255,0,0);
07        ResetPens();
08        pDoc->UpdateAllViews(NULL);
09    }
```

under the CMenuDrawView class, click on the new member function OnLinecolorRed to bring it into the Edit window. This is the function that will be executed each time that "Red" is clicked in the drop down menu. We need to reset m_Color whenever this happens and redefine the solid and dashed pens. The code shown in Table 6.7 will do this. Line 06 defines m_Color to correspond to the selected color red. Line 07 calls a function for resetting the colors of the solid and dashed pens which is described immediately below. And finally, line 08 redraws the window with the change in line color by calling UpdateAllViews.

The ResetPens function is shown in Table 6.8. It has been added as a member function of CMenuDrawView and makes use of the member variable m_Color as needed to reset the pen colors. Line 04 deletes the current solid pen and line 05 recreates the pen based on the current m_Color value. Lines 06 and 07 similarly update the dashed pen. The functions OnLinecolorGreen, OnLinecolorBlue and OnLinecolorBlack can now be completed in the same form as Table 6.7 but with values for

Table 6.8 Listing of ResetPens from MenuDrawView.cpp (Ver. 3.0)

```
01    /* This is the listing of ResetPens */
02    void CMenuDrawView::ResetPens(void)
03    {
04        m_SolidPen.DeleteObject();
05        m_SolidPen.CreatePen(PS_SOLID, 2, m_Color);
06        m_DashedPen.DeleteObject();
07        m_DashedPen.CreatePen(PS_DASH, 1, m_Color);
08    }
```

the arguments of the RGB function appropriate for the color selected (black, of course, corresponds to 0,0,0). The ResetPens function will also be used for the pen update from each of the functions. Once you have created and coded these functions, you can make an initial build and then execute your revision to see how it works. The only thing that is not yet included in the Version 3.0 program is the provision for check marks in the Line Color drop down menu.

6.3.2 Providing check marks

In drop down menus where various menu items are being selected or set, a "check mark" is placed next to those menu items which are currently active in an operating program. The placing of check marks is performed through updates of the Command User Interface. Messages of the form UPDATE_COMMAND_UI are used and appropriate functions for them may be generated using the Event Handler Wizard. In the case of the drop down menu, a message of this type is processed just before the menu is displayed and a check mark can be set next to any item that satisfies its check mark condition. The testing of the check mark condition (taking the color Red, for example) takes place in a function with the default name OnUpdateLinecolorRed in much the same way as the command from the Line Color > Red menu item is handled by the function with the default name OnLinecolorRed. The Event Handler Wizard establishes the function OnUpdateLinecolorRed and provides all of the internal linkages to the appropriate resources. A little bit of added coding within the function is all that is required to make it work.

Let's look at the process of setting the check mark for the Line Color > Red menu item. From the Resource View window, place the menu bar in the Edit window. Then click on the **Line Color** item to view the drop down menu. Right click on **Red** to obtain the options menu and click on **Add Event Handler**. The Event Handler Wizard window (as shown in Figure 6.18) will then open showing the Command name: ID_LINECOLOR_RED. In the Class list box select the class where you want the message handler to be a member function — in our case, this is the view class CMenuDrawView. Then, select the Message type:

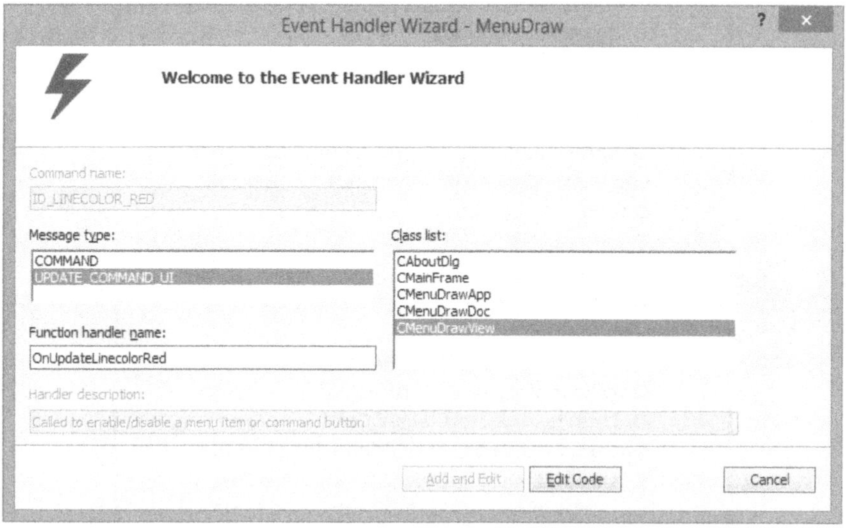

Figure 6.18 Adding the Update Command Function for "Red"

UPDATE_COMMAND_UI to indicate that it's the update function that we now want to create (of course, we've already created the command function). Also note that the default Function handler name: OnUpdateLinecolorRed is quite acceptable. When you are satisfied with the settings, click on the **Add and Edit** button to add the member function OnUpdateLinecolorRed to the class CMenuDrawView. This same process should also be repeated for Green, Blue and Black.

When you have added all of the update functions, use ClassView in the Workspace window to look at the full list of member functions (and member variables) for the CMenuDrawView class. Particularly check to be sure that you have the four new member functions for OnUpdateLinecolor... as well as the four member functions for OnLinecolor... which you have already created. Figure 6.19 shows our list of member functions and variables for CMenuDrawView. At this point we'll add code to the function OnUpdateLinecolorRed. Click on the function name in Class View to display it in the Edit window. Only one line needs to be added to OnUpdateLinecolorRed in order to call

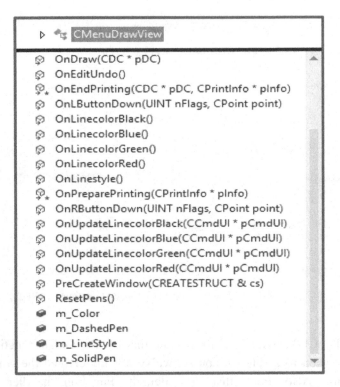

Figure 6.19 New Member Functions of the Class CMenuDrawView

Table 6.9 Listing of OnUpdateLinecolorRed from MenuDrawView.cpp (Ver. 3.0)

```
01    /* This is the listing of OnUpdateLinecolorRed */
02    void CMenuDrawView::OnUpdateLinecolorRed(CCmdUI* pCmdUI)
03    {
04        // TODO: Add your command update UI handler code here
05        pCmdUI->SetCheck(m_Color==RGB(255,0,0));
06    }
```

on the SetCheck function. Table 6.9 shows the completed function. Line 05 uses the command interface pointer as passed in the argument list of OnUpdateLinecolorRed and indicated in line 02. This pointer refers to the "Red" menu item in line 05 and the SetCheck function will place the checkmark next to "Red" if the condition on m_Color is satisfied. In this case m_Color is of type COLORREF and it is being compared against the full red color specified in the RGB function of line 05. Of course, if the color is red, the menu item will be shown as "checked".

The last revision task is to insert a line similar to line 05 (but with the appropriate RGB) into the update functions OnUpdateLinecolorGreen, OnUpdateLinecolorBlue, and OnUpdateLinecolorBlack which have already been created as member functions in the view class. When this critical statement has been added to each, the revision will be functionally equivalent to our project MenuDraw Version 3.0. Of course, the "About" dialog would also have to be revised to be completely equivalent to MenuDraw 3.0. Take a few minutes to exercise Version 3. Be sure to notice that the check marks in the drop down menu do record your most recent color selection. Also note the descriptions of the menu actions which appear in the status bar at the bottom of the window and correspond to the Prompt entries for each of the menu items.

6.4 Adding Toolbar Buttons (Version 4.0)

The next demonstration in our study of Windows tools is to develop a set of toolbar buttons that facilitates the selection of line colors and allows color changing with just a single mouse click. Our example project MenuDraw Version 4.0 contains the toolbar modification and you can find it in the folder *Chap6\4_MenuDraw*. Of course, if you build and execute it, you can study its operation and you should note that the toolbar buttons for the various colors correspond directly to the drop down menu items for Line Color.

In this section we will start with the Version 3 project as found in the folder *Chap6\3_MenuDraw*. We will then follow through the process of adding the color toolbar buttons to make it equivalent to Version 4. Bring MenuDraw 3.0 into the Visual C++ environment and begin the revision process with the Resource View window. Expand the MenuDraw resources and the Toolbar item so that you can double click on IDR_MAINFRAME. This will place the project toolbar in the Edit

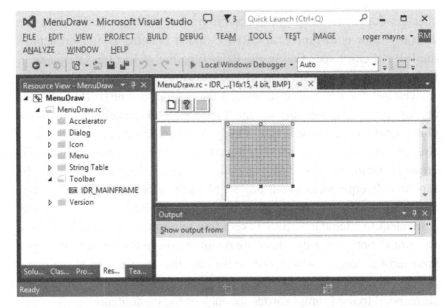

Figure 6.20 Initial Editing of a New Toolbar Button

window so that you can design your own toolbar buttons. If you click on the blank toolbar button to the right of the "?" button, this new button will appear enlarged and ready for editing as shown in Figure 6.20. A set of editing tools automatically becomes available in the environment when the project toolbar enters the Edit window. This allows the selection of various drawing tools for the button design process. You will also want to see the Colors window to select colors for your button designs. You can display it with a right click in the Edit window to produce an options window and then click on Show Colors Window. Figure 6.21 shows the editing process for the "Red" button. Notice the Colors window and the separate window for editing tools. We began drawing by first selecting the white color and using the "Fill" tool (the bucket) to make the button completely white. Then the red color and the "Line" tool were selected to begin line drawing. Of course, if desired, the Edit window can be moved to full screen, by clicking on View > Full Screen from the menu bar (this command serves as a toggle so that clicking it again leaves the full screen mode).

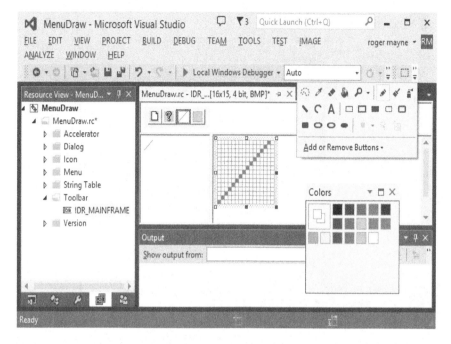

Figure 6.21 Designing the Red Toolbar Button

When you finish with your button design, you will want to associate the button with its corresponding command ID. To do this, you will need the Properties window for the toolbar button. Right click in the Edit window and then click on **Properties** in the pop-up options menu (or just double click in the Edit window) to display the Properties window. We show it in Figure 6.22 where you can also see our completed Red button. Initially the ID line will contain a default numbered ID. Click on the default ID to open a box containing a full set of command IDs. Scroll down until you find ID_LINECOLOR_RED and click it. The resulting ID should appear as in Figure 6.22. The Prompt line should now be filled with the prompt "Change line color to red" which we previously set for this command in Version 3.0. Figure 6.22 shows a small addition to the original command prompt. We have added a "\n" and a bit of text. The text appearing after the "\n" is used as the ToolTip prompt that appears

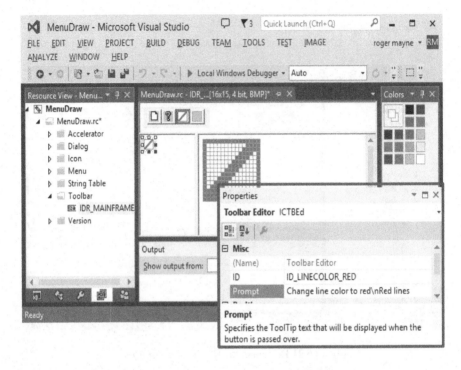

Figure 6.22 Toolbar Button Properties for the Red Button

when you let your cursor linger over the toolbar button in the operating program. In this case, we have written "Red lines" to serve as the ToolTip prompt. If you now close the Properties window, you have completed the addition of the red line toolbar button. You have drawn it, associated it with a command, and provided suitable text for both the status bar and the ToolTip prompts.

At this point, you may want to build and execute your program to show that the red line toolbar button does indeed function. However, you will also want to add additional toolbar buttons for the green, blue and black colors. Simply follow the same procedure as for the red button. You will also want to arrange the buttons in a standard looking format. This can be done by clicking and dragging on the individual buttons to move them to the desired position on the toolbar. Separations between buttons can be useful for grouping them. You can provide a separation by just clicking on a button in the Edit window and then sliding it along the toolbar about a half button width. We have grouped the color buttons together and separated them from the "New" button and the "?". Figure 6.23 shows the final arrangement.

This completes our addition of the color line toolbar buttons. Toolbar creation is very powerful and surprisingly easy. When executing MenuDraw 4.0, you can now change colors just by clicking on the new buttons. Take a moment to observe the status bar and pop-up prompts as your mouse cursor moves from button to button along the toolbar.

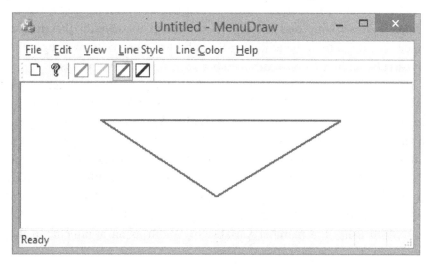

Figure 6.23 Final Toolbar for MenuDraw 4.0

6.5 Creating and Using a Dialog Window (Version 5.0)

Pop-up dialog windows are a standard feature in many PC programs and the use of an edit box in a dialog window is the most familiar way to input information and numbers into an operating program. To illustrate the process of creating and programming a dialog window with Visual C++, we have extended our series of MenuDraw programs to Version 5.0. This version includes a Line Dialog menu item with a drop down menu that allows changes in the drawing line width. You will find MenuDraw 5.0 in the folder *Chap6\5_MenuDraw*. Of course, you can build and execute it to become familiar with its operation. Clicking on **Line Dialog > Line Width** displays a dialog window and allows you to enter the desired line width in pixels.

6.5.1 Preparing for line width adjustment

As in the earlier examples in this chapter, we will carry out the revisions necessary to create MenuDraw Version 5.0 by revision of the previous version. We will start with MenuDraw 4.0 in the folder *Chap6\4_MenuDraw* and modify it as needed to develop the dialog. Since we are going to be adjusting the solid line pen width, we begin the revision by adding a line width member variable to the view class.

Display the Class View window in the workspace area and right click on CMenuDrawView. Then click on **Add > Add Variable** and specify an integer variable with the name m_Width. You should see this appear in the list of member variables for CMenuDrawView. We then set an initial line width in the revised constructor function CMenuDrawView (Table 6.10 contains the new listing). Line 07 of Table 6.10 shows m_Width being set to the initial two pixel pen width that we have been using for solid lines. The CreatePen function call in line 10 sets the solid line width using the member variable m_Width as an argument. In the

Table 6.10 Listing of CMenuDrawView from MenuDrawView.cpp (Ver. 5.0)

```
01    /* This is the listing of CMenuDrawView */
02    CMenuDrawView::CMenuDrawView()
03    //: m_LineStyle(_T(""))
04    //: m_Width(0)
05    {
06        // TODO: add construction code here
07        m_Width = 2;
08        m_LineStyle = "Solid";
09        m_Color = RGB(0,0,255);
10        m_SolidPen.CreatePen (PS_SOLID, m_Width, m_Color);
11        m_DashedPen.CreatePen (PS_DASH, 1, m_Color);
12    }
```

same way, the ResetPens function listed back in Table 6.8 must be modified to use the CreatePen statement for the solid pen in the form of line 10. By introducing the member variable m_Width into the ResetPens function, any color change by clicking a Line Color menu item or a toolbar button, permits ResetPens to maintain the appropriate line width as the color is changed.

6.5.2 Creating a menu item for the dialog window

The first step in the creation of a dialog window is to create a menu item and a corresponding function that displays the dialog window when the menu item is clicked. The function then activates the dialog window. Afterward, when the OK button of the dialog window is clicked, the function processes the information that was entered into the dialog. We will start this next step in the revision process by adding a Line Dialog item to the menu bar. You should display the Resource View window in the workspace area and expand it to show the MenuDraw resources. Then click on Menu and double click on IDR_MAINFRAME to bring the menu bar into the Edit window. Go to the "Type Here" to the right of "Help" and enter "Line & Dialog" to give the item a title and a shortcut key.

We'll now set up the drop down menu item for the line width dialog. Click on the Line Dialog item on the menu bar and in the "Type Here" which appears below it. Enter a caption such as Line &Width to provide a name and shortcut key. The Properties window for the Line Width item can be seen by right clicking on Line Width and then selecting **Properties** in the resulting options menu. The Edit window should now appear as in Figure 6.24 with the included Properties window for the Line Width menu item. Notice the Caption entry and the default ID entry of ID_LINEDIALOG_LINEWIDTH (which we will accept). We have also entered a Prompt of "Change line width". We now need to add a function which is activated by the LineWidth item. To do so, close the Properties window. Right click again on Line Width and now select **Add Event Handler**. The Event Handler Wizard will then appear. Click on CMenuDrawView in the Class list and click on Command in the

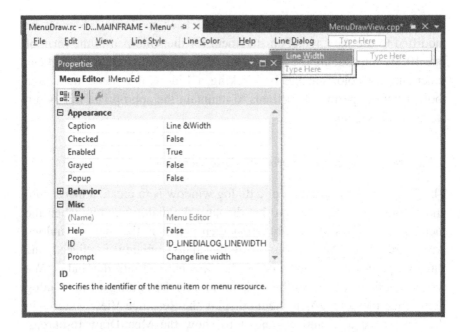

Figure 6.24 The Line Width Properties Window

Message type. Also accept the default function handler name OnLinedialogLinewidth. Close the Wizard by selecting the Add and Edit button.

At this point the Line Width item has been created on a drop down menu from the Line Dialog menu bar item and we have added the function OnLinedialogLinewidth which will be activated when it is clicked. We are now ready to develop the dialog window which will be displayed by the ·function OnLinedialogLinewidth and which will be used to obtain line width input from the user. We realize that this whole process may seem a bit complicated but when you have done it a few times, it becomes quite natural.

6.5.3 Developing the dialog window for line width

The next step in the dialog process is to make use of resource editing to create the dialog window. As the window is created, it is associated with a dialog class. A function available within the dialog class is used in displaying the dialog window during program execution and allows the exchange of data between the dialog window and the program itself.

Let's continue our revision and progress toward Version 5 by returning to the Resource View window. This time we right click on the Dialog folder to pop-up an options window and we click **Insert Dialog**. As shown in Figure 6.25, a dialog window now appears ready for editing and the dialog list expands to include the default dialog identifier IDD_DIALOG1 as an additional dialog item in Resource View. Initially the new dialog window contains only OK and Cancel buttons and the default name "Dialog". You can start editing the dialog by right clicking on the dialog window itself and then selecting **Properties**.

This pops-up a dialog Properties window for editing the dialog's ID box if desired. But IDD_DIALOG1 works fine so it can be left in place. You will, however, want to change the window caption so click into the Caption box where we have entered "Line Width Dialog". Close the

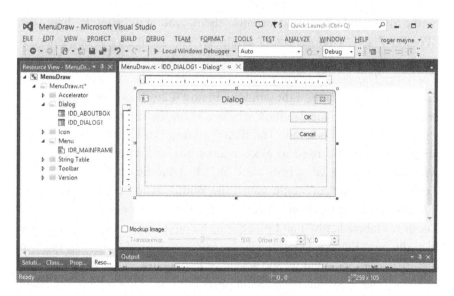

Figure 6.25 Creating a Dialog Window

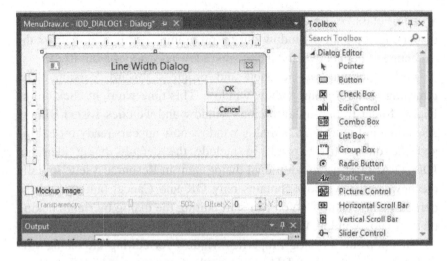

Figure 6.26 Editing the Window for Line Width Dialog

dialog Properties window and you should see your dialog window with its new caption as shown in Figure 6.26. To add some additional features to the dialog window and arrange them, you will want to have the "Toolbox" and "Dialog Editor" available. The Toolbox can be displayed on the right side of the development environment by clicking on **View >
Toolbox**. The dialog editing tools are automatically available when the dialog window is in the Edit window. Figure 6.26 shows the arrangement ready for editing. The Toolbox window is on the right and contains the various dialog components. The dialog editing tools contain a variety of alignment aids. We need to place a label box and an edit control in the window. To add a label box, click and drag the Static Text icon in the Toolbox (labeled "Aa") onto your Line Width Dialog window and place it in a convenient location. Click and drag the Edit Control icon from the Toolbox (labeled "abl") and place it in a convenient location to provide the edit box. Place a label inside the text box by right clicking on it to pop-up an options window and selecting **Properties**.

When the Properties window appears, you have the option to change all of the properties but we only need to edit the caption. So move to the Caption line and enter a suitable label that will serve as a useful description of the content of your edit box. We've used "Enter line width in pixels" (see Figure 6.27).

Close the text Properties window and then right click on the Edit Control box to pop-up a menu and select **Properties**. The edit control Properties window will appear and if you scroll down to find the ID line you will find a default entry such as IDC_EDIT1. We've found it useful to customize the edit control IDs and, to illustrate the process, we have changed this ID to read IDC_LineWidth. You can see this in Figure 6.27 along with our final form for the Line Width Dialog window. In editing the Line Width Dialog window, you can reposition, resize and realign the boxes and buttons as you prefer. Experiment with the alignment tools for dialog editing. A grid can be toggled on and off to guide you, the shift key can be used to highlight and align multiple items, etc.

The next step in completing the development of the Line Width Dialog window that we have created is to associate it with a class. To get the window shown in Figure 6.28, right click on the Line Width Dialog window and select **Add Class**. The MFC Class Wizard window will open. In Figure 6.28 we have entered the class name CLineWidthDialog

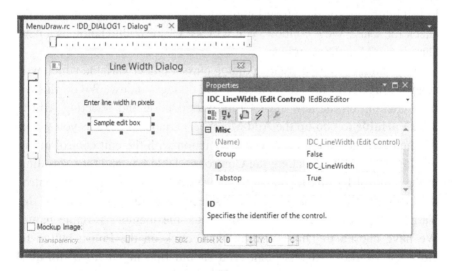

Figure 6.27 Edit Control Properties Window

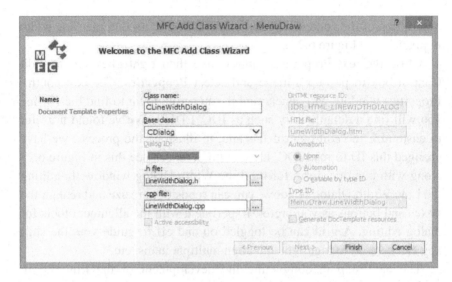

Figure 6.28 Entering the Class CLineWidthDialog

and the base class should be set to CDialog. The default dialog ID of
IDD_Dialog1 is appropriate. The header and source files to contain the
class are also given default names which we will accept. Clicking the
Finish button closes the Wizard window and creates the class. If you now
check the Class View window, you will see CLineWidthDialog as a new
class in the MenuDraw project.

To continue, we will create a dialog class member variable which will
connect directly to the edit control in the dialog window. We do this by
right clicking on the new class CLineWidthDialog and selecting **Add >
Add Variable** to pop-up the Add Member Variable Wizard as you see in
finished form in Figure 6.29. The association with the edit control in the
window is made by checking the Control variable box and then scrolling
in the Control ID box to find IDC_LineWidth which is the edit control
ID. Next, scroll the Category box to select Value and move over to the
Variable type to select "int". Finally enter the member variable name.
We have chosen m_DialogWidth. Then, click on the Finish button to
close the window. At this point, you should find m_DialogWidth as a
new member variable in the class CLineWidthDialog. A right click on

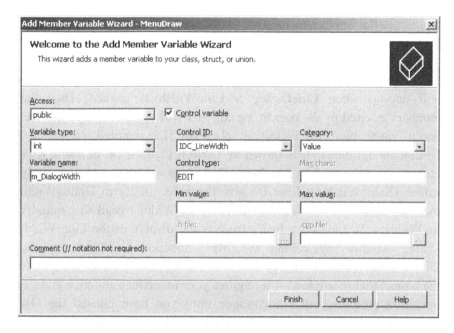

Figure 6.29 Adding a Member Variable to CLineWidthDialog

m_DialogWidth will allow you to select its Properties window and you should be able to note that the edit control IDC_LineWidth is associated with the variable m_DialogWidth.

6.5.4 Code for the function OnLinedialogLinewidth

At this point we have created a dialog window titled Line Width Dialog. It is to be a pop-up dialog window which will appear when the user clicks on **LineDialog > LineWidth** from the menu bar. The Line Width Dialog window contains an edit control to accept adjustments in line width which we want to apply to solid lines in the current drawing. The member variable m_Width that we added to the class CMenuDrawView is expected to carry this information to functions in the view class. The member variable m_DialogWidth used in the CLineDialog class represents the line width information for dialog purposes and provides the link to the edit control box in the Line Width Dialog window.

By properly coding the OnLinedialogLinewidth function of the view class (which we have already created), the Line Width Dialog window will pop-up when **LineDialog > LineWidth** is clicked. Then the numbers inserted by the user in the edit box will update the drawing line width when the OK button is clicked. The required coding for OnLinedialogLinewidth is shown in Table 6.11. Line 06 of Table 6.11 creates an object of the CLineWidthDialog class which we have simply called DialogWindow. Line 07 sets the value of its m_DialogWidth member variable to the current value of m_Width (recall that initially m_Width = 2). Line 08 actually triggers the display of the Line Width Dialog window by calling the MFC function DoModal for the DialogWindow object. This generates a "modal" dialog window which is the typical dialog window — it requires your immediate attention and the operating program will not continue until you have clicked the OK button to carry out its operation or the Cancel button to cancel the dialog. The value of m_DialogWidth set by line 07 is initially placed in the edit control box of the window. After the user modifies the contents of the edit box to define the desired width and clicks the OK button, the

Table 6.11 Listing of OnLinedialogLinewidth from MenuDrawView.cpp (Ver. 5.0)

```
01    /* This is the Listing of OnLinedialogLinewidth */
02    void CMenuDrawView::OnLinedialogLinewidth()
03    {
04        // TODO: Add your command handler code here
05        CMenuDrawDoc* pDoc = GetDocument();
06        CLineWidthDialog DialogWindow;
07        DialogWindow.m_DialogWidth = m_Width;
08    if (DialogWindow.DoModal()==IDOK)
09        {
10        m_Width = DialogWindow.m_DialogWidth;
11        }
12        m_SolidPen.DeleteObject();
13        m_SolidPen.CreatePen (PS_SOLID, m_Width, m_Color);
14        pDoc->UpdateAllViews(NULL);
15    }
```

window closes. And line 10 of the if statement sets the new m_Width value to the value of m_WidthDialog from the Edit box. With this new line width, lines 12 and 13 recreate the solid pen with the new width and line 14 updates the drawing.

There is one last thing to do before building and executing. The Application Wizard has created a special header file for the class CLineWidthDialog. It is located in LineWidthDialog.h and must be available for the function OnLinedialogLinewidth. This is assured by adding the statement

#include "LineWidthDialog.h"

near the top of the file MenuDrawView.cpp and after the other include statements. If you build and execute after this adjustment, the executing program will allow you to change line width by clicking on **LineDialog > LineWidth** and entering the desired value for line width. In case you

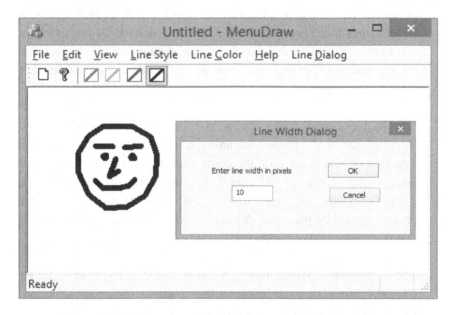

Figure 6.30 The MenuDraw Window with a Line Width of 10 Pixels

have had any difficulty with your revision, the completed MenuDraw Version 5.0 is available in *Chap6\5_MenuDraw*. Figure 6.30 shows the resulting MenuDraw program after our revision process above. The Line Width Dialog window is shown along with a simple line drawn image using an appropriate line width. As a last step in your revision process you may want to move the Help item to the end of the menu bar to have a standard appearance.

6.6 Exercises

1. The project MenuDraw Version 1.0 in the folder *Chap6\1_MenuDraw* contains a drop down menu item (Edit > Delete Line) for removing the last line drawn. Add a new item to the drop down menu under the Edit menu bar item. This new drop down item should be labeled Undelete Line and should have an accelerator key Ctrl+U. An unadvertised right arrow key should also serve as an accelerator. Of course, a descriptive status bar prompt should also be provided. Add an appropriate event handler with code which will restore lines that may have been previously deleted by the user and automatically update the drawing. You should include some basic error protection. For example, you do not want to restore lines that were never created.

2. The folder *Chap6\3_MenuDraw* contains the project MenuDraw Version 3.0. This project contains a drop down menu for the selection of line color. Add the color magenta as a drop down menu item so that it may be selected This corresponds to RGB (255, 0, 255). Of course, an event handler and an informative status bar prompt should be provided. A check mark should be activated in the drop down menu when appropriate.

3. The project MenuDraw Version 4.0 in the folder *Chap6\4_MenuDraw* includes toolbar buttons for color selection. Based on the drop down menu addition of Exercise 2 above, add a magenta toolbar button which is linked to the magenta drop down

menu item and also shows a suitable ToolTip prompt when the mouse cursor is on the toolbar button.

4. The modification to MenuDraw Version 1.0 discussed in Exercise 1 above results in a drop menu with items for Delete and Undelete. Create two toolbar buttons which activate these two commands. Design simple icons which can be used for the buttons.

5. The project MenuDraw Version 5.0 in the folder *Chap6\5_MenuDraw* contains a menu bar item for Line Dialog. Its drop down menu shows Line Width and produces a dialog window which allows the solid line width to be adjusted. Add a Line Color item to this drop down menu so that clicking on **Line Dialog > Line Color** produces a dialog window with three nicely labeled edit boxes which allow the RGB values of line color to be individually specified. Clicking on OK in this dialog should then update the window using the new line color.

6. Change the project MenuDraw 5.0 so that "line color" is a property of each line and so that each line is always drawn with the line color that is active when it is first drawn. Of course, the project should have full Windows functionality so that when the window is maximized, minimized, etc. the line drawn image is appropriately redrawn.

7. Modify the project MenuDraw 5.0 so that it can draw circles and rectangles as well as lines. Create a menu bar item with a drop down menu to allow selection of drawing mode. For each drop down menu item, provide basic drawing instructions for line, circle or rectangle in the status bar prompt. Create toolbar buttons to activate the desired drawing mode with a single click. It should also be possible to delete the last line, circle or rectangle drawn with a delete operation under the Edit menu bar item.

Chapter 7

More Adventures with Windows Tools

In Chapter 6 we began to create programs that have the look and feel of the Windows programs that we are all familiar with as PC users. This chapter continues exploring the Windows tools that are part of the Microsoft Foundation Classes and can be used in the development of fully functional Windows programs.

We begin by returning to one of our earlier projects from Chapter 5, that is, the SimpleDrawSnap project of Section 5.6. We'll now change the name of the project to SnapDraw to recognize that as we modify it throughout this chapter it will not appear to be quite so "simple". The new SnapDraw project has been created as a multiple document project so that it can handle multiple windows, normally one window for each open document. Overall, the general format of this chapter follows the pattern of Chapter 6. We will take the SnapDraw project from its Version 0.0 form on through a series of revisions. For each revision we will describe the changes made in detail, including all the pointing and clicking necessary for you to move from one version to the other on your own. As we proceed, several new capabilities will be considered for the SnapDraw program. These include: customizing icons to represent SnapDraw and its files, the creation and use of a dialog window that contains multiple edit boxes, the capture of the current window size and its use in graphics programming, the use of radio buttons to control program features, the development of text file formats as an alternative output format, and the performance of drawing operations in the multiple document format.

7.1 SnapDraw (Version 0.0)

Version 0.0 of SnapDraw is in the folder *Chap7\0_SnapDraw*. This SnapDraw project was created as a Visual C++ MFC Application using the default "Multiple Document Interface" and selecting MFC Standard style. However, the program code, member variables, etc. within SnapDraw duplicate the original program code of the SimpleDrawSnap project of Section 5.6. SnapDraw was created using the standard settings of the MFC Application Wizard with the exception of "Document Template Properties" where we have entered "snp" in the File extension box and "Drawing" in the box for Doc type name as shown in Figure 7.1. This figure also shows a variety of options for window captions, default file names, etc. which are commonly used in the multiple document environment. Except for our "Drawing" entry, we have simply accepted the default forms suggested by the Application Wizard. For some applications it may be useful to carefully select and edit the names.

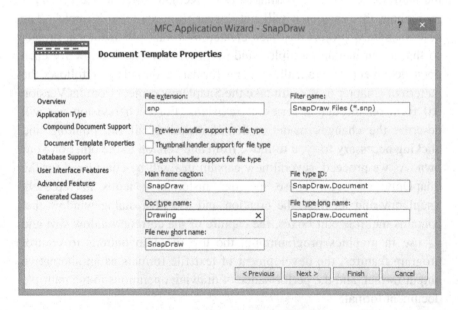

Figure 7.1 Setting the File Extension

When you build and execute Version 0.0 of SnapDraw, you will find that it contains the snap-to-grid features of SimpleDrawSnap and its file saving capability. However, you will also notice the multiple document format in which a window is opened for each current document. All of the familiar Windows management tools are available here. As you open a new document by clicking on **File > New** (or by clicking on the new document icon on the toolbar), a new window will automatically appear within the main program window containing the name of the document it represents. Each individual window is initially titled by default using the document name of "Drawing" followed by an appropriate number. The main title bar contains the mainframe caption as well as the document name for the active window. Figure 7.2 shows the program SnapDraw containing two windows with the default captions Drawing1 and Drawing2. We have drawn a simple figure in each and the document Drawing2 is active. Correspondingly, the main title bar contains the caption SnapDraw – Drawing2. You can readily exercise the windows by minimizing, maximizing or resizing them. Clicking on **Window > Cascade** or **Window > Tile** will automatically arrange the windows for the currently open documents. You can also try clicking on **Window > New Window** to pop up alternative "views" of documents but, to be useful, this feature requires specialized programming which is outside the scope of our interests. We will delete the Window > New Window command when we tidy up our menu bar and toolbar in moving on to Version 1.0.

7.1.1 Customizing the SnapDraw icons

In the Windows environment, we are familiar with "icons" or small figures which are used to represent programs and files. At a glance these icons immediately provide information about the nature of a program or file that we may see on the desktop or in a folder. Programs developed by using the Application Wizard use a set of default icons for the program itself and for files written by the program. The familiar "MFC" in building block form has been the icon used for all of our example programs up to this point.

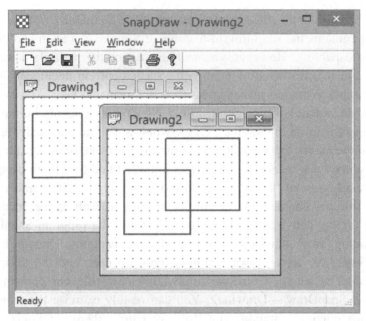

Figure 7.2 SnapDraw Displaying Two Documents

It is actually quite simple to modify the MFC icons and also the default file icons for Application Wizard programs. The process begins by displaying the Resource View window in the workspace area of the development environment. Expanding the SnapDraw resources and then "Icon" shows the two icon items for the SnapDraw program with the resource IDs of IDR_DrawingTYPE and IDR_MAINFRAME. If no icon revision has taken place, clicking on IDR_MAINFRAME will put the familiar MFC default program icon into the Edit window ready for editing. Similarly, clicking on the item IDR_DrawingTYPE before any revision places the default file icon into the Edit window. The icon shown in Figure 7.3 is the default program icon provided by the Application Wizard. It is shown in an enlarged grid form ready for editing while the smaller forms to the left indicate normal icon size and appearance. A right click in the Edit window will pop-up an options menu as also shown in Figure 7.3. This menu includes an item for the Show Colors Window and clicking on it will display the choice of colors for editing the icon. The item for Current Icon Image Types (as seen in Figure 7.3) displays the different icon formats available. In this case, for example, there is a 32x32 pixel icon size (shown) and a 48x48 pixel icon size, both with 4 bits of color choices (i.e. 16 colors). If you are customizing icons, you'll want to create icons of different sizes for the different displays needed. However, there are many icon image types available and you may find it convenient to remove some so that you have a simple set. The options menu item Delete Image Type is useful for this. For this example, we have used a small set of sixteen color (i.e. 4 bit) icons to simplify icon creation.

In Figure 7.4 we show the Colors window and the Image Editor toolbar which are used for selecting tools and colors in icon design. The Image Editor items typically appear on the toolbar and the Colors window typically appears in the toolbox location. Also shown in Figure 7.4 is our modified program icon edited into a "checkerboard" form. The editing of the icon was performed on a pixel-by-pixel basis using the graphics tools and colors included in the Edit window of Figure 7.4. The checkerboard is intended to be representative of the pixel grid used in the various SnapDraw versions here in Chapter 7.

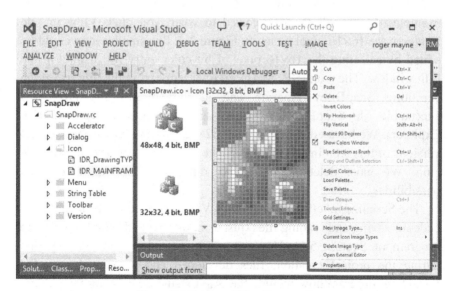

Figure 7.3 Ready to Edit a Program Icon

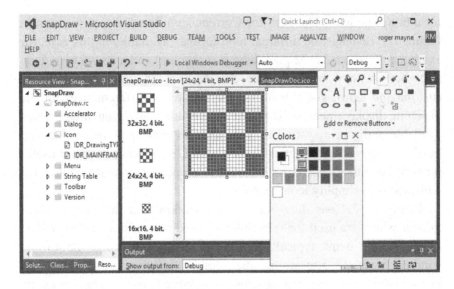

Figure 7.4 Editing a 24×24 Program Icon

The icon shown for editing in Figure 7.4 is the 24×24 pixel icon with 16 colors. Icons of varying size are required for the various displays within the program window, on the desktop or "File Explorer". For example, the "Small Icons" referred to when you click **View** in File Explorer are 16×16 pixel icons. In Figure 7.4, this smaller icon could be edited by selecting the 16×16 pixel, 4 bit color entry for display in the Edit window. The icon IDR_MAINFRAME appears in the title bar of the executing SnapDraw program and also represents the program's executable file SnapDraw.exe whenever it is displayed (e.g. in File Explorer). We have edited the 48×48, 32×32, 24×24 and the 16×16 pixel versions of this icon in 16 colors to create the blue checkerboard program icon. We have deleted the various other icon options offered as possibilities.

The Serialize function of SnapDraw Version 0.0 contains the program code for saving and reading files (just as in the original SimpleDrawSnap program of Section 5.6). However, with the .snp extension specified during the project creation, files developed and associated with the SnapDraw program now include the .snp extension. In using SnapDraw, documents containing drawings can be saved easily by clicking on **File > Save** or **File > Save As** when appropriate. When a window contains a stored document, the window name takes on the file name. This can be seen in Figure 7.5 where the main window for SnapDraw contains two open windows with saved files named 1Square.snp and 3Square.snp (of course, one square is drawn in 1Square.snp and three squares are drawn in 3Square.snp). Also shown in Figure 7.5 is the "Open" window displayed after clicking **File > Open** on the menu bar. Three files are shown in the Open window with the file 2Square.snp ready to be opened and displayed.

Figure 7.5 contains icons that were developed for SnapDraw. The title bar of the main window shows the checkerboard icon for SnapDraw which replaced the MFC blocks. The document windows for 1Square.snp and 3Square.snp each contain the file icon (IDR_DrawingTYPE) at the upper left corner of the window. Finally, the file names listed in the Open window also contain the file icon to the left of each file name. Both the program and file icons (large and small) are stored in pixel form in the icon files located in the subfolder "res" of the project folder.

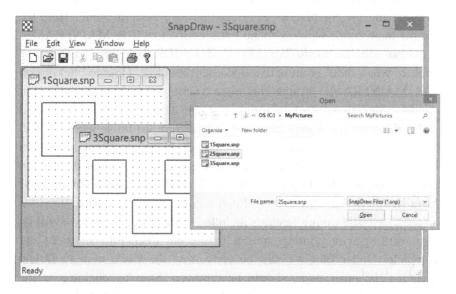

Figure 7.5 SnapDraw Window with Customized Icons

7.2 First Revision of SnapDraw (Version 1.0)

As described above, the program code of SnapDraw 0.0 duplicates the programming of SimpleDrawSnap discussed in Section 5.6. The initial changes that were made in developing the SnapDraw 0.0 program were described in Section 7.1 and included adding the multiple document feature, the .snp file extension, and customizing the program icons. We will now describe the revision of Version 0.0 to create SnapDraw 1.0 which you will find in the folder *Chap7\1_SnapDraw*. If you build and execute SnapDraw 1.0, you will find that it continues to be in the multiple document form and that the customized icons are still in use. You will also find that the menu bar and toolbar have been cleaned up so that options which we will not be using have been removed. In addition, an Edit > Delete Line command has been added to remove the last line drawn and the "scissors" or "cut" button on the toolbar has been connected to the delete line command.

We will briefly describe our revision of SnapDraw 0.0 to obtain the Version 1.0 form. In doing this we will follow a process similar to that described in Section 6.1. First, we bring SnapDraw 0.0 into the development environment and display the Resource View window. We then expand the SnapDraw resources and also expand Menu. Here we see the main frame window menu bar identified as IDR_MAINFRAME. We also see the menu bar identified as IDR_DrawingTYPE which appears when there is an active document window. Double clicking on IDR_MAINFRAME brings the main frame menu bar into the Edit window. Reviewing each of the drop down items under File, View and Help, all of the items may be useful to us before we finish working with SnapDraw and no revisions are required. Now, double clicking on IDR_DrawingTYPE brings up the menu bar effective when there is an active window. The drop down menus for this menu bar contain some extra items. However, the drop down menu under File is fine since we already have file saving features included in the program and we will be also working with printing options before our SnapDraw revisions are complete. Under Edit we will be converting the Undo item to Delete Line but the other items should be removed. Start by clicking on the "separator line" positioned below the Undo item so that the line is highlighted. Then press the Delete key to remove the line and continue to press Delete until all of the remaining items are removed from the Edit drop down menu and Undo remains alone.

We continue moving down the menu bar to View. This drop down menu contains only the Toolbar and Status Bar items which we would like to retain. Under Window, the New Window item requires specialized programming to use effectively. Since we do not intend to explore this, we delete New Window by clicking on it to highlight it and pressing Delete. This leaves us with Cascade, Tile and Arrange Icons under the Window drop down menu. All of these are useful in arranging windows and will be left in place. The Help item on the menu bar need not be revised.

We will return to the menu bar shortly to add the Delete Line item to Edit. But, for now, let's move on to the toolbar. In the Resource View window, we expand the Toolbar item and under it, we click on IDR_MAINFRAME to bring the toolbar into the Edit window. We would like to retain the buttons for New, Open, Save, Cut, Print and About (the question mark). Only the Copy and Paste buttons should be removed from the toolbar. This is done by clicking on each button and dragging it off into white space. After eliminating the Copy and Paste buttons, the toolbar is reorganized by grouping the file manipulation buttons together (i.e. New, Open and Save). Then, following a separator line, the Print button appears followed by another separator line and then the Cut button. The About button appears after a last separator. These rearrangements can all be made by clicking and dragging the buttons within the Edit window. Be careful not to drop one into white space or it may disappear. If this does happen, you may find the Visual Studio environment's Edit > Undo command to be quite useful. Separations between buttons can be made in the Edit window by clicking on a button and dragging it along the toolbar about half a button width.

Figure 7.6 shows our final toolbar configuration in the Edit window. At this point, you can build and execute the SnapDraw program (click on **Build > Rebuild Solution** if necessary). It will execute normally with multiple windows, etc. but the Cut button on the toolbar (the scissors) will be gray since it is not yet functional. If you click on Edit on the menu bar, you will also find that its drop down menu item is grayed out.

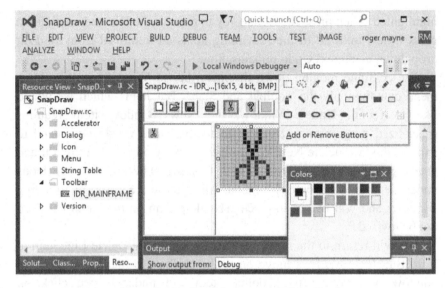

Figure 7.6 Toolbar Window with Editing Tools

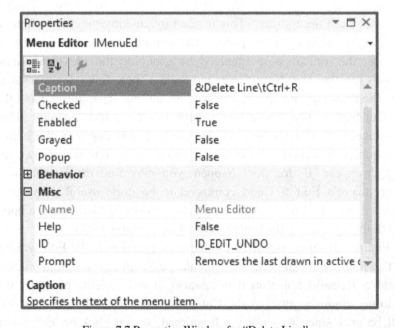

Figure 7.7 Properties Window for "Delete Line"

In both cases, this is because programming code has not yet been provided for the commands. We now use the same process followed in Section 6.1.4 to create a Delete Line command under the Edit menu item. In the Resource View window expand Menu and click on IDR_DrawingTYPE to bring the menu bar into the Edit window. In the Edit window, click on Edit to find its drop down menu. Then right click on Undo to bring up the options menu and select **Properties**. In the Properties window (Figure 7.7), the Caption should be edited to reflect the Delete Line operation and the Ctrl+R accelerator key. We have also put in place a suitable prompt line which appears in the Prompt box. Figure 7.7 shows the finished Properties window. Before closing the Properties window, note that ID_EDIT_UNDO is retained as the ID for the Delete Line command.

An event handler function, of course, is required for the Delete Line operation. To create it, we click on Delete Line in the Edit window to highlight it, right click to bring up the options menu and then select **Add Event Handler**. The Event Handler window appears with ID_EDIT_UNDO as the command name and (as in Section 6.1.4) we make sure that the view class is highlighted in the Class list box. We also select Command in the Messages box and note that OnEditUndo is the default function handler name. Clicking the Add and Edit button brings the new OnEditUndo function into the Edit window. This function requires the same code here that we saw in Table 6.1 except for the class name in line 02. After adding the code, you should be able to build and execute SnapDraw. At this point you should be able to draw a few lines and delete them one at a time by clicking **Edit > Delete Line** on the menu bar or by pressing Alt+E+D to use the shortcut keys.

The last items to complete for Version 1.0 are to connect the toolbar "scissors" button to Delete Line and to implement Ctrl+R and the left arrow key as accelerator keys. The accelerator keys are adjusted in the Resource View window by expanding Accelerator and clicking on IDR_MAINFRAME. Then follow the procedure previously described in Section 6.1.5 to adjust the accelerator keys for the ID_EDIT_UNDO command. Finally, expand the Toolbar item in the Resource View window and click on IDR_MAINFRAME under Toolbar. This will bring the toolbar into the Edit window. Click on the "scissors" to highlight the cut button, then right click to see the options menu and select **Properties**.

The Properties window will appear for the cut button as shown in Figure 7.8. Scroll through the commands in the ID box and select ID_EDIT_UNDO as you see in Figure 7.8. This associates the delete line command with the cut button. The Prompt box is also shown in the cut button Properties window and the text appearing after the "\n" will be displayed when the mouse cursor pauses on the cut button. We have simply entered "Delete line" to describe the button action. You can now close the Properties window and build and execute the SnapDraw program. You should find that it has all the features of SnapDraw Version 1.0. As you exercise the program, notice that you can draw in any active window within the program's main window. Also notice that the delete line operation works in the active window from the cut button and that you can carry out save operations for the active window by clicking on the Save button on the toolbar. Of course, you can try **File > Print Preview** or even **File > Print** but don't expect very satisfactory results at this point. Printing will be much more useful after Section 7.5.

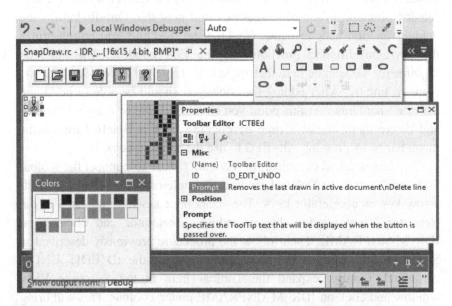

Figure 7.8 Toolbar Button Properties for the "Scissors"

7.3 Grid Size Adjustment and OnSize (Version 2.0)

The next step in revising the SnapDraw program is to add an adjustable grid size and to improve the process of drawing the pixel grid into a window. These features have been added to SnapDraw in its Version 2.0 form which you can find in the folder *Chap7\2_SnapDraw*. In the discussion below we will follow the process of revising SnapDraw to update it to Version 2.0. But first you'll want to check out the new features by building and executing SnapDraw 2.0. You will quickly notice that the menu bar now includes a new item for grid size dialog. If you click on **Grid Size** on the menu bar, a dialog window labeled Set Grid Size appears. This dialog window allows the selection of the grid size in pixels for both the vertical and horizontal directions. If you try it a few times, you will see that it allows the pixel grid to be changed for the active window. And if you have more than one window opened at a time, you can control the grid size in a particular window by making it the active one. Carry out a few drawing operations to check out the snap-to-grid process and notice how it functions with different grid sizes.

7.3.1 Creating the menu item Grid Size and its function

To begin the revision of SnapDraw 1.0, we bring it into the development environment and move to the Resource View window. We expand the Menu item and then double click on IDR_DrawingTYPE to bring the active menu bar into the Edit window. We need to create a GridSize menu item which will activate an OnGridSize function. We will then arrange for OnGridSize to display the dialog window which allows the selection of both the vertical and horizontal grid sizes. The process to be followed is very much related to that used in Section 6.5 for creating the earlier Line Width Dialog window. However, in this case we will be dealing with two separate inputs in the dialog window and the adjustment of two variables simultaneously. Once you have followed this procedure through to its conclusion, you will be able to create and utilize dialog windows with several edit boxes.

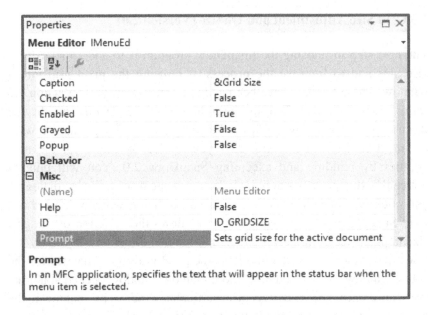

Figure 7.9 Properties Window for "Grid Size"

From the Resource View window, place the menu bar in the Edit window (IDR_DrawingTYPE) and enter &Grid Size in the Type Here box on the right of the menu bar. Double click this entry to pop-up its Properties window and change the Pop-up line in the Properties window to "False" (we want to go directly to the dialog window here, without a drop down menu). Also note the entry on the ID line. If it is blank, close the Properties window and then again double click on the new Grid Size menu item. The Properties window should show the command identification ID_GRIDSIZE on the ID line. Figure 7.9 shows the Properties window at this point after we have also entered suitable text into the Prompt line. Once again, close the Properties window.

We now create a function activated by the GridSize command using the usual process. A right click on the GridSize item pops up an options menu and we click on **Add Event Handler**. When the window appears for the Event Handler Wizard, notice that ID_GRIDSIZE is in the Command name box and that "COMMAND" is highlighted in the

Message type box. The suggested name for the event handler function is OnGridSize. We want to place this function in the view class so click on CSnapDrawView in the Class list box. Finally, click on the Add and Edit button to close the window and create the OnGridSize function. You should now be able to find OnGridSize as a member function of the class CSnapDrawView. You may also want to build and execute the program at this stage to be sure there are no errors. When the program executes, you should see the Grid Size menu item but it will not function if you click it.

We will return to the OnGridSize function shortly but first we need to create the dialog window that it will use.

7.3.2 Creating the dialog window Set Grid Size

To create the Set Grid Size dialog window of Figure 7.10, we will follow the general strategy already described in Section 6.5 in considerable detail. This begins in the Resource View window where we right click on Dialog and then select Insert Dialog from the pop-up options window. A general dialog box then appears in the Edit window ready for editing. The dialog window caption is inserted by right clicking on the initial Dialog caption and selecting **Properties** from the pop-up menu. In the resulting Properties window, enter Set Grid Size on the caption line and then close the Properties window. We will use the default dialog identification IDD_DIALOG1. From the Toolbox window, click and drag two Static Text boxes (labeled Aa) into your dialog window. Also click and drag two Combo Boxes (with small scroll icons) into the dialog window. One at a time, right click the static text boxes and choose **Properties** to access their Properties windows. On the Caption line of each, enter suitable labels which will be used to identify the combo boxes. We've used "Vertical grid in pixels" and "Horizontal grid in pixels".

One at a time, right click the combo boxes and select **Properties** to see the Properties window for the boxes. We have changed the combo box IDs to become IDC_VertGrid and IDC_HorizGrid for the vertical box and horizontal box respectively. The combo boxes will allow the selection of the grid spacing in the horizontal and vertical directions.

This selection will be made by clicking on one of several choices provided in a drop down list or by a direct entry from the keyboard. The entries in the list are entered into the Properties window for the combo box on the Data line using a semicolon after each entry. We have entered 2;5;10;20;25;50. To allow this list to be displayed as written, you must select "False" on the Sort line of the Properties window. After completing this process for both combo boxes, you can adjust the appearance of the dialog window, rearranging the boxes and buttons as you like. Resizing the dialog window may facilitate this arrangement process. Resizing the combo boxes will affect the appearance of the drop down lists. Note that you can also test the operation of the dialog window by clicking on **Format > Test Dialog** from the menu bar of the development environment. Our final arrangement is in Figure 7.10 and is shown with the drop down list for the horizontal grid.

Just as in Section 6.5, we must have a class associated with the Set Grid Size dialog window. The class is defined by right clicking on the Set Grid Size dialog in the Edit window and selecting **Add Class** in the resulting options menu. The Class Wizard window then appears. Note that IDD_DIALOG1 is the identifier for the dialog window. Set the base class to CDialog and also enter a name for the class to be associated with

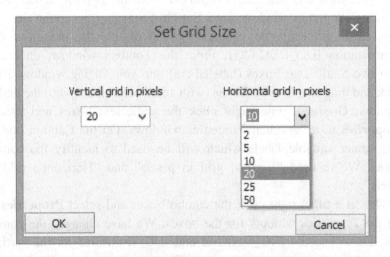

Figure 7.10 Testing the Set Grid Size Dialog Window

the dialog window. We have used CGridSizeDialog which results in file names for the class program code of GridSizeDialog.h and GridSizeDialog.cpp. Clicking the Finish button then closes the Class Wizard and creates the new class (check the Class View window).

Member variables must now be created in the dialog class for each of the combo boxes in the Set Grid Size dialog window. This can be done from the Class View window by right clicking on the class CGridSizeDialog and selecting **Add > Add Variable** to display the Add Member Variable Wizard. Then check the "Control variable" box in the Wizard window and select IDC_VertGrid in the Control ID box (to refer to the left most combo box in the dialog window). Also select Value in the Category box and leave CString in the box for Variable type. Finally, enter the member variable name that you would like associated with this combo box. We have used m_DialogVGrid. You should now repeat this process for the other combo box that we identified earlier as IDC_HorizGrid. Figure 7.11 shows our Add Member Variable window after declaring m_DialogHGrid. When you have finished, expand the CDialogGridSize class in the Class View window to be sure that you have been successful. You should now see m_DialogVGrid and m_DialogHGrid as member variables. Keep in mind that these are objects of the CString class.

7.3.3 Programming the function OnGridSize

The event handler function OnGridSize is activated by clicking on the menu bar item **Grid Size**. We want to use OnGridSize to display the Set Grid Size dialog window, to initialize the combo box variables in the dialog window, and to receive the newly changed variables when the dialog window's OK button is clicked. We have created two view class member variables to handle the grid size selection. These have been declared by right clicking in the Class View window on the class name CSnapDrawView and selecting **Add > Add Variable**. We have inserted m_VGrid and m_HGrid as integer member variables. In the constructor function CSnapDrawView we have overridden the default initialization and set m_VGrid and m_HGrid to initial values of ten. This corresponds

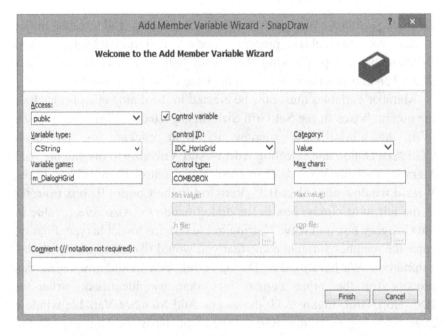

Figure 7.11 Adding m_DialogHGrid to the CGridSizeDialog Class

to the grid spacing that we have been using for snap-to-grid operations in SnapDraw Version 1.0.

With the member variables m_HGrid and m_VGrid declared and initialized, we can consider the program code for the OnGridSize function as shown in the listing of Table 7.1. In this code, line 05 declares DialogWindow as an object of our CGridSizeDialog class. Lines 06 and 07 create the CString object "buffer" and load it with the character string corresponding to the current grid size value m_VGrid. Line 08 then sets the value of the dialog CString variable m_DialogVGrid to correspond to the current m_VGrid. Similarly, lines 09 and 10 set the CString object m_DialogHGrid in the dialog to correspond to the integer view class variable m_HGrid. In this way both combo boxes in the Set Grid Size dialog window are initialized for the opening of the dialog window. The if statement of line 11 calls the DoModal function for DialogWindow. When the OK button is struck

Table 7.1 Listing of OnGridSize from SnapDrawView.cpp (Ver. 2.0)

```
01    /* This is the listing of OnGridSize */
02    void CSnapDrawView::OnGridsize()
03    {
04        // TODO: Add your command handler code here
05        CGridSizeDialog DialogWindow;
06        CString buffer;
07        buffer.Format(L"%d",m_VGrid);
08        DialogWindow.m_DialogVGrid = buffer;
09        buffer.Format(L"%d",m_HGrid);
10        DialogWindow.m_DialogHGrid = buffer;
11    if (DialogWindow.DoModal()==IDOK)
12        {
13        m_VGrid = _wtoi(DialogWindow.m_DialogVGrid);
14        m_HGrid = _wtoi(DialogWindow.m_DialogHGrid);
15        }
16        CSnapDrawDoc* pDoc = GetDocument();
17        pDoc->UpdateAllViews(NULL);
18    }
```

after user inputs, lines 13 and 14 reset m_VGrid and m_HGrid to the values left in the combo boxes. The function _wtoi() is used to convert the CString objects to their integer values (wide character strings to integers). Finally, lines 16 and 17 update the window for the document. To make the CGridSizeDialog class available to the OnGridSize function, be certain that #include "GridSizeDialog.h" has been added near the top of the SnapDrawView.cpp file. It should be right after the other include statements.

This is a good place to check your programming. You should be able to build and execute your revision. When you do, the Grid Size menu bar item should be in place and if you click it, the Set Grid Size dialog window should appear with initial values of ten for the combo box entries. If you enter different numbers and click OK, your grid size won't change yet (we haven't added the code). But, if you again click the Grid Size menu bar item, the Set Grid Size dialog window should reappear containing the updated values in the combo boxes.

7.3.4 Making use of m_VGrid and m_HGrid

We now have everything in place for the final programming which will display grid size changes and which will allow the snap-to-grid operations to take place at the adjustable grid size. The pixel grid is displayed, of course, in the OnDraw function of the class CSnapDrawView as indicated in Table 7.2. This program code is very similar to that shown earlier in Table 5.24. There is a set of nested for loops from line 07 to line 11 that displays the pixels. The only modification required has been to change the increment in each of these loops from the fixed value of ten by introducing the m_VGrid and m_HGrid variables.

In addition to displaying the pixels properly for the adjustable grid size, the program must also "snap" to the new pixel positions. This requires a change to the NearestGridPoint member function as shown in Table 7.3. This has a similar form to that shown previously in Table 5.26. In this case there is again a set of nested for loops from line 08 to line 23 that must now be incremented by m_HGrid and m_VGrid in lines 08 and 10, respectively. In addition, there is an if statement in the

Table 7.2 Listing of OnDraw from SnapDrawView.cpp (Ver. 2.0)

```
01    /* This is the Listing of OnDraw */
02    void CSnapDrawView::OnDraw(CDC* pDC)
03    {
04        CSnapDrawDoc* pDoc = GetDocument();
05        ASSERT_VALID(pDoc); if(!pDoc)return;
06        // TODO: add draw code for native data here
07    for (int xp=0;xp<1000; xp += m_HGrid)   {
08    for (int yp=0;yp<800;yp += m_VGrid)   {
09        pDC->SetPixel(xp,yp,0);
10        }
11        }
12        pDC->SelectObject(&m_BluePen);
13    for (int i=0; i < pDoc->NumLines; i++)   {
14        pDC->MoveTo(pDoc->FPoint[i]);
15        pDC->LineTo(pDoc->LPoint[i]);
16        }
17    }
```

Table 7.3 Listing of NearestGridPoint from SnapDrawView.cpp (Ver. 2.0)

```
01    /* This is the listing of NearestGridPoint */
02    void CSnapDrawView::NearestGridPoint(CPoint * PtClickedPoint)
03    {
04         double SavSqDis = 1.0E06;
05         int SavX, SavY, dx, dy;
06         int PointX = PtClickedPoint->x;
07         int PointY = PtClickedPoint->y;
08    for (int xp=0;xp<1000;xp=xp+m_HGrid)
09         {
10    for(int yp=0;yp<800;yp=yp+m_VGrid)
11         {
12         dx = abs(xp - PointX);
13         dy = abs(yp - PointY);
14    if(dx < m_HGrid && dy < m_VGrid)     {
15         double SqDis = dx*dx + dy*dy;
16    if (SqDis < SavSqDis)   {
17         SavSqDis = SqDis;
18         SavX = xp;
19         SavY = yp;
20         }
21         }
22         }
23         }
24         PtClickedPoint->x = SavX;
25         PtClickedPoint->y = SavY;
26    }
```

distance testing at line 14 which also requires insertion of the adjustable grid variables m_HGrid and m_VGrid as shown. After making the programming changes to OnDraw and NearestGridPoint, the adjustable grid portion of SnapDraw is ready to function properly. However, before building and executing, you should visit the Resource View window once more. Display the menu bar in the Edit window and click and drag the Grid Size menu item until it is just inside the Window and Help items. Having Window and Help appear at the end of the menu bar is quite standard. With this change, you are ready for a build and execute to check the adjustment of the display of pixel spacing and to check the snap-to-grid operation with adjustable spacing. Figure 7.12 shows the SnapDraw revision running with two windows of different grid spacing.

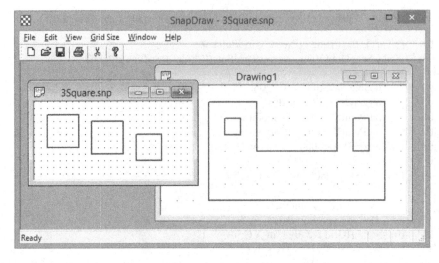

Figure 7.12 Grid Size Adjustment in SnapDraw

7.3.5 The OnSize function

The many functions and messages built into the Microsoft Foundation Classes provide assistance for drawing and imaging in the Windows environment. The Windows message WM_SIZE is a simple example that can be used nicely in our SnapDraw program. This message makes window dimensions available within a program whenever a window is displayed.

In the OnDraw function (Table 7.2) of our SnapDraw program you may have noticed that the pixel grid is always drawn over a fixed range of x (up to 1000) and y (up to 800). Similarly, when the NearestGridPoint function (Table 7.3) searches for the nearest grid point, it also operates over the same fixed range of x and y values. These operations take place identically for small windows or large windows and the fixed ranges need to be set large enough to cover the largest window anticipated. In this case, many extra operations take place when a small window is actually displayed. These issues can be avoided by identifying the size of the window and only considering the pixel range within the window. This feature has been included in SnapDraw 2.0.

The first step toward using an adjustable pixel range in this revision of SnapDraw is to make the OnSize function a member of the CSnapDrawView class. This is done by using the Properties window of the class CSnapDrawView and the WM_SIZE message in the same way as we used the messages WM_KEYDOWN, WM_LBUTTONDOWN, WM_MOUSEMOVE, etc. back in Chapters 4 and 5. With your current SnapDraw program in the development environment, display the Class View window and right click on **Properties**. Then click on messages in the Properties window and scroll down to WM_SIZE in the Messages box to select it. Click to its right to add the OnSize message handler function to the member list for CSnapDrawView.

To make use of the OnSize function we need to have view class member variables that represent the x and y dimensions of the window. Add the integer member variables m_XLimit and m_YLimit to the class CSnapDrawView. These variables can then be used in the OnSize function as shown in Table 7.4. Whenever a window is about to be displayed, OnSize executes and the variables cx and cy in the argument list of line 02 receive the x and y dimensions of the window in pixels. Then, in lines 06 and 07 of OnSize, the view class member variables m_XLimit and m_YLimit are set to the values of cx and cy. To draw just enough pixels to fill the current window, we then make a few small changes to the OnDraw function of Table 7.2. In line 07 of the OnDraw function we change the x limit on the for loop to m_XLimit (previously 1000) and in line 08 we change the y limit to m_YLimit (previously 800). In this way, the pixel grid changes size to match the current window. Similarly, to keep the nearest grid point search in the range of the window, we change the NearestGridPoint function of Table 7.3 at line 08 and at line 10 to use m_XLimit and m_YLimit as the limits for the search. After these changes, the listings of Tables 7.2 and 7.3 are in their completed Version 2.0 form.

As you exercise SnapDraw 2.0, you may notice the difference in drawing the pixel grid in large windows or small windows. Since there are more pixels to place in a large window, you may notice the delay in

Table 7.4 Listing of OnSize from SnapDrawView.cpp (Ver. 2.0)

```
01    /* This is the listing of OnSize */
02    void CSnapDrawView::OnSize(UINT nType, int cx, int cy)
03    {
04        CView::OnSize(nType, cx, cy);
05        // TODO: Add your message handler code here
06        m_XLimit = cx;
07        m_YLimit = cy;
08    }
```

the pixel drawing process especially at small grid size. If you have trouble seeing the difference and wonder if the OnSize function is doing its job, try setting the limits in OnSize to something smaller than the window size (e.g. try XLimit = cx – 100). With a build and execute, and a few adjustments of window size, you should be able to see that, in fact, the limits are working.

7.4 Using Radio Control Buttons (Version 3.0)

Version 3 of SnapDraw includes radio control buttons which turn snap-to-grid on and off and which control the appearance of the pixel grid. You can find SnapDraw 3.0 in the folder Chap7\3_SnapDraw. When you build and execute the program, you will see that a menu bar item has been added with the label Snap and Grid. If you click on this item a dialog window appears which contains two groups of radio buttons. One set controls the snap-to-grid process, the other switches the pixel display to a light gray color or turns the pixels off completely. The buttons are referred to as radio control buttons because they mimic the behavior of older radios (particularly car radios) with mechanical buttons. Only one button could be depressed at a time. Pressing a second button caused the first to "pop out". Exercise the program. Notice that the initial default is to have snap "on" and a black pixel grid. Also note that the snap-to-grid and pixel grid controls are separate so that, for example, you can turn off the pixels and still have snap-to-grid.

7.4.1 The programming changes

We will start with Version 2.0 and describe the process of carrying out the revision to create SnapDraw 3.0. The first step is to add two member variables to the CSnapDrawView class. The variables should be integers and we have used the names m_SnapGrid and m_PixGrid. We expect that with m_SnapGrid = 1, the snap process will be active and with m_SnapGrid = 0, the process will be turned off. Similarly, m_PixGrid = 2 corresponds to black pixels, m_PixGrid = 1 corresponds to gray pixels and with m_PixGrid = 0, no pixels will be drawn. The variables are initialized in the constructor function CSnapDrawView at the point where the initializations of the grid sizes and the blue pen take place. Values of m_SnapGrid = 1 and m_PixGrid = 2 are the initial values.

We also need to provide the code to carry out the changes to the snap-to-grid and pixel drawing processes depending on the values of m_SnapGrid and m_PixGrid. For the snap-to-grid process, there are two locations where adjustment is required. In the OnLButtonDown and OnRButtonDown functions of the view class, the statement:

```
NearestGridPoint(&point);
```

should be replaced by:

```
if (m_SnapGrid == 1) {NearestGridPoint(&point);}
```

With this change, the NearestGridPoint function will be called only when snap-to-grid is turned on. The pixel drawing process takes place in the OnDraw function of CSnapDrawView. Here the simple statement:

```
pDC->SetPixel(xp,yp,0);
```

should be replaced by the two statements:

```
if (m_PixGrid == 2){pDC->SetPixel(xp,yp,RGB(0,0,0));}
if (m_PixGrid == 1){pDC->SetPixel(xp,yp,RGB(150,150,150));}
```

In these new statements the calls to the SetPixel function use the RGB function to set the color of the pixels. The RGB values of 0,0,0 correspond to black pixels, the RGB values of 150,150,150 correspond to gray pixels. Notice that with these if statements in place, pixels will not be displayed if m_PixGrid = 0.

7.4.2 Creating the radio button dialog

A menu item must be added to activate a function that displays the radio button dialog. We do this under Menu in the Resource View window by double clicking on IDR_DrawingTYPE to bring the menu bar into the Edit window. The menu item "Snap and Grid" is created by entering text into the Type Here box on the menu bar in the Edit window. A right click on the new Snap and Grid item displays the pop-up options menu where **Properties** should be selected. In the resulting Properties window the caption can be further edited, appropriate text should be entered on the Prompt line and the Popup line should be set to False so that a pop-up menu is not activated. Also, note the default ID of ID_SNAPANDGRID for this menu bar item (if the ID is not yet set, close the Properties window and reopen it). When you leave the Properties window it should appear as in Figure 7.13. On the menu bar, click and drag the Snap and Grid menu bar item to the left of the Window item. You'll also need a function associated with Snap and Grid. Right click on it to display the options menu and select **Add Event Handler**. When the Event Handler Wizard appears, note the Command name ID_SNAPANDGRID and the default Function handler name OnSnapandgrid. Select the Message type COMMAND and select CSnapDrawView from the Class list. Clicking the **Add and Edit** button will create the new handler function in the view class. We will use the OnSnapandgrid function to display and manage the radio button dialog window.

The radio button dialog window is developed by right clicking on Dialog in the Resource View window and choosing Insert Dialog from the options. The new dialog appears in the Edit window ready for editing. Begin by displaying the Properties window for the dialog and

Figure 7.13 Menu Item Properties for Snap and Grid

setting its Caption line to read Set Snap and Grid. Close the Properties window and then grab a corner of the Set Snap and Grid dialog window to enlarge it. Position the OK and Cancel buttons near the bottom corners. Click on one of the Radio Buttons in the Toolbox window and drag and drop it onto the dialog toward the left side of the window. Drag and drop another radio button into the same area and place it below the first. Now click on the Group Box item in the Toolbox window and then move back to the dialog window where you can click and drag the box around your two buttons.

The Set Snap and Grid window should now be similar to Figure 7.14. These will be the "snap buttons". At this point, right click on the group box and display its Properties window. Enter "Set Snap" on the Caption line and also set the Group line to True. Right click on the first radio button and bring up its Properties window. Its Caption line should be set

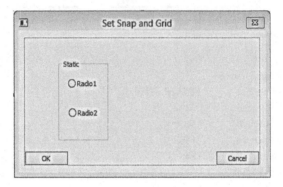

Figure 7.14 The Initial Grouping of Radio Buttons

to Snap On. Its ID box should be set to IDC_SnapOn so that this control can be identified more easily as we develop the dialog. Close the Properties window for the first button. Then, right click on the second radio button and obtain its Properties window. Set its Caption to Snap Off and its ID to IDC_SnapOff. This completes the first group of buttons. You can test it by clicking on **Format > Test Dialog** from the menu bar of the development environment. As you click the Snap On and Snap Off buttons in the test window, when one turns on, the other should turn off. Close the test window by clicking OK.

Let's move on to the second group of buttons. Click and drag three radio buttons (one at a time, of course) from the Toolbox window on to your growing dialog window for Set Snap and Grid. Click on the Group Box icon on the Toolbox window and then click and draw a box around your three new buttons. Right click on the new group box to display its Properties window and enter Set Grid on its Caption line and be sure to set the Group line to True. At this point, click **Format > Test Dialog** and check the two groups of buttons. Each group should be independent of the other and as one button is clicked "on", the previously "on" button should go "off". If you have difficulties at this point, you can remove a radio button or a group box by clicking to highlight it and hitting delete. You can then repeat the process above, following the directions as closely as possible. When your buttons are operating satisfactorily, right

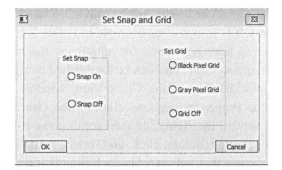

Figure 7.15 The Completed Radio Button Dialog

click on each of the new radio buttons, bringing up their Properties windows to change their captions and IDs. The top button caption should read Black Pixel Grid and have an ID of IDC_BPGrid. The second should be labeled Gray Pixel Grid with an ID of IDC_GPGrid and the third should be Grid Off with an ID of IDC_GridOff. When you finish, position and align the buttons and groups as you like. Our final arrangement is shown in Figure 7.15.

When you have everything arranged, right click on the overall Set Snap and Grid dialog and select **Add Class** from the options window. You should see the Class Wizard window ready to create a new class for your dialog resource. We have entered CSnapGridDialog in the Class name box and CDialog should be selected in the Base class box. Note the default Dialog ID and file names of SnapGridDialog.h and SnapGridDialog.cpp for the class. Click the Finish button to create the class. A check of the Class View window should confirm its presence. At this point, a function must be added for each radio button. Bring the Set Snap and Grid dialog window back into the Edit window. Right click on the first radio button (Snap On) and select **Add Event Handler** from its Properties window. In the Event Handler Wizard, select BN_CLICKED in the Message type box and accept the default function name OnBnClickedSnapon making sure that CSnapGridDialog is selected in the Class list. Click the Add and Edit button to create the function. Continue the process of adding functions for IDC_SnapOff,

IDC_BPGrid, IDC_GPGrid and IDC_GridOff. The Event Handler window for Grid Off is shown as an example in Figure 7.16.

We also need to have a function for initializing the radio buttons in the dialog Set Snap and Grid. This can be established by right clicking on the class CSnapGridDialog in the Class View window and selecting **Properties**. In the Properties window, click on the Overrides button of the toolbar (it's toward the right) and then scroll down to OnInitDialog. On the right of OnInitDialog, click and select "Add" to create an OnInitDialog function that will execute each time that the Set Snap and Grid dialog is displayed. This function will be used to initialize the radio buttons appropriately as the dialog is displayed. At this point use ClassView to inspect the CSnapGridDialog class. You should see the "BnClicked" member functions for the five buttons and the member function OnInitDialog. We'll also need two member variables for use in the dialog operations. They can be added by right clicking on the CSnapGridDialog and selecting **Add > Add Variable** from the options window. The integer variables m_DialogPixGrid and m_DialogSnap should be added to serve as counter parts to the view class variables m_PixGrid and m_SnapGrid.

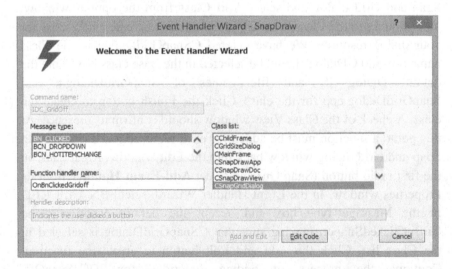

Figure 7.16 Adding the Handler Function for the Grid Off Button

7.4.3 Preparing code for the dialog

With all of the functions and variables now in place, we can begin adding program code. First we consider the function OnSnapandgrid which will create the dialog object, display it and then implement the results of the dialog. Table 7.5 shows the function listing. Line 05 declares the object DialogWindow of the class CSnapGridDialog. Lines 06 and 07 then initialize m_DialogSnap and m_DialogPixGrid to be used in displaying the radio buttons. Line 08 calls the DoModal function that displays the dialog window for Set Snap and Grid. After the OK button is clicked to close the dialog, lines 10 and 11 set the closing values for m_SnapGrid and m_PixGrid. Lines 13 and 14 then update the document window.

When the DoModal function is called in line 08 of Table 7.5, the OnInitDialog function of the class CSnapGridDialog automatically executes to initialize the dialog window. The function that we have used for OnInitDialog is shown in Table 7.6 where the code that has been added consists of the five if statements of lines 06–10. Here you can see that the variables m_DialogSnap and m_DialogPixGrid are being used in setting the radio buttons. In each case, the function CheckDlgButton

Table 7.5 Listing of OnSnapandgrid from SnapDrawView.cpp (Ver. 3.0)

```
01    /* This is the Listing of OnSnapandgrid */
02    void CSnapDrawView::OnSnapandgrid()
03    {
04        // TODO: Add your command handler code here
05        CSnapGridDialog DialogWindow;
06        DialogWindow.m_DialogSnap = m_SnapGrid;
07        DialogWindow.m_DialogPixGrid = m_PixGrid;
08    if (DialogWindow.DoModal() == IDOK)
09        {
10        m_SnapGrid = DialogWindow.m_DialogSnap;
11        m_PixGrid = DialogWindow.m_DialogPixGrid;
12        }
13        CSnapDrawDoc* pDoc = GetDocument();
14        pDoc->UpdateAllViews(NULL);
15    }
```

Table 7.6 Listing of OnInitDialog from SnapGridDialog.cpp (Ver. 3.0)

```
01    /* This is the listing of OnInitDialog */
02    BOOL CSnapGridDialog::OnInitDialog()
03    {
04         CDialog::OnInitDialog();
05         // TODO: Add extra initialization here
06         if (m_DialogSnap == 1)      {CheckDlgButton (IDC_SnapOn,1);}
07         if (m_DialogSnap == 0)      {CheckDlgButton (IDC_SnapOff,1);}
08         if (m_DialogPixGrid == 2)   {CheckDlgButton (IDC_BPGrid,1);}
09         if (m_DialogPixGrid == 1)   {CheckDlgButton (IDC_GPGrid,1);}
10         if (m_DialogPixGrid == 0)   {CheckDlgButton (IDC_GridOff,1);}
11         return TRUE;  // return TRUE unless you set the focus to a control
12         // EXCEPTION: OCX Property Pages should return FALSE
13    }
```

executes when the if statement is satisfied. The button IDs define the specific buttons and the argument "1" indicates that the button should be "on". Recall that we have initialized m_SnapGrid = 1 and m_PixGrid = 2 so that the first time through, lines 06 and 08 will set the appropriate radio buttons in the dialog. After the first pass, the values from the last use of the box are passed back to OnInitDialog according to lines 06 and 07 of Table 7.5. The dialog then reactivates with the reset buttons.

The last step in the programming process is to define the actions that take place as each radio control button is clicked. These are the BN_CLICKED message functions that we established in the CSnapGridDialog class. The code is very simple with each function changing one of the variables to a value appropriate for the button clicked. The OnBnClickedSnapOff function is shown in Table 7.7 as an example. The only line of added code here is line 05 which shows m_DialogSnap = 0. Similarly, the OnBnClickedSnapOn function sets m_DialogSnap = 1, while the OnBnClickedBPGrid function results in m_DialogPixGrid = 2, etc.

Before compiling, be sure that you insert an include statement for the file SnapGridDialog.h in the SnapDrawView.cpp file. This is required to make the dialog class and functions available to the view class.

Table 7.7 Listing of OnBnClickedSnapOff from SnapGridDialog.cpp (Ver. 3.0)

```
01   /* This is the listing of OnBnClickedSnapOff */
02   void CSnapNGridDialog::OnBnClickedSnapOff()
03   {
04       // TODO: Add your control notification handler code here
05       m_DialogSnap = 0;
06   }
```

Figure 7.17 shows the SnapDraw program with four open documents in a tiled arrangement (obtained by selecting **Window > Tile**). The active window Drawing1 has a coarse pixel grid and shows a simple figure drawn with snap-to-grid turned off. The 1Square.snp document has the grid set to black pixels. The document 2Square.snp shows gray pixels while the document 3Square.snp shows the pixel grid turned off.

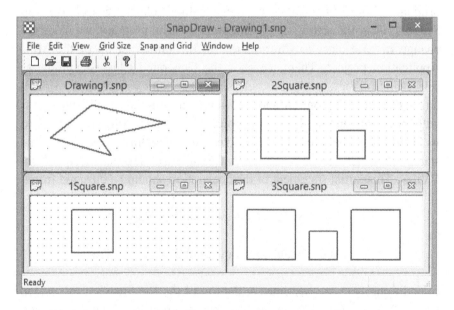

Figure 7.17 Tiled Windows with Varied Snap and Grid Settings

7.5 Scrolling with Multiple Documents (Version 4.0)

We now move on to develop Version 4.0 of SnapDraw which includes the ability to scroll over each of the document windows operating in the program window and to carry out the full size printing of a standard page in landscape orientation. The new revision is located in the folder *Chap7\4_SnapDraw*. As you build and execute it, notice the scroll bars in each window which allow you to scroll over the document's pixel grid. Also, when you select landscape orientation and print a document, you will see it in its proper size. By clicking **File > Print Preview**, you will see the full landscape page. This version of SnapDraw is based on our earlier introduction of the MM_LOENGLISH mapping mode for the program SimpleDrawPrint discussed in Section 5.7.

The revision of SnapDraw 3.0 to obtain SnapDraw 4.0 requires a few coding changes to change the base class of CSnapDrawView from the original default of CView to the scrolling class CScrollView. In Section 5.7, while setting up the SimpleDrawPrint program, we made the change in base class to CScrollView in the initial set up of the MFC Application project. There we used the Generated Classes window to select CScrollView as the base class. At this point we are now working on an established program and we would like to change the base class without reconstructing the whole project. To do this with minimal effort, we start near the top of the header file SnapDrawView.h with the statement which declares the class CSnapDrawView as derived from CView. This initial statement of the declaration should be changed from:

class CSnapDrawView : public CView

to:

class CSnapDrawView : public CScrollView

In addition, there are two lines at the top of the file SnapDrawView.cpp (right after the "include" statements) that also require a change to reflect the new base class. These two lines should be edited to read:

IMPLEMENT_DYNCREATE(CSnapDrawView, CScrollView)
BEGIN_MESSAGE_MAP(CSnapDrawView, CScrollView)

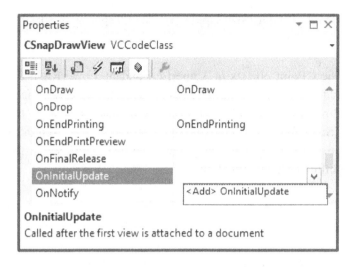

Figure 7.18 Adding the Function for OnInitialUpdate

Now, in order to provide the coding to initialize scrolling, an OnInitialUpdate function is required in the view class. This was automatically provided for us in Section 5.7 but here we must specifically add it as an "override". To do so, enter the Class View window, right click on CSnapDrawView, and select **Properties**. In the Properties window, as shown in Figure 7.18, click on the Overrides button on the toolbar (toward the right) and then scroll down through the override possibilities until you find OnInitialUpdate. At this point click to its right and select <Add> OnInitialUpdate to add the function. Close the window and notice that OnInitialUpdate now appears as a member function of CSnapDrawView.

With the OnInitialUpdate function in place, the final steps of this revision proceed as follows (following the pattern described in Section 5.7 for SimpleDrawPrint):

1.   Coding is added to OnIntialUpdate just as shown in Table 5.28 to prepare for the range of pixels over the landscape oriented page. We also call SetScrollSizes to choose the

MM_LOENGLISH mapping mode and specify the desired scrolling size.

2. The CPoint objects m_UpperLeft and m_LowerRight are added as member variables to the class CSnapDrawView. However, their default initialization in the CSnapDrawView constructor function can be removed (just comment them out) since they are being set in the OnInitialUpdate function.

3. The OnDraw function is modified to correspond to Table 5.29 in Section 5.7. However, variable grid sizes must be included in place of the fixed grids. The NearestGridPoint function must be similarly modified to adjust the range for the grid in the snap-to-grid process.

4. As in Table 5.30, the OnLButtonDown and OnRButtonDown mouse handler functions need to be edited. The functions OnPrepareDC(&aDC) and aDC.DPtoLP(&point) must be inserted to make the conversion from cursor position in pixels (device units) to MM_LOENGLISH (logical units).

5. Finally, the m_XLimit and m_YLimit member variables are no longer being used in OnDraw. To keep your coding neat, they can be removed from the declaration of CSnapDrawView in the file SnapDrawView.h and deleted from the OnSize function.

7.6 Writing Output Files in Text Format (Version 5.0)

This section will conclude our development of the SnapDraw program. The last feature which we will include provides a convenient approach to changing the output file format of SnapDraw. For the file output, we continue use of the Serialize function of the document class (as introduced in Section 5.6) with its archiving operators. These facilities very conveniently permit direct access to the Windows filing system. You'll find SnapDraw Version 5.0 in the folder *Chap7\5_SnapDraw* and, of course, you can build and execute it easily. You'll see that Version 5.0 has a new "File Format" entry on the menu bar. In its drop down menu, you can select from the Default, Text or Spread Text formats.

The "Default" format is the ordinary binary file format which is furnished by the archiving process. It has been used in the original SimpleDrawSnap of Section 5.6 and in the previous SnapDraw programs of this chapter. The "Text" format uses the archiving process to store program data in a very simple text format which enters one number on each line of the file. This text file can then be viewed directly by Microsoft's Notepad or Excel programs. The "Spread Text" format records the drawing data by entering four numbers on each line of the file. The x and y coordinates of the first point (FPoint) on a drawn line are entered and then the x and y coordinates of the last point (LPoint) on the drawn line. "Tab" delimiting is used in between. When the Spread Text file is read by Notepad or Excel, the point coordinates are conveniently spread across a line of text. In Excel, each entry occupies its own cell.

7.6.1 Installing the File Format item on the menu bar

Starting from Version 4 of SnapDraw, the first step in creating the text file capability is to insert a member variable in the document class to identify the current file format. We have used the integer variable m_FileForm. It was added with a right click in the Class View window on the class CSnapDrawDoc and then selection of **Add > Add Variable**. We have also provided an initialization of m_FileForm = 0 in the OnNewDocument function of CSnapDrawDoc. We will let this zero value for m_FileForm correspond to the default file structure.

We now move on to the Resource View window and click on IDR_DrawingTYPE under Menu to bring the menu bar into the Edit window. We've entered File For&mat on the Type Here location to create an "m" shortcut key. Then, in the drop down Type Here, we have entered &Default followed by &Text and &Spread Text. We have also dragged the File Format item down the menu bar to install it next to File. At this point, we add function handlers for each of the drop down menu items by right clicking on the menu item and then selecting **Add Event Handler**. In this case, we ask the Event Handler Wizard to place the functions in the document class (this is convenient, since it's where Serialize is located). Be sure that CSnapDrawDoc is highlighted in the Class list box and also highlight the Message type COMMAND. The first function handler to be added is OnFileformatDefault. Returning to the Edit window, we repeat this process for the Message type UPDATE_COMMAND_UI which adds another handler function OnUpdateFileformatDefault. This process should then be continued until OnFileformatText, OnUpdateFileformatText, OnFileformatSpreadtext and OnUpdateFileformatSpreadtext have all been added as member functions to the document class CSnapDrawDoc.

7.6.2 Adding code

With the handler functions all in place, a bit of code is required to set m_FileForm appropriately and to keep the check marks in order on the drop down items. As an example, Table 7.8 shows the handler function for OnFileformatText with the single added line of code setting the value of M_FileForm = 1. Table 7.9 shows the handler function for the update command OnUpdateFileformatText. This will turn on the check mark on the drop down menu item Text if m_FileForm = 1.

The critical coding added in the creation of Version 5.0 contains the program lines which actually write the output to a file and, of equal importance, the lines of code which read the data back from a previously written file. All of this coding appears in the Serialize function which is broken up into two parts. The first portion deals with writing to files, the second with reading from files. In principle, the overall approach is as described in Section 5.6. The FPoint and LPoint data are written to the file to save the document and the document data is recovered when the file is read back. In our multi-format arrangement, as a file is written, it is labeled with the current value of m_FileForm. As the file is read back, m_FileForm is the first thing read. This identifies the file format and

Table 7.8 Listing of OnFileformatText from SnapDrawDoc.cpp (Ver. 5.0)

```
01    /* This is the listing of OnFileformatText */
02    void CSnapDrawDoc::OnFileformatText()
03    {
04         // TODO: Add your command handler code here
05         m_FileForm = 1;
06    }
```

Table 7.9 Listing of OnUpdateFileformatText from SnapDrawDoc.cpp (Ver. 5.0)

```
01    /* This is the listing of OnUpdateFileformatText */
02    void CSnapDrawDoc::OnUpdateFileformatText(CCmdUI *pCmdUI)
03    {
04         // TODO: Add your command update UI handler code here
05         pCmdUI->SetCheck(m_FileForm == 1);
06    }
```

allows the appropriate reading strategy to be applied. The code for writing m_FileForm is at the top of the "storing" portion of the Serialize function and is shown below:

```
CString buffer;
buffer.Format(L"%10d\r\n",m_FileForm);
ar.WriteString(buffer);
```

This formats the CString object buffer with m_FileForm as a decimal integer followed by the "\r\n" control sequence that produces a new line. The archiving function WriteString in the last statement above inserts buffer into the file. Similarly, at the top of the "reading" portion of Serialize, the value of m_FileForm is read with the code:

```
CString buffer;
ar.ReadString(buffer);
m_FileForm = _wtoi(buffer);
```

Here, the archiving function ReadString reads the first item from the file as the CString buffer and the function _wtoi (for "wide" to integer) sets the value of m_FileForm to the value specified by the text in buffer.

When m_FileForm = 0, the default file operations in Serialize are as as shown in Section 5.6. When m_FileForm = 1, output is in a single column using the format above with the WriteString archive function. The most intricate of the storing and reading code is for m_FileForm = 2 as shown in Tables 7.10 and 7.11. The storing code fragment in Table 7.10 is executed when the if statement shown in line 02 is satisfied. Here NumLines is written in line 06 by the WriteString function and followed by the fresh line also provided in buffer. The for loop of lines 07–15 then creates output for each of the drawn lines. The coordinates of the first and last points on each line are clearly identified as four outputs in lines 09–12. Line 13 formats them into buffer as integers using "tab" characters after each and followed by "\r\n" to move on to a new line. Line 14 then writes buffer to the file with WriteString.

Table 7.11 shows the portion of the Serialize function that deals with reading the file in the case of m_FileForm = 2. After the first line of the file is read and m_FileForm = 2 is recognized, the code continues at

Table 7.10 A Portion of the Serialize Function from SnapDrawDoc.cpp (Ver. 5.0)

```
01    /* An excerpt from the "storing" portion of Serialize in CSnapDrawDoc.cpp*/
02    if (m_FileForm == 2)
03    {
04        int Out1, Out2, Out3, Out4;
05        buffer.Format(L"%10d\r\n",NumLines);
06        ar.WriteString(buffer);
07    for (int i = 0; i<NumLines; i++)
08        {
09        Out1=FPoint[i].x;
10        Out2=FPoint[i].y;
11        Out3=LPoint[i].x;
12        Out4=LPoint[i].y;
13        buffer.Format(L"%10d\t%10d\t%10d\t%10d\r\n",Out1,Out2,Out3,Out4);
14        ar.WriteString(buffer);
15        }
16    }
```

Table 7.11 Additional Code from Serialize in SnapDrawDoc.cpp (Ver. 5.0)

```
01   /* An excerpt from the "reading" portion of Serialize in CSnapDrawDoc.cpp*/
02   if (m_FileForm == 2)
03   {
04       ar.ReadString(buffer);
05       NumLines = _wtoi(buffer);
06   for (int i = 0; i<NumLines; i++)
07       {
08       ar.ReadString(buffer);
09       int spot = buffer.Find('\t');
10       FPoint[i].x = _wtoi (buffer.Left(spot));
11       buffer.Delete(0,spot+1);
12       spot = buffer.Find('\t');
13       FPoint[i].y = _wtoi(buffer.Left(spot));
14       buffer.Delete(0,spot+1);
15       spot = buffer.Find('\t');
16       LPoint[i].x = _wtoi(buffer.Left(spot));
17       buffer.Delete(0,spot+1);
18       LPoint[i].y = _wtoi(buffer);
19       }
20       FPoint[NumLines]=LPoint[NumLines-1];
21   }
```

lines 04 and 05 by reading the next line in the file using the ReadString function and _wtoi to obtain the integer value NumLines. Then the for loop of lines 06–19 executes to bring in the data for each of the drawn lines. After each use of the ReadString function at line 08, the line from the file must be dissected. This is performed by using the CString "Find" function at line 09 to locate the tab delimiter. And in line 10, the CString Left function is used with _wtoi to obtain the x coordinate of the first point. In this process, the Find function identifies the position of the tab character and the function Left recovers the text up to that point in the file line. After this, line 11 then trims off everything from position 0 up to and including the tab character. Now lines 12 and 13 can recover the y coordinate of the first point and a Delete in line 14 continues to move us through the data in the file. Finally at line 18, everything has been trimmed from buffer so that only the y coordinate of the last point remains and can be converted by again using the function _wtoi. Each

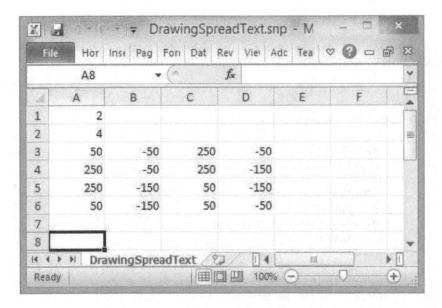

Figure 7.19 Viewing the "Spread Text" Format with Excel

drawn line in the figure is brought into the document by repetition of the for loop starting at line 06. Afterward, line 20 is used to set an initial value for the first point on the next line which might be drawn after updating the display.

As you test out the SnapDraw 5.0 program, be sure that you make a drawing and then save it in each of the file formats. Inspect the resulting files with Notepad or with Excel. In Figure 7.19, we've used Excel to display the output data from SnapDraw 5.0 for a simple rectangle drawn near the upper left corner of the window. Notice that the identifying 2 is in the first row of the file to indicate the Spread Text format. The next row shows a 4 since the square has four lines. The rest of the rows show the FPoint and LPoint values for the lines of the square. Notice that all of the numbers appearing for y coordinates are negative since any positive y values would be off the screen in the MM_LOENGLISH mapping mode.

7.7 Exercises

1. The project SnapDraw Version 0.0, which is located in the folder *Chap7\0_SnapDraw*, is a restructuring of the project SimpleDrawSnap originally presented in Section 5.5. Starting a new project in Visual C++, create your own multiple document version of SimpleDrawSnap. Give this new project a customized name, specify your own file extension and define your own customized icons to represent the program and its document files. As you develop this new project, you will need to create view class and document class member variables and functions including message and event handlers. But you can cut and paste code as you think appropriate from the original SimpleDrawSnap program (located in *Chap5\6_SimpleDrawSnap*).

2. In Version 2.0 of SnapDraw (*Chap7\2_SnapDraw*), the OnSize function was introduced and discussed in Section 7.3.5. Modify SnapDraw 2.0 to make use of the OnSize function information and the OnDraw function to maintain a red framing boundary just inside the program window. This boundary should consist of four straight lines drawn with a red pen around the inside of the window, each line should be ten pixels from the window's edge. Whenever the window is refreshed or resized, the red frame boundary should be redrawn — again ten pixels from the window edge.

3. Modify Version 3.0 of SnapDraw (*Chap7\3_SnapDraw*), to add color selection using a dialog window. The dialog window should be displayed in response to a click on a menu bar item called Line Color which should be located between View and Grid Size on the menu bar. The dialog window should contain six radio buttons and provide the user with six choices for line color (red, green, blue, yellow, cyan and magenta). After the user selects the line color and closes the dialog box, the drawing should be updated showing all of its lines in the new color.

4. Modify Version 3.0 of SnapDraw (*Chap7\3_SnapDraw*) to add the arc drawing capability. Use a drop down menu bar item labeled Drawing Mode and containing "Lines" or "Arcs" as the drawing mode options. You may use your own arc drawing function modeled on DrawCirc introduced in Section 5.5 or use an appropriate MFC function. A convenient way to draw arcs is for a right mouse click to define the arc center, then a left mouse click can define both the radius and starting point of the arc and finally a second left click can define the angular sweep of the arc. Of course, you should have full windows functionality for your arcs so that window resizing (minimizing or maximizing) will still redisplay both your arcs and your lines. You should also be able to store a drawing containing both arcs and lines in a file and retrieve it when desired. In addition, you should be able to draw arcs beginning in any quadrant (the math function "atan2" will be useful for this). During development of this arc drawing process, it may be convenient for you to inhibit the snap-to-grid operation. But reactivate it as you finish.

5. We have now introduced many of the concepts needed to create an amateur CAD package. Work with SnapDraw in the form of Version 3.0 (pixel coordinates) or Version 5.0 (LoEnglish coordinates) and create a two-dimensional drawing program that can draw lines, circles, rectangles and arcs. The user should be able to change colors, save files, etc. Rubber-banding in each drawing mode would be an optional challenge. Also consider drawing individual lines, arcs, etc. in desired colors and maintaining and saving those colors for redisplay.

Chapter 8

Classes, Objects and Animation

In previous chapters, we have described the basic strategies for writing Windows programs including the many MFC tools that are part of Windows programming. Of course, classes and objects play a major role in this process and we have used the document/view classes and other standard MFC classes as an integral part of our programs. At this point, it's time to consider the creation and use of our own classes in the Windows environment and to develop strategies for integrating the classes into useful programs.

We will begin by developing our own "points" class for use in very basic graphics operations. Then we'll add the class to an MFC Application program and use it in a simple calculation and a graphical display. Based on this initial class we extend the approach to a class for two-dimensional shapes which allows 2D shapes to be conveniently created, moved, and displayed. Then the concept of the "shapes" class is further developed to create specific classes for circular and rectangular shapes. We apply these ideas in animation programs to demonstrate their use. A planet simulation shows planets revolving around the sun with the moon revolving around the earth. A robot animation includes a jaw which appears to open and close during a motion cycle. At the end of this chapter, you should have a good understanding of the process of creating and using your own classes in the Windows environment. You'll also have a small library of useful classes and functions for displaying and animating two-dimensional objects.

8.1 Adding a Class to an MFC Application

Our first example program using homemade classes introduces a class for two dimensional points called C2DPoints. The class declaration is shown in Table 8.1. The class structure is very simple with member variables m_x and m_y declared as double precision variables in line 04 and an empty constructor function shown in line 06. The m_x and m_y variables have been made double precision because the C2DPoints class is intended for use in later graphics operations where that level of precision will be important. The empty constructor function will facilitate the use of point objects from the class C2DPoints as member variables of other classes. In line 07, the member function Adjust2DPoint is defined to set the values of m_x and m_y. The function Show2DPoint in line 08 serves as a display function to show the pixel corresponding to the coordinates m_x and m_y for C2DPoints objects. Notice that a device context pointer is passed to Show2DPoint and is used to allow SetPixel to access the proper display.

We would now like to introduce the C2DPoints class into an MFC Application. To describe the process, we start by creating a new single document MFC Application project called TwoDPoints. The application has MFC Standard style and Native Windows visual style along with default project settings. After the project is created, a file can be made to contain the class C2DPoints by clicking on **Project > Add New Item**. The file should be a Visual C++ header file using the suggested file name TwoDPointsClass.h. After the file has been added to the project, the

Table 8.1 Listing of a Class for Two-Dimensional Points

```
01    /* Listing of the file TwoDPointsClass.h */
02    class C2DPoints
03    {
04         double m_x, m_y;
05         public:
06         C2DPoints () {}
07         void Adjust2DPoint(double x, double y) { m_x = x; m_y = y; }
08         void Show2DPoint(CDC* pDC) { pDC->SetPixel(int(m_x),int(m_y),0); }
09    };
```

code in Table 8.1 can be typed into it or can be added by a copy and paste operation. In either case, as soon as the code is in the file, you can look into the Class View window and the class C2DPoints should appear along with the more familiar view class, document class, etc. Figure 8.1 shows the Class View window at this point with the class C2DPoints expanded so its member functions and variables are displayed.

With this new class in place, it is relatively easy to add the code to create the example project TwoDPoints as contained in the folder *Chap8\1_TwoDPoints*. An important step in adding objects of the C2DPoints class to the project is to be sure that the class header file TwoDPointsClass.h appears in an "include" statement in the document

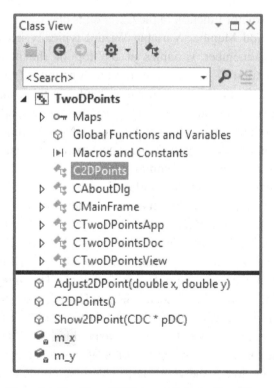

Figure 8.1 The Class C2DPoints as Seen in Class View

header file TwoDPointsDoc.h. This will be done automatically if you add a member variable to the document class with a right click on the document class in Class View and select **Add > Add Variable** from the options menu. Then, when the class C2DPoints is entered as the "variable type" for the new member variable, the Add Member Variable Wizard inserts an include statement for the file TwoDPointsClass.h into the file TwoDPointsDoc.h. It also inserts the code declaring the object into the declaration of the class CTwoDPointsDoc in the same file. Note, however, that manually adding (i.e. without the Add Variable Wizard) all of the C2DPoints objects as member variables of CTwoDPointsDoc would also require the manual insertion of the include statement as well. The C2DPoints objects can be directly declared as member variables of the document class using simple declarations because of the inclusion of the empty constructor function in the C2DPoints class.

The MFC Add Member Variable Wizard typically inserts a default initialization of member variables at the top of the document class constructor function — in this case into the function CTwoDPointsDoc of the file TwoDPointsDoc.cpp. In our examples in this chapter, we will override any default initializations in the document class and perform the appropriate initializations directly in the OnNewDocument function. These initializations then apply as new documents are generated within the program by the File > New command.

At this point, let's open the folder *Chap8\1_TwoDPoints* and bring the prepared example TwoDPoints into the development environment. With Class View, you can see the document class member variable Point1 of the C2DPoints class. The array PointArray[500] of the C2DPoints class is another document class member (recall that the array size is inserted manually into the declaration). The integer variable NumRandPoints has also been declared. Overall, the program TwoDPoints is not complicated. The class file TwoDPointsClass.h has been added to the project. But, other than this, code has only been inserted in the OnNewDocument function of the document class and in the OnDraw function of the view class. There are no view class member variables. Table 8.2 shows the OnNewDocument function. In Table 8.2, Line 07 initializes Point1 at the coordinates (100,100). Lines 08–14

Table 8.2 Listing of OnNewDocument from TwoDPointsDoc.cpp

```
01   /* This is the listing of OnNewDocument */
02   BOOL CTwoDPointsDoc::OnNewDocument()
03   {
04       if (!CDocument::OnNewDocument()) return FALSE;
05       // TODO: add reinitialization code here
06       // (SDI documents will reuse this document)
07       Point1.Adjust2DPoint(100,100);
08       NumRandPnts = 500;
09   for (int i = 0; i < NumRandPnts; i++)
10       {
11       int RandX = 200 + rand()%100;
12       int RandY =  50 + rand()%100;
13       PointArray[i].Adjust2DPoint(RandX,RandY);
14       }
15       return TRUE;
16   }
```

then randomly generate 500 points with x values from 200 to 300 and y values from 50 to 150. Lines 11 and 12 use the rand() function and the notation after the "+" sign in each line yields a random number with a uniform distribution between 0 and 100.

As this program runs, the OnNewDocument function executes to set all of the point coordinates and then the OnDraw function displays them. The OnDraw function is shown in Table 8.3.

Table 8.3 Listing of OnDraw from TwoDPointsView.cpp

```
01   /* This is the listing of OnDraw */
02   void CTwoDPointsView::OnDraw(CDC* pDC)
03   {
04       CTwoDPointsDoc* pDoc = GetDocument();
05       ASSERT_VALID(pDoc); if(!pDoc)return;
06       // TODO: add draw code for native data here
07       pDoc->Point1.Show2DPoint(pDC);
08   for (int i = 0; i < pDoc->NumRandPnts; i++)
09       {
10       pDoc->PointArray[i].Show2DPoint(pDC);
11       }
12   }
```

Line 07 in OnDraw makes use of the document pointer to access Point1 and then displays it at (100,100) using Show2DPoint. Then the for loop of lines 08–11 cycles through all of the randomly generated points in PointArray and displays each of them with Show2DPoint. The window for TwoDPoints after execution is shown in Figure 8.2 where the single pixel of Point1 at (100,100) is clearly visible and the 500 points in PointArray seem to form a square. The program does not include a provision for user interaction but a click of the "new document" button on the toolbar will re-execute OnNewDocument and then OnDraw to generate and display another 500 random points (still in the same square).

8.2 A Class for Two-Dimensional Shapes

In this section we continue our development of classes for use in two-dimensional graphic presentations and basic animations. The class that is developed here will be used to display and manipulate

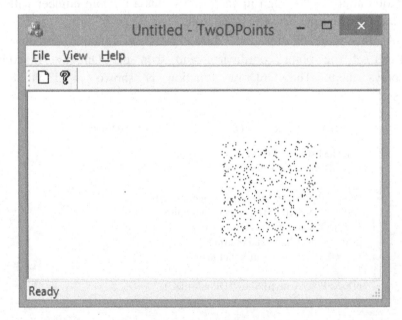

Figure 8.2 Execution of TwoDPoints

two-dimensional graphical shapes. The class is called C2DShapes and it makes use of objects of the C2DPoints class described in Section 8.1 above. We will begin the discussion of the class C2DShapes by considering its member variables:

> int m_NumPnts
> C2DPoints m_PointArray[25]
> double m_xBP, m_yBP

In this list of class member variables, the integer variable m_NumPnts defines the number of points contained in a two dimensional shape object. The array of points specified in m_PointArray is intended to describe the two dimensional shape relative to a local coordinate system. We are specifically using the class C2DPoints from Section 8.1 to provide double precision coordinate values and a simple show function for the points. The member variables m_xBP and m_yBP define the position of the shape in a global coordinate system by specifying the global coordinates for the origin of the local coordinate system used to specify the shape. Figure 8.3 illustrates the situation. It shows the global coordinate system of the screen (x_G, y_G) and also the local coordinate system (x_L, y_L) in which the points defining the vertices of the two dimensional shape are defined.

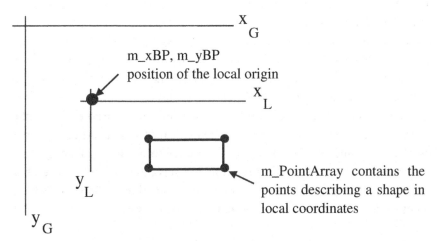

Figure 8.3 Coordinate Systems for Shape Definition

The member functions of the C2DShapes class are as follows:

C2DShapes()
Adjust2DShape (int numpnts, CPoint* PtPointArray)
Show2DPoints(CDC* pDC)
Show2DShape(CDC* pDC)
Fill2DShape(CDC* pDC)
Move (double Mvx, double Mvy)
DMove (double DMvx, double DMvy)
LRotate(double Theta)
GRotate(double Theta, double xRotate, double yRotate)

As shown in the list of member functions, the class contains an empty constructor function as well as the function Adjust2DShape which serves to define member variables for the class. Additional functions which allow objects of the C2DShapes class to be displayed, moved and rotated are also included. We will discuss several of the functions which are shown along with detailed coding in Table 8.4. The coding details for all of the functions can be found in the example program folder *Chap8\2_TwoDShapes* where the file TwoDShapesClass.h contains the full class declaration and function definitions. This file was added to the TwoDShapes project in the same way that we added TwoDPointsClass.h to the TwoDPoints project in Section 8.1. The advantage of placing both the class declarations and function definitions in the header file is that only a single file needs to be added to a project to make the classes available. Notice that we have also included the C2DPoints class in the same header file along with the C2DShapes class.

The Adjust2DShape function shown in Table 8.4 is used to define the member variables of the class C2DShapes. It receives, as arguments, the number of points in the shape and a pointer to an array of points that describes the shape. Line 03 of the function sets the m_NumPnts member variable and lines 04 and 05 assign the initial position of the shape's base point to be at the origin of the global coordinate system. The for loop of lines 06–10 then assigns the member variables in m_PointArray (recall that these are C2DPoints objects with double precision coordinate values). Notice that lines 08 and 09 use the pointer received as an input parameter to address the coordinates of the input shape.

The function Move is also shown in Table 8.4 and is used in positioning the 2D graphical objects. The function is very simple. It receives two coordinate values as input arguments in line 01. In lines 03 and 04 it uses these values to set the base point member variables for the object and thus moves its position within the global coordinate system shown in Figure 8.3. Animated motion of the 2D objects can be achieved with these base point movements just as we used "NoseTip" information for the SimpleAnimate project of Section 5.4. The function DMove is not shown in Table 8.4 but operates similarly to make incremental changes in the base point coordinates.

There are three functions provided in the class C2DShapes for displaying its 2D graphical objects. The function Show2DPoints displays the individual points which make up the object, the function Show2DShape draws the shape by using lines to connect the points and

Table 8.4 Selected Functions from the Class C2DShapes

```
01   void C2DShapes::Adjust2DShape (int numpnts, CPoint* PtPointArray)
02   {
03         m_NumPnts = numpnts;
04         m_xBP = 0;
05         m_yBP = 0;
06     for (int i=0; i<m_NumPnts; i++)
07         {
08         m_PointArray[i].m_x = (PtPointArray+i)->x;
09         m_PointArray[i].m_y = (PtPointArray+i)->y;
10         }
11   }


01   void C2DShapes::Move (double Mvx, double Mvy)
02   {
03         m_xBP = Mvx;
04         m_yBP = Mvy;
05   }
```

Table 8.4 (*Continued*)

```
01    void C2DShapes::Show2DShape(CDC* pDC)
02    {
03        pDC->MoveTo(int(m_xBP + m_PointArray[0].m_x), int(m_yBP +
04            m_PointArray[0].m_y));
05      for (int j =1; j < m_NumPnts; j++)
06        {
07        pDC->LineTo(int(m_xBP + m_PointArray[j].m_x),int(m_yBP +
08                m_PointArray[j].m_y));
09        }
10        pDC->LineTo(int(m_xBP + m_PointArray[0].m_x), int(m_yBP +
11                m_PointArray[0].m_y));
12    }

01    void C2DShapes::LRotate(double Theta)
02    {
03        Theta=Theta/57.296;
04        double SinTheta = sin(Theta);    double CosTheta = cos(Theta);
05      for (int i=0; i<m_NumPnts; i++)
06        {
07        double savx = m_PointArray[i].m_x;
08        double savy = m_PointArray[i].m_y;
09        m_PointArray[i].m_x = savx * CosTheta - savy * SinTheta;
10        m_PointArray[i].m_y = savx * SinTheta + savy * CosTheta;
11        }
12    }
```

the function Fill2DShape draws the object and fills its interior. Show2DShape appears in Table 8.4 as an example. There, you can see in line 01 that its only input parameter is a device context pointer to tell Show2DShape where to draw. It then draws the specified 2D object by making use of its m_PointArray for shape definition and by using its base point member variables to position it. Specifically, lines 03 and 04 carry out a MoveTo operation to reach the first point of the object. Notice that the base point coordinates m_xBP and m_yBP are added to the coordinates in m_PointArray in this process. The for loop of lines 05–09 then draws lines for the shape and lines 10 and 11 draw in the last line making the connection back to the first point to close the polygon.

The trigonometric operations required for rotation are included in the functions LRotate and GRotate. The code for LRotate is shown in Table 8.4 and performs local rotations of the 2D object about its coordinate origin (the base point) where the input argument Theta is the desired angle of rotation in degrees. The function GRotate also rotates the 2D object but it performs a global rotation about a specified point in the global coordinate system. Figure 8.4 shows the distinction between the local and global rotations for a specific point of interest on an object. The angle shown as ThetaL refers to local rotation of the point of interest within its local coordinate system. The angle shown as ThetaG refers to a global rotation of the point of interest and the coordinate position xRotate, yRotate defines the point of rotation for the global rotation.

Let's now look at the basis for the trigonometry in the function LRotate as shown in Table 8.4. Figure 8.5 describes the situation in a set of traditional (X,Y) coordinates (with Y positive upward). Figure 8.5a shows a point positioned at (x,y) being rotated through an angle θ to its new coordinate position at (x',y'). We can find an expression for the x' and y' coordinate values by separately considering the x and the y components of the original point. Figure 8.5b shows the x component being rotated through θ and resulting in a point positioned at (x $\cos\theta$, x $\sin\theta$). Similarly, Figure 8.5c shows the y component of the original point being rotated through the angle θ to result in a point at (-y $\sin\theta$, y $\cos\theta$). Since the rotation of the original point involves both components

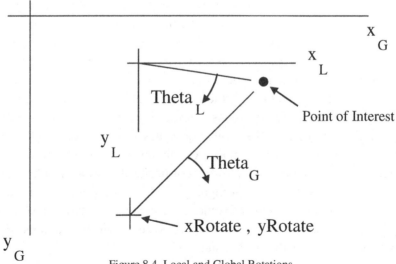

Figure 8.4 Local and Global Rotations

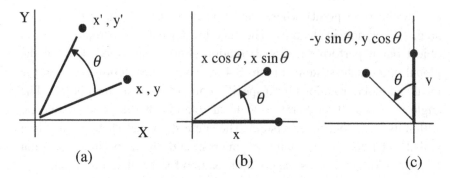

Figure 8.5 Rotation of a Point

x and y, the overall rotation result is the sum of the component results so that

$$x' = x \cos \theta - y \sin \theta$$

$$y' = x \sin \theta + y \cos \theta$$

With this result in mind, we can take a closer look at the coding in the LRotate function of Table 8.4. In line 01, you can see that the input parameter to the function is the rotation angle and in line 03, the angle is converted to radians ready to be used by the trigonometric functions. The statements in Line 04 take the sine and cosine and save them as SinTheta and CosTheta. Using line 04 calls each trigonometric function only once for the shape rotation. Then, the for loop of lines 05–11 rotates all of the points in the 2D shape through the desired angle where lines 09 and 10 actually implement the equations above. Note that the rotation takes place about the origin of the local coordinates which we have called the base point. Note also that a positive rotation with the y axis directed downward (the default Windows coordinate direction) results in a clockwise rotation as shown in Figure 8.4. If the coordinate y axis were upwards, a positive rotation would be counter-clockwise as seen in Figure 8.5. Both of these results are consistent with the familiar sign convention known as the "right hand rule".

We have not shown the code for the function GRotate (it can be inspected in the folder *Chap8\2_TwoDShapes*). GRotate operates very much the same as the LRotate function, starting with a local rotation of the points in the m_PointArray. But it also rotates the base point globally about the specified rotation point xRotate, yRotate as shown in Figure 8.4. This results in an effective global rotation of the 2D shape about xRotate, yRotate and also preserves the local coordinates in the m_PointArray for the rotated shape relative to the basepoint.

8.2.1 Example use of the class C2DShapes

The development of the class C2DShapes provides some very basic graphics tools for manipulating two dimensional shapes. In this section we review the structure and operation of the program in the folder *Chap8\2_TwoDShapes*. This example shows the use of C2DShapes and its functions. In order to become familiar with the features of the program, you should build and execute it. Try the Show Options and Rotate menu bar items and use the arrow keys to translate the shape.

Table 8.5 Listing of OnNewDocument from TwoDShapesDoc.cpp

```
01   /* This is the listing of OnNewDocument*/
02   BOOL CTwoDShapesDoc::OnNewDocument()
03   {
04       if (!CDocument::OnNewDocument())
05       return FALSE;
06       // TODO: add reinitialization code here
07       // (SDI documents will reuse this document)
08       CPoint PointArray[8];
09       int NumPoints = 8;
10       PointArray[0].SetPoint( 20,  0);   PointArray[1].SetPoint( 20,100);
11       PointArray[2].SetPoint( 10,110); PointArray[3].SetPoint(-10,110);
12       PointArray[4].SetPoint(-20,100); PointArray[5].SetPoint(-20,  0);
13       PointArray[6].SetPoint(-10,-10); PointArray[7].SetPoint( 10,-10);
14       Shape1.Adjust2DShape (NumPoints, PointArray);
15       Shape1.Move (500,150);
16       return TRUE;
17   }
```

Inspecting the document class in the Class View window, you'll see that Shape1 is its only member variable where Shape1 is an object of the class C2DShapes. The OnNewDocument function shown in Table 8.5 defines Shape1 and initially positions it at the window coordinates (500,150). This begins in line 08 where the vector of CPoint objects called PointArray is declared. Then, lines 10–13 use the SetPoint member function of the CPoint class to set the coordinate values for each of the eight PointArray entries. Shape1 has been declared as a member variable of the document class. Line 14 calls the Adjust2DShape function for Shape1. It acts to define Shape1, specifying the number of points in the shape and supplying the PointArray name to serve as a pointer to the vector of points. Finally, line 15 uses the Move function to locate Shape1 at its initial position coordinates.

Of course, after the execution of OnNewDocument, Shape1 is not yet displayed. It only exists as data in the new document. As the program starts, the OnDraw function executes after OnNewDocument completes. It displays Shape1 following the code in Table 8.6 where line 04 obtains the document pointer. A brush (for filling the polygon) and a pen are then selected for the display. These are view class member variables and were initialized in the view class constructor function. Lines 09–11 use the value of the view class member variable m_ShapeMode (a CString object) to select the appropriate function to display the filled shape, the shape outline or the shape points on the screen.

Table 8.6 Listing of OnDraw from TwoDShapesView.cpp

```
01    /* This is the listing of OnDraw*/
02    void CTwoDShapesView::OnDraw(CDC* pDC)
03    {
04        CTwoDShapesDoc* pDoc = GetDocument();
05        ASSERT_VALID(pDoc); if(!pDoc)return;
06        // TODO: add draw code for native data here
07        pDC->SelectObject(&m_RedBrush);
08        pDC->SelectObject(&m_BlackPen);
09        if (m_ShapeMode == "Filled")pDoc->Shape1.Fill2DShape(pDC);
10        if (m_ShapeMode == "Lines")pDoc->Shape1.Show2DShape(pDC);
11        if (m_ShapeMode == "Points")pDoc->Shape1.Show2DPoints(pDC);
12    }
```

As the program starts, m_ShapeMode is initialized to "Filled". After the initial display of Shape1, clicking on the Show Options menu bar item and selecting from the resulting drop down menu entries activates functions which set m_ShapeMode to either "Filled", "Lines" or "Points". The function OnShowPoints is typical of these. It simply sets m_ShowShape to "Points" and calls the function UpdateAllViews to execute OnDraw and redisplay Shape1 in its new form. Figure 8.6 shows a variation of the TwoDShapes program. It was modified especially for the Figure 8.6 to display Shape1 at three different locations using the three show functions. Fill2DShape is on the left, Show2DShape is in the center and Show2DPoints is on the right. In normal operation of the TwoDShapes program, only one image of Shape1 appears and the menu bar items control its motion. The Local Rotate item executes the function OnLocalrotate which calls Shape1.LRotate (to make a -30° rotation) and then calls UpdateAllViews to redisplay the shape rotated about its base point. Notice that the negative rotation corresponds to a counter-clockwise direction. Quite similarly, a click on the Global Rotate

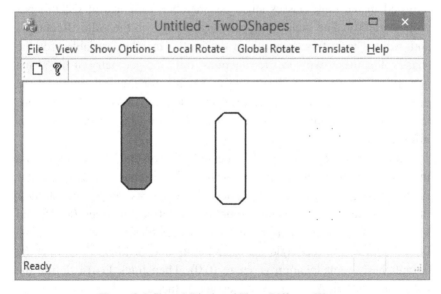

Figure 8.6 Shape1 Displayed Three Different Ways

menu bar item executes the function OnGlobalrotate which uses the function call Shape1.GRotate (-30,350,200) to globally rotate Shape1 about a central point in the window at the coordinates of (350,200). A click on the Translate menu bar item provides the instruction to use the arrow keys for translation. The OnKeyDown function is set to call Shape1.DMove with appropriate arguments to incrementally move Shape1 up, down, right or left with strokes of the arrow keys.

8.3 Forming Other Shapes Classes

Based on the class C2DShapes described in the previous section, it is quite easy to form additional and more specific classes for two-dimensional shapes using the tools that C2DShapes provides. The folder *Chap8\3_TwoDShapes+* contains the file TwoDShapes+Classes.h with the added classes CRectangles and CCircles for displaying and manipulating rectangular and circular shapes. Each of these classes is derived from the C2DShapes class so that the additional coding required for the new classes is quite minimal. In fact, no member variables are required in the new classes since the member variables of C2DShapes work perfectly. The major programming effort is in the AdjustRectangle and AdjustCircle functions which define the member variables for the shapes. For these two specific functions, only the geometry of the shape is required as input, i.e. the height and width for the rectangle and the diameter for the circle. The AdjustRectangle and AdjustCircle functions are written to define the member variables for each object from this information.

Table 8.7 shows the full class declaration for the CRectangles class including the function definitions. In line 02 it is clear that CRectangles is derived from C2DShapes. Line 05 shows its empty constructor function. The AdjustRectangle function is defined in lines 06–15 and here the definition of each of the member variables can be seen. In line 08, of course, the rectangle has four points and in lines 09 and 10 the default base point location is set to (0,0). Then lines 11–14 define the entries in m_PointArray using the center of the rectangle as the origin of

Table 8.7 Listing of the Class CRectangles from TwoDShapes+Classes.h

```
01   /* This is the listing of the CRectangles Class*/
02   class CRectangles : public C2DShapes
03   {
04       public:
05       CRectangles (){ }
06       void CRectangles::AdjustRectangle (double ht, double wd)
07       {
08       m_NumPnts = 4;
09       m_xBP = 0;
10       m_yBP = 0;
11       m_PointArray[0].m_x = -wd/2.;  m_PointArray[0].m_y = -ht/2.;
12       m_PointArray[1].m_x = -wd/2.;  m_PointArray[1].m_y = ht/2.;
13       m_PointArray[2].m_x = wd/2.;   m_PointArray[2].m_y = ht/2.;
14       m_PointArray[3].m_x = wd/2.;   m_PointArray[3].m_y = -ht/2.;
15       }
16       void CRectangles::Move (double Mvx, double Mvy)
17           {C2DShapes::Move(Mvx, Mvy);}
18       void CRectangles::DMove (double DMvx, double DMvy)
19           {C2DShapes::DMove(DMvx, DMvy);}
20       void CRectangles::ShowRect(CDC* pDC)
21           {C2DShapes::Show2DShape (pDC);}
22       void CRectangles::FillRect(CDC* pDC)
23           {C2DShapes::Fill2DShape(pDC);}
24       void CRectangles::ShowRectPoints(CDC* pDC)
25           {C2DShapes::Show2DPoints(pDC);}
26       void CRectangles::LRotate(double Theta)
27           {C2DShapes::LRotate(Theta);}
28       void CRectangles::GRotate(double Theta, double xRotate, double yRotate)
29           {C2DShapes::GRotate(Theta, xRotate, yRotate);}
30   };
```

the local coordinate system and using the given height and width to set the coordinate values. The remainder of the function definitions in lines 16–29 of Table 8.7 create the move, rotate and show functions for the CRectangles class. These functions simply call the C2DShapes functions previously developed for the same purposes and able to make direct use of the member variables describing CRectangles objects. We do not show the CCircles class here but it is structured in the same way as the CRectangles class and also derived from C2DShapes. Its AdjustCirc function uses the approach of DrawCirc discussed in Section 5.5 to generate an array of points forming a circle. The local origin is at the circle center. You can certainly see all of the details by viewing the CCircles class in the project TwoDShapes+.

Based on the new CCircles and CRectangles classes and the original C2DShapes class, the project in the folder *Chap8\3_TwoDShapes+* creates several 2D shapes and illustrates the use of the various functions for their manipulation. You should, of course, build and execute TwoDShapes+. To test its operation, click on the menu bar items to carry out a few global and local rotations and also use the arrow keys. To explore the coding for this project, begin by looking at the document class through the Class View window and notice that six 2D shapes are declared as member variables of the document class. Shape1 and Shape2 are objects of the C2DShapes class, Rect1 and Rect2 are CRectangles objects and Circle1 and Circle2 are CCircles objects. These shapes are defined in the OnNewDocument function as shown in Table 8.8. Lines 08–13 define Shape1 just as in the previous example using an array of the CPoint class. Line 14 moves Shape1 to the desired position on the screen. Then, line 15 defines Shape2 to be the same as Shape1 and located in exactly the same position. Lines 16 and 17 define and position Rect1 and line 18 defines Rect2 as its duplicate. Similarly, lines 19 and 20 define and position Circle1 and line 21 defines its duplicate as Circle2.

After the objects have been defined and positioned, they are displayed by OnDraw as shown in Table 8.9. Lines 07 and 08 of Table 8.9 select a red brush and black pen. Lines 09–14 then display the six shapes. Shape1, Rect1 and Circle1 are all displayed as filled shapes and are colored with the red brush. Shape2 and Rect2 are simply drawn by lines and Circle2 is shown only by drawing its points. Of course, since Shape1, Rect1 and Circle 1 are initially positioned over the other shapes, displaying them as filled shapes hides the simpler displays of Shape2, Rect2 and Circle2. The menu bar items and arrow keys allow rotations of the first set of shapes.

Table 8.8 Listing of OnNewDocument from TwoDShapes+Doc.cpp

```
01    /* This is the listing of the OnNewDocument function*/
02    BOOL CTwoDShapesDoc::OnNewDocument()
03    {
04        if (!CDocument::OnNewDocument())
05        return FALSE;
06        // TODO: add reinitialization code here
07        // (SDI documents will reuse this document)
08        CPoint PointArray[8];
09        PointArray[0].SetPoint( 20, 0);  PointArray[1].SetPoint( 20,100);
10        PointArray[2].SetPoint( 10,110); PointArray[3].SetPoint(-10,110);
11        PointArray[4].SetPoint(-20,100); PointArray[5].SetPoint(-20, 0);
12        PointArray[6].SetPoint(-10,-10); PointArray[7].SetPoint( 10,-10);
13        Shape1.Adjust2DShape (8, PointArray);
14        Shape1.Move (200,200);
15        Shape2 = Shape1;
16        Rect1.AdjustRectangle(40, 100);
17        Rect1.Move (400,50);
18        Rect2 = Rect1;
19        Circle1.AdjustCircle(100);
20        Circle1.Move (600,250);
21        Circle2 = Circle1;
22        return TRUE;
23    }
```

Table 8.9 Listing of OnDraw from TwoDShapes+View.cpp

```
01    /* This is the listing of the OnDraw function*/
02    void CTwoDShapesView::OnDraw(CDC* pDC)
03    {
04        CTwoDShapesDoc* pDoc = GetDocument();
05        ASSERT_VALID(pDoc); if(!pDoc)return;
06        // TODO: add draw code for native data here
07        pDC->SelectObject(&m_RedBrush);
08        pDC->SelectObject(&m_BlackPen);
09        pDoc->Shape1.Fill2DShape(pDC);
10        pDoc->Shape2.Show2DShape(pDC);
11        pDoc->Rect1.FillRect(pDC);
12        pDoc->Rect2.ShowRect(pDC);
13        pDoc->Circle1.FillCirc(pDC);
14        pDoc->Circle2.ShowCircPoints(pDC);
15    }
```

The GRotatePlus and GRotateMinus menu bar items perform ten degree global rotations of Shape1, Rect1 and Circle1 (with the GRotate functions). Similarly, LRotatePlus and LRotateMinus on the menu bar result in ten degree local rotations (with the LRotate functions). The arrow keys also activate these rotations. As an example of the functions for the rotate buttons, we have included the OnGrotateminus function from the view class in Table 8.10. This function is associated with the GRotateMinus menu bar item.

Line 05 of the function obtains the pDoc pointer which is used in lines 06–08 to call the GRotate functions for the Shape1, Rect1 and Circle1 objects. Then in line 09, calling the UpdateAllViews function results in an execution of OnDraw to redraw the objects in their new position. The negative rotation of -10 degrees is about the point (400,250) near the center of the window. Figure 8.7 shows the result of a few clicks of the GRotateMinus menu bar item. Notice that after the movement of the filled shapes, the outline drawings of Shape2 and Rect2 and the point display of Circle2 become visible. Of course, Shape2, Rect2 and Circle2 were not rotated by the coding in the function OnGrotateminus and remain in their original positions. The -10 degree global rotation has also been coded into the OnKeyDown function to occur after striking the "up arrow" key. The other arrow keys are similarly active for other rotations.

Table 8.10 Listing of OnGrotateminus from TwoDShapes+View.cpp

```
01    /* This is the listing of the OnGrotateminus function*/
02    void CTwoDShapesView::OnGrotateminus()
03    {
04        // TODO: Add your command handler code here
05        CTwoDShapesDoc* pDoc = GetDocument();
06        pDoc->Shape1.GRotate(-10,400,250);
07        pDoc->Rect1.GRotate(-10, 400,250);
08        pDoc->Circle1.GRotate(-10, 400,250);
09        pDoc->UpdateAllViews(NULL);
10    }
```

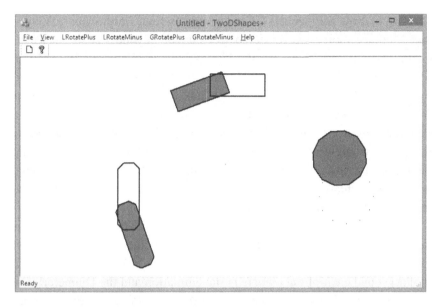

Figure 8.7 Display of the Six Objects after Global Rotation

8.4 A Planet Simulation

The previous sections in this chapter have introduced the use of classes as a basic tool for graphics displays. Our examples so far have been for demonstration purposes and particularly to illustrate the control and display of multiple graphics objects. This example carries the use of our graphics objects into a simple animation of a scaled down solar system. The Planets project is in the folder *Chap8\4_Planets*. If you build and execute the project, you can operate it using the start and stop menu bar items and see the planets and moon revolving about the sun.

The Planets project includes the file TwoDShapes+Classes.h as described in the previous sections and containing the class information for the shapes classes. The CCircles class is used here to define the two-dimensional planet representations needed in the solar system animation. A check of the Class View window for the document class reveals the document member variables and the various objects necessary for the animation. You will see the CCircles objects Sun, Earth, Moon, Venus, and Mercury (sorry we don't go to Mars or beyond). Also shown as document class members are the circles objects oSun, oEarth, oMoon, oVenus, and oMercury. This second set of objects (with names preceded by an "o") describes a set of the planets in initial reference positions which is repeatedly used during the animation. The double precision variable PhiEarth is also included as a member variable. This represents the position angle of the earth in its circular orbit and is the driving parameter for the animation. As you will see, PhiEarth is incremented during the animation and the other planet position angles (as well as the moon) are defined in terms of PhiEarth.

Our "solar system" is configured in the OnNewDocument function as program execution begins. Table 8.11 shows the code. Line 07 of OnNewDocument declares the diameter variables to be used for the sun, the moon and each of the planets in the animation and the DiameterScale of 2 pixels per thousand kilometers is set in line 08. Accordingly, lines 09–12 set the planet and moon diameters to be used in the animation. Lines 13 and 14 set the sun diameter (DiamS) including an "adjustment factor" to keep the size of the sun from being excessively large in the display. Based on the appropriate diameter values, lines 15–19 use the AdjustCircle function of the CCircles class to define a set of circle objects which will represent the planets, moon and sun during the animation. Notice at this point that all of the objects are simply positioned at the origin of the global coordinates.

In the next block of code, line 20 declares the orbital distance variable (the radius) for each of the revolving bodies and then line 21 sets the DistanceScale for the display at 2 pixels per million kilometers. Notice that the scale values used for DiameterScale (line 08) and DistanceScale (line 21) are different. Equal values would, of course, produce a more accurate animation but unfortunately the moon and planets would then appear no larger than a pixel (distances in the solar system are vast compared to the size of the bodies). Accordingly, lines 22–24 then set the planet orbital distances. Lines 25 and 26 are used to set the moon's orbital distance using another "adjustment factor" to keep the moon orbiting well outside of the earth's scaled diameter. At this point the

Table 8.11 Listing of OnNewDocument from PlanetsDoc.cpp

```
01   /* This is the listing of the OnNewDocument function*/
02   BOOL CPlanetsDoc::OnNewDocument()
03   {
04       if (!CDocument::OnNewDocument())   return FALSE;
05       // TODO: add reinitialization code here
06       // (SDI documents will reuse this document)
07       double DiamMcy, DiamV, DiamE, DiamMn, DiamS;
08       double DiameterScale = 2.;        // 2 pixels/thousand km
09       DiamE = DiameterScale * 13.;      //EarthDiameter = 13 thousand km
10       DiamV = DiameterScale * 12.;      //VenusDiameter = 12
11       DiamMcy = DiameterScale * 5.;     //MercuryDiameter = 5
12       DiamMn = DiameterScale * 3.5;     //MoonDiameter = 3.5
13       double SunFudge = 1./40.;
14       DiamS = SunFudge * DiameterScale * 1390.;     //SunDiameter = 1390;
15       oEarth.AdjustCircle (DiamE);
16       oVenus.AdjustCircle (DiamV);
17       oMercury.AdjustCircle (DiamMcy);
18       oMoon.AdjustCircle (DiamMn);
19       oSun.AdjustCircle (DiamS);
20       double RadMcy, RadV, RadE, RadMn;
21       double DistanceScale = 2.;        // 2 pixels/million km
22       RadE = DistanceScale * 150.;      //EarthDistance = 150 million km
23       RadV = DistanceScale * 108.;      //VenusDistance = 108
24       RadMcy = DistanceScale * 58.;     //MercuryDistance = 58
25       double MoonFudge = 40.;
26       RadMn = MoonFudge * DistanceScale * 0.39;   // MoonDistance = 0.39
27       oEarth.Move(RadE, 0);
28       oVenus.Move(RadV, 0);
29       oMercury.Move(RadMcy, 0);
30       oMoon.Move(RadE+RadMn, 0);
31       PhiEarth = 0;
32       return TRUE;
33   }
```

orbital distances are used in lines 27–30 to call the CCircles Move function for positioning the planets and the moon relative to the sun. Finally, line 31 initializes the value of PhiEarth to zero. Note that as we leave the OnNewDocument function, the sun of our initialized solar system is at the global origin (based on its default base point position) and the planets and moon are arranged in a straight line extending along the x axis.

After OnNewDocument has executed, the OnDraw function begins and creates the initial display window for the Planets program. The OnDraw function is shown in Table 8.12. The first added line of code in the OnDraw function appears in line 07, where the document class function PositionBodies is called to position the solar system bodies and prepare them for display. This is a critical line of code in the OnDraw function and the operation of the PositionBodies function will be described in detail directly below. First, however, note that the remaining lines in the OnDraw function of Table 8.12 are completely devoted to drawing the sun, planets and moon into the window. Lines 08 and 09 select a black pen and a red brush. Line 10 then draws the red sun as a filled circle with a black outline. Line 11 provides a blue brush and line 12 draws in the "blue planet". Finally, lines 13–16 draw the remaining planets and moon in black.

Let's now consider operation of the PositionBodies function from the CPlanetsDocClass. This function is called when the solar system is first

Table 8.12 Listing of OnDraw from PlanetsView.cpp

```
01    /* This is the listing of the OnDraw function*/
02    void CPlanetsView::OnDraw(CDC* pDC)
03    {
04        CPlanetsDoc* pDoc = GetDocument();
05        ASSERT_VALID(pDoc); if(!pDoc)return;
06        // TODO: add draw code for native data here
07        pDoc->PositionBodies(m_CenterX, m_CenterY);
08        pDC->SelectObject(&m_BlackPen);
09        pDC->SelectObject(&m_RedBrush);
10        pDoc->Sun.FillCirc(pDC);
11        pDC->SelectObject(&m_BlueBrush);
12        pDoc->Earth.FillCirc (pDC);
13        pDC->SelectObject(&m_BlackBrush);
14        pDoc->Venus.FillCirc (pDC);
15        pDoc->Mercury.FillCirc (pDC);
16        pDoc->Moon.FillCirc (pDC);
17    }
```

drawn into the window and is also called at every step of the animation. With each animation step, the document class member variable PhiEarth is incremented to a new value by the view class OnTimer function which also calls UpdateAllViews. This executes the OnDraw function so that PositionBodies operates once again, acting as a keystone of the animation with the incremented PhiEarth. Table 8.13 shows the code for the PositionBodies function.

The argument list for PositionBodies shows it receiving the integer variables CenterX and CenterY when the function is called. In OnDraw, the arguments inserted in PositionBodies are member variables of the view class (m_CenterX and m_CenterY). They are set by the OnSize function to represent the center coordinates of the current window. The PositionBodies function ultimately makes use of CenterX and CenterY to position the center of the animated solar system (i.e. the sun) in the center of the window. However, the function begins with the code of lines 04–08 retrieving the initialized representations of the planets, sun and moon (oEarth, oVenus, etc.). As stated earlier, the orbital position angle of the earth is the key animation parameter and lines 09–12 calculate the position angles of the other bodies in terms of PhiEarth using the orbital period for the angular adjustment. In this way, for example, the angular position of Venus (line 10) increases 62 percent faster than the angular position of the earth.

After the orbital position angle of each body is calculated, lines 13–15 then globally rotate (i.e. revolve) each of the planets around the sun which, at this point, is still positioned at the origin of the window coordinates. Lines 16–18 similarly position the moon in its orbit around the earth. Finally, after all of the planets and the moon are properly positioned in their orbits relative to the sun, lines 19–23 use CenterX and CenterY in the DMove functions for each of the objects. This shifts the whole assembly so that the sun is at the center of the window with the planets and the moon properly positioned around it. At the end of the PositionBodies function, the CCircles objects Sun, Earth, Venus, Mercury and Moon have all been updated to positions appropriate for the current value of PhiEarth. The OnDraw function then continues on to draw the solar system into the window. When the program begins,

Table 8.13 Listing of PositionBodies from PlanetsDoc.cpp

```
01    /* This is the listing of the PositionBodies function*/
02    void CPlanetsDoc::PositionBodies(int CenterX, int CenterY)
03    {
04         Earth = oEarth;
05         Venus = oVenus;
06         Mercury = oMercury;
07         Sun = oSun;
08         Moon = oMoon;
09         double PhiMcy, PhiV, PhiMn;
10         PhiV = PhiEarth * 365./225.;      //VenusYear = 225 days
11         PhiMcy = PhiEarth * 365./88.;     //MercuryYear = 88 days
12         PhiMn = PhiEarth * 365./27.;      //LunarMonth = 27 days
13         Earth.GRotate(PhiEarth, 0, 0);
14         Venus.GRotate(PhiV, 0, 0);
15         Mercury.GRotate(PhiMcy, 0, 0);
16         double RadMn = oMoon.m_xBP - oEarth.m_xBP;
17         Moon.Move(Earth.m_xBP + RadMn, Earth.m_yBP);
18         Moon.GRotate(PhiMn, Earth.m_xBP, Earth.m_yBP);
19         Earth.DMove(CenterX,CenterY);
20         Venus.DMove(CenterX,CenterY);
21         Mercury.DMove(CenterX,CenterY);
22         Sun.DMove(CenterX,CenterY);
23         Moon.DMove(CenterX,CenterY);
24    }
```

the earth angle is initialized to PhiEarth = 0 and the planets and moon are displayed in a straight line to the right of the sun with the sun centered in the window. Clicking on the Start Animation menu bar item executes the SetTimer function to start the timer. In the OnTimer function each tick then increments PhiEarth by -2.5 degrees. A negative value is used so that a counter-clockwise rotation takes place. Figure 8.8 shows the solar system animation about "six months" after clicking Start. At any time, clicking on the menu bar item Stop and Reset will turn off the timer and reposition the solar system to its initial in-line position by setting PhiEarth = 0.

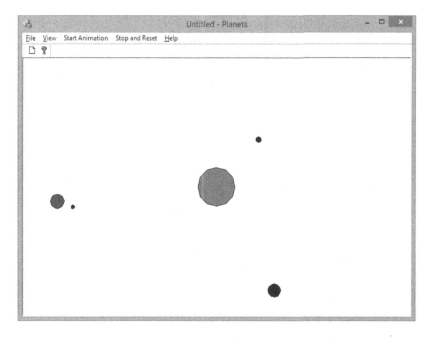

Figure 8.8 The Planet Simulation "Six Months" After Start Up

8.5 A Simple Robot Animation

The solar system animation in Section 8.4 provides an introduction to the animation process. It also demonstrates the advantage of using C++ classes and objects to conveniently organize the animation operations. In this section we will extend these concepts to describe the animation of a simple robot in two dimensions. This project is in the folder *Chap8\5_MiniRobot* and, of course, you should build and execute it to become familiar with its operation. Clicking on the menu bar Start button will initiate an animation sequence with the robot picking up a ball and dropping it into a hole. Figure 8.9 shows the robot at several points in the animation. The animation process is continuous, recycling until the Stop

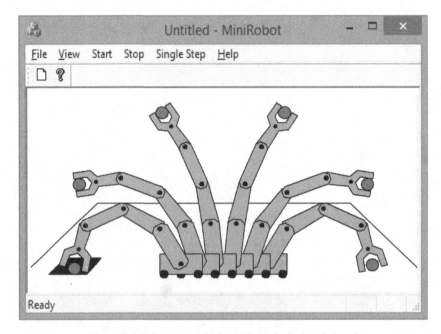

Figure 8.9 A Sequence of Images from the Robot Animation

button on the menu bar is clicked. The Single Step button on the menu bar allows a single step in the animation to take place. Notice also that the arrow keys allow the whole image to be moved around the window. We will now describe the program operation rather carefully but in order to appreciate the full detail you will have to carefully explore the project files in *Chap8\5_MiniRobot*.

8.5.1 The robot model

The OnNewDocument function for the MiniRobot is shown in Table 8.14. It begins in lines 07 and 08 with an initial definition of the document member variables BaseXo and BaseYo which serve to locate the overall image in the window. Lines 09–19 are then used to define a pair of two dimensional polygons in window coordinates which are intended to give the impression of a three dimensional floor with a hole in it. You can see the floor and the hole representation in Figure 8.9. Line 20 in Table 8.14 calls the function InitializeRobot which creates and initializes the robot, preparing it for the animation. Line 21 initializes the variable MotionParam to zero. MotionParam is used as a parameter to govern the overall animation. As MotionParam is incremented in steps through a range of values from zero to five, the robot animation cycle takes place. The animation becomes a repetitive process by resetting MotionParam to zero whenever it becomes greater than five. In this arrangement, the actual range of values for MotionParam is arbitrary. We have selected the zero to five range to define the animation cycle and, as you will see, we have tuned the robot movement for that range of values.

The InitializeRobot function is called at line 20 of OnNewDocument. The last portion of InitializeRobot is shown in Table 8.15 and includes its more important lines of code. Lines 02–10 in Table 8.15 define the

Table 8.14 Listing of OnNewDocument from MiniRobotDoc.cpp

```
01   /* This is the listing of the OnNewDocument function*/
02   BOOL CMiniRobotDoc::OnNewDocument()
03   {
04       if (!CDocument::OnNewDocument()) return FALSE;
05       // TODO: add reinitialization code here
06       // (SDI documents will reuse this document)
07       BaseXo = 600;
08       BaseYo = 450;
09       CPoint FloorArray[4];
10       FloorArray[0].SetPoint(-700,700);
11       FloorArray[1].SetPoint(700,700);
12       FloorArray[2].SetPoint(300,300);
13       FloorArray[3].SetPoint(-300,300);
14       Floor.Adjust2DShape(4,FloorArray);
15       FloorArray[0].SetPoint(-65,75);
16       FloorArray[1].SetPoint(25,75);
17       FloorArray[2].SetPoint(60,35);
18       FloorArray[3].SetPoint(-25,35);
19       FloorHole.Adjust2DShape(4,FloorArray);
20       InitializeRobot();
21       MotionParam = 0.;
22       return TRUE;
23   }
```

coordinates of points that describe the robot's last link as an open jaw. This link is identified as the JawOpenArray. SetPoint is used to define the point coordinates for JawOpenArray in lines 03–10, creating the shape shown in Figure 8.10. The coordinate system used is in the form of the windows coordinate system (with y positive downward) and the fifteen points making up the open jaw shape are labeled as points 0–14 in Figure 8.10. Notice that the other link geometries (including the closed jaw) have been created earlier in InitializeRobot. A vertical orientation has been assumed and the shapes have been defined in local coordinates. The actual global position of the open jaw is specified by its base point coordinates which can be adjusted with Move and DMove function calls. Any use of the functions LRotate or GRotate will change its orientation.

Table 8.15 A Portion of InitializeRobot from MiniRobotDoc.cpp

```
01    /* Last portion of the listing of the InitializeRobot function*/
.
02    CPoint JawOpenArray[15];
03    JawOpenArray[0].SetPoint ( 15,0);      JawOpenArray[1].SetPoint ( 7,10);
04    JawOpenArray[2].SetPoint ( -7,10);     JawOpenArray[3].SetPoint (-15,0);
05    JawOpenArray[4].SetPoint (-12,-55);    JawOpenArray[5].SetPoint (-32,-70);
06    JawOpenArray[6].SetPoint (-35,-110);   JawOpenArray[7].SetPoint (-20,-110);
07    JawOpenArray[8].SetPoint (-17,-80);    JawOpenArray[9].SetPoint (0,-70);
08    JawOpenArray[10].SetPoint (17,-80);    JawOpenArray[11].SetPoint (20,-110);
09    JawOpenArray[12].SetPoint (35,-110);   JawOpenArray[13].SetPoint (32,-70);
10    JawOpenArray[14].SetPoint (12,-55);
11    oLink1.Adjust2DShape(8,Link1Array);
12    oLink2.Adjust2DShape(8,Link2Array);
13    oLink3.Adjust2DShape(8,Link3Array);
14    oJawClosed.Adjust2DShape(15,JawClosedArray);
15    oJawOpen.Adjust2DShape(15,JawOpenArray);
16    Base.AdjustRectangle(50,100);
17    Ball.AdjustCircle(30);
18    WheelL.AdjustCircle(20);
19    WheelR.AdjustCircle(20);
20    Bearing1.AdjustCircle(10);
21    Bearing2.AdjustCircle(10);
22    Bearing3.AdjustCircle(10);
23    Bearing4.AdjustCircle(10);
24    Bearing5.AdjustCircle(8);
25    }
```

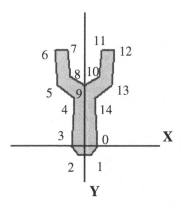

Figure 8.10 Layout of the Open Jaw from the Robot Animation

In the InitializeRobot function of Table 8.15, the code before line 02 (but not shown) defines the arrays Link1Array, Link2Array, Link3Array and JawClosedArray as needed to describe the geometry of the other robot parts. Lines 11–15 of Table 8.15 then make use of these arrays and the JawOpenArray to define the objects oLink1, oLink2, oLink3, oJawClosed and oJawOpen which will be used to represent these robot parts and preserve their initially specified vertical orientation. Line 16 of Table 8.15 defines the rectangular base of the robot. Finally, lines 17–24 make use of CCircles objects to define the ball to be handled by the robot, the wheels of the base, and the bearings to be used for the robot joints. Since the angular orientation of these circular items is not critical for appearance, we have not had to arrange to preserve their initial orientation as we did for the links and jaw.

8.5.2 Displaying the robot

Table 8.16 is a listing of the OnDraw function for the MiniRobot. Before drawing any portion of the robot scene, however, line 07 of this code calls the document class function PositionParts. This function orients and locates each robot part based on the current state of the animation and serves the same purpose as the PositionBodies function did in the Planets project. We will discuss the PositionParts function shortly. But once

Table 8.16 Listing of OnDraw from MiniRobotView.cpp

```
01    /* This is the listing of the OnDraw function*/
02    void CMiniRobotView::OnDraw(CDC* pDC)
03    {
04        CMiniRobotDoc* pDoc = GetDocument();
05        ASSERT_VALID(pDoc); if(!pDoc)return;
06        // TODO: add draw code for native data here
07        pDoc->PositionParts();
08        pDC->SelectObject(&m_BlackPen);
09        pDC->SelectObject(&m_BlackBrush);
10        pDoc->Floor.Show2DShape(pDC);
11        pDoc->FloorHole.Fill2DShape(pDC);
12        pDC->SelectObject(&m_GrayBrush);
13        pDoc->Base.FillRect(pDC);
14        pDoc->Link2.Fill2DShape(pDC);
15        pDoc->Link1.Fill2DShape(pDC);
16        pDoc->Jaw.Fill2DShape(pDC);
17        pDoc->Link3.Fill2DShape(pDC);
18        pDC->SelectObject(&m_RedBrush);
19        pDoc->Ball.FillCirc(pDC);
20        pDC->SelectObject(&m_BlackBrush);
21        pDoc->Bearing1.FillCirc(pDC);
22        pDoc->Bearing2.FillCirc(pDC);
23        pDoc->Bearing3.FillCirc(pDC);
24        pDoc->Bearing4.FillCirc(pDC);
25        pDoc->Bearing5.FillCirc(pDC);
26        pDoc->WheelL.FillCirc(pDC);
27        pDoc->WheelR.FillCirc(pDC);
28    }
```

it has been called to position the parts, the OnDraw function then continues the display process. Lines 08–11 select a black pen and brush and then draw the floor for the scene along with the hole in the floor. The robot links are drawn in with a gray brush in lines 12–17 where the order of drawing for the links has been adjusted to give the impression that certain links are located behind others. For example, by being drawn after Base, Link1 appears on the viewer's side of the Base. While Link2 is drawn early so that it appears behind both Link1 and Link3. Lines 18 and 19 draw the robot's red ball and then lines 20–27 use a black brush to draw in all of the robot bearings and the wheels of the base.

8.5.3 Positioning and orienting the robot parts

The PositionParts function can be seen in its entirety in the folder *Chap8\5_MiniRobot*. We have shown some selected code in Table 8.17 where you can see that lines 06–13 set the angular position of each of the robot links according to the current value of MotionParam. For example, PhiLink1, the angle of Link1 varies from 30 degrees to negative 30 degrees as MotionParam varies from zero to two. Similarly, the jaw angle PhiJaw varies for the same range of MotionParam from 165° to -165°. Lines 07–13 apply to the first portion of the animation as controlled by the if statement of line 06. During an animation, the OnTimer function increments MotionParam in steps of 0.1 over its range from zero to five. When single stepping, each click of the Single Step button also creates an increment of 0.1 in MotionParam. In lines 06–13 the robot is advancing as MotionParam increases to a value of two. Lines 14–22 take over in the next motion phase, fixing the positions of the robot links and its base while moving the ball back into the scene from the right hand side. The next phase of robot motion with MotionParam increasing from three to five (this has not been included in Table 8.17) moves the robot back to the right ready to pick up the ball when the animation cycle begins again.

The first portion of the PositionParts function defines the link and jaw angles in terms of MotionParam. The next stage is to define the exact link positions at each increment in MotionParam. Lines 25–34 contain the statements defining the x and y base point coordinates of each link. These coordinate values represent the positions for the links and are used in Move functions to position the links at each step. Line 25 sets the variable LinkL = 100 since each of the links that we have in our MiniRobot (including the jaw) has been defined with a length of 100 from center to center of the robot joints. DpRad is used to convert angles in degrees to angles in radians.

Table 8.17 Selected Code From PositionParts in MiniRobotDoc.cpp

```
01    /* These are segments of code from the PositionParts function*/
02    void CMiniRobotDoc::PositionParts(void)
03    {
04        .
05        .
06    if (MotionParam < 2.05)
07        {
08        PhiLink1 = 30 - MotionParam * 30;
09        PhiLink2 = 60 - MotionParam * 60;
10        PhiLink3 = 115 - MotionParam * 115;
11        PhiJaw = 165 - MotionParam * 165;
12        BaseX = BaseXo - MotionParam *100;
13        }
14    if ((MotionParam > 2.05) && (MotionParam < 3.05))
15        {
16        PhiLink1 = -30;
17        PhiLink2 = -60;
18        PhiLink3 = -115;
19        PhiJaw = -165;
20        BaseX  = BaseXo - 200;
21        BallX = BaseXo + 950 - (MotionParam - 2)* 700;
22        }
24        .
25        double LinkL = 100;      double DpRad = 180./3.14159;
26        Link1X = BaseX;          Link1Y = BaseY;
27        Link2X = Link1X+LinkL*sin(PhiLink1/DpRad);
28        Link2Y = Link1Y-LinkL*cos(PhiLink1/DpRad);
29        Link3X = Link2X+LinkL*sin(PhiLink2/DpRad);
30        Link3Y = Link2Y-LinkL*cos(PhiLink2/DpRad);
31        JawX = Link3X+LinkL*sin(PhiLink3/DpRad);
32        JawY = Link3Y-LinkL*cos(PhiLink3/DpRad);
33        BallJawX = JawX+LinkL*sin(PhiJaw/DpRad);
34        BallJawY = JawY-LinkL*cos(PhiJaw/DpRad);
35        .
36        Link2 = oLink2;
37        Link2.Move(Link2X, Link2Y);
38        Link2.LRotate(PhiLink2);
39        .
40        Jaw = oJawOpen;
41        if ((MotionParam > .05) && (MotionParam < 1.85)) Jaw = oJawClosed;
42        Jaw.Move(JawX, JawY);
43        Jaw.LRotate(PhiJaw);
44        .
```

In line 26, the coordinates of Link1 are set to the coordinates of the Base. Lines 27 and 28 use trigonometry to swing Link1 through the angle PhiLink1 to find its endpoint coordinates and set the values of Link2X and Link2Y for the base point position of Link2. Similarly, lines 29 and 30 use the end point coordinates for Link2 and determine Link3X and Link3Y to position the base point of Link3. Lines 31 and 32 then position Jaw at the end of Link3. And lines 33 and 34 provide the location where the ball should be positioned to be within the jaw.

Lines 36–38 in the PositionParts function are typical of the code used to position each link. Line 36 sets Link2 equal to oLink2 in order to recover the initial vertical orientation of the link. Line 37 moves Link2 to locate it at its calculated end position. Then line 38 calls LRotate to perform the local rotation of Link2 about its base point into its appropriate orientation. Lines 40–43 handle the positioning of Jaw in a similar way. In this case, lines 40 and 41 recover the oJawOpen or oJawClosed configuration (each with vertical orientation) according to the value of MotionParam. Line 42 moves Jaw to its calculated end position and line 43 performs the local rotation which completes the orientation. Figure 8.11 provides some insight into this process. Figure 8.11a shows the resulting robot appearance if the LRotate of line 38 were removed and Figure 8.11b shows the resulting appearance if the LRotate of line 43 were excluded.

The programming described above handles the robot definition and animation operations. The basic user interactions provided by the project include Start, Stop and Single Step. Each of these is implemented by simple functions. When the "Start" button is clicked on the menu bar, its function simply starts the timer. The OnTimer function increments MotionParam by 0.1 with each tick and if MotionParam has exceeded five, it resets MotionParam to zero. After this, OnTimer concludes by calling UpdateAllViews, executing OnDraw to reposition and redisplay the robot. If the user clicks "Stop", the timer is stopped. And, if the user clicks "Single Step" on the menu bar, MotionParam is incremented by 0.1 with each click and UpdateAllviews is called.

In addition to controlling the robot animation, the position of the whole image in the window can be adjusted by use of the arrow keys on

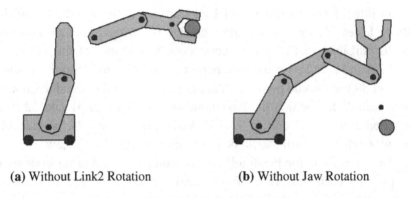

(a) Without Link2 Rotation   **(b)** Without Jaw Rotation

Figure 8.11 Robot Images with Excluded Link Rotations

the keyboard. This feature has been provided by using the document class member variables BaseXo and BaseYo which were initially defined in OnNewDocument. All of the floor and robot images are presented relative to these coordinates (for example, see lines 12 and 20 of Table 8.17). In this way, the OnKeyDown function responds to an arrow key input by incrementing BaseXo (left or right arrows) or incrementing BaseYo (up and down arrows). Following an arrow keystroke, a call to UpdateAllViews redraws the whole image at the new location.

8.6 Exercises

1. Modify the TwoDPoints project in the folder *Chap8\1_TwoDPoints* so that the Show2DPoint member function of the class C2DPoints can display points with a specified color. Add an argument to the Show2DPoint function (see Table 8.1) using the variable type COLORREF and new coding which displays the points in the color specified by the COLORREF variable. Modify the OnDraw function using your new Show2DPoint function appropriately to make the following displays: (a) all of the points in blue, (b) half of the points in blue, half of the points in red and (c) all of the points in random colors by using the rand() function and the RGB function.

2. Change the shape in the TwoDShapes project located in the folder *Chap8\2_TwoDShapes*. Make it a simple "L" shape with six vertex points, equal leg lengths of 100 pixels, and a leg width of 25 pixels. The local origin should be at the outside corner of the "L".

3. Develop a new shape class called CLShape. Similar to the other shape classes, it should have an empty constructor function, an AdjustLShape function and rotate and translate capability. The AdjustLShape function should accept arguments for leg length and leg width. Exercise your new class by (a) using it in a program which will allow local rotations, global rotations and translations similar to the TwoDShapes project of *Chap8\2_TwoDShapes*. And by (b) creating a program that will place three different LShapes across a window (one a filled shape, one a line drawn shape and one drawn only with points). Allow the shapes to be rotated and translated by keyboard or menu bar items.

4. Create and animate a "top view" of a vehicle moving around a simple race track. Use line drawings of CCircle objects to create the track. Use a CRectangle object for the top view of the vehicle body and four CRectangle objects for the tires. Of course, the tires are to be properly positioned relative to the vehicle body and the vehicle assembly then is to be positioned appropriately on the track. When the up arrow key is struck, a timer should start moving the vehicle around the track. When the down arrow key is struck, the vehicle should stop and return to its initial position.

5. As an exercise to consider the details of the MiniRobot project in *Chap8\5_MiniRobot*, change the project so that the robot's operation is reversed. Adjust the code in the project to have the robot retrieve balls from the black hole on the left of the screen and deposit them on the floor at the right side of the screen where they roll off the screen further to the right. The robot should then move back to the left, retrieve another ball from the hole, etc.

Chapter 9

Classes for Graphs, Plotting and Calculations

In Chapter 8 we considered the creation of our own classes for use in Visual C++/MFC programming and we demonstrated strategies for integrating those classes into animation programs. The focus in Chapter 8 was on developing classes for display and manipulation of two-dimensional geometric shapes. In this chapter we extend the use of classes and objects to the representation of graphs and curves and we show how these tools can be used effectively by integrating them into example technical calculations.

This chapter begins by developing a class structure to describe graphs including a process for easily plotting data onto a graph. Issues of positioning, scaling, and drawing the graph must all be considered. Using the graph class, it is easy to generate multiple graph objects and we include an example for handling an array of graphs. Next, the addition of a class for text labels makes it convenient to place and manipulate text to be used for labeling graphs and also for labeling other items on a display. We return to the planet animation of Chapter 8 where we add a pair of labeled graphs and continuously display them during the animation. The chapter closes by addressing the problem of color contour plotting and we develop classes and functions which facilitate color contour plotting. The final illustrative example applies our contour plotting tools to represent a typical stress distribution in a beam.

9.1 Developing Classes for Graphs and Curves

The ability to plot graphs is an essential part of computing, analysis, and the performance of technical calculations. The project found in

Chap9\1_Grapher provides an example of plotting graphs in the object-oriented Windows environment. Building and executing the Grapher program should result in the graph shown in Figure 9.1. The graph can be easily positioned in the window by clicking the left mouse button to relocate its lower left corner. Scaling of the graph is also easily performed, using a right mouse click to move the upper right corner of the graph while the lower left corner stays in place. Similarly, the left and right arrow keys move the graph left and right while the up and down arrow keys rescale the graph. We will now discuss the programming behind this example.

The Grapher program relies on a set of classes contained in the file GraphClasses.h which has been included in the project folder of *Chap9\1_Grapher*. The strategy used in this object-oriented approach to drawing graphs is to separate the structure of the graph and its axes from

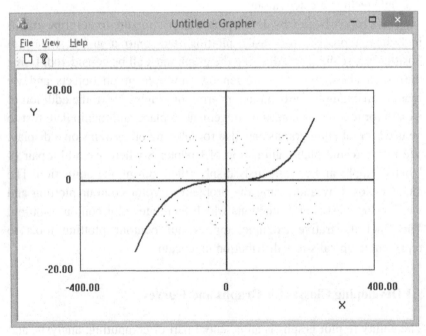

Figure 9.1 The Grapher Window after Position and Scale Adjustments

the data that is to be plotted onto the graph. We create both a class for the graphs (called CGraphs) and a class for the curves that may be plotted on the graphs (called CCurves). Working together, these classes provide a set of convenient tools for plotting graphs. With appropriate modification, the approach can be used for a variety of graph plotting needs. Let's begin the discussion of the class arrangement by considering the CGraphs class where the following member variables are declared:

int m_xBP, m_yBP;
int m_xDisplayLength, m_yDisplayLength;
double m_xVarMin, m_ xVarMax;
double m_ yVarMin, m_yVarMax;

The member variables m_xBP and m_yBP define the base position of a graph object by specifying the x and y window coordinates for the lower left graph corner as it will be drawn in the window. These are the usual window coordinates in pixels with the origin at the upper left of the window. The next set of variables defines the size of the graph as it is to be drawn into the window. The extent of the x axis in pixels is given by m_xDisplayLength and the extent of the y axis is defined by m_yDisplayLength. Scaling of the graph is based on the next set of member variables that define the ranges of x and y to be plotted on the graph. The range for the x variable is from m_xVarMin to m_xVarMax and the range for the y variable is from m_yVarMin to m_yVarMax. Notice that these are double precision variables. Additional variables describing the pens to be used in drawing the graph and curves are defined in appropriate member functions when needed.

In addition to the member variables above, the member functions below have also been provided to manipulate objects of the class CGraphs:

CGraphs
AdjustGraph
ShowGraph
PlotPoints
PlotLines

MoveGraph
DMoveGraph
NewUpRghtCorner
StretchGraph

The member function CGraphs is an empty constructor function while the AdjustGraph function actually serves to define graph objects of the CGraphs class. ShowGraph is used to draw the graph axes and labels onto the display and PlotPoints places data points onto the graph. Similarly, PlotLines connects data points on the graph with straight lines. MoveGraph and DMoveGraph provide the ability to reposition a graph on the display by resetting m_xBP and m_yBP. The functions NewUpRghtCorner and StretchGraph allow graphs to be re-scaled by adjusting member variables m_xDisplayLength and m_yDisplayLength. In the discussion below, we won't be able to describe all of these functions in detail but we will discuss the more important ones. Of course, you can always explore the project folder *Chap9\1_Grapher* to see all of the CGraphs code. The graph classes, functions, etc. are all located in the file GraphClasses.h.

The CGraphs member function AdjustGraph is shown in Table 9.1. This is the function that initializes member variables for graph objects. In Table 9.1, lines 05 and 06 of AdjustGraph set the graph's base position coordinates m_xBP and m_yBP from the CPoint input parameter DisplayOrigin. Similarly, lines 07 and 08 define the x and y display lengths in terms of the CSize input parameter DisplaySize. Then lines 09–12 set the range of x and y variables for the plot directly from the corresponding input arguments.

9.1.1 Displaying a graph

The member variables of CGraphs, as defined by the AdjustGraph function are sufficient to describe the basic character of a graph. With this information, it is possible to display the graph on the screen ready to

Table 9.1 Listing of AdjustGraph from GraphClasses.h

```
01   /* This is the Listing of AdjustGraph */
02   void CGraphs::AdjustGraph (CPoint DisplayOrigin, CSize DisplaySize,
03          double xvarmin, double yvarmin, double xvarmax, double yvarmax)
04   {
05          m_xBP = DisplayOrigin.x;
06          m_yBP = DisplayOrigin.y;
07          m_xDisplayLength = DisplaySize.cx;
08          m_yDisplayLength = DisplaySize.cy;
09          m_xVarMin = xvarmin;
10          m_yVarMin = yvarmin;
11          m_xVarMax = xvarmax;
12          m_yVarMax = yvarmax;
13   }
```

have curves plotted onto it. The basic graph drawing operations are provided in the ShowGraph function of the CGraphs class. Table 9.2 contains the more significant lines of code for the graph drawing process in the ShowGraph function. In Table 9.2, the device context pointer pDC is received by ShowGraph as an input parameter in line 02. Lines 04–08 declare several variables and create one and two pixel pens. Then, using pDC, line 09 selects the one pixel pen width and line 10 moves the pen to the lower left corner of the graph area. Lines 11–14 then draw a box around the graph area using the member variables for base position coordinates and the x and y display lengths.

In the if statement of line 15, the range of y values is considered. If the line y = 0 falls within the graph and is to be drawn, line 16 establishes the scale for the y axis and line 17 determines the scaled location of y = 0 within the graph. The statements of lines 18 and 19 begin the process of placing the y = 0 line into the graph by displaying the "0" label at the proper position. Lines 20–23 then define the pixel coordinates of the beginning and end of the line to be drawn. Line 24 selects the wider pen for drawing and lines 25 and 26 draw the y = 0 line into the graph as a heavier line than the box of lines 11–14. Quite similarly, the if statement of line 28 checks the range of x values and if the x = 0 line is to be drawn, lines 29–38 proceed to draw it and label it.

Table 9.2 Partial Listing of Show Graph from GraphClasses.h

```
01   /* Partial Listing of ShowGraph */
02   void CGraphs::ShowGraph(CDC* pDC)
03   {
04          double xLineStart, yLineStart, xLineEnd, yLineEnd; int ex,wye;
05          CPen m_Pen1Pix, m_Pen2Pix; CString buffer;
06          m_Pen1Pix.DeleteObject();  m_Pen2Pix.DeleteObject();
07          m_Pen1Pix.CreatePen(PS_SOLID, 1, RGB(0, 0, 0));
08          m_Pen2Pix.CreatePen(PS_SOLID, 2, RGB(0, 0, 0));
09          pDC->SelectObject(&m_Pen1Pix);
10          pDC->MoveTo(m_xBP,m_yBP);
11          pDC->LineTo(m_xBP+m_xDisplayLength,m_yBP);
12          pDC->LineTo(m_xBP+m_xDisplayLength,m_yBP-m_yDisplayLength);
13          pDC->LineTo(m_xBP,m_yBP-m_yDisplayLength);
14          pDC->LineTo(m_xBP,m_yBP);
15   if((m_yVarMax>0)&&(m_yVarMin<=0))  {
16          double yScale=m_yDisplayLength/(m_yVarMax-m_yVarMin);
17          double yScaledOrigin = m_yBP-yScale*(0.0 - m_yVarMin);
18          ex=int (m_xBP-20);  wye=int( yScaledOrigin-10);
19          if(m_yVarMin<0) pDC->TextOut(ex,wye,L"0");
20          xLineStart=double(m_xBP);
21          yLineStart=yScaledOrigin;
22          xLineEnd=m_xBP+m_xDisplayLength;
23          yLineEnd=yScaledOrigin;
24          pDC->SelectObject(&m_Pen2Pix);
25          pDC->MoveTo(int(xLineStart),int(yLineStart));
26          pDC->LineTo(int(xLineEnd),int(yLineEnd));
27   }
28   if((m_xVarMax>0)&&(m_xVarMin<=0))  {
29          double xScale=m_xDisplayLength/(m_xVarMax-m_xVarMin);
30          double xScaledOrigin = m_xBP+xScale*(0.0 - m_xVarMin);
31          ex=int(xScaledOrigin-5);  wye=int(m_yBP+15);
32          if(m_xVarMin<0) pDC->TextOut(ex,wye,L"0");
33          xLineStart=xScaledOrigin;  yLineStart=m_yBP;
34          xLineEnd=xScaledOrigin;  yLineEnd=m_yBP-m_yDisplayLength;
35          pDC->SelectObject(&m_Pen2Pix);
36          pDC->MoveTo(int(xLineStart),int(yLineStart));
37          pDC->LineTo(int(xLineEnd),int(yLineEnd));
38   }
39          ex=m_xBP-20; wye=m_yBP+15;
40          buffer.Format(L"%6.2f",m_xVarMin);
41          pDC->TextOut(ex,wye,buffer);
42   .
43   .
44   .
```

The last portion of the ShowGraph function completes the display of the graph (without yet plotting any data) by placing labels on the x and y axes. As an example of the labeling, lines 39–41 use the value of m_xVarMin as the label for the lower limit of the x axis. Following this, the upper limit of x is also displayed along with the y axis limits and finally nominal labels of "x" and "y" are inserted to identify the axes. The sample graph of Figure 9.1 contains the box outlining the range of the graph, the x and y axes and the basic set of labels.

9.1.2 The CCurves class

In the previous sections we described the CGraphs class and discussed its member function ShowGraph as a means for drawing the graph area and the graph axes along with simple labels. In this section we will look at a class for conveniently handling data to be plotted onto a graph. This is the CCurves class with its declaration as shown in Table 9.3. The member variables m_NumCrvPnts, m_XPlot and m_YPlot in lines 04–06 store the number of data points on the curve and provide arrays to store the x and y coordinates of each of the data points.

Table 9.3 Listing of the CCurves Class from GraphClasses.h

```
01   /* This is the class CCurves */
02   class CCurves {
03   public:
04        int m_NumCrvPnts;
05        double m_XPlot[500];
06        double m_YPlot[500];
07   public:
08        CCurves () {}
09   void CCurves::AdjustCurve (int numpnts, double* PtXPlot, double* PtYPlot)
10        {
11             m_NumCrvPnts = numpnts;
12             for (int i = 0; i < m_NumCrvPnts; i++) {
13                  m_XPlot[i] = *(PtXPlot + i);
14                  m_YPlot[i] = *(PtYPlot + i);
15             }
16        }
17   };
```

Line 08 shows the empty constructor function. The AdjustCurve function beginning at line 09 of Table 9.3 is used to define the member variables for individual curve objects. The input arguments in line 09 include pointers to arrays containing the x and y data point coordinates. The member variable m_NumCrvPnts for the number of data points is set in line 11 based on the input parameter and the for loop of lines 12–15 sets the values of the arrays m_XPlot and m_YPlot for the x and y coordinates provided.

9.1.3 Plotting in the CGraphs class

The CGraphs class contains a PlotPoints function for the direct plotting of data points onto a graph. Data points are contained in a CCurves object and are plotted into a CGraphs object. The PlotPoints function of CGraphs is shown in Table 9.4. Line 02 shows the input arguments as a pointer to a device context and a pointer to a CCurves object. Lines 04 and 05 establish the scales of the x and y axes based on the member variable values for the current graph. The for loop of lines 06–15 then processes each of the points on the curve. Lines 07 and 08 obtain the x and y coordinate values for each data point. Then, the if statement of

Table 9.4 Listing of CGraphs::PlotPoints from GraphClasses.h

```
01    /* This is the  Listing of CGraphs::PlotPoints */
02    void CGraphs::PlotPoints(CDC* pDC, CCurves* pCurve)
03    {
04            double xScale = m_xDisplayLength/(m_xVarMax-m_xVarMin);
05            double yScale = m_yDisplayLength/(m_yVarMax-m_yVarMin);
06            for (int i=0;i<pCurve->m_NumCrvPnts;I++)  {
07            double TempX=pCurve->m_XPlot[i];
08            double TempY=pCurve->m_YPlot[i];
09            if ((TempX<m_xVarMax)&&(TempX>m_xVarMin)&&
10                 (TempY<m_yVarMax)&&(TempY>m_yVarMin)) {
11            int xScaledPoint = int (m_xBP+xScale*(TempX-m_xVarMin));
12            int yScaledPoint = int (m_yBP-yScale*(TempY-m_yVarMin));
13            pDC->SetPixel(xScaledPoint,yScaledPoint,0);
14            }
15            }
16    }
```

lines 09 and 10 checks to see if the point falls within the graph area. If it does, lines 11 and 12 scale it accordingly and position it relative to the graph base position. Line 13 then places a pixel at the appropriate data point position. After the for loop completes its execution for all of the data points (m_NumCrvPnts), plotting of the curve is completed and points falling outside the graph area have been excluded. The sine curve shown in Figure 9.1 was plotted by the PlotPoints function. The cubic curve plotted with a solid line in Figure 9.1 was plotted with the member function PlotLines which is also contained in the file GraphClasses.h. It will not be discussed here but its operation is very similar to the PlotPoints function.

9.2 Operation of the Grapher Program

The basic tools for plotting graphs have been provided in the CGraphs class and the CCurves class as discussed in Section 9.1 above. The Grapher program in the folder *Chap9\1_Grapher* makes use of these classes to present the basic graph shown as an example in Figure 9.1. We will now explore the coding in Grapher to see how the classes are utilized. You will want to have the Grapher project loaded into the Visual Studio development environment so that you can follow the discussion below.

In the Class View window, expanding CGrapherDoc shows the document class member variables Curve1 and Curve2 which are objects of the CCurves class. GraphA of the CGraphs class also appears as a member variable. The OnNewDocument function is shown in Table 9.5 and serves to define Curve1and Curve2 so that the curves are ready for plotting. It also defines the graph object GraphA so that it is ready to display the curves. Line 07 in Table 9.5 declares two arrays to hold data point values and line 08 sets Npoints = 100. The for loop of lines 09–12 then defines the x and y coordinate values for the 100 data points. Line 10 generates 100 x values beginning at x = -250 and line 11 generates 100 y values as a sinusoidal function of x. After these data points have

Table 9.5 Listing of OnNewDocument from GrapherDoc.cpp

```
01   /* This is the  Listing of OnNewDocument */
02   BOOL CGrapherDoc::OnNewDocument()
03   {
04        if (!CDocument::OnNewDocument()) return FALSE;
05        // TODO: add reinitialization code here
06        // (SDI documents will reuse this document)
07        double xPlot[100], yPlot[100];
08        int Npoints = 100;
09        for (int i = 0; i < Npoints; i++)  {
10        xPlot[i] = -250 + 5 * i;
11        yPlot[I] = 10. * sin (.05 * xPlot[i]);
12        }
13        Curve1.AdjustCurve(Npoints,xPlot,yPlot);
14        Npoints = 50;
15        for (i = 0; i < Npoints; i++)  {
16        xPlot[i] = -250 + 10 * i;
17        yPlot[i] = pow(xPlot[i], 3) * 1.e-06;
18        }
19        Curve2.AdjustCurve(Npoints,xPlot,yPlot);
20        double xMin = -400;    double xMax = 400;
21        double yMin = -20;     double yMax = 20;
22        CPoint Origin(200,300); CSize GraphSize (300,200);
23        GraphA.AdjustGraph (Origin, GraphSize, xMin, yMin, xMax, yMax);
24        return TRUE;
25   }
```

all been generated, line 13 uses AdjustCurve to define the member variables of Curve1 so that it contains the data points generated by the for loop.

After Curve1 has been defined, line 14 resets Npoints to 50 and the for loop of lines 15–18 prepares another data set. Line 16 sets the x values, again beginning with x = -250. Line 17 then sets the y values as a cubic function of x. After execution of the for loop, we have 50 data points representing the cubic function. Line 19 uses AdjustCurve so that the curve object Curve 2 contains this data. You might notice that Curve1 and Curve2 have been scaled so that the range of x and y coordinate values for each is approximately the same. The remaining statements of OnNewDocument are now used to define GraphA to be suitable for displaying Curve1 and Curve2. The statements of lines 20 and 21 define suitable ranges for x and y to contain the data. Line 22 specifies the position and the size of the graph. The graph's origin will be at (200,300) in the usual pixel coordinates and, as specified by GraphSize, the graph area will extend 300 pixels in the x direction and 200 pixels in the y direction. Line 23 of Table 9.5 uses AdjustGraph and the information from lines 20–22 to define GraphA accordingly.

With the available CGraphs and CCurves classes and with the definitions of Curve1, Curve2 and GraphA made in OnNewDocument, we can now look at the OnDraw code of Table 9.6. This initiates the plotting of the graph and curves in the display window. OnDraw contains only three added lines of code. Line 07 uses the document pointer pDoc to call the ShowGraph function for GraphA. This displays the graph area and labeled axes. Line 08 calls the PlotPoints function for GraphA with a pointer to Curve1 as an argument. This plots the Curve1 data as points on GraphA. Finally, line 09 calls the function PlotLines to plot Curve2 on GraphA with its data points joined by straight lines. This sequence of statements places the initial graph in the window as the program starts. Adjustments in the graph sizing and positioning are then made with mouse clicks or by striking the arrow keys.

The function OnLButtonDown in Table 9.7 indicates how a graph can be manipulated. The code shown carries out the repositioning of the graph. Line 06 is the key statement here and calls the MoveGraph function for GraphA to move its base position to the mouse cursor coordinates received with the left button click. The MoveGraph function adjusts the base position member variables for GraphA. When line 07

Table 9.6 Listing of OnDraw from GrapherView.cpp

```
01   /* This is the Listing of OnDraw */
02   void CGrapherView::OnDraw(CDC* pDC)
03   {
04       CGrapherDoc* pDoc = GetDocument();
05       ASSERT_VALID(pDoc); if(!pDoc)return;
06       // TODO: add draw code for native data here
07       pDoc->GraphA.ShowGraph(pDC);
08       pDoc->GraphA.PlotPoints(pDC,&(pDoc->Curve1));
09       pDoc->GraphA.PlotLines(pDC,&(pDoc->Curve2));
10   }
```

Table 9.7 Listing of OnLButtonDown from GrapherView.cpp

```
01    /* This is the  Listing of OnLButtonDown */
02    void CGrapherView::OnLButtonDown(UINT nFlags, CPoint point)
03    {
04        // TODO: Add your message handler code here and/or call default
05        CGrapherDoc* pDoc = GetDocument();
06        pDoc->GraphA.MoveGraph(point.x,point.y);
07        pDoc->UpdateAllViews(NULL);
08        CView::OnLButtonDown(nFlags, point);
09    }
```

executes the UpdateAllViews function, the function OnDraw is re-executed and redraws the graph in its new position. The function OnRButtonDown operates in much the same way but calls on the function NewUpRghtCorner to re-scale the graph while leaving the base position unchanged. The OnKeyDown function similarly responds to key strokes on the arrow keys. Horizontal repositioning is performed by calling the function DMoveGraph with strokes of the left or right arrow keys. Re-scaling is performed by calling the function StretchGraph in response to the up or down arrow keys. All of these functions are in the file GraphClasses.h and can be inspected through Class View for the Grapher project.

9.3 Working with an Array of Graphs

The CGraphs and CCurves classes introduced in Section 9.1 and applied in Section 9.2 are convenient tools for manipulating families of graph or curve objects. The folder *Chap9\2_Grapher+* provides an example of dealing with multiple graphs by using those tools. If you build and execute the program Grapher+, you should see a display similar to Figure 9.2. The six graphs in Figure 9.2 show Curve1 and Curve2 of the previous section viewed with various scales for the x and y axes. The graphs can be manipulated by the program's drop down menu bar items. Clicking on **Display Graphs** allows the individual graphs to be toggled on and off in the display. Clicking on **Position Graphs** produces a

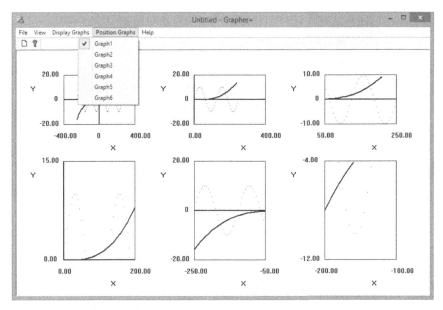

Figure 9.2 Selecting a Graph for Positioning with Grapher+

dropdown menu as shown in Figure 9.2 and allows a graph to be selected for positioning. Left mouse clicks move the base position of the selected graph and right mouse clicks change the graph scale and size.

The GraphClasses.h file described in Section 9.1 is part of the Grapher+ project so that the CGraphs and CCurves classes are available. This can be seen easily if you have Grapher+ in the Visual C++ environment and explore its Class View window. There you can see that the classes CGraphs and CCurves are part of the project structure. In the discussion below, we will describe the use of these classes to provide the graphing capabilities evident in Figure 9.2 for the Grapher+ program. Let's begin by considering the member variables in the document class. Looking carefully at the ClassView window for CGrapher+Doc shows the member variables Curve1 and Curve2 as objects of the CCurves class. The array of objects of the CGraphs class simply called Graph has also been included as a member variable. With the array Graph dimensioned at 10, up to ten graphs can be handled within the project.

Table 9.8 Partial Listing of OnNewDocument from Grapher+Doc.cpp

```
01    /* This is a  Partial Listing of OnNewDocument */
02    BOOL CGrapherDoc::OnNewDocument()
03    {
04        if (!CDocument::OnNewDocument()) return FALSE;
05        // TODO: add reinitialization code here
06        // (SDI documents will reuse this document)
07            .
08            .
09            .
10        CPoint Origin(100,150);      CSize GraphSize (150,100);
11        Graph[0].AdjustGraph (Origin, GraphSize, -400, -20, 400, 20);
12        Origin.SetPoint(375, 150);
13        Graph[1].AdjustGraph (Origin, GraphSize, 0, -20, 400, 20);
14        Origin.SetPoint(650, 150);
15        Graph[2].AdjustGraph (Origin, GraphSize, 50, -10, 250, 10);
16        Origin.SetPoint(100, 425); GraphSize.SetSize(150,200);
17        Graph[3].AdjustGraph (Origin, GraphSize, 0, 0, 200, 15);
18        Origin.SetPoint(375, 425);
19        Graph[4].AdjustGraph (Origin, GraphSize, -250, -20, -50, 20);
20        Origin.SetPoint(650, 425);
21        Graph[5].AdjustGraph (Origin, GraphSize, -200, -12, -100, -4);
22        return TRUE;
23    }
```

Table 9.8 shows most of the OnNewDocument function for Grapher+. It is used to define curves and graphs for the project just as it was for the original Grapher project. The three "dots" shown in Table 9.8 at lines 07–09 represent the definition of Curve1 (the sine curve) and Curve2 (the cubic) exactly as presented earlier in Table 9.5. In the remainder of Table 9.8, lines 10–21 define the six graphs seen in Figure 9.2. Lines 10 and 11 define Graph[0] ready to be placed in the upper left hand corner of the window. Similarly, lines 12–15 define Graph[1] and Graph[2] to fill out the top row of graphs. Then, lines 16–21 create the three graphs that will be placed in the bottom row.

The graphs are all drawn in the view class by OnDraw with the coding shown in Table 9.9. Here the for loop of lines 07–13 cycles through each of the graphs. Line 09 draws the graph area, axes and labels

Table 9.9 Listing of OnDraw from Grapher+View.cpp

```
01   /* This is the  Listing of OnDraw */
02   void CGrapherView::OnDraw(CDC* pDC)
03   {
04       CGrapherDoc* pDoc = GetDocument();
05       ASSERT_VALID(pDoc); if(!pDoc)return;
06       // TODO: add draw code for native data here
07   for (int i = 0; i < 6; i++)  {
08   if (m_DisplayGraph[i]=="Yes")  {
09        pDoc->Graph[i].ShowGraph(pDC);
10        pDoc->Graph[i].PlotPoints(pDC,&(pDoc->Curve1));
11        pDoc->Graph[i].PlotLines(pDC,&(pDoc->Curve2));
12        }
13        }
15   }
```

into the window. Lines 10 and 11 then plot Curve1 and Curve2 appropriately. After completion of the for loop, all six graphs are displayed. Of course, the display of any individual graph depends on whether the if statement of line 08 is satisfied. The array m_DisplayGraph is a member variable of the view class and each of its entries are initially set to "Yes" in the constructor CGrapherView so that all of the graphs are displayed at the start of the program.

An individual graph may be turned off by clicking on the menu bar item **Display Graphs** and then clicking the graph number to be removed in the resulting drop down menu,. These actions set the appropriate m_DisplayGraph entry to "No" and re-execute OnDraw. The function OnDisplaygraphsGraph1 is shown in Table 9.10 as an example. Here you can see lines 06–08 simply toggling the "Yes" and "No" values for m_DisplayGraph[0]. Line 08 executes an UpdateAllViews to redraw the window. In this way, repeated clicks of **Display Graphs > Graph1** will turn the first graph off and on in the display. The program code to toggle display of the other graphs is very much the same.

Repositioning of the individual graphs in Grapher+ is controlled through the view class member variable m_PositioningGraph. This variable is initialized at zero in the constructor CGrapherView to allow positioning of the first graph in Figure 9.2. It may be changed by clicking

Table 9.10 Listing of OnDisplaygraphsGraph1 from Grapher+View.cpp

```
01    /* This is the  Listing of OnDisplaygraphsGraph1 */
02    void CGrapherView::OnDisplaygraphsGraph1()
03    {
04        // TODO: Add your command handler code here
05        CGrapherDoc* pDoc = GetDocument();
06        if (m_DisplayGraph[0]=="Yes") {m_DisplayGraph[0]="No";}
07            else {m_DisplayGraph[0]="Yes";
08        }
09        pDoc->UpdateAllViews(NULL);
10    }
```

on the menu item **Position Graphs** and then the drop down menu entry. The event handler function for the corresponding graph simply sets m_PositioningGraph to the value for that graph to be positioned. Then, with left clicks, the code in the mouse function OnLButtonDown applies MoveGraph to reposition the desired graph. Similarly, with right clicks, OnRButtonDown uses NewUpRghtCorner for re-scaling the graph.

9.4 Adding Graphs and Text to the Planet Simulation

This section combines the graphing capability described in Sections 9.1 and 9.3 with the planet animations of Chapter 8. We also develop the class CTextBoxes as a convenient approach to manipulating and displaying text labels. The example program for this section is in the folder *Chap9\3_GTPlanets*. The program is very similar to the Planets project of Section 8.4 with the addition of a pair of graphs in the upper left and right corners and several text labels. Figure 9.3 shows the program window for the GTPlanets simulation after the earth has traveled two simulated revolutions (720 degrees) about the sun. The first graph plots the distance between Venus and Earth during the two revolutions and the second graph plots the distance between Mercury and Earth. The animation cycle has been adjusted to end and reset the planets after two revolutions of the earth.

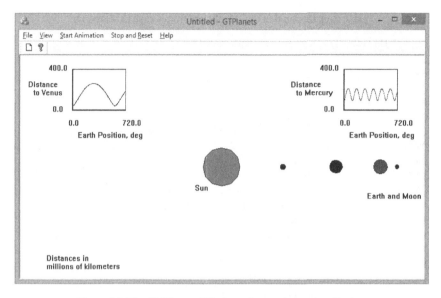

Figure 9.3 The GTPlanets Window after an Animation Cycle

9.4.1 The class CTextBoxes

The class CTextBoxes has been developed as a simple approach to placing and moving text labels during program execution. In Figure 9.3, text box objects are used as supplementary graph labels, as labels for the animation and to identify the distance units. The class CTextBoxes has been added to the file of CCurves and CGraphs classes and the file has been renamed GraphTxtClasses.h in the GTPlanets project. The class CTextBoxes can be seen in the Class View window of GTPlanets. Its declaration including functions is shown in Table 9.11. The member variables in lines 03 and 04 of Table 9.11 include the CString variable m_Text to hold a text string and the integer variables m_TextX and m_TextY to position the text. There is an empty constructor function in line 06. The AdjustTextBox function of lines 07–11 serves to define the string m_Text for a text box object and also its initial position m_TextX and m_TextY. The text box can then be moved by its Move function as

Table 9.11 Declaration of CTextBoxes from GraphTxtClasses.h

```
01    /* This is the Declaration of CTextBoxes */
02    class CTextBoxes {
03        CString m_Text;
04        int m_TextX, m_TextY;
05        public:
06        CTextBoxes::CTextBoxes(){};
07        void CTextBoxes::AdjustTextBox (int textx, int texty, CString textin) {
08            m_TextX = textx;
09            m_TextY = texty;
10            m_Text = textin;
11        }
12        void CTextBoxes::Move (int Mvx, int Mvy) {
13            m_TextX = Mvx;
14            m_TextY = Mvy;
15        }
16        void CTextBoxes::DMove (int DMvx, int DMvy) {
17            m_TextX += DMvx;
18            m_TextY += DMvy;
19        }
20        void CTextBoxes::ShowTextBox(CDC* pDC) {
21            pDC->TextOut(m_TextX, m_TextY, m_Text);
22        }
23    };
```

in lines 12–15 or function DMove in lines 16–19. The ShowTextBox function of lines 20–22 is used to display the text by calling the standard TextOut function in line 21. CTextBoxes is a very simple class but it provides a convenient approach to defining, positioning and displaying text labels and also arrays of text labels.

9.4.2 Modifying the planet simulation

Adding the file GraphTxtClasses.h to the planet simulation makes the classes CCurves, CGraphs and CTextBoxes all available within the project. This is readily apparent in the GTPlanets project folder *Chap9\3_GTPlanets* when you explore its Class View window. All of the member variables and functions for the added classes can be viewed through Class View. Let's now see how these new tools are used to combine the animation, graph plotting and labeling.

The first step is to consider the extra member variables used in the document class. These can be seen by expanding CGTPlanetsDoc in the Class View window. We have added the member variables GraphA and GraphB for the two graphs and Curve1 and Curve2 for the curves to be plotted. You will see that Curve1 carries the Earth-to-Venus distance data and Curve2 carries the Earth-to-Mercury data. For labeling we use an array of text boxes called Label and the number of active textboxes is NumLabels. The new member variable m_DistanceScale makes the distance scale for the planets available in any document class function.

All of the new member variables are initialized in the OnNewDocument function for GTPlanets as shown in Table 9.12. In this function, the "dots" of lines 07–09 represent the preparation of the original solar system member variables as shown previously in the OnNewDocument function of Table 8.11 for the basic planet simulation. Recall that the display is window centered and uses the OnSize function in placing the sun and planets in the center. Beginning in line 10 of Table 9.12, the graph and text variables are initialized. Lines 10–13 define GraphA while GraphB is defined in lines 14 and 15. The position of GraphA is to be near the upper left corner of the window and its pixel coordinates are given with respect to the window origin in line 12.

Table 9.12 Listing of OnNewDocument from GTPlanetsDoc.cpp

```
01   /* This is a Partial Listing of OnNewDocument */
02   BOOL CGTPlanetsDoc::OnNewDocument()
03   {
04       if (!CDocument::OnNewDocument()) return FALSE;
05       // TODO: add reinitialization code here
06       // (SDI documents will reuse this document)
07       .
08       .
09       .
10       double xMin=0; double xMax=720;
11       double yMin=0; double yMax=400;
12       CPoint OriginA(100,100); CPoint SizeA(100,75);
13       GraphA.AdjustGraph (OriginA, SizeA, xMin, yMin, xMax, yMax);
14       CPoint OriginB (0,0); CPoint SizeB (100,75);
```

Table 9.12 (*Continued*)

```
15      GraphB.AdjustGraph (OriginB, SizeB, xMin, yMin, xMax, yMax);
16      double InitialXs[500] = {0};  double InitialYs[500] = {0};
17      Curve1.AdjustCurve(0,InitialXs, InitialYs);
18      Curve2.AdjustCurve(0,InitialXs, InitialYs);
19      NumLabels = 10;
20      Label[0].AdjustTextBox(110,137, L"Earth Position, deg");
21      Label[1].AdjustTextBox(15,45, L"Distance");
22      Label[2].AdjustTextBox(25,60, L"to Venus");
23      Label[3].AdjustTextBox(0,0, L"Sun");
24      Label[4].AdjustTextBox(0,0, L"Earth Position, deg");
25      Label[5].AdjustTextBox(0,0, L"Distance");
26      Label[6].AdjustTextBox(0,0, L"to Mercury");
27      Label[7].AdjustTextBox(0,0, L"Earth and Moon");
28      Label[8].AdjustTextBox(0,0, L"Distances in");
29      Label[9].AdjustTextBox(0,0, L"millions of kilometers");
30      return TRUE;
31   }
```

GraphB, however, is intended to appear at the upper right of the window. Its coordinates depend on window size and are specifically set in the function PositionBodiesEtc just before drawing of the graph takes place. In lines 14 and 15, its position is temporarily set to (0,0). Lines 16–18 initialize Curve1 and Curve2. In line 19, NumLabels is set to 10 for the ten text labels used in the program. Lines 20–29 then initialize the labels. Label[0]–Label[2] are initialized in lines 20–22 and are used to label GraphA, these labels are positioned directly in pixel coordinates. The positions of all of the other labels depend on window size (just as the GraphB position and the solar system). They are set in the function PositionBodiesEtc just before they are displayed. For now, lines 23–29 of OnNewDocument set these initial label positions to (0,0).

During program start up, after OnNewDocument is finished, the OnDraw function of GTPlanets executes to place the initial display in the program window and it also executes whenever window adjustments take place. In addition, as in the original planet simulation, the OnDraw function executes at every stage of the animation whenever a tick of the animation clock activates OnTimer. The first action of OnDraw (as you will see in Table 9.14) is to make a call to the document class function PositionBodiesEtc where the new body positions are calculated and also

Table 9.13 Listing of PositionBodiesEtc from GTPlanetsDoc.cpp

```
01    /* This is a Partial Listing of PositionBodiesEtc */
02    void CGTPlanetsDoc::PositionBodiesEtc(int CenterX, int CenterY)
03    {
04        .
05        .
06        .
07        double Distance=(Earth.m_xBP-Venus.m_xBP)*(Earth.m_xBP-Venus.m_xBP)
08                      + (Earth.m_yBP-Venus.m_yBP)*(Earth.m_yBP-Venus.m_yBP);
09        Distance = sqrt(Distance)/m_DistanceScale;
10        Curve1.m_YPlot[Curve1.m_NumCrvPnts] = Distance;
11        Curve1.m_XPlot[Curve1.m_NumCrvPnts] = -PhiEarth;
12        Curve1.m_NumCrvPnts++;
13        Distance = (Earth.m_xBP-Mercury.m_xBP)*(Earth.m_xBP-Mercury.m_xBP)
14                      + (Earth.m_yBP-Mercury.m_yBP)*(Earth.m_yBP-Mercury.m_yBP);
15        Distance = sqrt(Distance)/m_DistanceScale;
16        Curve2.m_XPlot[Curve2.m_NumCrvPnts] = -PhiEarth;
17        Curve2.m_YPlot[Curve2.m_NumCrvPnts] = Distance;
18        Curve2.m_NumCrvPnts++;
19        GraphB.MoveGraph (2*CenterX - 150, 100);
20        Label[3].Move(int(Sun.m_xBP - 50), int(Sun.m_yBP + 30));
21        Label[4].Move(2*CenterX - 140, 137);
22        Label[5].Move(2*CenterX - 250 , 45);
23        Label[6].Move(2*CenterX - 240 , 60);
24        Label[7].Move(int(Earth.m_xBP - 25), int(Earth.m_yBP + 45));
25    if(Earth.m_yBP > CenterY) {
26        Label[7].Move(int(Earth.m_xBP-25), int(Earth.m_yBP-60));  }
27        Label[8].Move(50, 2*CenterY - 45);
28        Label[9].Move(50, 2*CenterY - 30);
29    }
```

the graph and label positions are determined. Table 9.13 shows the function PositionBodiesEtc. The function begins by positioning the solar system bodies exactly as in the original PositionBodies function of Table 8.13 and this is represented by the dots of lines 04–06 shown in Table 9.13 for PositionBodiesEtc.

Lines 07–18 update Curve1 and Curve2 at each step of the animation. Lines 07–09 calculate the distance between Venus and Earth and lines 10 and 11 set the x and y values for Curve1 at the current earth position (recall that the counter clockwise rotation of the planets requires negative values for PhiEarth). With a new point, line 12 increments the number of points in Curve1. Lines 13–18 operate in the same way to calculate the Mercury-to-Earth distance and update the Curve2 data. The remainder of the function PositionBodiesEtc handles graph and label positioning. The pixel coordinates of the center of the current window (CenterX and CenterY) are received as arguments by PositionBodiesEtc as shown in line 02 of Table 9.13. In line 19, the MoveGraph function is applied to GraphB to change its coordinates using the CenterX variable. This statement positions the origin of GraphB 150 pixels from the right side of the window and 100 pixels down from the top. Line 20 positions Label[3] (the "sun" label) just to the lower left of the sun. Lines 21–23 control the positioning of the labels for GraphB and make use of the Move function for text in order to position them appropriately relative to GraphB. Lines 24–26 position the label which follows the Earth and Moon motions. Finally lines 27 and 28 place the information note about units in the lower left corner of the window.

The OnDraw function for GTPlanets is relatively simple. It is shown in Table 9.14 and serves to display the planet simulation as reflected in the current document data. As indicated previously, its first action in line 07 calls the PositionBodiesEtc function above to update the simulation status and the positions of objects, labels, etc. Lines 08 and 09 display GraphA and place Curve1 on it. Lines 10 and 11 plot the Curve2 data onto GraphB. The for loop of lines 12–15 then puts the Label array on the display. The last lines of code in OnDraw are represented in Table 9.14 by the dots of lines 16–18. This code places the sun, planets and

Table 9.14 Listing of OnDraw from GTPlanetsView.cpp

```
01    /* This is a Partial Listing of OnDraw */
02    void CGTPlanetsView::OnDraw(CDC* pDC)
03    {
04        CGTPlanetsDoc* pDoc = GetDocument();
05        ASSERT_VALID(pDoc);  if(!pDoc)return;
06        // TODO: add draw code for native data here
07        pDoc->PositionBodiesEtc(m_CenterX, m_CenterY);
08        pDoc->GraphA.ShowGraph(pDC);
09        pDoc->GraphA.PlotPoints(pDC,&(pDoc->Curve1));
10        pDoc->GraphB.ShowGraph(pDC);
```

Table 9.14 (*Continued*)

```
11        pDoc->GraphB.PlotPoints(pDC,&(pDoc->Curve2));
12        for(int i = 0; i<pDoc->NumLabels ; i++)
13              {
14                    pDoc->Label[i].ShowTextBox(pDC);
15              }
16              .
17              .
18              .
19    }
```

moon into the window and is exactly as shown in the original OnDraw
function of Table 8.12. Notice we have specifically drawn the graphs and
labels first in the new OnDraw function. In this way, the animated
planets are drawn into the display after the graphs so that the labels are
already in place and do not cover the planets.

9.5 Color Contour Plotting

Computer graphics has provided an ability to conveniently visualize data
and information for many different applications. The color contour plot
is one of the most popular approaches for bringing life to numerical data

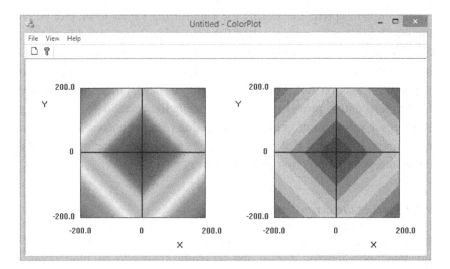

Figure 9.4 Examples of Color Contour Plots

and is an important example of the effective use of color computer graphics. In this section we will present a strategy for developing color contour plots by extending the object-oriented approach that we have developed through Chapters 8 and 9. Our color plotting example program is in Figure 9.4 and can be found in the folder *Chap9\4_ColorPlot*. You can build and execute the program ColorPlot to see the resulting display of Figure 9.4. The plot shown in both graphs is for the simple algebraic function

$$F(x, y) = |x| + |y|$$

In these plots, the values of F have been scaled from their minimum value to their maximum value and colors have been assigned from deep blue for the smallest values of F occurring in the graph through deep red for the largest values of F. When the graph is plotted, the appropriate color is shown at each x and y position within the graph. As you will see later in this section, the graph on the left uses one hundred different colors in displaying the range of values for F over the graph's range while the graph on the right only uses eight distinct colors to represent F over the same range of x and y.

Our discussion of the color plotting process begins below by describing an approach to storing the data for the values to be plotted on the graph using a new class called CArrays which is included in the file GraphTxtClasses.h introduced in Section 9.4. We have also added two new functions to the class CGraphs which was first introduced and applied in Section 9.1. The first of these new functions is called ColorInterp and it provides a color interpolation method for specifying RGB color values in proportion to the value of a parameter. The second new function is called ColorPlot. It creates color contour plots using the color interpolation function and stored array data.

9.5.1 Storing the array data

In Section 9.1 we introduced the CCurves class to provide an object-oriented approach for storing and handling curves to be plotted on a graph. In this section, we describe the class CArrays which allows the data for color contour plotting to be readily available. Table 9.15 shows the declaration of the CArrays class where we provide member variables to store the various values necessary for the display of a color contour plot including a two-dimensional array of data. Line 04 in Table 9.15 declares the floating point array m_PlotMatrix to provide the two-dimensional array of values to be represented by the color plot (notice that the maximum dimensions provided here are 100x100). The type float can be used instead of double because the accuracy requirements for this plotting are limited. Line 05 declares m_NumRows and m_NumCols to describe the size of the array m_PlotMatrix being used for plotting. In line 06, the range of x and y covered by the array is described through the member variables m_xMin, m_xMax, m_yMin,

Table 9.15 Declaration of CArrays from GraphTextClasses.h

```
01   /* This is the declaration of the class CArrays */
02   class CArrays {
03   public:
04         float m_PlotMatrix[100][100];
05         int m_NumRows, m_NumCols;
06         double m_xMin, m_xMax, m_yMin, m_yMax;
07         float m_MatrixMin, m_MatrixMax;
08         CArrays () { };
09         void CArrays::AdjustArray (int NRows, int NCols, double xMin, double yMin,
10                    double xMax, double yMax, float* PtArray)
11         {
12                    m_NumRows = NRows;        m_NumCols = NCols;
13                    m_yMax = yMax;            m_yMin = yMin;
14                    m_xMax = xMax;            m_xMin = xMin;
15                    m_MatrixMin = 1e+20f;     m_MatrixMax = -1e+20f;
16            for (int i=0;i<m_NumRows;i++) {
17            for (int j=0;j<m_NumCols;j++) {
18                    m_PlotMatrix[i][j] = *(PtArray + m_NumRows*i + j);
19                    float Func = m_PlotMatrix[i][j];
20                    if (Func < m_MatrixMin)  m_MatrixMin = Func;
21                    if (Func > m_MatrixMax)  m_MatrixMax = Func;
22            }
23            }
24         }
25   };
```

and m_yMax. Line 07 declares m_MatrixMin and m_MatrixMax as member variables which represent the minimum and maximum values over all of the data contained in the array m_PlotMatrix. These minimum and maximum values are needed for the process of scaling the entries in the array over the range of colors to be used in the color plot.

Line 08 provides an empty constructor function for the CArrays class. The member function AdjustArray shown in lines 09–24 serves to define the member variables for objects of the CArrays class using its list of arguments in lines 09 and 10. In the argument list, the pointer PtArray passes an array address into the function so that m_PlotMatrix can be defined for the data at hand. Definition of the member variables begins in lines 12–14 where the size and the range variables are set for the array. Line 15 shows the initialization of m_MatrixMin and m_MatrixMax to arbitrary extreme values. Then the nested for loops of lines 16–24 make use of the array input data accessible through the pointer PtArray. Line 18 fills in the values of m_PlotMatrix[i][j] as the for loops execute. At each step, lines 20 and 21 compare the entry in the matrix against the current values of m_MatrixMin and m_MatrixMax so that these member variables will contain the extreme values of the array when the loop execution is complete.

9.5.2 Using color quantitatively

The key step in the development of color contour plots is the "colorizing" of the parameter to be plotted. The plot is established by displaying pixels of appropriate color at the x,y coordinates corresponding to specific graph positions. The function values F(x,y) are made available in m_PlotMatrix for the CArrays class and the member variables m_MatrixMin and m_MatrixMax indicate the full range of F(x,y) in the array. A convenient way to provide a parameter covering the range of values is to scale the entries in the array so that a parameter value of zero corresponds to m_MatrixMin and a parameter value of one corresponds to m_MatrixMax. Each value of F(x,y) then scales to a parameter value between zero and one. Let's now look at a strategy for defining an appropriate color for each of these parameter values.

As we have seen at many points in the preceding chapters, colors can be specified by providing values for the red, green and blue components in an RGB format. The colorizing of a parameter can be implemented by defining the red, green and blue components at each parameter value. Of course, this can be done in many ways. The approach shown in Figure 9.5 is quite representative. In this figure, the red, green and blue components are described by a sequence of points with a linear interpolation performed between points. The first graph in Figure 9.5 shows the red RGB component at zero for small parameter values with a growing red component starting at 0.5. As the parameter approaches unity, the red component again decreases to approach a dark red. The second graph shows the green RGB component which reaches its peak

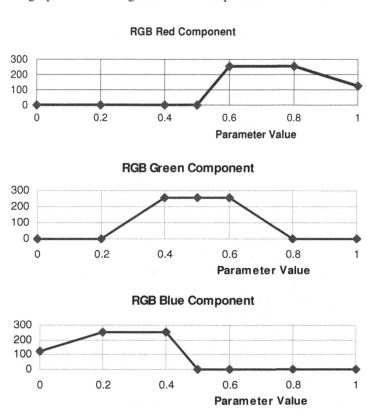

Figure 9.5 RGB Components vs Parameter Values

with the parameter value in the range of 0.5 and is symmetric about that point. Finally, the graph at the bottom of Figure 9.5 shows the blue RGB component starting at a level of deep blue for a parameter value of zero, increasing to a bright blue and then falling off to zero at 0.5. The blue values are the mirror image of the red values.

At any parameter value the RGB color result is the combination of the three graphs. The overall effect approximates a sweep through the color spectrum from blues through green through yellows, oranges and reds for the zero through one parameter range. The RGB pattern of Figure 9.5 is carried out by the member function ColorInterp of the CGraphs class as shown in Table 9.16. The argument list for this function in line 02 of Table 9.16, accepts the parameter value Param and the number of colors NColors. It then returns a COLORREF variable that contains the colorized representation of the parameter. Lines 06–08 of the ColorInterp function define vectors which control the linear color

Table 9.16 Listing of CGraphs::ColorInterp from GraphTextClasses.h

```
01    /* This is a listing of the function CGraphs::ColorInterp */
02    COLORREF CGraphs::ColorInterp(double Param, int NColors)
03    {
04        double RedValue, GreenValue, BlueValue;
05        COLORREF Color;
06        double Red[7]   = {   0,    0,    0,   0, 225, 255, 125};
07        double Green[7] = {   0,    0, 255, 255, 255,   0,   0};
08        double Blue [7] = {125, 255, 225,   0,   0,   0,   0};
09        double Break[7] = {   0, 0.20, 0.40, 0.50, 0.60, 0.80, 1.0};
10        if (Param >=1.0)  Param = 0.999;
11        Param = int(NColors*Param)/double(NColors) + .5/double(NColors);
12    for (int i = 0; i < 6; i++) {
13    if (Param >= Break[i] && Param <= Break[i+1]) {
14        double BrkLnth = Break[i+1]-Break[i];
15        RedValue = Red[i] + (Red[i+1]-Red[i]) * (Param-Break[i]) / BrkLnth;
16        GreenValue = Green[i] + (Green[i+1]-Green[i]) * (Param-Break[i]) / BrkLnth;
17        BlueValue = Blue[i] + (Blue[i+1] - Blue[I]) * (Param - Break[i]) / BrkLnth;
18        }
19        }
20        Color = RGB (RedValue, GreenValue, BlueValue);
21        return (Color);
22    }
```

interpolation. The interpolation corresponds to the RGB values shown by the data points in Figure 9.5. But, of course, this interpolation is a flexible arrangement and could be adjusted to achieve any particular effect. Line 09 defines the parameter "break points" for the interpolation, again corresponding to the graphs of Figure 9.5. In ColorInterp, a provision has been made to use a discrete number of colors (as indicated by NColors) in the colorizing process. Line 11 is the key to providing this capability by adjusting the value of Param accordingly. The first term in the equation of line 11 identifies the parameter value at the beginning of a particular color band. The second term in line 11 then adjusts the value of Param to the center of the color band. If the value of NColors is large, the color distribution will appear essentially continuous as seen on the left side of Figure 9.4 (NColors = 100).

If NColors is small, the coloring will appear in bands as on the right side of Figure 9.4 (NColors = 8). The for loop in lines 12–19 of ColorInterp actually carries out the color interpolation for the adjusted value of Param. Within this loop, the if statement of line 13 identifies the active interpolation region for each value of Param and the interpolated red, green and blue components are set appropriately in lines 15–17. The COLORREF variable Color is declared in line 05. The RGB function in line 20, at the end of the for loop, sets the value of Color based on the interpolated color components. Line 21 then returns Color as the output of the ColorInterp function.

9.5.3 A function for color plotting

In Section 9.5.1 and 9.5.2, we introduced the CArrays class and the function ColorInterp. We will now discuss the function ColorPlot of the CGgraphs class which utilizes CArrays and ColorInterp to actually place the color contour plot on the display. ColorPlot is a member of the CGraphs class and when it acts on a CGraphs object it has the member variables of the graph object available for scaling and positioning the plot appropriately. Table 9.17 provides a listing of the ColorPlot function. Its argument list in line 02 shows that it will receive a pointer to a display context to tell it where to plot, a pointer to an object of

Table 9.17 Listing of CGraphs::ColorPlot from GraphTextClasses.h

```
01    /* This is a listing of the function CGraphs::ColorPlot */
02    void CGraphs::ColorPlot(CDC* pDC,CArrays* pArray, int NumColors)
03    {
04        double xScale=m_xDisplayLength/(m_xVarMax-m_xVarMin);
05        double yScale=m_yDisplayLength/(m_yVarMax-m_yVarMin);
06        double xInc = (pArray->m_xMax - pArray->m_xMin)/(pArray->m_NumCols-1);
07        double yInc = (pArray->m_yMax - pArray->m_yMin)/(pArray->m_NumRows-1);
08        double xLL = pArray->m_xMin;
09        double yLL = pArray->m_yMin;
10        double xUR = xLL + xInc;
11        double yUR = yLL + yInc;
12        int i, j;
13        double AverageFunc, NormAverageFunc;
14        double FuncMin = pArray->m_MatrixMin;
15        double FuncRange = pArray->m_MatrixMax - pArray->m_MatrixMin;
16        COLORREF SaveBkColor = pDC->GetBkColor();
17    for (i=0;i<pArray->m_NumRows-1;i++)  {
18    for (j=0;j<pArray->m_NumCols-1;j++)  {
19        int ScaledxLL = m_xBP + int(xScale*(xLL - m_xVarMin));
20        int ScaledyLL = m_yBP - int(yScale*(yLL - m_yVarMin));
21        int ScaledxUR = m_xBP + int(xScale*(xUR - m_xVarMin));
22        int ScaledyUR = m_yBP - int(yScale*(yUR - m_yVarMin));
23        AverageFunc = (pArray->m_PlotMatrix[i][j] + pArray->m_PlotMatrix[i][j+1]
24            + pArray->m_PlotMatrix[i+1][j] + pArray->m_PlotMatrix[i+1][j+1])/4.;
25        NormAverageFunc = (AverageFunc - FuncMin)/FuncRange;
26        COLORREF BoxColor = ColorInterp(NormAverageFunc, NumColors);
27        if ((xLL+xInc/2.>=m_xVarMin)&&(xUR - Inc/2.<=m_xVarMax)&&
28            (yLL+yInc/2.>=m_yVarMin)&&(yUR - yInc/2.<=m_yVarMax))  {
29        pDC->FillSolidRect(CRect (ScaledxLL,ScaledyUR, ScaledxUR,
30            ScaledyLL),BoxColor);
31        }
32        xLL+=xInc;
33        xUR+=xInc;
34        }
35        xLL = pArray->m_xMin;
36        xUR = xLL + xInc;
37        yLL += yInc;
38        yUR += yInc;
39        }
40        pDC->SetBkColor(SaveBkColor);
41    }
```

the CArrays class to tell it what to plot and an input of NumColors to indicate how many colors to use in the plot. The function begins in lines 04 and 05 where the scaling variables are set for the x and y axes depending on the member variables for the display length and the x and y ranges.

The color contour plot consists of many small rectangles each individually calculated from the CArray member variables for the range of x and y values in the array and the number of columns and rows that it contains. Lines 6 and 7 define the size of small rectangles that will be placed on the graph. Lines 08–11 define the first of the rectangles with xLL and yLL indicating the lower left corner of the rectangle. The upper right corner corresponds to xUR, yUR. Lines 14 and 15 extract the minimum function value and the function range from the member variables of the CArrays object developed from the argument list. Line 16 saves the current background color for the display so that it can be restored at the end of the function. This is necessary because the MFC FillSolidRect function used for rectangle plotting changes the background color.

The nested for loops of lines 17–39 cycle through all of the rows and columns of the array, putting a colored rectangle in place at each step. Lines 19–22 scale the lower left and upper right coordinates of the rectangles and also add in the base point coordinates of the graph so that ScaledxLL and ScaledyLL become the pixel coordinates of the rectangle's lower left corner. Similarly, ScaledxUR and ScaledyUR are the pixel coordinates of the upper right corner. Lines 23 and 24 average the function values at the rectangle corners and line 25 normalizes the function value relative to the minimum function value and the range of the function across the array. Notice that NormAverageFunc will be between zero and one. This is exactly the parameter that we want to colorize.

The colorizing operation is performed in line 26 where the ColorInterp function is called and BoxColor becomes the interpolated RGB color. The if statement in lines 27 and 28 checks to be sure that the scaled rectangle falls inside the graph. If it does, the rectangle is filled with the appropriate color using the MFC function FillSolidRect which is called in lines 29 and 30. Lines 32 and 33 increment xLL and xUR as the inner for loop marches across the array. At the conclusion of the inner loop, lines 35 and 36 reset xLL and xUR back to the first column and lines 37 and 38 increment yLL and yUR to move on to the next row. After both loops have completed execution, the color contour plot has been drawn. Line 40 then resets the original background color for the display.

9.5.4 Using the plotting tools

The tools needed to create a color contour plot are now in place. This section applies the CArrays class and the new additions to the CGraphs class to create the plots that we presented in Figure 9.4. We use these tools in the OnNewDocument function where the member variables m_Array1, m_GraphA and m_GraphB are part of the document class. These will be used in the plotting process where m_Array1 is an object of the CArrays class to be plotted on m_GraphA and m_GraphB (which are objects of the CGraphs class). The listing of OnNewDocument is shown in Table 9.18. The line 07 statements in OnNewDocument declare the array size using the integer constants NumYs (for the number of rows) and NumXs (for the number of columns). Line 08 then uses these constants to declare the two-dimensional array Matrx (of type float) which will be used to create m_Array1. The upper and lower limits of the x and y variables for the array are specified in lines 09 and 10.

Line 11 initializes Ax and Ay at the minimum coordinates for the array. These form the basis for generating function values to insert into the array. Then, lines 12 and 13 calculate the values of AxInc and AyInc to be used for incrementing Ax and Ay while filling the array. The nested for loops of lines 14–21 cycle through each row and each column, calculating and inserting function values into the array. Line 15 resets Ax to its minimum value as each new row is started. The inner for loop beginning at line 16 moves across the rows. Line 17 sets the value of the entry in Matrx by summing absolute values of x and y. Recall that this was our equation for F(x,y) used in Figure 9.4. Of course, more complicated calculations or a call to a function could also appear here.

Table 9.18 Listing of OnNewDocument from ColorPlotDoc.cpp

```
01   /* This is a listing of the function OnNewDocument */
02   BOOL CColorPlotDoc::OnNewDocument()
03   {
04       if (!CDocument::OnNewDocument()) return FALSE;
05       // TODO: add reinitialization code here
06       // (SDI documents will reuse this document)
07       const int NumYs = 100;      const int NumXs = 100;
08       float Matrx[NumYs][ NumXs];
09       double AxMin=-200;       double AxMax=200;
10       double AyMin=-200;       double AyMax=200;
11       double Ax = AxMin;       double Ay = AyMin;
12       double AxInc = (AxMax-AxMin)/(NumXs-1);
13       double AyInc = (AyMax-AyMin)/(NumYs-1);
14   for ( int i=0;i<NumYs;i++)  {
15       Ax = AxMin;
16   for (int j=0;j<NumXs;j++)  {
17       Matrx[i][j] = float (fabs(Ax)+fabs(Ay));
18       Ax = Ax + AxInc;
19       }
20       Ay = Ay + AyInc;
21       }
22       m_Array1.AdjustArray(NumYs,NumXs,AxMin,AyMin,
23              AxMax,AyMax,Matrx[0]);
24       CPoint Origin(100,275);
25       CSize GraphSize(225,225);
26       m_GraphA.AdjustGraph (Origin, GraphSize, AxMin,
27              AyMin, AxMax, AyMax);
28       m_GraphB.AdjustGraph (Origin, GraphSize, AxMin,
29              AyMin, AxMax, AyMax);
30       m_GraphB.MoveGraph(450,275);
31       return TRUE;
32   }
```

Line 18 increments Ax to move across the row and line 20, at the end of the outer loop, increments Ay to move to the next row. After the end of the loops at line 21, Matrx is filled and ready to be passed into m_Array1. This is done in lines 22 and 23 where the AdjustArray function is called. It defines the size and range in the x and y directions and passes Matrx[0], the pointer to the matrix.

Table 9.19 Listing of OnDraw from ColorPlotView.cpp

```
01    /* This is the listing of OnDraw */
02    void CColorPlotView::OnDraw(CDC* pDC)
03    {
04        CColorPlotDoc* pDoc = GetDocument();
05        ASSERT_VALID(pDoc); if(!pDoc)return;
06        // TODO: add draw code for native data here
07        pDoc-> FillWindow(pDC);
08    }
```

The description of the graphs to be plotted by the program is shown in lines 24 through 29. Line 24 declares a CPoint object to serve as the graph origin and locates the graph toward the left side of the window. Line 25 declares a CSize object to define the size of the graph as 225x225 pixels. The AdjustGraph function in lines 26 and 27 is used to define m_graphA, with ranges of the coordinates corresponding to those used for m_Array1. Lines 28 and 29 define m_GraphB in the same way and then line 30 moves m_GraphB to the right side of the window.

At this point we have performed some simple calculations and have created an array to carry the resulting data. We have also defined two graphs that are appropriate for color contour plotting of the array. Our next step is to arrange for the display of the graphs in the window as the program starts. Table 9.19 shows the OnDraw function for this program. It is a very simple function with the only added line of code at line 07 calling the document class function FillWindow. This is a different approach to executing display operations than we have been using. It is an approach that can be used conveniently to avoid repeated passing of document class information to the view class. With this strategy we carry out the drawing operations in the FillWindow function and since it is in the document class, all of the document class member variables are readily available for use. Notice, of course, that the display context pointer is passed into the FillWindow function so it knows where to draw.

The FillWindow function prepared here for the document class is listed in Table 9.20. The first statement in line 04 declares NumColors

Table 9.20 Listing of FillWindow from ColorPlotDoc.cpp

```
01    /* This is the listing of CColorPlotDoc::FillWindow */
02    void CColorPlotDoc::FillWindow(CDC* pDC)
03    {
04         int NumColors = 100;
05         m_GraphA.ColorPlot(pDC, &m_Array1, NumColors);
06         m_GraphA.ShowGraph(pDC);
07         NumColors = 8;
08         m_GraphB.ColorPlot(pDC, &m_Array1, NumColors);
09         m_GraphB.ShowGraph(pDC);
10    }
```

and sets it to 100. Then line 05 calls the ColorPlot function for m_GraphA using the data of m_Array1. Line 06 calls ShowGraph for m_GraphA, drawing its axes and labels on top of the color contour plot. Line 07 now switches to NumColors = 8. The function ColorPlot is called in line 08 for m_GraphB to create a new color contour plot of m_Array1 using only eight colors. Finally, in line 09, the call to the ShowGraph function for m_GraphB puts its axes and labels in place on the contour plot.

Figure 9.4 is the result of executing this program. The example folder *Chap9\4_ColorPlot* contains the full program structure, classes and functions described in the preceding sections. The CArrays class and the new CGraphs functions may all be found in the upgraded file GraphTxtClasses.h. The contour plots described by Figure 9.4 are for a very simple absolute value function. But much more complicated functions can be handled in the same way. Section 9.6 is the conclusion of this graphing discussion and presents a graphing program in a rather complete format.

9.6 One Last Graphing Example

We conclude this chapter on graph plotting with a final example using basic calculations from engineering mechanics. This program can be found in the folder *Chap9\5_StressPlots*. Building and executing the program will result in the window displayed in Figure 9.6. The drawing, graphs and text displayed in the figure make direct use of the programming strategies and classes that we have just described. This final section provides an example of how Visual C++ along with basic classes and functions can be used to create customized output displays to support interactive calculations.

At the top of Figure 9.6, you can see a schematic drawing of a cantilever beam. The beam is completely fixed at the left end and free to deflect at the right end. A ten-pound load is applied to the free end and this load creates stresses (which are not material dependent) throughout the beam. The beam is 25 inches long. It has a height of one inch and a one-half inch depth. From this information, relatively standard

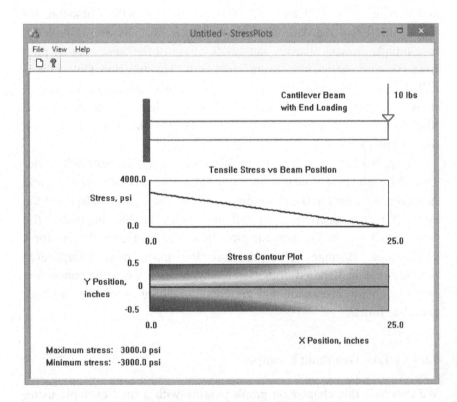

Figure 9.6 Graphs Based on Stress Calculations

engineering equations (presented in Section 9.6.2) can be used to calculate the stresses in the beam. The graph at the middle of Figure 9.6 shows the tension stress calculated for the top surface of the beam. It indicates that the stress level is zero at the free end of the beam and reaches its largest tension value of 3000 psi (pounds per square inch) at the fixed end. Although the calculated stress levels are not dependent on the material, if the material is not strong enough to support the stress, failure will result.

The graph at the bottom of the window is a color contour plot of the stresses in the beam. In this plot, the stresses are scaled from the minimum of -3000 psi to the maximum of +3000 psi. The color scaling was performed as described in Section 9.5 and results in blue colors representing the negative stresses and red colors representing the most positive stresses. Stresses near zero appear as green in the plot. The contour plot clearly shows the maximum stresses (tension) appearing at the fixed upper corner of the beam and minimum stresses (compression) appearing at the fixed lower corner of the beam.

9.6.1 Organization of the program

The overall structure of the StressPlots program will become apparent as you bring it into the Visual C++ environment and explore the document and view classes. Since the program has not been constructed with significant user interaction, the view class CStressPlotsView is relatively empty without added member variables or functions. Most of the work here is performed by the document class CStressPlotsDoc. The OnDraw function directly passes the drawing operations on to the document class function FillWindow (just as in Section 9.5 for the ColorPlot example). In this way, the member variables of the document class are easily available for display operations.

The header file TwoDShapes+Classes.h presented in Section 8.3 and the file GraphTxtClasses.h (Section 9.4) have also been included in the StressPlots project. If you use Class View to inspect the project, you can see the various classes readily available for geometry and graphing. Also in ClassView, you can expand the document class CStressPlotsDoc to see its full set of member variables and member functions. Member variables have been provided to handle an array, a curve, text labels, graphs and, of course, the beam characteristics.

The OnNewDocument function for the StressPlots program is shown in Table 9.21. The function has relatively few statements since we have created and used several additional functions to perform the calculations and prepare the graphs. Lines 07–11 define the beam characteristics and the load force for the calculations and place them in document class member variables. The sequence of function calls begins at line 12 where the schematic at the top of the graph is defined. The stresses plotted in the simple graph at the center of the display are calculated in the function call at line 13. The document member variable m_Array1 is filled at line 14, ready to be used for color contour plotting. Line 15 defines the labels for the display.

Table 9.21 Listing of OnNewDocument from StressPlotsDoc.cpp

```
01    /* This is a listing of the function OnNewDocument */
02    BOOL CStressPlotsDoc::OnNewDocument()
03    {
04        if (!CDocument::OnNewDocument()) return FALSE;
05        // TODO: add reinitialization code here
06        // (SDI documents will reuse this document)
07        m_BeamLength = 25.;
08        m_BeamHeight = 1.;
09        m_BeamWidth = 0.5;
10        m_Load = 10;
11        m_BeamMomInertia = m_BeamWidth*pow(m_BeamHeight , 3.) / 12.;
12        CreateSchematicData();
13        CreateCurvePlotData();
14        CreateContourPlotData();
15        CreateLabelData();
16        return TRUE;
17    }
```

9.6.2 Preparing the data

The OnNewDocument function in Table 9.21 uses several functions to provide a simplified organization for the required calculations. Each of these is a member function of the document class and has direct access to the document member variables to obtain geometric information for the beam or any other required data that may be needed. While they are executing, the functions can readily deposit their results in the member variables provided. In the Visual C++ environment, you can easily explore the member variables and member functions of the document class. We will discuss two of the functions below as examples.

The first of the functions, CreateSchematicData, is called in line 12 of OnNewDocument (Table 9.21). Its purpose is to develop data for the schematic drawing by filling the arrays m_FPoint and m_LPoint and the variables m_NumLines, m_Rectangle1 and m_Rectangle2. These are all document class member variables. CreateSchematicData is shown in Table 9.22. The code in lines 04–12 defines the arrow at the end of the beam. Line 13 defines m_Rectangle1, which represents the beam itself, while line 14 positions it. Similarly, the vertical colored rectangle

Table 9.22 Listing of CreateSchematicData from StressPlotsDoc.cpp

```
01    /* This is the listing of CStressPlotsDoc:: CreateSchematicData */
02    void CStressPlotsDoc::CreateSchematicData(void)
03    {
04        m_NumLines = 4;
05        m_FPoint[0].x=600;   m_FPoint[0].y= 80;
06        m_LPoint[0].x=610;   m_LPoint[0].y= 70;
07        m_FPoint[1].x=610;   m_FPoint[1].y= 70;
08        m_LPoint[1].x=590;   m_LPoint[1].y= 70;
09        m_FPoint[2].x=590;   m_FPoint[2].y= 70;
10        m_LPoint[2].x=600;   m_LPoint[2].y= 80;
11        m_FPoint[3].x=600;   m_FPoint[3].y= 20;
12        m_LPoint[3].x=600;   m_LPoint[3].y= 70;
13        m_Rectangle1.AdjustRectangle(30,400);
14        m_Rectangle1.Move(400,95);
15        m_Rectangle2.AdjustRectangle(100,10);
16        m_Rectangle2.Move(195,95);
17    }
```

supporting the beam is m_Rectangle2 which is defined and positioned by lines 15 and 16.

The function CreateContourPlotData called in line 14 of the OnNewDocument function will be described in conjunction with Table 9.23. It has the job of filling m_Array1 by performing stress calculations for the cantilever beam. These stress calculations use a few algebraic equations based on the theory of solid mechanics (typically part of a second year course for many engineering students).

The bending stress within the beam can be represented as:

$$\text{Stress} = \text{Load} * (\text{BeamLength} - x) * y / \text{BeamMomInertia}$$

where the Load is the force applied at the end of the beam and the BeamLength represents the total length of the beam. The distance to the stress calculation point as measured from the fixed end of the beam is given by x and the distance from the center of the beam to the stress calculation point is given by y. In this way, the bottom of the beam at the free end corresponds to x = BeamLength while y = -BeamHeight / 2 and the top of the beam at the fixed end is at x = 0 with y = +BeamHeight / 2.

The dimensions of the cross section of the beam determine the moment of inertia of the beam. This is an important beam characteristic and is calculated relatively simply for a rectangular beam cross section as

$$\text{BeamMomInertia} = (1/12) \text{ BeamWidth} * (\text{BeamHeight})^3$$

This expression appears directly in line 11 of the OnNewDocument function to calculate the member variable m_BeamMomInertia. As the function CreateContourPlotData begins execution, all of the beam dimensions and the moment of inertia have been defined. It then uses the stress equation above to calculate the stresses throughout the beam.

The function CreateContourPlotData is shown in Table 9.23. Line 04 of CreateContourPlotData contains the statements defining the number of x and y entries in the matrix and corresponds to the stress calculation

Table 9.23 Listing of CreateContourPlotData from StressPlotsDoc.cpp

```
01   /* This is the listing of CStressPlotsDoc::CreateContourPlotData */
02   void CStressPlotsDoc::CreateContourPlotData(void)
03   {
04        const int NumYs = 50;      const int NumXs = 50;
05        float Matrx[NumYs][ NumXs];
06        double AxMin=0;     double AxMax = m_BeamLength;
07        double AyMin = - m_BeamHeight / 2.;
08        double AyMax = m_BeamHeight / 2.;
09        double AxInc = (AxMax-AxMin)/(NumXs-1);
10        double AyInc = (AyMax-AyMin)/(NumYs-1);
11        double Ax = AxMin;      double Ay = AyMin;
12   for (int i=0;i<NumYs;i++)  {
13        Ax = AxMin;
14   for (int j=0;j<NumXs;j++)  {
15        double Stress = m_Load * (m_BeamLength - Ax) * Ay / m_BeamMomInertia;
16        Matrx[i][j] = float (Stress);
17        Ax = Ax + AxInc;
18        }
19        Ay = Ay + AyInc;
20        }
21        m_Array1.AdjustArray(NumYs,NumXs,AxMin,AyMin,
22               AxMax,AyMax,Matrx[0]);
23        CPoint OriginB(200,385);
24        CPoint GraphSizeB(400,75);
25        m_GraphB.AdjustGraph (OriginB,GraphSizeB,AxMin,
26               AyMin,AxMax,AyMax);
27   }
```

points used across the beam. Line 05 declares a matrix which will hold the beam stress data as it is generated and uses the values of NumYs and NumXs from line 04 to define the dimensions of Matrx. Lines 06–08 define the range of coordinates (called Ax and Ay) of interest across the beam. Here, you can see, for example, that the Ax values will extend from zero to m_BeamLength. Lines 09 and 10 determine the increments in Ax and Ay to be used between calculation points. Line 11initializes the calculation position at the lower left corner of the beam. The pair of for loops from lines 12–20 move across and up the beam. At the top of the first for loop, line 13 sets the current Ax value to its minimum to prepare for each swing across the beam from left to right. Line 15 calculates the stress at each point. Line 16 places the calculated stress into the current matrix entry. Line 17 then increments Ax to move towards the end of the beam. Line 19 is executed when the inner loop completes and increments Ay to move toward the top of the beam. After the conclusion of the for loops, lines 21 and 22 define m_Array1 using the AdjustArray function. Lines 23–26 define the graph object m_GraphB which is sized to present a color plot of the stress data now loaded into m_Array1.

9.6.3 Generating the display

As described in Section 9.6.2, the OnNewDocument function prepares the data necessary for our plotting purposes by using the functions CreateSchematicData, CreateCurvePlotData, CreateContourPlotData, and CreateLabelData. At the conclusion of OnNewDocument, the OnDraw function of the view class executes and calls the FillWindow function of Table 9.24. This is the same strategy used in Section 9.5 for the previous graphing program. As shown in Table 9.24, the FillWindow function of the document class makes use of the display context pointer pDC to directly draw into the window.

The first steps in FillWindow draw the blue beam schematic using lines 04–11. Lines 04 and 05 select a blue pen and blue brush. These objects are document class member variables and were initialized in the constructor function. The for loop of lines 06–09 then draws the "load arrow" into the display. Line 10 displays the "beam" and line 11 displays the "support rectangle". The graph in the center of the display is drawn by lines 12 and 13 using the graph and data developed in the function CreateCurvePlotData. Lines 14–16 display the color contour plot for beam stresses and the for loop of lines 17–19 places the text boxes (from CreateLabelData) into the window.

Table 9.24 Listing of FillWindow from StressPlotsDoc.cpp

```
01    /* This is the listing of CStressPlotsDoc::FillWindow */
02    void CStressPlotsDoc::FillWindow(CDC* pDC)
03    {
04        pDC->SelectObject(&m_BluePen);
05        pDC->SelectObject(&m_BlueBrush);
06    for (int i=0; i < m_NumLines; i++) {
07        pDC->MoveTo(m_FPoint[i]);
08        pDC->LineTo(m_LPoint[i]);
09    }
10        m_Rectangle1.ShowRect(pDC);
11        m_Rectangle2.FillRect(pDC);
12        m_GraphA.ShowGraph(pDC);
13        m_GraphA.PlotLines(pDC, &m_Curve1);
14        int NumColors = 100;
15        m_GraphB.ColorPlot(pDC, &m_Array1, NumColors);
16        m_GraphB.ShowGraph(pDC);
17    for (int i=0; i < m_NumTextBoxes; i++) {
18        m_Label[i].ShowTextBox(pDC);
19    }
20    }
```

9.7 Exercises

1. Using the project Grapher (*Chap9\1_Grapher*) as a model, write a program to plot calculations based on the simple physics problem of a body moving with a constant acceleration. The equation you will need for velocity calculations is:

$$v = v_o + at$$

where

$a =$ constant acceleration level

$t =$ time of interest

$v_o =$ initial velocity

$v =$ velocity at time t

From an initial velocity of zero, select a suitable set of parameters and suitable scaling for a graph. Plot a graph of velocity vs. time using the CGraphs and CCurves classes. Now consider twice your chosen acceleration and three times your chosen acceleration. Develop CCurves objects for these cases and plot three velocity vs.

time curves on your graph — one for each acceleration value. Adjust your graph scale so that the curves fit the graph nicely.

2. Extend the plotting program of Exercise 1 above. Consider the position equation for a body moving from rest with constant acceleration so that:

$$p = p_o + \tfrac{1}{2}at^2$$

where

p_o = initial position

p = current position

Revise your program so that two graphs are plotted for your chosen set of parameters and for the three acceleration levels from an initial position and velocity of zero. Place the velocity vs. time graph from Exercise 1 on the left and the new position vs. time graph on the right.

3. In Section 9.4.1 we introduced a simple process of adding text to graphs and figures with the class CTextBoxes. Make use of this basic text capability to label the graphs and curves that you created in Exercises 1 and 2 above.

4. Expand your programs from Exercise 3 above to permit user interaction. Provide a menu bar item that displays a dialog window that allows a user to input the acceleration levels and the upper time limit of interest (assume that the lower time limit is zero). Based on user inputs through this dialog window, have your program recalculate data for the curves appropriately, automatically select the graph scales, modify the text labels and, of course, redisplay the graphs.

5. Consider the project GTPlanets in the folder *Chap9\3_GTPlanets*. This program displays a Venus-to-Earth distance graph on the upper left of the screen and a Mercury-to-Earth distance graph on the upper right. Add a nicely labeled graph to plot the Venus-to-Mercury

distance. (a) Have your initial program place this new graph on the left side of the window just below the Venus-to-Earth graph. (b) Then, revise your program to relocate the graph so that the distance plot for Venus-to-Mercury is in the lower right hand corner of the window.

6. Figure 9.4 was generated by the project ColorPlot located in *Chap9\4_ColorPlot*. The absolute value function that it contains creates the straight line pattern shown in the figure. Modify the program to plot the simple function

$$F(x, y) = x^2 + y^2$$

In this form, you should expect to see a family of circles centered about the origin. Modify the equation and revise your program to produce a family of circles with a center point displaced from the origin.

7. The project StressPlots (*Chap9\5_StressPlots*) presents a schematic, a line graph and a color contour plot for a cantilever beam with an end load. Modify this program to consider a simply supported beam loaded at its center point as indicated below:

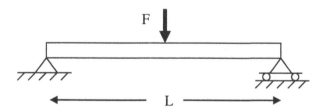

Using dimensions similar to those in StressPlots, have your program draw a schematic to represent the beam and its loading. Present a graph of maximum beam tensile stress vs. position along the beam. Also include a color contour plot showing stress level as a function of position within the beam. Each of these figures should be nicely labeled. Notice that the stress in a simply supported beam can be calculated as follows:

Stress = BendMoment * y / BeamMomInertia

where y is vertical position within the beam measured from the beam center line (positive up). The bending moment for a position x along the beam and measured from its midpoint is:

BendMoment = $-(1 - 2x/L)$ FL/4, for $0 \le x \le L/2$

and

BendMoment = $-(1 + 2x/L)$ FL/4, for $-L/2 \le x \le 0$

Chapter 10

Introducing Touch Screen Programming

The first nine chapters of this book have provided an introduction to Visual C++ Windows programming and Microsoft Foundation Class applications. This second edition has updated the material of the first edition in those chapters using the most recent version of Visual C++ at this writing (Version 2013). The material in Chapters 1–9 shows a progression from very basic programming skills in the console environment to an introduction of Windows programming and finally to the development of more complex graphics programming using classes, objects and animations.

Since the writing of the first edition, touch screen capabilities have become an ever more important part of the modern computing environment. Microsoft's Visual C++ and MFC programming tools have adapted to this environment by providing appropriate resources to allow user interaction with the touch screen. The purpose of this chapter is to offer an introduction to the programming capabilities provided within MFC for the touch screen environment.

We will begin this discussion of touch screen programming with a few general comments on the evolution of computing environments since the first edition. An example of gesture programming is then provided to introduce the basic strategy of using a gesture function. This is followed by a more detailed look at the operation of the various gesture functions provided within MFC applications. Finally, we will consider the use of registered touch input functions as a very direct way to manage the touch screen interface without the "gesture" context. This provides a flavor of the flexibility (and the detail) that might be the result of managing touch screen operations without the gesture tools. Chapter 11 will further develop touch screen programming, emphasizing the gesture functions and their use in the context of drawing and other graphics operations from our earlier chapters.

10.1 Comments on Touch Screen Programming

Over the decade since the preparation of the first edition of this book, there have been vast improvements in the computational power and capabilities of small computers. Most especially, there have been major improvements in terms of cost for computational ability. Among the many other developments, perhaps the most notable is the continual expansion of the touchscreen as the communication interface between the computer and its user.

The smart phone, of course, is the shining example of the success of the touchscreen. Coupled with the increased computational capability at the micro-scale and the ability to use the touchscreen as the only interface, the smartphone has become a convenient computational device for internet access, gaming, navigation, photography, simple word processing, etc. At the same time that growth in smart phones occurred, the tablet computer has also found a very major place in the world. In many ways it has become a larger version of the smart phone. But, with the increased size of their display screens, tablets have very naturally been used much more for computer-type activities (internet access, gaming, navigation, simple word processing...) and much less frequently for voice communication.

It is clear that advances in computational and touch screen capabilities have made the popularity and utility of smartphones and tablets possible. It is also clear that these devices have not become actual replacements for traditional personal computers. Instead, they are used primarily as devices for viewing content and consuming information — often for entertainment. At the same time, personal computers have remained the major tool for generating content, creating information and actually "doing work". In a technical/engineering context personal computers are still the dominant choice and often the only choice. As just one example, personal computers are important tools used in the engineering design of smart phones and tablets but the reverse, of course, could not be true.

At the time of this writing, the competition in the cell phone and tablet world has become very intense with Google's Android operating system and Apple's iOS operating system leading the way. Microsoft has provided a Windows phone operating system and Windows RT as a tablet environment. However, the latest development by Microsoft and a number of manufacturers in the new world of smart devices has been a movement toward a more integrated personal computer/tablet environment with the release of Windows 8.1. The release of this revision of the Windows operating system has led major manufacturers to create Windows devices which offer tablet operation for viewing or consuming content but which also operate conveniently in a desktop mode. They provide a touch screen with the availability of a keyboard and mouse pad to allow traditional personal computer applications including content creation and the possibility of actually "doing work". The new devices are being marketed as one device for "work and play" with such phrases as "all in one" or "two in one".

At this point, the culmination of the developments in smart devices and personal computers is that the traditional desktop application programs that have been the focus of Chapters 1–9 in this book can now be used on an increasing number of platforms ranging from 7 inch Windows 8.1 tablets to large scale desktop computers. Recent versions of Visual C++ programming tools and the Microsoft Foundation Class applications have adapted to the modern touch screen environment by providing expanded programming capabilities. These capabilities allow desktop programs to be easily created that provide touch screen features whenever they can be used to advantage.

10.2 An Example Program Using the Zoom Gesture

Our first example of gesture programming is shown in the project *Chap10\1_FirstGesture*. This example has taken the simple face of the SimpleAnimate project of Chapter 5 and developed it with the function

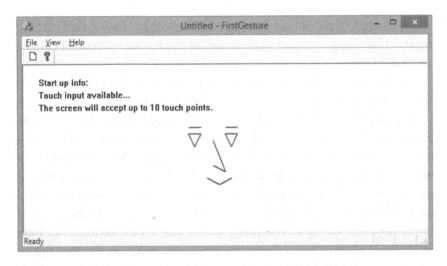

Figure 10.1 Start-up View of the FirstGesture Program

OnGestureZoom so that the face can be "zoomed" or "pinched" with the two-fingered gesture that we all know from the phone/tablet environment. Of course, this zooming or pinching will increase or decrease the image size.

If you bring the FirstGesture project into Visual C++ and build and execute it, the initial screen appears as shown in Figure 10.1. Here you see the simple face from SimpleAnimate in the middle of the window with a start-up statement that touch screen operations are possible (assuming you have a touch screen) appearing at the upper left. At this point, a normal zoom/pinch gesture on your touch screen display will enlarge or shrink the simple face image. After a gesture takes place, the start-up information is removed so that only the face appears at its adjusted size and still near the middle of the window. Figure 10.2 shows the resulting window for the FirstGesture program after a zoom gesture has taken place. As you exercise this program, notice that limits have been placed on the pinch and zoom extremes.

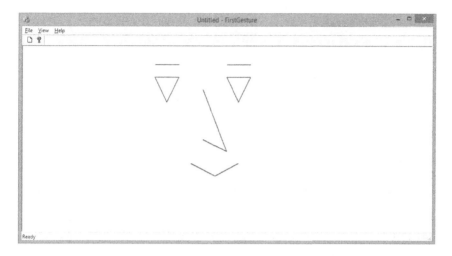

Figure 10.2 View of FirstGesture after Zooming

10.2.1 Basic programming concepts for gestures

At this point we can consider the programming details necessary for creating the zoom gesture behavior. In the recent versions of Visual C++, the MFC application format provides virtual functions for gestures as part of the class CWnd. The view class for a project is derived from the CWnd class and the gesture functions can be accessed to serve as the handlers for each supported gesture when corresponding virtual functions have also been added to the view class for the project.

In the case of this FirstGesture example project, exploring the Class View window, as in Figure 10.3, shows the base classes for the class CFirstGestureView. It can be seen that CFirstGestureView is derived from CView and that the base class of CView is CWnd. Clicking on CWnd in the Class View window allows the list of the functions for the CWnd class to appear in the bottom portion of the Class View window. Scrolling through these functions will show the various "OnGesture..." functions which have been provided to handle gesture events. Here we are considering the OnGestureZoom function. Make a right click on that

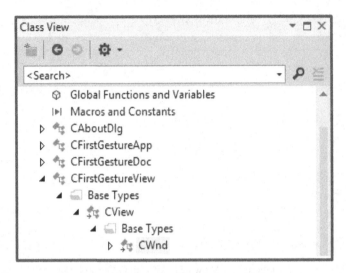

Figure 10.3 Class View of the FirstGesture Project

function (in CWnd) and then a left click on "Go To Declaration" in the resulting options menu. This will display the declaration for the handler function "OnGestureZoom" (from the file afxwin.h). The declaration and comments are in a standard format which is provided for each of the gesture behaviors. This format shows a series of comment statements describing the nature of the gesture function and its arguments. As shown below, these statements are then followed by the single line of code which declares the virtual gesture function itself:

```
/// The method is called upon a gesture zoom event</summary>
/// <returns>
/// TRUE if application processes this event; otherwise FALSE.
/// <param name="ptCenter">Zoom center point. In client coordinates.
/// <param name="lDelta">The distance from the center point. In pixels.
virtual BOOL OnGestureZoom(CPoint ptCenter, long lDelta);
```

In addition to the default declaration in the CWnd class, the OnGestureZoom function must also be added appropriately to the class CFirstGestureView as a virtual function in order for it to be accessible and specifically defined within the FirstGesture project. This can be done by placing a copy of the declaration statement into the file FirstGestureView.h and then a re-declaration statement into FirstGestureView.cpp ready to define the code for OnGestureZoom as a handler function. However, a much more convenient approach for adding the OnGestureZoom function into the FirstGestureView class is to use the Add Member Function Wizard as described below.

For the FirstGesture project, the OnGestureZoom function has been added by clicking on the CFirstGestureView class in the Class View window and selecting Add Function. As expected, this brings up the Add Member Function Wizard. The OnGestureZoom function was then added carefully to the CFirstGestureView class as a virtual function to be compatible with the initial declaration of OnGestureZoom provided in the CWnd class. Figure 10.4 shows the Add Member Function Wizard as prepared and ready for the Finish button to be clicked. Notice that the "virtual" box has been checked, that the return variable is BOOL and that CPoint ptCenter and long lDelta have been shown as the function arguments. After clicking Finish, OnGestureZoom was added to

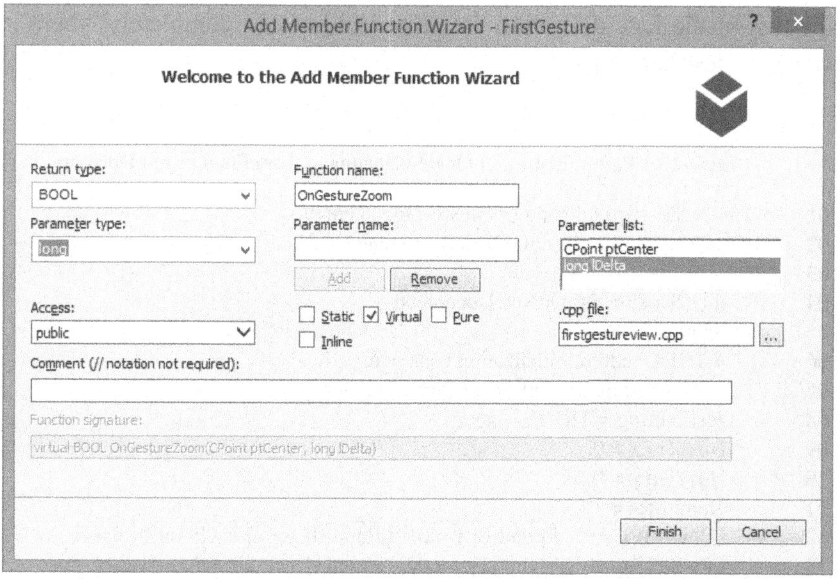

Figure 10.4 Adding OnGestureZoom to the Class CFirstGestureView

the CFirstGestureView.cpp file ready for coding to be inserted. A declaration of OnGestureZoom was also added to the file FirstGestureView.h. With the function now in place, we can discuss the overall programming of the project to create the zoom/pinch behavior for the program operation.

10.2.2 Program structure for zoom and pinch in FirstGesture

To view the structure of the FirstGesture project, we will begin with a look at the OnNewDocument function. This will initialize the data for the project each time that the program is executed or the New icon on the tool bar is clicked. Code from the OnNewDocument function is in Table 10.1. The function creates and stores the simple face, very much the same as originally shown for SimpleAnimate in Section 5.4. We have added a document member variable called JustStarting (line 08) to identify the fact that the program is just starting to run and we will use this variable in displaying the touch screen status as the program window first appears. In lines 09 and 10 NoseTip is zeroed and following this the twelve line face is defined. We use dots in lines 14 and 15 to represent the rest of the face definition data that can be seen completely where it was first described in Table 5.13.

Table 10.1 Partial Listing of OnNewDocument from FirstGestureDoc.cpp

```
01    /* This is the  partial listing of OnNewDocument */
02    BOOL CFirstGestureDoc::OnNewDocument()
03    {
04         if (!CDocument::OnNewDocument())
05         return FALSE;
06         // TODO: add reinitialization code here
07         // (SDI documents will reuse this document
08         JustStarting = TRUE;
09         NoseTip.x = 0;
10         NoseTip.y = 0;
11         NumLines = 12;
12         FPoint[0].x = 0;  FPoint[0].y = 0;  LPoint[0].x = -20; LPoint[0].y = -1
13         FPoint[1].x = 0;  FPoint[1].y = 0;  LPoint[1].x = -20; LPoint[1].y = -50;
14     .
15     .
```

Table 10.2 Listing of OnDraw from FirstGestureView.cpp

```
01   /* This is the listing of OnDraw */
02   void CFirstGestureView::OnDraw(CDC* pDC)
03   {       CFirstGestureDoc* pDoc = GetDocument();
04           ASSERT_VALID(pDoc);
05           if (!pDoc) return;
06           // TODO: add draw code for native data here
07           if (pDoc->JustStarting == TRUE) StartUpDisplay();
08           pDoc->JustStarting = FALSE;
09           pDC->SelectObject(&m_BluePen);
10           pDoc->NoseTip.x = m_CenterX;
11           pDoc->NoseTip.y = m_CenterY;
12   for (int i = 0; i < pDoc->NumLines; i++)  {
13           int Fx = int(m_ZoomMult*pDoc->FPoint[i].x) + pDoc->NoseTip.x;
14           int Fy = int(m_ZoomMult*pDoc->FPoint[i].y) + pDoc->NoseTip.y;
15           int Lx = int(m_ZoomMult*pDoc->LPoint[i].x) + pDoc->NoseTip.x;
16           int Ly = int(m_ZoomMult*pDoc->LPoint[i].y) + pDoc->NoseTip.y;
17           pDC->MoveTo(Fx, Fy);
18           pDC->LineTo(Lx, Ly);
19           }
20   }
```

We will now consider the OnDraw function of FirstGesture. It can be seen in Table 10.2. The first added code in line 07 of OnDraw checks the document variable JustStarting to see if the program has just begun running. If so, it calls the view class function StartUpDisplay to check on the availability of touch screen operations and displays the status (we will look carefully at StartUpDisplay shortly). Line 08 then sets JustStarting to False so that the start-up information will not reappear. Of course, line 09 readies the blue pen. Then lines 10 and 11 set the values for the NoseTip point so that the face will be maintained at the window center. The view class variables m_CenterX and m_CenterY are set at half of the screen width and height in the message handler OnSize (the reader is left to verify this by inspecting the OnSize function).

Next, the for loop of lines 12–19 draws the face on the screen with the nose tip at the center of the window. Lines 13–16 adjust the coordinates appropriately for the first and last point of each line. In these statements, notice that the view class variable m_ZoomMult controls the size of the face image as it multiplies the coordinate values. The last statements of the for loop then use a MoveTo and a LineTo to place each scaled line on the screen. The variable m_ZoomMult was initially set to m_ZoomMult = 1 in the view class constructor function so that the first drawing of the face is at normal size as defined in the OnNewDocument function. As the touch screen is used, OnGestureZoom will make adjustments to m_ZoomMult.

The function StartUpDisplay shown in line 07 of OnDraw outputs an initial display of start-up information after it performs a check of the touch screen capabilities. Table 10.3 shows the coding of the StartUpDisplay function which was simply added to the view class as a member function. In Table 10.3, line 04 identifies the current window preparing to write the start-up information. Line 07 uses the Windows API function GetSystemMetrics. This function is available in MFC to

Table 10.3 Listing of StartUpDisplay from FirstGestureView.cpp

```
01   \*Listing of StartUpDisplay */
02   void CFirstGestureView::StartUpDisplay()
03   {
04       CClientDC aDC(this);
05       CString Buffer;
06       int nInputs = 0;
07       nInputs = GetSystemMetrics(SM_MAXIMUMTOUCHES);
08   if (nInputs == 0)  {
09       Buffer.Format(L"Start up info:");
10       aDC.TextOut(25, 20, Buffer);
11       Buffer.Format(L"Touch input not available.");
12       aDC.TextOut(25, 40, Buffer);
13       }
14   if (nInputs > 0)  {
15       Buffer.Format(L"Start up info:");
16       aDC.TextOut(25, 20, Buffer);
17       Buffer.Format(L"Touch input available...");
18       aDC.TextOut(25, 40, Buffer);
19       Buffer.Format(L"The screen will accept up to %d touch points.", nInputs);
20       aDC.TextOut(25, 60, Buffer);
21       }
22       m_ZoomMult = 1.;
23   }
```

identify characteristics of the system on which the program is running. In this case, we wish to find the touch capability of the system. Calling the function GetSystemMetrics using the index parameter SM_MAXIMUMTOUCHES returns the number of finger touches that the screen can process. If the number is zero, touch screen is not supported, nInputs = 0 and lines 08–13 output the information that touch screen is not available. If touch screen is supported, nInputs reflects the number of possible touches and is output by lines 14–21. Finally, line 22 sets m_ZoomMult to unity to support instances where the new document option is clicked in a running program.

At this point we have developed the setting in which the FirstGesture project can demonstrate programming for zoom/pinch operations. We began the discussion by showing where the declaration of the virtual function OnGestureZoom resides in the CWnd class (Figure 10.3). We then indicated the process of forming an accessible version of the OnGestureZoom function by using the Add Function Wizard (Figure 10.4). We also created the data for a simple image (Table 10.1) and we have shown the code for placing the image on the screen in OnDraw (Table 10.2). Of course, the for loop that draws our simple face contains a zooming variable m_ZoomMult to scale the image. As just discussed, OnDraw also calls a start-up function (Table 10.3) which checks on the availability of touch screen support and displays that in the initial program window.

We are now ready to explore our OnGestureZoom function to see the manipulation of the variable m_ZoomMult for adjusting the image size with zoom and pinch gestures. The function is shown in Table 10.4. Of the arguments shown in line 02, ptCenter captures the center of the finger placements making the zoom gesture while the argument lDelta identifies the movement made by the fingers making the gesture. In Section 10.3 below we will look more closely at parameter values in the various OnGesture functions. Now, for the FirstGesture project, we only consider the lDelta argument. In this case, the nose tip position is fixed at the window center and lDelta is used for adjusting image size as zooming takes place. This is first seen in line 04 where we use the variable

Table 10.4 Listing of OnGestureZoom from FirstGestureView.cpp

```
01    /* This is the  listing of OnGestureZoom */
02    BOOL CFirstGestureView::OnGestureZoom(CPoint ptCenter, long lDelta)
03    {
04        double ZoomInc = lDelta;
05        double ZoomIncLim = 5.; double ZoomScale = 0.025;
06        if (ZoomInc > ZoomIncLim) ZoomInc = ZoomIncLim;
07        if (ZoomInc < -ZoomIncLim) ZoomInc = -ZoomIncLim;
08        m_ZoomMult += ZoomScale * ZoomInc;
09        if (m_ZoomMult > 5)  m_ZoomMult = 5;
10        if(m_ZoomMult < 1./5.)  m_ZoomMult = 1./5.;
11        RedrawWindow();
12        return TRUE;
13    }
```

ZoomInc to capture the value of lDelta. Line 05 sets a limiting value for the zooming increment and also sets a scaling variable to be used in incrementing the zoom factor. Lines 06 and 07 test ZoomInc against positive and negative limits on the increment and line 08 increments (or decrements) the member variable m_ZoomMult accordingly. Lines 09 and 10 control the limits of the zooming variable so that the image does not become unreasonably large or small.

The function OnGestureZoom is continually called while a zoom gesture is in action so that the zooming increment of line 08 quite rapidly changes the image size. The sensation of zoom speed can be varied easily by changes in ZoomScale and/or ZoomIncLim. A zoom function in the form of Table 10.4 results in a smooth zooming operation which is easily controlled by the user's gesture. Notice that the OnDraw function is executed by the call to RedrawWindow in line 11 to produce a newly scaled image. The RedrawWindow function redraws the current window and, in this context, is equivalent to the UpdateAllViews function that we have used frequently in earlier chapters.

10.3 A Detailed Look at the Gesture Functions

The gesture handler functions that are available within the Microsoft Foundation Classes include:

- OnGesturePan
- OnGestureTwoFingerTap
- OnGesturePressAndTap
- OnGestureRotate

as well as the OnGestureZoom function that we discussed at length and demonstrated in Section 10.2. Each of these functions has its own argument list reflecting the nature of the gesture that it interprets. Each also has a Boolean return variable that is set to true within the function to indicate that the gesture is being processed. These details are described as comments where the gesture handler functions first appear in the CWnd class declaration in the file afxwin.h. To help in understanding the very specific nature of these functions we have prepared the example project in *Chap10\2_GestureDetails*. If you click on the .sln file in that directory you will see the structure of our GestureDetails project. Building and executing the project will show start-up information regarding touch screen capability similar to the text of Figure 10.1 that opened the FirstGesture project (Section 10.2). However, touching the window in this program will now trigger the various gesture functions. After a touch, the start-up information dissolves and the parameter values of the triggered gesture will be displayed during the gesture.

Figure 10.5 shows the display for the handler function OnGestureRotate. You can see its arguments displayed including the coordinates in pixels of the center point of the rotation gesture and the angle (in radians) of the amount of rotation since the gesture began. If a rotation gesture is applied in the window, the parameter values will be continuously updated and displayed. Similarly, if you make other gestures in the window, the type of gesture detected and its parameter values will be displayed. Try a two finger tap gesture, or try the zoom gesture used in Section 10.2 and you will see the parameter values of the gesture function displayed in response to the gesture.

It must be mentioned here that mouse clicks are, of course, a form of graphical interaction for any operating Windows program. With an MFC program operating on a touch screen, the touch of a single finger is normally interpreted as a left button mouse click and the pixel touched is

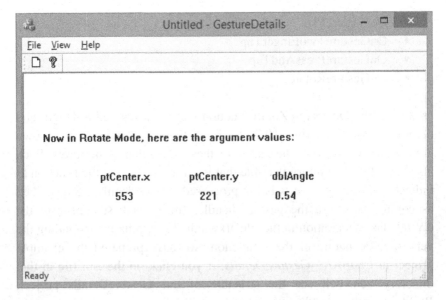

Figure 10.5 Sample Output from GestureDetails

recorded as the cursor position. The GestureDetails project displays mouse button information and mouse cursor location in response to both mouse clicks and finger touches. If you make a few mouse clicks, the results will be represented in the GestureDetails display. In this program, single finger touches also produce a mouse response but may also activate the panning gesture. We will discuss more of these details below. But, first, we will consider the structure of the GestureDetails project.

10.3.1 Programming of GestureDetails

The focus of this project is to display information about the detailed nature of touch screen inputs provided in the gesture functions that are part of the Microsoft Foundation Classes. We display these details by placing "messages" within each of the gesture functions, the OnDraw function then displays the messages in the program window to illustrate

Table 10.5 Listing of OnDraw from GestureDetailsView.cpp

```
01   /* This is a listing of OnDraw */
02   void CGestureDetailsView::OnDraw(CDC* pDC)
03   {
04       CGestureDetailsDoc* pDoc = GetDocument();  ASSERT_VALID(pDoc);
05       if (!pDoc) return;
06       // TODO: add draw code for native data here
07       if (pDoc->JustStarting == TRUE) StartUpDisplay();
08       pDoc->JustStarting = FALSE;
09       pDC->TextOut(25, 75, m_Message1);
10       pDC->TextOut(100, 125, m_Message2);
11       pDC->TextOut(100, 150, m_Message3);
12       pDC->TextOutW(25, 200, m_MessageUp1);
13       pDC->TextOut(100, 250, m_MessageUp2);
14       pDC->TextOut(100, 275, m_MessageUp3);
15       m_MessageUp1.Format(L"                    ");
16       m_MessageUp2 = m_MessageUp1; m_MessageUp3 = m_MessageUp1;
17   }
```

the parametric values associated with a currently active gesture. Table 10.5 shows the OnDraw function for the GestureDetails project. The first added code is at line 07 where the JustStarting variable from the document class is tested in order to execute the function StartUpDisplay (to be discussed next). This provides start-up information, as in the previous FirstGesture project and also performs some required initialization. Lines 09–14 of OnDraw then output messages (in the form of CString member variables) which are received from the gesture handler functions and also from the message handlers for left button down and left button up. The final code in lines 15 and 16 clears a few messages that should only appear when needed.

The function StartUpDisplay is shown in Table 10.6. The core of this function uses the GetSystemMetrics function in line 08 to test for the availability of touch input, and lines 09–18 display the results of the touch input test. However, another very important task for StartUpDisplay is to enable the operation of the rotate gesture. The rotate gesture is the only gesture that requires an enabling operation. The others are enabled and active by default (as long as the appropriate gesture handling functions

Table 10.6 Listing of StartUpDisplay from GestureDetailsView.cpp

```
01    /* This is a listing of StartUpDisplay */
02    void CGestureDetailsView::StartUpDisplay()
03    {
04         CGestureConfig FixRotate;
05         FixRotate.EnableRotate();
06         SetGestureConfig(&FixRotate);
07         CClientDC aDC(this);   CString Buffer;
08         int nInputs = GetSystemMetrics(SM_MAXIMUMTOUCHES);
09    if (nInputs == 0)  {
10         Buffer.Format(L"Start up info:"); aDC.TextOut(25, 20, Buffer);
11         Buffer.Format(L"Touch input not available."); aDC.TextOut(25, 40, Buffer);
12         }
13    if (nInputs > 0)  {
14         Buffer.Format(L"Start up info:"); aDC.TextOut(25, 20, Buffer);
15         Buffer.Format(L"Touch input available..."); aDC.TextOut(25, 40, Buffer);
16         Buffer.Format(L"The screen will accept up to %d touch points.", nInputs);
17         aDC.TextOut(25, 60, Buffer);
18         }
19         m_Message1.Format(L"                                              ");
20         m_Message2 = m_Message1; m_Message3 = m_Message1;
21    }
```

have been prepared in the view class). The lines 04–06 in Table 10.6 activate the rotate gesture. Line 04 declares an object of the class CGestureConfig which we've called FixRotate. Line 05 then uses the EnableRotate function to set FixRotate appropriately and then the function SetGestureConfig is called in line 06 to actually enable the rotate gesture. This enabling sequence must be completed for the OnGestureRotate handler function to operate. The sequence can be provided in any appropriate location including OnDraw, but it only needs to execute once as the program begins operation. The last few lines of StartUpDisplay in Table 10.6 assure that unnecessary information does not appear when the start-up touch screen message is displayed.

Perhaps the simplest of the gesture functions is the two finger tap. It is implemented by the function OnGestureTwoFingerTap and is triggered, of course, by two fingers tapping the screen. The parameters transmitted to the function are simply the coordinates of the midpoint

Table 10.7 Listing of OnGestureTwoFingerTap from GestureDetailsView.cpp

```
01   /* This is the listing of OnGestureTwoFingerTap */
02   BOOL CGestureDetailsView::OnGestureTwoFingerTap(CPoint ptCenter)
03   {
04        m_Message1.Format(L"Two Finger Tap, here are the argument values:");
05        m_Message2.Format(L"ptCenter.x        ptCenter.y");
06        m_Message3.Format(L"%8d           %8d", ptCenter.x, ptCenter.y);
07        RedrawWindow();
08        return TRUE;
09   }
```

between the two fingers. The function executes only once as a tap is received and, as expected, the results of the tap are controlled by the code placed in the function OnGestureTwoFingerTap. Table 10.7 shows the function as coded for this example of GestureDetails. In this case, the function creates three messages to be written by OnDraw. Lines 04–06 fill the CString member variables. The variable m_Message1 indicates that the tap was received. Then m_Message2 provides a label for the tap coordinates of ptCenter (in pixels) contained in m_Message3. Line 07 redraws the window and line 08 returns true after execution. Of course, in a real program, this function would do something useful, typically applying the value of the ptCenter coordinates.

The OnGestureTwoFingerTap function is a gesture function which executes only once for the tap event. When the tap is received, it is triggered and its code is followed. This is also the process for the function OnGesturePressAndTap which executes when a finger is pressing on the screen and a second finger performs a tap. This executes only once for the event and makes the coordinates of the pressed point available (ptPress) as well as the distance from the pressed point. In this example we simply create messages to display that information but, normally the data would be available for program functionality.

The other gesture functions OnGestureZoom, OnGestureRotate and OnGesturePan all result from a touch behavior that is not a single event but has some aspect of continuity to it. These functions do not just execute a single time but continue to execute as long as the gesture behavior continues. We demonstrated the operation of the OnGestureZoom function in the FirstGesture example of Section 10.1. You can see the behavior of its parameters here in the executing GestureDetails program by carrying out a zoom or pinch behavior and watching the alphanumeric values displayed. Notice that there are continual variations in the data while the gesture is in effect.

Table 10.8 shows an example of code for a continually varying gesture. Provided that the rotation gesture has been enabled, whenever a rotation is detected, the OnGestureRotate function will repeatedly execute as long as the action continues. In an application program, the gesture location and rotation angle can be used to rotate an image or a scene. In this example, we only display the parameters defined by the gesture — the rotation center point and the angle of rotation in radians. In Table 10.8, line 04 produces the message that "rotate" is active and the message of line 05 labels the parameter values to be written. Line 06 then outputs the coordinates of the center point and the current angle of rotation. In executing the program and performing a rotation, notice the behavior of the rotation angle displayed as you rotate your fingers. The rotation angle starts at zero as the gesture begins. It increases or decreases during movement and tracks the rotation relative to the position where the gesture was originally detected.

Table 10.8 Listing of OnGestureRotate from GestureDetailsView.cpp

```
01   /* This is a listing of OnGestureRotate */
02   BOOL CGestureDetailsView::OnGestureRotate(CPoint ptCenter, double dblAngle)
03   {
04        m_Message1.Format(L"Now in Rotate Mode, here are the argument values:");
05        m_Message2.Format(L"ptCenter.x        ptCenter.y        dblAngle");
06        m_Message3.Format(L"%8d  %8d  %8.2lf", ptCenter.x, ptCenter.y, dblAngle);
07        RedrawWindow();
08        return TRUE;
09   }
```

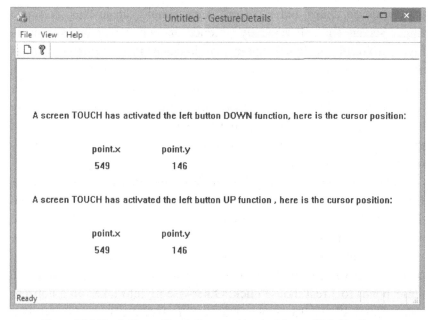

Figure 10.6 Single Finger Touch Processed by the Mouse Click Handlers

10.3.2 Considering mouse clicks

Until the advent of touch screens, the accepted method for graphical interaction was the mouse and the mouse click. In our MFC programs, the left button click that we use so normally activates the OnLButtonDown message handler function. It also passes the cursor coordinates at the time of the click into the message handler for the program to manage appropriately. In the touch screen environment, a simple tap of the screen in an MFC program is typically treated as a left button mouse click. In a program prepared for gesture interaction, the user's gestures can be directly recognized and a finger tap may be handled as a default mouse click or can be overridden as desired.

Our GestureDetails demonstration program has included left button down and left button up message handlers to illustrate the mouse click situation. While running the GestureDetails program, perform some left button mouse clicks and carry out some simple screen taps. A single finger screen tap will typically produce an output that appears as in Figure 10.6. In that figure, the display indicates that a screen touch has activated both the left button down and left button up message handlers and the cursor coordinates are shown. In this case the cursor coordinates for both down and up are the same. Of course, if you carry out a mouse button left click, you will see a similar display to Figure 10.6 except that the activation will be described as resulting from a mouse button click rather than a screen touch.

Table 10.9 shows the left button down function of GestureDetails. Here you can see (in lines 6 and 7 and in lines 09 and 10) the two different messages for a screen touch and a "real" mouse click. The if statement of line 08 decides between the two possibilities based on the value of m_Info. The MFC function GetMessageExtraInfo is used in line 05 to set the value of m_Info. As seen in line 08, a value of m_Info = 0 corresponds to a real mouse click. Otherwise m_Info takes on a nonzero value. Lines 12 and 13 prepare messages to indicate the cursor position of the mouse click and line 14 redraws the window. If you look at the OnLButtonUp function in GestureDetails, you will see the same coding structure as above but the m_Info value obtained in OnLButtonDown is

Table 10.9 Listing of OnLButtonDown from GestureDetailsView.cpp

```
01    /* This is a listing of OnLButtonDown */
02    void CGestureDetailsView::OnLButtonDown(UINT nFlags,CPoint point)
03    {
04         // TODO: Add your message handler code here and/or call default
05         m_Info = GetMessageExtraInfo();
06         m_Message1.Format(L"A screen TOUCH has activated the left button
07                DOWN function, here is the cursor position:");
08    if (m_Info == 0)  {
09         m_Message1.Format(L"A mouse CLICK has activated the left button
10                DOWN function, here is the cursor position:");
11         }
12         m_Message2.Format(L"    point.x         point.y");
13         m_Message3.Format(L"%8d            %8d", point.x, point.y);
14         RedrawWindow();
15         CView::OnLButtonDown(nFlags, point);
16    }
```

used for the decision process (m_Info is a member variable of the view class).

The introduction of the panning gesture with its event handler OnGesturePan creates potential confusion with the OnMouseMove gesture when a finger touch is producing the "mouse" movement. While executing the GestureDetails program, you can explore the distinction between the two. While moving your finger across the screen, observe the messages displayed. Typically a generally vertical finger motion will result in a message from OnGesturePan while a horizontal swipe produces a message from OnMouseMove. You should also note that a two finger movement is quite reliably detected as a panning gesture. Of course, a simple finger tap will correspond to the straight-forward mouse click information displayed in Figure 10.6. It is helpful to keep these guidelines in mind to avoid confusion in programming for a single finger touch. In the project folder *2_GestureDetails*, you will find it useful to explore the functions OnGesturePan and OnMouseMove to see how their message displays have been programmed.

At this time there is not a touch gesture directly equivalent to a right button mouse click. Of course, by providing an OnRButtonDown function, real mouse clicks of the right button can be recognized and processed. However, in a touch screen environment, when a right button down equivalent is required, a specific gesture should be identified and appropriate coding provided so that the desired program action takes place. The press and tap gesture can be used as a right click equivalent with its function OnGesturePressAndTap. The two finger tap is also an alternative for use as a right button click.

At this point, we have discussed the GestureDetails program quite thoroughly. Each of the gesture handler functions has been included in the project with message displays to show the gesture parameters when the gesture is being detected. We have presented the details for OnGestureRotate and OnGestureTwoFingerTap as well as the OnLButtonDown function. Review of the remaining functions is left as a task for the reader. You will find the message creation to be quite similar. However, we do note that two additional variables have been included in the display messages for OnGesturePan. The calculated variables "dx" and "dy" represent the dynamics of the finger motion creating the panning gesture.

10.4 Using Gestures in the SimpleAnimate Example

We used the SimpleAnimate face to start our discussion of gestures in Section 10.1. We will continue to revisit the SimpleAnimate project now in developing a gesture version of the program that we originally introduced in Section 5.4.

Consider the example project *Chap10\3_TouchSimpleAnimate*. To begin our discussion of the program, click on the .sln file and bring it into the Visual C++ development environment. If you build and execute the project, you should see the touch screen announcement as a start-up display along with some gesture instructions similar to Figure 10.7. As described in the prompts, the simple face will respond to both mouse

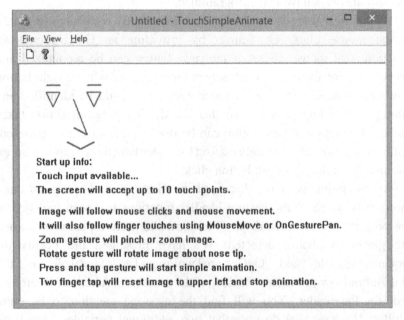

Figure 10.7 Opening Screen of TouchSimpleAnimate

inputs and touch gestures. Mouse clicks, of course, will also continue to function on the menu and tool bars. As you begin making gestures, the text will no longer display but the simple image will persist and you can manipulate it with gestures. With a few gestures, you should be able to create the display of Figure 10.8. If necessary, touching (or clicking) the New Document tool bar item will clear the display, initialize the simple face and repeat the prompts.

We will now look at the coding that supports the display and allows the various gestures to take effect. Of course, the OnNewDocument function is the starting point for the program. The listing is not shown here but you can find it in the development environment with a few clicks. For TouchSimpleAnimate, the function OnNewDocument is very much in the same form as previously presented in Table 10.1 for the FirstGesture project (based on the original SimpleAnimate in Table 5.13). The JustStarting variable is again initialized in OnNewDocument and it is used to manage the start-up display as can be seen in the OnDraw function of this project shown in Table 10.10. In line 07 of OnDraw, the JustStarting variable is tested and if true, the StartUpDisplay function is called. This function then enables the

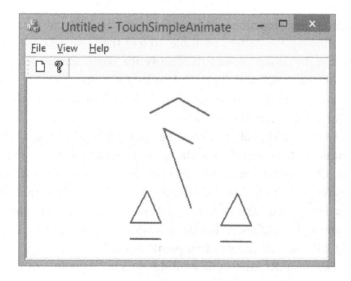

Figure 10.8 The Simple Face after a Few Gestures

Table 10.10 Listing of OnDraw from TouchSimpleAnimateView.cpp

```
01   /* This is a listing of OnDraw */
02   void CTouchSimpleAnimateView::OnDraw(CDC* pDC)
03   {
04        CTouchSimpleAnimateDoc* pDoc = GetDocument();
05        ASSERT_VALID(pDoc); if (!pDoc) return;
06        // TODO: add draw code for native data here
07        if (pDoc->JustStarting == TRUE) StartUpDisplay();
08        pDoc->JustStarting = FALSE;
09        pDC->SelectObject(&m_BluePen);
10        pDC->TextOut(25, 25, m_Message);
11        m_Message = "";
12        CPoint RFPoint[100];   CPoint RLPoint[100];
13        RotateFunc(pDoc->FPoint, pDoc->LPoint, RFPoint, RLPoint,
14                   pDoc->NumLines, m_RotAngle);
15   for (int i = 0; i < pDoc->NumLines; i++)  {
16        int Fx = int(m_ZoomMult*RFPoint[i].x) + pDoc->NoseTip.x;
17        int Fy = int(m_ZoomMult*RFPoint[i].y) + pDoc->NoseTip.y;
18        int Lx = int(m_ZoomMult*RLPoint[i].x) + pDoc->NoseTip.x;
19        int Ly = int(m_ZoomMult*RLPoint[i].y) + pDoc->NoseTip.y;
20        pDC->MoveTo(Fx, Fy);
21        pDC->LineTo(Lx, Ly);
22        }
23   }
```

OnGestureRotate function and tests for the availability of touch screen inputs following the pattern of Table 10.6 in the GestureDetails project. It produces the initial prompt to identify the touch screen possibilities. Then additional code in the StartUpDisplay function sends text output to the screen to provide the gesture instructions in the initial window of TouchSimpleAnimate shown in Figure 10.7.

In Table 10.10, after executing StartUpDisplay, line 08 sets JustStarting to false and then a blue pen is prepared for drawing. Lines 10 and 11 manage the message variable set in OnMouseMove or OnGesturePan which will be discussed in Section 10.4.3. Line 12 declares a new set of first and last points that are used to store the rotated image when the OnGestureRotate function becomes active. The array RFPoint will store the rotated first points of the lines defining our simple image. The array RLPoint will store the rotated last points of the image lines. Then the rotate function RotateFunc (see Table 10.11) is called by lines 13 and 14 to take the original image points and rotate them through the rotation angle m_RotAngle. The argument list for RotateFunc includes the FPoint and LPoint arrays for the image as well as RFPoint and RLPoint which will hold the rotated image lines. Of course, the last argument m_RotAngle is the desired angle of rotation for the image. Finally, the for loop of lines 15–22 draws the rotated image on the screen. Notice that lines 16–19 include the zoom multiplying factor m_ZoomMult and that the zoomed image continues to be positioned relative to the x and y coordinates of the nose tip.

10.4.1 Implementing image rotation

The rotate function as shown in Table 10.11 actually carries out the image rotation when the rotate gesture is recognized. The memory of the current rotation angle is carried by the view class member variable m_RotAngle. It is received as Angle in the argument list of RotateFunc (lines 02 and 03) in Table 10.11. Also shown as arguments are pointers to the array of start points for the lines (SPoint), the end points for the lines (EPoint), the rotated start points (RSPoint), and rotated end points (REPoint). Note that the SPoints and EPoints correspond to the

Table 10.11 Listing of RotateFunc from TouchSimpleAnimateView.cpp

```
01   /* This is a listing of RotateFunc */
02   void CTouchSimpleAnimateView::RotateFunc(CPoint* SPoint, CPoint* EPoint,
03          CPoint* RSPoint, CPoint* REPoint, int NumPoints, double Angle)
04   {
05          double SinAngle = sin(Angle);   double CosAngle = cos(Angle);
06          double sav1x, sav1y, sav2x, sav2y;
07   for (int i = 0; i<NumPoints; i++)   {
08          sav1x = SPoint[i].x; sav1y = SPoint[i].y;
09          sav2x = EPoint[i].x; sav2y = EPoint[i].y;
10          RSPoint[i].x = int(sav1x * CosAngle - sav1y * SinAngle);
11          RSPoint[i].y = int(sav1x * SinAngle + sav1y * CosAngle);
12          REPoint[i].x = int(sav2x * CosAngle - sav2y * SinAngle);
13          REPoint[i].y = int(sav2x * SinAngle + sav2y * CosAngle);
14          }
15   }
```

stored image and that the RSPoints and REPoints are used for display purposes. The sine and cosine of the rotation angle are obtained in line 05 and are applied in the for loop of lines 07–14. The familiar rotation equations (Section 8.2) are applied in lines 10–13 to obtain the arrays of rotated start and end points.

Another step in the rotation process of TouchSimpleAnimate is the control of the view class member variable m_RotAngle from the gesture function OnGestureRotate. The GestureDetails project in Section 10.3 allowed an inspection of the parameters in each gesture during the gesture operation. Close observation of the rotate gesture in Section 10.3 shows that the rotation angle (in radians) begins at zero with each rotation gesture and measures the gesture rotation angle until the gesture concludes. In this example we have used an incremental approach for the rotation gesture so that the image rotation appears smooth as the gesture takes place. In addition, the results of a rotation are preserved by the image orientation and a new image rotation begins where the last one concluded (without returning to the zero position).

Table 10.12 presents the listing of OnGestureRotate used to rotate our simple face. Here we are focused only on the angle of rotation and are not concerned with the center of rotation. Our rotations will take place about the nose tip as controlled by the RotateFunc and the display loop

Table 10.12 Listing of OnGestureRotate from TouchSimpleAnimateView.cpp

```
01   /* This is a listing of OnGestureRotate */
02   BOOL CTouchSimpleAnimateView::OnGestureRotate(CPoint ptCenter,
03        double dblAngle)
04   {
05        if (abs(dblAngle) < .01)  m_SavdblAngle = 0;
06        double DeltaAngle = dblAngle - m_SavdblAngle;
07        double LimDelta = 0.2;
08        if (DeltaAngle > LimDelta)DeltaAngle = LimDelta;
09        if (DeltaAngle < -LimDelta)DeltaAngle = -LimDelta;
10        m_SavdblAngle = dblAngle;
11        m_RotAngle = m_RotAngle - DeltaAngle;
12        RedrawWindow();
13        return TRUE;
14   }
```

of OnDraw. Line 05 of Table 10.12 initializes the variable m_SavdblAngle as the rotate gesture starts. Line 06 then calculates the change in angle "DeltaAngle" since the last cycle of the gesture function. Recall that the OnGestureRotate function continues to cycle as long as a rotate gesture is recognized. At each cycle, line 11 increments the m_RotAngle variable and line 12 results in redrawing the image so that the face rotation tends to follow the gesture rotation. Lines 07–09 serve to limit spurious rotations by bounding DeltaAngle. Line 10 captures the current value of the rotation angle for use by line 06 in the next cycle of OnGestureRotate. Notice that when a rotation gesture concludes and a new rotation gesture is begun, the variable m_SavdblAngle will be reset to zero. The variable m_RotAngle will be unchanged (holding the face in place) until the new gesture proceeds and cycling through the gesture function begins again.

10.4.2 Considering the other gesture functions

The rotate gesture strategy described above is the most complex of the gesture implementations for this project which brings touch screen controls to our simple animation example. The pinch/zoom operation based on the function OnGestureZoom follows the pattern of Section 10.2.2 for the FirstGesture project. The OnGestureZoom function used here is identical to that presented earlier in Table 10.4 and the coding in

Table 10.13 Listing of OnGesturePressAndTap from TouchSimpleAnimateView.cpp

```
01   /* This is a listing of OnGesturePressAndTap */
02   BOOL CTouchSimpleAnimateView::OnGesturePressAndTap(CPoint ptPress,
03        long lDelta)
04   {
05        CTouchSimpleAnimateDoc* pDoc = GetDocument();
06        pDoc->NoseTip = ptPress;
07        SetTimer(1, 500, NULL);
08        pDoc->UpdateAllViews(NULL);
09        return TRUE;
10   }
```

lines 16–19 in the OnDraw function of Table 10.10 also follows the pattern of the FirstGesture project of Section 10.2.

Two of the remaining gesture functions used in this project are OnGestureTwoFingerTap and OnGesturePressAndTap. We use the press and tap gesture to start the simple animation. The two finger tap is used to reset the image to its starting point in the upper left corner of the window and to stop the animation (if it is running).

The code for OnGesturePressAndTap is shown in Table 10.13. It consists of a just a few important statements that will activate the animation. Line 06 sets the nose tip position to the place where the "press" touch took place. Line 07 sets timer number one to 500 milliseconds and line 08 updates the window resulting in the face movement to the pressed point. As the timer "ticks", the OnTimer message handler is called and actually carries out the animation beginning at the new position. The OnTimer function used here is identical to that in Section 5.4 where we first discussed the SimpleAnimate project (Table 5.18).

Table 10.14 presents the code for OnGestureTwoFingerTap. The purpose of this function is to reset the image to the start point and remove zooming and rotation from the image. Exploring the function, we see that line 05 stops the animation by killing the timer and that lines 06

Table 10.14 Listing of OnGestureTwoFingerTap from TouchSimpleAnimateView.cpp

```
01    /* This is a listing of OnGestureTwoFingerTap */
02    BOOL CTouchSimpleAnimateView::OnGestureTwoFingerTap
03        (CPoint ptCenter)
04    {
05        KillTimer(1);
06        m_ZoomMult = 1;
07        m_RotAngle = 0;
08        CTouchSimpleAnimateDoc* pDoc = GetDocument();
09        pDoc->NoseTip.x = 100;
10        pDoc->NoseTip.y = 100;
11        pDoc->UpdateAllViews(NULL);
12        return TRUE;
13    }
```

and 07 return the zoom factor to unity while setting the rotation angle to zero. After identifying the document, lines 09 and 10 return the image to the upper left corner and finally, line 11 updates the view.

10.4.3 Managing the mouse operations

As has been mentioned, this TouchSimpleAnimate project has been developed to use gestures as well as mouse motion for movement of the face image. Clicks of the traditional mouse button are processed by OnLButtonDown and OnLButtonUp which are unchanged from Chapter 5 (see for example Table 5.15). A quick single finger tap will also trigger these functions and the image will follow the taps. Moving the mouse with the left button down will trigger OnMouseMove (Table 10.15) and the image will follow the mouse as in the earlier SimpleAnimate project. Line 07 assigns the nose tip position as the mouse moves and line 09 redraws the window while the mouse is moving. We have also inserted a "message" at line 08 so that OnDraw can display "Now in MouseMove" in the program window (line 10 of Table 10.10). This message has been inserted because a single finger horizontal swipe will typically trigger the OnMouseMove function and the user can control the face position with a single finger gesture. The message is intended to identify when OnMouseMove is active.

Table 10.15 Listing of OnMouseMove from TouchSimpleAnimateView.cpp

```
01   /* This is a listing of OnMouseMove */
02   void CTouchSimpleAnimateView::OnMouseMove(UINT nFlags, CPoint point)
03   {
04       // TODO: Add your message handler code here and/or call default
05       CTouchSimpleAnimateDoc* pDoc = GetDocument();
06   if (m_LeftDown == "Yes")  {
07       pDoc->NoseTip = point;
08       m_Message.Format(L"Now in MouseMove!");
09       pDoc->UpdateAllViews(NULL);
10       }
11   CView::OnMouseMove(nFlags, point);
12   }
```

On the other hand, a single finger motion in a generally vertical direction will typically trigger the OnGesturePan function which we show in Table 10.16. This function will also be triggered when a two finger panning gesture is recognized. We have included both OnMouseMove and OnGesturePan in this project so that a finger touch will reliably result in movement of the simple face. We have included display messages in both functions so that this example project can demonstrate the differences in the activation of the two functions.

Referring now to the OnGesturePan function of Table 10.16, we can see in line 02 that the CPoint objects ptFrom and ptTo are passed into the function when the gesture is recognized. They are updated as long as the gesture continues. Line 05 uses the CPoint object Delta to obtain the change in panning position and lines 06 and 07 make incremental changes in the nose tip position at each cycle through the function. When line 09 updates the window, the image appears to move in proportion to the panning motion. Of course, the message generated in line 08 indicates that OnGesturePan is active.

We used the difference in ptFrom and ptTo of OnGesturePan to control motion of the face. As a result the face moves in proportion to the panning gesture but the nose tip does not exactly follow the finger position. Either ptFrom or ptTo could be used to position the nose tip during panning so that face position could be controlled by the panning finger. We have used the "Delta" strategy because spurious or incidental finger touches during zooming or rotating can trigger the panning

Table 10.16 Listing of OnGesturePan from TouchSimpleAnimateView.cpp

```
01   /* This is a listing of OnGesturePan */
02   BOOL CTouchSimpleAnimateView::OnGesturePan(CPoint ptFrom, CPoint ptTo)
03   {
04       CTouchSimpleAnimateDoc* pDoc = GetDocument();
05       CPoint Delta = ptTo - ptFrom;
06       pDoc->NoseTip.x += Delta.x;
07       pDoc->NoseTip.y += Delta.y;
08       m_Message.Format(L"Now Panning!");
09       pDoc->UpdateAllViews(NULL);
10       return TRUE;
11   }
```

gesture and result in accidental changes of the face position. With the Delta strategy, accidental triggering of the panning gesture has a much less notable effect. Limits on Delta could also be applied if desired.

10.5 Touch Interactions with "RegisterTouchWindow"

The gesture functions discussed in Section 10.2–10.4 offer a very convenient approach to managing touch screen inputs for user interactions. However, there is an alternative path available which relies on directly detecting and responding to each touch of the display screen. The functions used to implement this direct approach are OnTouchInputs and OnTouchInput. They are made available in an MFC project by calling the function RegisterTouchWindow as a program begins execution. These functions offer a very flexible (but perhaps less convenient) approach to managing touch screen inputs compared to gesture functions. It should be noted, however, that activation of this option through a call to RegisterTouchWindow currently excludes the possibility of also using the gesture function approach.

In the sub-sections below we will consider the two functions OnTouchInputs and OnTouchInput. We will demonstrate the characteristic behavior of the functions by displaying their parameter values during touch screen interaction. Finally, we will focus on the approach offered by the OnTouchInput function and consider that function further with two examples in Section 10.6.

10.5.1 Exploring the function OnTouchInputs

The example program TouchArray has been prepared to show the touch detail that is available from the function OnTouchInputs. The project can be found in *Chap10\4_TouchArray*. Clicking on the solution file will, of course, allow you to explore it in the development environment. Building and executing it will show its operation and a sample of the very detailed information it provides. Figure 10.9 shows example text output from the program including the screen coordinates of each contacting finger. We

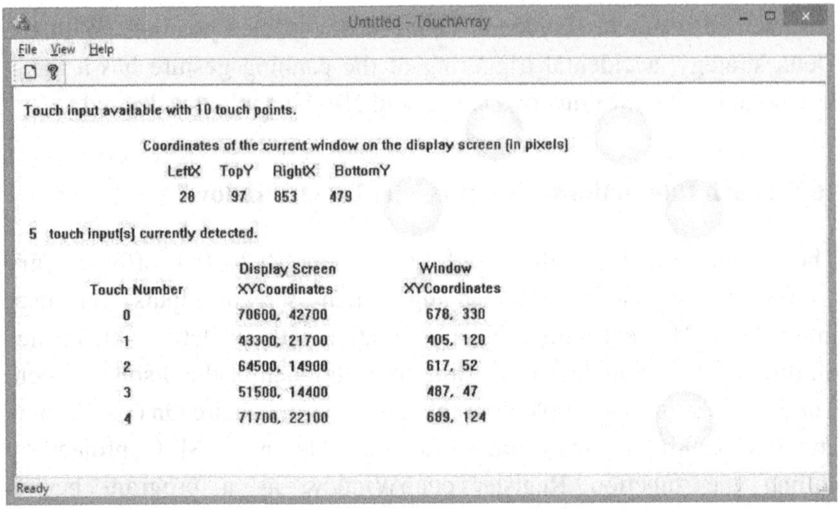

Figure 10.9 Display of TouchArray with Five Touch Points

will look carefully at the programing shortly. But, briefly, the display shows the screen coordinates of the program window itself and also indicates the number of current touch points (in this case five). The touch number of each active contact is then shown along with the coordinates of each touch point (in two forms). As you run this program and touch the screen yourself, you will see all of the values changing appropriately when you move your fingers.

The critical item in developing this project is the creation of the virtual function OnTouchInputs. Following the pattern of the OnGesture functions of the previous projects (e.g. Section 10.2), the initial declaration of OnTouchInputs is in the base class CWnd. It can be seen by finding it in the function list of CWnd and right clicking to locate its declaration. Our implementation of OnTouchInputs was created by adding a virtual function to the view class using the same approach as used earlier for the OnGesture functions (Figure 10.4). Table 10.17 shows the details of the OnTouchInputs function for the TouchArray project. The argument list contains an integer variable for the number of touch inputs currently being received (nInputsCount) and a pointer (PTOUCHINPUT) to an array of input data (pInputs).

Table 10.17 Listing of OnTouchInputs from TouchArrayView.cpp

```
01   /* This is a listing of OnTouchInputs */
02   BOOL CTouchArrayView::OnTouchInputs(UINT nInputsCount,
03       PTOUCHINPUT pInputs)
04   {
05       m_NumTouches = nInputsCount;
06   for (int i=0; i < m_NumTouches; i++)  {
07       m_TouchArray[i].x = pInputs[i].x;
08       m_TouchArray[i].y = pInputs[i].y;
09       }
10       RedrawWindow();
11       return true;
12   }
```

Entries in the pInputs array are in a structure format which contains several details about each current screen touch point. The first two items in the structure are the touch coordinates and are of primary interest to us. The remaining items are beyond the scope of this effort but are important for more advanced programming strategies. The array entries pInputs[i].x and pInputs[i].y represent the location of each touched point in display screen coordinates where the upper left hand corner of the overall screen (not just the window) is at 0,0. The coordinate units are in hundredths of pixels. Our for loop of lines 06–09 in Table 10.17 stores the touch point coordinates in the array of CPoint objects m_TouchArray to make them available as member variables of the view class. The member variable m_NumTouches contains the number of active touches (line 05). The OnTouchInputs function continually cycles as long as there is at least one touch point occurring. Line 10 executes the call to RedrawWindow at each cycle. In this case we have simply used OnTouchInputs to capture the function parameters as view class member variables for display by OnDraw. But, of course, there are many other possibilities.

The OnDraw function for TouchArray is now shown in Table 10.18. The first line of added code in line 07 calls the function RegisterTouchWindow. This function call is required to activate the OnTouchInputs function and its partner function OnTouchInput which

Table 10.18 Listing of OnDraw from TouchArrayView.cpp

```
01   /* This is a listing of OnDraw */
02   void CTouchArrayView::OnDraw(CDC* pDC) {
03   CTouchArrayDoc* pDoc = GetDocument();
04   ASSERT_VALID(pDoc);
05   if (!pDoc)  return;
06   // TODO: add draw code for native data here
07   RegisterTouchWindow();
08   CRect WinRect; int nInputs;
09   GetWindowRect(WinRect);
10   nInputs = GetSystemMetrics(SM_MAXIMUMTOUCHES);
11   CString Buffer;
12   Buffer.Format(L"Touch input available with %d touch points.", nInputs);
13   pDC->TextOut(10, 15, Buffer);
14   Buffer.Format(L" Coordinates of the window on the display screen (in pixels)");
15   pDC->TextOut(125, 50, Buffer);
16   Buffer.Format(L" LeftX     TopY     RightX     BottomY ");
17   pDC->TextOut(150, 75, Buffer);
18   Buffer.Format(L"  %d       %d       %d        %d", WinRect.left,
19       WinRect.top, WinRect.right, WinRect.bottom);
20   pDC->TextOut(150, 100, Buffer);
21   Buffer.Format(L" %d   touch input(s) currently detected.", m_NumTouches);
22   pDC->TextOut(10, 135, Buffer);
23   Buffer.Format(L"                  Display Screen            Window ");
24   pDC->TextOut(130, 170, Buffer);
25   Buffer.Format(L"Touch Number      XYCoordinates          XYCoordinates ");
26   pDC->TextOut(75, 190, Buffer);
27   for (int i = 0; i < m_NumTouches; i++) {
28   Buffer.Format(L" %d       %d, %d", i, m_TouchArray[i].x, m_TouchArray[i].y);
29   pDC->TextOut(100, 215 + 25 * i, Buffer);
30   }
31   for (int i = 0; i < m_NumTouches; i++) {
32       int TouchedX = m_TouchArray[i].x / 100 - WinRect.left;
33       int TouchedY = m_TouchArray[i].y / 100 - WinRect.top;
34       Buffer.Format(L"%d, %d", TouchedX, TouchedY);
35       pDC->TextOut(415, 215 + 25 * i, Buffer);
36       }
37   SetTimer(1, 250, NULL);
38   }
```

we will discuss in the next section. It should be noted that calling RegisterTouchWindow disables the OnGesture functions which we have been considering and which will be discussed more extensively in

Chapter 11. Lines 08–10 gather information on the screen position of the current window rectangle and the number of touch points available. Lines 12–20 then output this information in a labelled format. We are interested in the window position because the raw coordinate values from pInputs are in screen (rather than window) coordinates. Lines 21–36 display and label the member variable data obtained from the OnTouchInputs function. Lines 21 and 22 output the current number of active touches m_NumTouches. The for loop of lines 27–30 displays the touch number and the raw coordinate values directly from OnTouchInputs. These displayed values are clearly in hundredths and referenced to the screen. Lines 31–36 process the m_TouchArray by dividing by 100 and shifting the reference coordinates from the top left of the screen to the top left of the current window.

The very last line of code in OnDraw at line 37 in Table 10.18 sets a timer. The corresponding OnTimer function simply sets m_NumTouches to zero and redraws the window. While a screen touch is occurring, OnDraw is being repeatedly executed by the cycling of OnTouchInputs. This repeatedly updates the window image. When the screen touch is removed, OnTouchInputs does not execute and the last touch information will remain in the window unless it is cleared. With SetTimer(1,250, NULL) taking effect at the end of OnDraw, the OnTimer function will execute 250 milliseconds after the last touch. This will refresh the display with m_NumTouches set to zero. Of course, when OnTouchInputs is cycling with a screen touch in place, OnDraw is being repeatedly called and line 37 simply continues to reset the timer at each cycle until the last touch is removed. Careful observation of the project window (Figure 10.9) during program operation will show the brief delay in clearing of the output as a screen touch concludes.

10.5.2 Considering the OnTouchInput function

The previous section introduced the possibility of using direct touch functions for touch screen interaction. We particularly discussed the function OnTouchInputs in some detail. The alternative function made available by calling RegisterTouchWindow is OnTouchInput. This

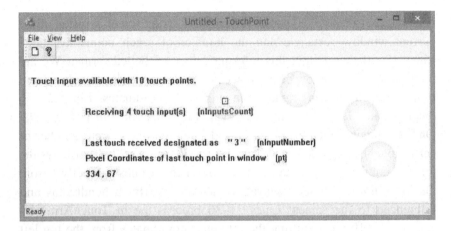

Figure 10.10 Display of TouchPoint with Four Touch Points

function operates much like the OnTouchInputs function of Section 10.5.1. However, it focuses only on one touch point at a time and is somewhat easier to manage. We have prepared the example project in *Chap10\5_TouchPoint* to demonstrate its operation. Building and executing this project and making a few screen touches will result in a window similar to Figure 10.10. In this case, the display indicates that four finger touches are being received. The designation of the most recent touch as number "3" is also shown along with its window coordinates in pixels (of course, number "0" would be the first touch). A small square with a pixel is drawn at the last touch point received.

We can now consider the programming for project TouchPoint beginning with Table 10.19 containing the listing of the virtual function OnTouchPoint. This was added to the view class using Add Function in the same way as the OnGesture functions were added (e.g. Section 10.2). The function declaration (lines 2 and 3) of Table 10.19 shows the current point coordinates in pt, the input number of the latest point nInputNumber, the number of current inputs nInputsCount and the PTOUCHPOINT data structure of the most recent point pInput. The coordinates in pt are in pixels relative to the window origin. The coordinates in pInput are in hundredths of pixels and relative to the

Table 10.19 Listing of OnTouchInput from TouchPointView.cpp

```
01    /* This is a listing of OnTouchInput */
02    BOOL CTouchPointView::OnTouchInput(CPoint pt, int nInputNumber,
03        int nInputsCount, PTOUCHINPUT pInput)
04    {
05        m_InNum = nInputNumber;
06        m_InCount = nInputsCount;
07        m_TouchPoint = pt;
08        RedrawWindow();
09        return true;
10    }
```

display screen origin. Our code added to this function as lines 05–07 simply uses the member variables m_InNum, m_InCount and m_TouchInput to capture the corresponding function parameters during the cycles of OnTouchInput while a touch is being received. Line 08, of course, continually redraws the window as long as a touch is detected.

The OnDraw function is shown in Table 10.20 and maintains the display of the touch screen results. Line 07 of OnDraw activates RegisterTouchWindow. Then lines 08–12 obtain and display the touch screen capability. In lines 13–15, the number of current inputs are displayed along with a reminder of the parameter name from OnTouchInput. The if statement of line 16 will execute as long as current touch inputs are cycling the OnTouchInput function. In this way lines 17–24 will present the number and coordinate values for the last touch point received. Lines 25–28 display a pixel at the last touch point, showing a small square around it. The SetTimer function in line 29 allows the OnDraw function to reset after finger touches are removed. The OnTimer function simply sets m_InCount to zero and redraws the window so that the touch screen text is cleared. We have left the pixel and square behind so that the last finger touch released can be seen.

Table 10.20 Listing of OnDraw from TouchPointView.cpp

```
01    void CTouchPointView::OnDraw(CDC* pDC)
02    {
03        CTouchPointDoc* pDoc = GetDocument();
04        ASSERT_VALID(pDoc);
05        if (!pDoc) return;
06        // TODO: add draw code for native data here
07        RegisterTouchWindow();
08        int nInputs;
09        nInputs = GetSystemMetrics(SM_MAXIMUMTOUCHES);
10        CString Buffer;
11        Buffer.Format(L"Touch input available with %d touch points.", nInputs);
12        pDC->TextOut(10, 25, Buffer);
13        Buffer.Format(L"Receiving %d touch input(s)    (nInputsCount)",
14                m_InCount);
15        pDC->TextOut(100, 75, Buffer);
16    if (m_InCount > 0)  {
17        Buffer.Format(L"Last touch received designated as   \" %d \"
18                (nInputNumber)", m_InNum);
19        pDC->TextOut(100, 125, Buffer);
20        Buffer.Format(L"Pixel Coordinates of last touch point in window    (pt)");
21        pDC->TextOut(100, 150, Buffer);
22        Buffer.Format(L"%d , %d", m_TouchPoint.x, m_TouchPoint.y);
23        pDC->TextOut(100, 175, Buffer);
24        }
25        CPoint RectPoint = m_TouchPoint;
26        pDC->Rectangle(RectPoint.x - 5, RectPoint.y - 5, RectPoint.x + 5,
27                RectPoint.y + 5);
28        pDC->SetPixel(RectPoint, 0);
29        SetTimer(1, 250, NULL);
30    }
```

10.6 Drawing Examples Using OnTouchInput

We expect that most readers of this book will find the OnGesture function approach to be the most convenient way to manage touch screen inputs. For that reason we have made gesture functions the focus of Chapter 11. However, the RegisterTouchWindow strategy may be attractive for certain applications and so we are including here two examples of drawing programs making use of the OnTouchInput function. The first of these should be reminiscent of the drawing projects introduced in Chapter 5. In contrast, the second example is in a format intended to be convenient for tablet applications. It allows the drawing of continuous curves as well as cursive shapes.

10.6.1 Line drawing using the touch screen

The example project contained in *Chap10\6_TouchLines* is a touch screen drawing project (Figure 10.11). It is based on using the function OnTouchInput to detect and respond to screen touches. In this case we have not provided mouse click interaction and, within the display window, the program will only respond to screen touches. However, the menu bar and tool bar will still react to mouse inputs. Figure 10.11 shows the TouchLines window with an example drawing. The program provides start-up information to indicate the availability of touch screen operations and a few instructions — especially to indicate that a finger touch will draw a line and that a press and tap will start a new line. This is analogous to the left click/right click approach in our original drawing programs of Chapters 5–7. The TouchLines program also includes an array of pixels at 50 unit intervals and a snap-to-grid operation so that

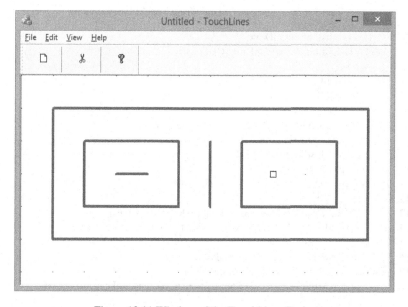

Figure 10.11 Window of the TouchLines Project

straight lines are easily drawn. A Delete Line operation has also been included. It follows the pattern of Section 6.1.4 and uses the event handler OnEditUndo much the same as shown in Table 6.1. In the TouchLines project, notice that the tool bar buttons have been enlarged (via Resource View) to facilitate touch screen interaction. The "cut" button activates Delete Line. A small rectangle may be seen in the right hand box of Figure 10.11. This marker is provided to indicate the start point for the line to be drawn with the next finger touch.

We will now look at the programming of TouchLines by focusing on its OnDraw function and OnTouchInput. In Table 10.21 line 08 of the OnDraw function is checking the JustStarting variable initialized in OnNewDocument. In the spirit of the earlier Table 10.6, the function StartUpDisplay provides a check on the touch screen capability and a few brief prompts. In addition, it also calls the RegisterTouchWindow function to activate OnTouchInput. A grid of reference pixels are placed across the window by lines 10–12 in OnDraw. The size of the grid is established by m_SizeX and m_SizeY which were set in the OnSize function. The pixel grid is then used in the snap-to-grid process

Table 10.21 Listing of OnDraw from TouchLinesView.cpp

```
01   /* This is a listing of OnDraw */
02   void CTouchLinesView::OnDraw(CDC* pDC)
03   {
04       CTouchLinesDoc* pDoc = GetDocument();
05       ASSERT_VALID(pDoc);
06       if (!pDoc) return;
07       // TODO: add draw code for native data here
08       if (pDoc->JustStarting) StartUpDisplay();
09       pDoc->JustStarting = false;
10   for (int xp = 0; xp<m_SizeX; xp += 50)  {
11   for (int yp = 0; yp<m_SizeY; yp += 50)  {pDC->SetPixel(xp, yp, 0); }
12       }
13       CPoint RectDraw = pDoc->FPoint[pDoc->NumLines];
14       pDC->Rectangle(RectDraw.x - 5, RectDraw.y - 5, RectDraw.x + 5,
15              RectDraw.y + 5);
16       pDC->SelectObject(&m_BluePen);
17   for (int i = 0; i < pDoc->NumLines; i++)  {
18       pDC->MoveTo(pDoc->FPoint[i]);  pDC->LineTo(pDoc->LPoint[i]);
19       }
20   }
```

supported by the view class function NearestGridPoint. We did this originally in Section 5.6, where NearestGridPoint is described in Table 5.26. Lines 13–15 draw the small rectangle which is used to represent the first point of the line to be drawn with the next finger touch. Finally, lines 16–19 use the blue pen to draw the stored image.

Table 10.22 presents the listing of the OnTouchInput function. Notice that line 07 immediately changes the touch input to the nearest grid point. The if statement of lines 08–12 checks to see if the point has changed since the last touch. If so, the member variable m_TouchPoint is updated and Change is set to "yes". If this is a second finger touch (for press and tap), then nInputsCount = 2 and New is set to "yes" by line 11 to indicate the start of a new line. If Change is "yes" and New is "no",

Table 10.22 Listing of OnTouchInput from TouchLinesView.cpp

```
01   /* This is a listing of OnTouchInput */
02   BOOL CTouchLinesView::OnTouchInput(CPoint pt, int nInputNumber,
03                   int nInputsCount, PTOUCHINPUT pInput)
04   {
05       CString Change, New;
06       Change = "no"; New = "no";
07       NearestGridPoint(&pt);
08       if (pt != m_TouchPoint) {
09           m_TouchPoint = pt;
10           Change = "yes";
11           if (nInputsCount > 1) New = "yes";
12       }
13       CTouchLinesDoc* pDoc = GetDocument();
14       if ((Change == "yes") && (New == "no")) {
15           pDoc->LPoint[pDoc->NumLines] = m_TouchPoint;
16           pDoc->FPoint[pDoc->NumLines + 1] = m_TouchPoint;
17           pDoc->NumLines++;
18           pDoc->SavNumLines = pDoc->NumLines;
19       }
20       if ((Change == "yes") && (New == "yes")) {
21           pDoc->NumLines = pDoc->SavNumLines - 1;
22           pDoc->FPoint[pDoc->NumLines] = pDoc->LPoint[pDoc->NumLines];
23       }
24       RedrawWindow();
25       return true;
26   }
```

the if statement of line 14 allows a line is to be added to the line data base in the document and the number of lines is incremented. Line 18 at the end of the if statement saves the current number of lines in the drawing. Lines 20–23 start a new line (when New = "yes") by removing the last line drawn and updating FPoint for the new line. Notice that this approach allows an extra line to appear briefly on the display until the second finger touch (the "tap") is received. It might be noted that the steps of checking to see if a point change has occurred (line 08) and introducing the SavNumLines variable (line 18) are necessary because of the rapid cycling of the OnTouchInput function whenever a finger touch is in place. OnTouchInput does not cycle just once like an event handler but is executing as long as a touch occurs. Finally, of course, the RedrawWindow of line 24 maintains a continuing update of the drawn image.

10.6.2 Drawing continuous curves with Scribble

The project in *Chap10\7_Scribble* illustrates the process of drawing continuous lines using the OnTouchInput function. Building and executing the project will allow you to simply draw or write into its window. An example showing it in tablet format is in Figure 10.12. Pen width is adjustable through use of the W+ or W- toolbar buttons. The "cut" button will carry out deletion line by line.

As with most of the projects in this book, Scribble was created as a single document MFC project. It was modified, however, to have a more tablet friendly appearance by considering the "User Interface Features" of the MFC Application Wizard. On the page for User Interface Features we have removed most of the check marks under "Mainframe styles", leaving only "Maximized" and "System menu" as checked. To the right on that page we have left the default classic menu and classic toolbar items in place. The additional adjustment that we have made is to increase the size of the toolbar buttons. With these adjustments, the program launches in maximized form. Its window fills the screen and the more prominent tool bar buttons make them more touch friendly.

Figure 10.12 The Scribble Project Running in a Tablet Environment

As a first step in exploring the Scribble project, let's consider the OnDraw function of Table 10.23. Line 07 tests the document class JustStarting variable and runs the StartUpDisplay function if appropriate. The start-up function tests for the touch capability and runs the RegisterTouchWindow function as well as other initializations. It also displays a few operating instructions for the program. Line 08 updates the JustStarting variable. Lines 09–11 draw a small simple rectangle at the first point on the next line to be drawn to provide a bit of guidance to the user. The last lines 12–15 draw the line image stored in the document each time that the OnDraw function executes. It might be noted that the arrays FPoint and LPoint have been increased in size considerably from earlier drawing examples in order to accommodate the short lines that make up individual curves and cursive or print lettering.

The key function in this Scribble project is the OnTouchInput function shown in Table 10.24. This function serves several purposes. It receives a single touch input and it determines if that touch represents

Table 10.23 Listing of OnDraw from ScribbleView.cpp

```
01    /* This is a listing of OnDraw */
02    void CScribbleView::OnDraw(CDC* pDC) {
03        CScribbleDoc* pDoc = GetDocument();
04        ASSERT_VALID(pDoc);
05        if (!pDoc) return;
06        // TODO: add draw code for native data here
07        if (pDoc->JustStarting) StartUpDisplay();
08        pDoc->JustStarting = false;
09        CPoint RectDraw = pDoc->FPoint[pDoc->NumLines];
10        pDC->Rectangle(RectDraw.x - 5, RectDraw.y - 5, RectDraw.x + 5,
11                RectDraw.y + 5);
12        pDC->SelectObject(&m_BluePen);
13    for (int i = 0; i < pDoc->NumLines; i++) {
14        pDC->MoveTo(pDoc->FPoint[i]); pDC->LineTo(pDoc->LPoint[i]);
15        }
16    }
```

the start of a new line or a continuation of the previous line. It also draws a continuing line if that is appropriate and it moves on to begin a new line, refreshing the full line drawn image if that is required. In Table 10.24, as a touch input is being processed, lines 05–07 prepare to store data by obtaining the document pointer and also prepare to draw lines by getting the client device context and selecting the blue pen. Lines 08–11 then initialize a few variables used in deciding on an appropriate response to the touch input. Lines 12–20 are active if the touch (or movement of a touch) represents a new point on the screen. Line 12 is specifically checking the current touch point against the last touch point. If a changed point is being processed, lines 14–18 then consider whether the change represents a BigChange. Line 19 then updates the member variable m_LastPoint.

The next segment of the OnTouchPoint function deals with a change which is not a big change by drawing a line to the new point. If the change is a big change, the current drawing is redrawn and the first point of the next line is established. Lines 22–27 deal with the small change case. Lines 23 and 24 update the coordinates of LPoint and the next FPoint to the touched point values. Line 25 draws a line to the current

Table 10.24 Listing of OnTouchInput from ScribbleView.cpp

```
01    /* This is a listing of OnTouchInput */
02    BOOL CScribbleView::OnTouchInput(CPoint pt, int nInputNumber,
03                   int nInputsCount, PTOUCHINPUT pInput)
04    {
05        CScribbleDoc* pDoc = GetDocument();
06        CClientDC aDC(this);
07        aDC.SelectObject(&m_BluePen);
08        double DistSq, Dist;
09        double BigDef = 20;
10        CString Change, BigChange;
11        Change = "no"; BigChange = "no";
12    if (pt != m_LastPoint) {
13        Change = "yes";
14        int dx = pt.x - m_LastPoint.x;
15        int dy = pt.y - m_LastPoint.y;
16        DistSq = dx*dx + dy*dy;
17        Dist = sqrt(DistSq);
18        if (Dist > BigDef) BigChange = "yes";
19        m_LastPoint = pt;
20        }
21        int i = pDoc->NumLines;
22    if ((Change == "yes") && (BigChange == "no")) {
23        pDoc->LPoint[i] = m_LastPoint;
24        pDoc->FPoint[i + 1] = m_LastPoint;
25        aDC.MoveTo(pDoc->FPoint[i]); aDC.LineTo(pDoc->LPoint[i]);
26        pDoc->NumLines++;
27        }
28    if ((BigChange == "yes") || (Change == "no")) {
29        pDoc->FPoint[i] = m_LastPoint;
30        RedrawWindow();
31        }
32        return TRUE;
33    }
```

touched point (without using OnDraw). Line 26 increments NumLines. If a big change has occurred, line 29 begins a new line by updating FPoint and line 30 redraws the window executing OnDraw. The sensation that the user should receive is that finger motion results in the drawing of a continuous line while picking up the finger and touching again allows the beginning of a new line. We use the drawing functions in line 25 to draw the new line without delay because the use of OnDraw to refresh the full image as each line segment is drawn disrupts the sensation of continuity. In drawing curved lines each of the line segments is necessarily short and for this reason the array sizes for the document class variables FPoint and LPoint have been increased considerably.

Another feature of this program is the ability to delete the last line drawn by using the event handler OnEditUndo. This follows the pattern of several of our earlier drawing programs (e.g. Section 6.1.4). We have also used the cut button on the tool bar to activate a delete line. Another item that has been provided in this project is the adjustment of line width as used in earlier projects (e.g. Section 6.5). But in this case we are incrementing the line width +/-2 pixels with OnLineWidthIncrease and OnLineWidthDecrease as activated by the tool bar W+ and W- buttons.

10.7 Exercises

1. The FirstGesture project carries out zooming operations for the simple face located at the window center. Modify this project by adding an OnGestureRotate function to also rotate the face about this center point. Then, add a two finger tap function which will move the position of the face and maintain it at the tapped point.

2. Modify the GestureDetails project to add a simple line drawing. Use OnGesturePressAndTap to move to a start point for a line and use OnGestureTwoFingerTap to draw a line. Clear and refresh the screen if a left mouse click is received but does not respond to a single finger screen touch.

3. The project TouchSimpleAnimate uses OnMouseMove to have the nose tip of the simple face follow a touching finger tip. As coded, the panning gesture (OnGesturePan) only moves the face proportional to the finger motion. Change OnGesturePan to use ptFrom or ptTo directly so that the nose tip tracks the finger tip when panning. Consider the effect of this change on the zooming and rotating gestures. Do you now see spontaneous movements of the face caused by incidental touches at the start of a zoom or rotate gesture?

4. Add a simple line drawing operation to the project OnTouchInputs. When four touch inputs are received, draw a line between the first touch point and the fourth touch point. The line drawing should clear when touches are removed.

5. Modify the Touchlines project to allow adjustable grid size. The grid size should increase or decrease in response to mouse clicks (or finger taps) on tool bar buttons.

6. Add line drawing capability to the Scribble project. Press and tap should start a new line and a single finger tap should draw a straight line. Of course, Scribble should still work for drawing arbitrary curves.

Chapter 11

Additional Topics in Gesture and Touch Screen Programming

The basic ideas of Windows touch screen programming were introduced in Chapter 10. In this chapter we will look further at strategies for using the touch screen in a variety of graphics applications. You will find that we have focused on programming with the OnGesture functions since that is probably the most convenient approach for general application programming. The examples presented here describe techniques for integrating gesture and touch screen concepts into the object-oriented programming that we introduced in Chapters 8 and 9. In particular, you will see that we have used those homemade classes developed for geometric and graphing applications in several examples that make use of the touch screen environment.

The first of our examples in this chapter revisits the drawing programs of Chapter 6 using the touch screen to allow zooming and panning during the drawing operations. We then move on to manipulating and animating two-dimensional objects using the classes that we developed initially in Chapter 8. Graphs were the focus of Chapter 9 and we conclude this chapter by introducing examples that bring our graph classes into the touch screen environment.

The examples in this chapter and the previous chapter generally follow the pattern of the earlier chapters of the book. We have used the single document interface and default MFC formatting during project creation. This way, the operating programs that have resulted have the typical look and feel of traditional Windows programs. The Scribble project of Section 10.6 was an exception where we maximized the program window and reduced features that create the standard Windows appearance. As a result, it was possible to create a much more tablet friendly appearance for a program intended to run in a tablet mode. The photo in Figure 10.12 illustrates this. The reader should keep in mind that there is flexibility in formatting during project creation. If you would like to create a program using MFC applications that has a nonstandard look or a tablet-like feel, experiment with the formats available during project creation.

This chapter concludes with the project TouchGrapher+ in Section 11.4 as another example of a tablet oriented program. You will see that we have again removed much of the Window appearance and that we have also emphasized touch screen operation. The addition of a swiping mode has been added to provide the kind of behavior that we have all become familiar with on touch screen devices. However, while shifting to a tablet friendly format, we have still retained mouse functionality so the program also runs nicely without a touch screen.

11.1 Zooming and Panning in a Drawing Project

The first project in this concluding chapter further explores strategies for touchscreen programming. It is a revisit of our drawing projects originally presented in Chapter 5 but now with the addition of zooming and panning as tools for facilitating the drawing process. You should find the example project in *Chap11\1_ZoomDraw* to be reminiscent of the SimpleDraw project of Section 5.2. When you bring the ZoomDraw project into the development environment and build and execute it, you will be able to draw lines just as we did in our initial Windows programs. A right mouse click readies the program to draw a new line. A left mouse click draws a line and successive left mouse clicks draw a sequence of connected lines. A command to "remove the last line drawn" has also been provided under the Edit menu bar item and can be activated by clicking (or touching) the "scissors" icon on the tool bar button or by pressing the left arrow key. Of course, there are now additional capabilities added to take advantage of the touch screen. Panning can be used to move the image around the program window. A zoom action can be used for zooming or pinching a target area in the window and a two finger tap will reset the drawn image to its original display position and remove the zoom.

Figure 11.1 shows a simple image created with ZoomDraw. This image is shown in the default size where it is difficult to appreciate the detail in the image. The simple line drawing was begun by creating the

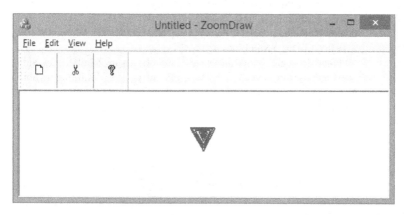

Figure 11.1 View of a Sample ZoomDraw Image at Default Size

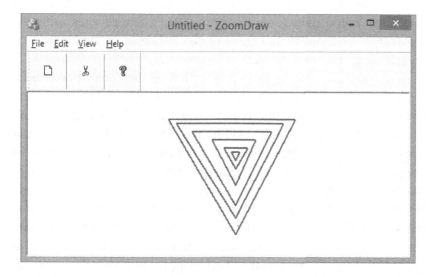

Figure 11.2 View of the ZoomDraw Sample with Zoom

Table 11.1 Listing of OnDraw from ZoomDrawView.cpp

```
01   /* This is a listing of OnDraw */
02   void CZoomDrawView::OnDraw(CDC* pDC
03   {
04        CZoomDrawDoc* pDoc = GetDocument();
05        ASSERT_VALID(pDoc);    if (!pDoc) return;
06        // TODO: add draw code for native data here
07        if (pDoc->JustStarting == true)StartUpDisplay();
08        pDoc->JustStarting = false;
09        double NFPointX[100], NFPointY[100], NLPointX[100], NLPointY[100];
10   for (int i = 0; i < pDoc->NumLines; i++)   {
11        NFPointX[i] = m_ZoomMult*pDoc->FPoint[i].x + m_ZShiftX + m_ShiftX;
12        NFPointY[i] = m_ZoomMult*pDoc->FPoint[i].y + m_ZShiftY + m_ShiftY;
13        NLPointX[i] = m_ZoomMult*pDoc->LPoint[i].x + m_ZShiftX + m_ShiftX;
14        NLPointY[i] = m_ZoomMult*pDoc->LPoint[i].y + m_ZShiftY + m_ShiftY;
15        }
16        pDC->SelectObject(&m_BluePen);
17   for (int i = 0; i < pDoc->NumLines; i++)   {
18        pDC->MoveTo(int(NFPointX[i]), int(NFPointY[i]));
19        pDC->LineTo(int(NLPointX[i]), int(NLPointY[i]));
20        }
21   }
```

external triangle with this default size. Then the interior detail was completed with a tight zoom in effect. After a few gestures using the capabilities for zooming and panning, the full detail of the Figure 11.1 triangle image becomes apparent in Figure 11.2.

We'll now consider the programming behind the ZoomDraw project. Following our normal pattern, we will discuss details of the most critical aspects of the code with the reader invited to further explore the full detail of the project coding within the Visual Studio development environment. The OnNewDocument function has minimal content in ZoomDraw. It simply sets the JustStarting variable to true and initializes (to zero) the other document variables NumLines, FPoint[0].x and FPoint[0].y. As the project continues to execute, the OnDraw function takes initial effect and then OnDraw frequently executes during program operation in response to touch screen gestures. OnDraw is shown in Table 11.1. Line 07 executes the StartUpDisplay function which tests for touch screen capability and displays a few prompts as a reference for gesture interactions. Line 08 sets JustStarting to false. Line 09 declares a set of new point coordinates. These are used in modifying and displaying the stored line image while incorporating the effect of zooming and panning operations. Lines 10–15 modify all of the stored lines by including the basic image shift (m_ShiftX, m_ShiftY) associated with panning gestures as well as an additional shift made for zoom correction (m_ZShiftX, m_ZShiftY). This is intended to maintain the appropriate screen position as zooming takes place. Notice, of course, that the variable m_ZoomMult is continually adjusting the image size (zooming or pinching) by multiplication in lines 11–14. Finally, the for loop of lines 17–20 in OnDraw places each of the lines on the display.

11.1.1 Implementing zooming and panning operations

In the ZoomDraw project, we have restricted drawing operations to normal mouse clicks. And we have reserved gestures for controlling the display of the line drawn image. Zooming takes place in the OnGestureZoom function where m_ZoomMult is adjusted while at the same time maintaining the position of the zoom region within the display as much as possible. Table 11.2 shows the details of OnGestureZoom for the project. Line 04 captures the location of the zoom gesture on the display in pixel coordinates using the variables ZPixX and ZPixY. Then lines 05 and 06 calculate the coordinates within the stored image (ZCoordX, ZCoordY) represented by the point (ZPixX, ZPixY). Adjustments are made for both the current zoom factor and the shift variable values. Line 07 sets a tentative value for ZoomInc. The if statement of line 08 tests whether a significant zoom gesture is in progress. If so, lines 09–14 then establish a value for the zoom factor including limitations to maintain a smooth zoom and maximum and minimum limits on the zoom factor. Lines 15 and 16 calculate the shifts m_ZShiftX and m_ZShiftY necessary to maintain the position of the zoom region on the screen when OnDraw executes. Line 17 prepares for possible panning as discussed below.

In this project we are using the OnZoomGesture function to not only zoom as defined in lines 08–16, but also to provide panning capability.

Table 11.2 Listing of OnGestureZoom from ZoomDrawView.cpp

```
01   /* This is a listing of OnGestureZoom */
02   BOOL CZoomDrawView::OnGestureZoom(CPoint ptCenter, long lDelta)
03   {
04        int ZPixX = ptCenter.x;   int ZPixY = ptCenter.y;
05        m_ZCoordX = (ZPixX - m_ZShiftX - m_ShiftX) / m_ZoomMult;
06        m_ZCoordY = (ZPixY - m_ZShiftY - m_ShiftY) / m_ZoomMult;
07        double ZoomInc = lDelta;
08   if (abs(ZoomInc) >= 1)  {
09        double ZoomIncLim = 5.;    double ZoomScale = 0.025;
10        if (ZoomInc > ZoomIncLim) ZoomInc = ZoomIncLim;
11        if (ZoomInc < -ZoomIncLim) ZoomInc = -ZoomIncLim;
12        m_ZoomMult += ZoomScale*ZoomInc;
13        if (m_ZoomMult > 5) m_ZoomMult = 5;
14        if (m_ZoomMult < 1. / 5.) m_ZoomMult = 1. / 5.;
15        m_ZShiftX = ZPixX - int(.5 + m_ZoomMult*m_ZCoordX) - m_ShiftX;
16        m_ZShiftY = ZPixY - int(.5 + m_ZoomMult*m_ZCoordY) - m_ShiftY;
17        m_SaveX = ZPixX;    m_SaveY = ZPixY;
18        }
19   if (abs(ZoomInc) < 1)  {
20        int dx = ZPixX - m_SaveX;
21        int dy = ZPixY - m_SaveY;
22        m_ShiftX = m_ShiftX + dx;
23        m_ShiftY = m_ShiftY + dy;
24        }
25        m_SaveX = ZPixX;
26        m_SaveY = ZPixY;
27        RedrawWindow();
28        return TRUE;
29   }
```

Panning within the zoom is implemented by lines 19–24 in Table 11.2. The if statement of line 19 identifies cases of limited zooming action even though a zoom operation is still being detected and the zoom function is still cycling. Lines 20 and 21 calculate the motion increment since the last cycle and lines 22 and 23 calculate the corresponding shift in the image (m_ShiftX, m_ShiftY). These values will move the image appropriately as OnDraw executes again. Lines 25 and 26 save the current pixel position and then line 27 refreshes the image displayed.

The sensation intended for the user during a zooming operation is that image zooming and panning should appear continuous. The interaction of the continuing cycle of OnGestureZoom and OnDraw tends to provide this. The equations of lines 11–14 of OnDraw (in Table 11.1) update the display coordinates and lines 17–19 draw the display as the zooming/redrawing cycle proceeds.

11.1.2 Panning with OnGesturePan

In addition to the possibility of panning during zooming operations, a user is very likely to simply touch the screen with the intent of moving the image displayed. For this case we have activated the OnGesturePan function as shown in Table 11.3. The function arguments ptFrom and ptTo very conveniently capture the movement implied by the panning gesture as the function executes. Lines 04 and 05 carry the change in x and y coordinates during this cycle of OnGesturePan (recalling that the function continues to cycle as long as the pan gesture is detected). Lines 06 and 07 then increment the shift member variables (m_ShiftX, m_ShiftY) accordingly and the window is refreshed by line 08. In this case, cycling between OnDraw and OnGesturePan provides the sensation of the displayed image moving in proportion to the panning gesture.

Table 11.3 Listing of OnGesturePan from ZoomDrawView.cpp

```
01    /* This is a listing of OnGesturePan */
02    BOOL CZoomDrawView::OnGesturePan(CPoint ptFrom,CPoint ptTo)
03    {
04        int dx = ptTo.x - ptFrom.x;
05        int dy = ptTo.y - ptFrom.y;
06        m_ShiftX = m_ShiftX + dx;
07        m_ShiftY = m_ShiftY + dy;
08        RedrawWindow();
09        return true;
10    }
```

11.1.3 Drawing and panning with mouse functions

We have used normal mouse interactions for drawing operations in the ZoomDraw project. This, of course, follows the pattern of our initial drawing projects of Chapter 5. However, in addition, we have added a few special considerations for touch screen operations. First, the GetMessageExtraInfo function has been used to inhibit drawing by an inadvertent touch of the screen (recall that a screen touch can be a left mouse click). Second, we have included corrections for zooming and panning so that when a mouse click is received, the intended image point is determined from the cursor position. And, third, we have made it possible to pan by screen touch when OnMouseMove is active.

Table 11.4 shows the message handler for OnLButtonDown. Here you can see in line 06 that we are concerned with obtaining button click details. As we have mentioned earlier, the Info variable is zero for a

Table 11.4 Listing of OnLButtonDown from ZoomDrawView.cpp

```
01   /* This is a listing of OnLButtonDown */
02   void CZoomDrawView::OnLButtonDown(UINT nFlags, CPoint point)
03   {
04       // TODO: Add your message handler code here and/or call default
05       CZoomDrawDoc* pDoc = GetDocument();
06       long Info = GetMessageExtraInfo();
07   if (Info == 0)  {
08       int i = pDoc->NumLines;
09       pDoc->LPoint[i].x = int ( .5 + ((point.x - m_ZShiftX - m_ShiftX) /
10           m_ZoomMult));
11       pDoc->LPoint[i].y = int ( .5 + ((point.y - m_ZShiftY - m_ShiftY) /
12           m_ZoomMult));
13       pDoc->FPoint[i + 1] = pDoc->LPoint[i];
14       pDoc->NumLines++;
15       pDoc->UpdateAllViews(NULL);
16       }
17   if (Info != 0)  {
18       m_LDown = true;
19       m_SaveX = point.x;
20       m_SaveY = point.y;
21       }
22       CView::OnLButtonDown(nFlags, point);
23   }
```

"real" mouse click. Thus the if statement of line 07 allows normal mouse drawing to proceed where we use the equations of line 09–12 to recover the intended image point correcting for both the current image shifting and the zooming status. Lines 13 and 14 save the next line's first point and update NumLines. Then line 15 refreshes the display including the new line.

In the case where OnLButtonDown has been activated by a screen touch instead of a mouse click, lines 17–21 in Table 11.4 exclude the possibility of drawing a line and instead prepare for a possible panning operation with OnMouseMove. Line 18 records that the left button is down and lines 19 and 20 save the cursor position (in this case, the touch point).

We will return shortly to the discussion of OnMouseMove and possible panning. But to complete the mouse drawing options, we do need the OnRButtonDown function shown in Table 11.5. This function is much the same as previous right button drawing functions and updates the FPoint coordinates to start a new line. In this case, however, the adjustment of the x and y coordinates included in lines 07–10 is required to correct for the zooming and image shifting that are part of the display. This is the same correction applied by lines 09–12 in Table 11.4 for the OnLButtonDown function.

Table 11.5 Listing of OnRButtonDown from ZoomDrawView.cpp

```
01   /* This is a listing of OnRButtonDown */
02   void CZoomDrawView::OnRButtonDown(UINT nFlags, CPoint point)
03   {
04       // TODO: Add your message handler code here and/or call default
05       CZoomDrawDoc* pDoc = GetDocument();
06       i  = pDoc->NumLines;
07       pDoc->FPoint[i].x = int( .5 + ((point.x - m_ZShiftX - m_ShiftX) /
08               m_ZoomMult));
09       pDoc->FPoint[i].y = int( .5 + ((point.y - m_ZShiftY - m_ShiftY) /
10               m_ZoomMult));
11       pDoc->UpdateAllViews(NULL);
12       CView::OnRButtonDown(nFlags, point);
13   }
```

Let's return now to the discussion of the possibility of panning with the OnMouseMove function. We consider this because of potential difficulties in detecting the panning gesture as distinctly different from a mouse click by screen touch. Typically a single finger screen touch is detected as a mouse click and a two finger panning motion is detected as the activator of OnGesturePan. Because of the similarity of these two touch events, we have implemented "panning" in this project by both the gesture function OnGesturePan and also by the OnMouseMove function as activated by a screen touch. This combination plus the inclusion of panning in OnGestureZoom provides a very reliable interpretation of panning gestures in the operation of ZoomDraw.

Table 11.6 shows the OnMouseMove function as written to carry out a panning operation. This function is active for our purpose after execution of lines 17–21 of OnLButtonDown in Table 11.4. Line 09 of OnMouseMove checks the status of the left button which remains "down" as long as the detected finger motion continues (it is reset in OnLButtonUp). Incrementing m_ShiftX and m_ShiftY in line 10 creates the panning effect as the RedrawWindow of line 11 allows cycling between OnMouseMove and OnDraw. With each finger movement OnMouseMove recycles so that lines 05–08 update the dx and dy increments as well as the current finger position (m_SaveX, m_SaveY).

Table 11.6 Listing of OnMouseMove from ZoomDrawView.cpp

```
01   /* This is a listing of OnMouseMove */
02   void CZoomDrawView::OnMouseMove(UINT nFlags, CPoint point)
03   {
04       // TODO: Add your message handler code here and/or call default
05       int dx = point.x - m_SaveX;
06       int dy = point.y - m_SaveY;
07       m_SaveX = point.x;
08       m_SaveY = point.y;
09   if (m_LDown == true)  {
10       m_ShiftX = m_ShiftX + dx;   m_ShiftY = m_ShiftY + dy;
11       RedrawWindow();
12       }
13       CView::OnMouseMove(nFlags, point);
14   }
```

This concludes our discussion of the ZoomDraw project and the intricacies of zooming and shifting. There are a few remaining details to be considered by the reader. The OnEditUndo function deletes the last line drawn and is in the same format as seen earlier in Chapters 5–7. The OnLButtonUp function simply resets the member variable m_LDown. Finally, the OnGestureTwoFingerTap function serves to remove zooming and shifting so that the drawing returns to its default size and position. It operates by simply setting m_ZoomMult to unity and all of the shift variables to zero.

11.2 Gesture Functions and Two-Dimensional Shapes

In Chapter 8 we described an approach to using classes and objects in graphics applications. We included several projects which illustrated the process of creating graphics classes with appropriate member variables and member functions. The purpose was to facilitate the creation, manipulation and display of two-dimensional graphics objects. Sections 8.4 and 8.5 concluded that chapter with a planet simulation and a robot simulation which demonstrated the effectiveness of the shapes classes and the object-oriented process.

At this point, we have the opportunity to integrate touch screen programming with the classes and objects introduced in Chapter 8. We will first return to the basics of the class C2DShapes introduced in Section 8.2 and manipulate a simple shape with gestures for zooming, rotating, etc. We will follow that with touch control of the earlier robot simulation.

11.2.1 Revisiting the class C2DShapes

The class C2DShapes was developed in Chapter 8 to provide the tools to create and manipulate two dimensional shapes. The class can be utilized by defining two dimensional shapes as objects of the class and then using the functions provided to move, rotate or display the objects. Display options are provided to show the vertices of the object, the basic 2D shape or a filled representation. The shapes are defined by specifying the coordinates of the object's vertices. Derived classes have also been provided to simplify the creation, manipulation and display of circles and rectangles. We do suggest that you briefly review Sections 8.1–8.3 before continuing with this section.

The material of Chapter 8 easily adapts to a touchscreen approach for manipulating and animating objects and assemblies of two-dimensional shapes. The first example of this can be found in the project *Chap11\2_Touch2DShapes*. Building and executing the program will show a start-up display similar to that in Figure 11.3. After a bit of manipulation involving rotating, panning and zooming, you should be able to reach a configuration similar to Figure 11.4. All of the manipulation functions needed for this project are provided in the original class C2DShapes except for the zooming capability. For this example project, we have added the capabilities for zooming operations into the class and expanded the original class file. The revised file for the project classes is TwoDShapes+ZClasses.h. This file can be seen in the project folder *Chap11\2_Touch2DShapes* and includes the zooming capability used in the Touch2DShapes project.

To create the zooming functions, we have supplemented the following original C2DShapes display functions: Show2DShape, Show2DPoints and Fill2DShape. The listing of the original Show2DShape function was presented in Table 8.7. There it can be seen that a device context pointer is the only argument passed into the function. Member variables for the 2D shape of interest are then used in calls to the MoveTo and DrawTo functions to display the 2D shape. Similar approaches are used for Fill2DShape and Show2DPoints. For this project, zooming capability has been provided by including the additional member functions ZoomShow2DShape, ZoomShow2DPoints and ZoomFill2DShape.

Table 11.7 shows the listing for the function ZoomShow2DShape. In this case, line 02 shows that the function accepts the variable "Zoom" as an argument along with the device context pointer. The statement in lines 04 and 05 then carries out a MoveTo to the first point on the object. Notice that this move includes multiplication of the local x and y coordinates of the first point on the object by the factor Zoom. The for

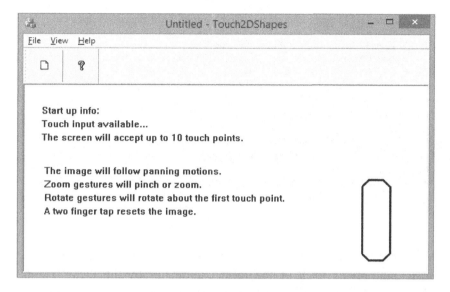

Figure 11.3 Initial Display of Touch2DShapes

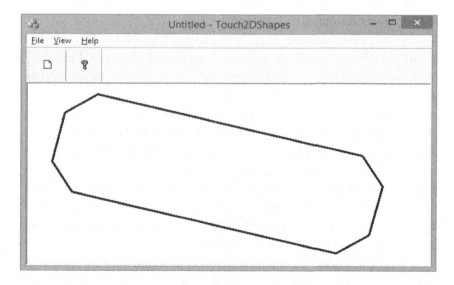

Figure 11.4 Touch2DShapes after Zooming, Rotating, Panning

Table 11.7 Listing of ZoomShow2DShape from TwoDShapes+ZClasses.h

```
01   /* This is a listing of ZoomShow2DShape */
02   void C2DShapes::ZoomShow2DShape(CDC* pDC, double Zoom )
03   {
04        pDC->MoveTo(int(m_xBP + Zoom * m_PointArray[0].m_x), int(m_yBP +
05             Zoom * m_PointArray[0].m_y));
06   for (int j = 1; j < m_NumPnts; j++)
07        {
08        pDC->LineTo(int(m_xBP + Zoom * m_PointArray[j].m_x), int(m_yBP +
09             Zoom * m_PointArray[j].m_y));
10        }
11        pDC->LineTo(int(m_xBP + Zoom * m_PointArray[0].m_x), int(m_yBP +
12             Zoom * m_PointArray[0].m_y));
13   }
```

loop of lines 06–10 draws lines to the remaining points on the shape, again multiplying each of the local coordinates by the factor Zoom. Finally, lines 11 and 12 close the shape by drawing a line back to its first point including the zoom multiplication. In this way, the size of the object is increased (or decreased) relative to its base point. Notice that the base point location has not been adjusted by the zoom multiplication so that this serves only as a local zoom.

The two other zooming/display functions ZoomShow2DPoints and ZoomFill2DShape follow the pattern of the coding shown in Table 11.7 for ZoomShow2DShape. Those functions can be seen as desired in the development environment for this Touch2DShapes project. We will continue to explore the code for Touch2DShapes by looking at its OnNewDocument function as shown in Table 11.8. There you can see that, as in recent examples, we are using a JustStarting variable (line 07) and that we then define the simple shape much as we did for the demonstration projects of Chapter 8. Line 08 declares PointArray and lines 09–13 fill the array with the local shape coordinates. Line 14 then defines the object Shape1 using PointArray and line 15 moves Shape1 to its initial position at (500, 150) in window coordinates.

We now consider the OnDraw function of Table 11.9 recalling that OnDraw not only provides the initial display but also is continually cycled as gestures occur. You can see in lines 07–11 that we execute a

Table 11.8 Listing of OnNewDocument from TouchTwoDShapesDoc.cpp

```
01   /* This is a listing of OnNewDocument */
02   BOOL CTouch2DShapesDoc::OnNewDocument()
03   {
04   if (!CDocument::OnNewDocument()) return FALSE;
05   // TODO: add reinitialization code here
06   // (SDI documents will reuse this document)
07       JustStarting = "Yes";
08       CPoint PointArray[10];
09       int NumPoints = 8;
10       PointArray[0].SetPoint(20, 0);  PointArray[1].SetPoint(20, 100);
11       PointArray[2].SetPoint(10, 110);  PointArray[3].SetPoint(-10, 110);
12       PointArray[4].SetPoint(-20, 100);  PointArray[5].SetPoint(-20, 0);
13       PointArray[6].SetPoint(-10, -10);  PointArray[7].SetPoint(10, -10);
14       Shape1.Adjust2DShape(NumPoints, PointArray);
15       Shape1.Move(500, 150);
16       return TRUE;
17   }
```

start-up function as in previous touch examples. In this case, the StartUpDisplay function tests for the availability of a touchscreen, enables the OnGestureRotate function, initializes display variables and provides a few initial prompts. Also at start-up, line 09 saves a copy of the initial shape in its starting position as a view class member variable. This will allow an easy reset to the start-up position after the program is running (using OnGestureTwoFingerTap). Line 12 in Table 11.9 provides the global rotation capability for the project. In response to a rotation gesture, the rotation angle and rotate center variables are defined through the OnGestureRotate function. Similarly, line 13 provides the differential move of the Shape1 with the member variables that are defined by panning operations. Line 14 resets the variables for incremental motion and lines 15 and 16 display Shape1 including the zoom level corresponding to m_ZoomMult. Notice that the complete OnDraw function as provided in the Touch2DShapes project folder contains extra lines of "commented-out" function calls to ZoomFill2DShape and ZoomShow2DPoints. You can use these statements to easily experiment with the other display options.

Table 11.9 Listing of OnDraw from Touch2DShapesView.cpp

```
01   /* This is a listing of OnDraw */
02   void CTouch2DShapesView::OnDraw(CDC* pDC)
03   {
04       CTouch2DShapesDoc* pDoc = GetDocument();
05       ASSERT_VALID(pDoc);   if (!pDoc) return;
06       // TODO: add draw code for native data here
07   if (pDoc->JustStarting == "Yes") {
08       StartUpDisplay();
09       m_SaveShape1 = pDoc->Shape1;
10       }
11       pDoc->JustStarting = "No";
12       pDoc->Shape1.GRotate(-m_DeltaAngle,m_RotateCenter.x,m_RotateCenter.y);
13       pDoc->Shape1.DMove(m_DeltaPoint.x, m_DeltaPoint.y);
14       m_DeltaPoint.x = 0;  m_DeltaPoint.y = 0;  m_DeltaAngle = 0;
15       pDC->SelectObject(&m_BlackPen);
16       pDoc->Shape1.ZoomShow2DShape(pDC, m_ZoomMult);
17   }
```

Rotate gestures are, of course, expected during execution of the Touch2DShapes project. When a rotate gesture is detected, the OnGestureRotate function presented in Table 11.10 continually interacts with the call to GRotate shown in the OnDraw function at line 13. The member variables m_DeltaAngle and m_RotateCenter are updated by OnGestureRotate at each cycle. Since the angular rotation of the GRotate function was established in degrees, we use m_DeltaAngle in degrees and perform a conversion from radians to degrees in line 05 of OnGestureRotate in Table 11.10. Line 06 is intended to set m_SavdblAngle to zero during the initial detection of a rotate gesture and line 07 continually updates the change in angle (m_DeltaAngle) as the rotation gesture proceeds. Lines 08 and 09 limit the magnitude of m_DeltaAngle to avoid spurious motions and then line 10 saves the current angle for use in the next cycle of OnGestureRotate during the rotation gesture. Finally, line 11 records m_RotateCenter as the rotation center point and line 12 calls the redraw function. You should notice that calls to the global rotate function GRotate at line 12 of OnDraw

Table 11.10 Listing of OnGestureRotate from Touch2DShapesView.cpp

```
01   /* This is a listing of OnGestureRotate */
02   BOOL CTouch2DShapesView::OnGestureRotate(CPoint ptCenter,
03                    double dblAngle)
04   {
05        dblAngle = dblAngle * 180 / 3.14156;
06        if (abs(dblAngle) < .1)  m_SavdblAngle = 0;
07        m_DeltaAngle = dblAngle - m_SavdblAngle;
08        if (m_DeltaAngle > 5)  m_DeltaAngle = 5;
09        if (m_DeltaAngle < -5)  m_DeltaAngle = -5;
10        m_SavdblAngle = dblAngle;
11        m_RotateCenter = ptCenter;
12        RedrawWindow();
13        return TRUE;
14   }
```

results in changing the coordinate variable values for Shape1 with each rotation. For this reason, the incremental angular change m_DeltaAngle is used in the rotations instead of using a specific angular orientation.

Line 13 of Table 11.9 for the OnDraw function interacts with the panning function OnGesturePan in much the same way as the rotation interactions just discussed. When a panning gesture is detected and the OnGesturePan function of Table 11.11 executes, the member variable m_DeltaPoint is updated in line 04 of Table 11.11 using the panning movement to define the change in position. Redrawing the window in line 05 then allows OnDraw to execute and the DMove function call in line 13 of OnDraw in Table 11.9 adjusts the Shape1 object by the increment in position before it is displayed.

In order to provide reliable panning motions in this project, we have also coded the message handler OnMouseMove to provide panning and adjust the m_DeltaPoint accordingly. This follows in the same spirit as the discussion for ZoomDraw in Section 11.1.3. There we mentioned the potential difficulty in detecting panning gestures as distinct from touch screen mouse movement. The OnMouseMove function provided here operates much the same as the function for ZoomDraw shown in Table 11.6. In this case, each mouse movement results in a calculation of position change which is then used by the DMove call of line 13 in

Table 11.11 Listing of OnGesturePan from Touch2DShapesView.cpp

```
01   /* This is a listing of OnGesturePan */
02   BOOL CTouch2DShapesView::OnGesturePan(CPoint ptFrom, CPoint ptTo)
03   {
04        m_DeltaPoint = ptTo - ptFrom;
05        RedrawWindow();
06        return TRUE;
07   }
```

OnDraw to move Shape1 appropriately. We will leave this as an exercise for the reader to inspect the OnLButtonDown function and the OnMouseMove function of the Touch2DShapes project to see the details.

11.2.2 Adding touch screen capability to the MiniRobot

The MiniRobot project of Section 8.5 demonstrated the use of the C2DShapes class as a tool for creating a rather complex animation. We created a variety of objects and developed the calculations that linked them together and provided an animated robot motion. In this section we begin with the original MiniRobot project and add gesture functions that enhance its operation. We do suggest that you review the MiniRobot development in Section 8.5 before exploring the touch screen enhancements below.

The project folder *Chap11\3_TouchMiniRobot* contains the modified MiniRobot project. If you click on the MiniRobot.sln file in this folder, you can bring it into the development environment and then build and execute the project. You will find the original robot appearance (Figure 8.9) and the original project features intact so that, for example, mouse clicks of the menu bar activate an animation or allow single stepping. In addition, two touch screen features have now been added and can be exercised. First, try a press and tap gesture and you will see that the center of the robot base at the start is repositioned to the press point. Then, swipe your fingers across the screen in a two finger panning gesture. The robot animation will follow your panning motion in swiping to the left or to the right. Notice that panning via OnMouseMove has not been included here (it has been left as an exercise). At this point, you will find that a panning gesture with two fingers most reliably triggers the robot motion.

In developing the touch screen version of MiniRobot, we have left in place all of the original MiniRobot coding from *Chap8\5_MiniRobot*. A few start-up prompts have been added to OnDraw. And the two gesture functions OnGesturePressAndTap and OnGesturePan have been added to the project. This direct modification of the original project explains why the file names in the TouchMiniRobot folder continue to appear as "MiniRobot" instead of showing the name of the current folder.

The functions OnGesturePressAndTap and OnGesturePan were both added to the MiniRobot project by the Add Function Wizard. They were added as virtual functions following the format of the original function declarations in the CWnd class. Table 11.12 shows the listing for the OnGesturePressAndTap function. The function contains only a few statements with line 04 obtaining a document pointer and then lines 05 and 06 setting the document variables BaseXo and BaseYo to the position of the pressed point. These variables position the nominal starting point of the robot base as the animation begins. Line 07 redraws the window. This gesture function only executes once when the press and tap gesture occurs and accordingly repositions the robot scene within the program window locating the robot base at the pressed point. The original arrow key adjustments continue to be available to move the scene position as well.

Table 11.12 Listing of OnGesturePressAndTap from MiniRobotView.cpp

```
01    /* This is a listing of OnGesturePressAndTap */
02    BOOL CMiniRobotView::OnGesturePressAndTap(CPoint ptPress, long lDelta)
03    {
04        CMiniRobotDoc* pDoc = GetDocument();
05        pDoc->BaseXo = ptPress.x;
06        pDoc->BaseYo = ptPress.y;
07        RedrawWindow();
08        return TRUE;
09    }
```

The OnGesturePan function is shown in Table 11.13. It controls the animated robot motion by incrementing the variable MotionParam as the panning gesture takes place. The pan gesture function executes continually as long as the gesture is detected. At each cycle it increments MotionParam. In Table 11.13, line 05 captures the change dx in horizontal motion resulting from the gesture movement during the current cycle of the pan function. The variable dx is then used in the incrementing of MotionParam at the end of the function in line 11. The variable MotionParam ranges from zero to five. In the normal animation, activated by the Start item on the menu bar, MotionParam is driven from zero to five with time steps controlled by the message handler OnTimer at each timer tick. When MotionParam reaches five, it is reset to zero. The coding in lines 06–10 of the OnGesturePan function shown in Table 11.13 varies MotionParam from zero to five under control of the panning gesture. Changing the direction of the gesture changes the direction of robot motion by changing the increment of MotionParam from positive to negative. The if statements in lines 06–10 hold MotionParam between the limits of zero and five. When necessary, the sign change of m_Sign in line 09 carries out a direction change. This takes place in line 11 where the MotionParam increment includes m_Sign as well as a

Table 11.13 Listing of OnGesturePan from MiniRobotView.cpp

```
01    /* This is a listing of OnGesturePan */
02    BOOL CMiniRobotView::OnGesturePan(CPoint ptFrom, CPoint ptTo)
03    {
04         CMiniRobotDoc* pDoc = GetDocument();
05         int dx = ptTo.x - ptFrom.x;
06         if (pDoc->MotionParam > 5)  pDoc->MotionParam = 0;
07    if (pDoc->MotionParam < 0)  {
08         pDoc->MotionParam = 0;
09         m_Sign = -1 * m_Sign;
10         }
11         pDoc->MotionParam += .01 * m_Sign * dx;
12         RedrawWindow();
13         return TRUE;
14    }
```

scaling multiplier (shown as 0.01) that adjusts the speed of the animation relative to the speed of the gesture motion.

11.3 Displaying Graphs in the Touch Screen Environment

In Section 11.2 we demonstrated the integration of our C2DShapes class with gesture functions and the touch screen environment. As we concluded our introductory material in Chapter 9, we extended the use of classes to plotting and displaying graphs using a class structure to manipulate objects representing curves and graphs themselves. In the same way, we now conclude this discussion of gesture and touch screen capability by showing how gesture and touch screen ideas can be combined effectively with object-oriented graphing tools. Our final example in Section 11.4 will demonstrate a graphing concept adapted for a Windows tablet application.

11.3.1 Extending the Grapher project to the touch screen

This material makes use of class structures introduced in Chapter 9. Before beginning this section, you will want to at least make a brief review of the classes and functions developed there for the manipulation and display of graphs and curves. The first graphing project we discussed in Chapter 9 was called Grapher. We have brought this project into the touch screen environment with the demonstration project in the folder *Chap11\4_TouchGrapher*. If you build and execute TouchGrapher you will see an initial graph plus start-up information confirming that touch input is available along with a few prompts for possible user inputs. Figure 11.5 shows the program window and its sample graph after a mouse click has cleared the start-up information. Gestures for a two finger tap and for press and tap will change the display of the graph. The zoom gesture is also active so that a pinch or zoom will shrink or expand the graph size.

The capabilities provided by the classes CGraphs and CCurves have been used for the interactive and touch screen display of the graph. The

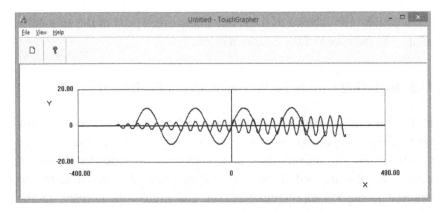

Figure 11.5 Display of a Sample Graph by TouchGrapher

first step in exploring the project is to consider its OnNewDocument function shown in Table 11.14. Here the JustStarting variable is set to begin the first of the added coding in line 07. The for loop of lines 10–13 defines the data for the sine curve at the center of Figure 11.5. Line 14 then uses that data to describe the Curve1 object. In a similar way, lines 16–20 define the Curve 2 object which is the growing sine curve in Figure 11.5. The graph itself is described at the end of OnNewDocument where lines 21 and 22 establish the range of x and y values and line 23 positions and sizes the graph in pixel coordinates. GraphA is then defined as an object by line 24.

Table 11.14 Listing of OnNewDocument from TouchGrapherDoc.cpp

```
01    /* This is a listing of OnNewDocument */
02    BOOL CTouchGrapherDoc::OnNewDocument()
03    {
04        if (!CDocument::OnNewDocument()) return FALSE;
05        // TODO: add reinitialization code here
06        // (SDI documents will reuse this document)
07        JustStarting = "Yes";
08        double xPlot[500];   double yPlot[500];
09        int Npoints = 100;  int i;
10    for (i = 0; i < Npoints; i++) {
11        xPlot[i] = -250 + 5 * i;
```

Table 11.14 (*Continued*)

```
12        yPlot[i] = 10. * sin(.05*xPlot[i]);
13        }
14        Curve1.AdjustCurve(Npoints, xPlot, yPlot);
15        Npoints = 300;
16   for (i = 0; i < Npoints; i++) {
17        xPlot[i] = -300 + 2 * i;
18        yPlot[i] = (1 + (5. / 300) * i) * sin(.25*xPlot[i]);
19        }
20        Curve2.AdjustCurve(Npoints, xPlot, yPlot);
21        double xMin = -400; double xMax = 400;
22        double yMin = -20; double yMax = 20;
23        CPoint Origin(150, 300);     CSize GraphSize(700, 150);
24        GraphA.AdjustGraph(Origin, GraphSize, xMin, yMin, xMax, yMax);
25        return TRUE;
26   }
```

With all of the details included in the OnNewDocument function, the OnDraw function of Table 11.15 is relatively simple. Testing for touch screen capability and providing the display of a few prompts at start-up is handled by the function call to StartUpDisplay in line 08. Line 10 draws the framework for GraphA using its ShowGraph member function. The curves are drawn into GraphA by lines 11 and 12 using the PlotLines member function for each curve. Notice that a pointer to a curve object is a required argument for PlotLines. In touch screen interactions, including OnGestureZoom, this OnDraw function can be repeatedly called without any special considerations.

The functions OnGestureTwoFingerTap and OnGesturePressAndTap allow positioning of the graph by touch gestures. The two finger tap relocates the lower left corner of the graph without changing the size of the graph. A press and tap gesture resizes the graph by changing the upper right corner of the graph while keeping the lower left graph corner in its place. Both of these functions are relatively simple in that they call a member function of the CGraphs class to adjust the graph and then redraw the window. Neither gesture function results in a repetitive operation. Table 11.16 shows the OnGesturePressAndTap function as an example. Here you can see lines 04 and 05 use the document pointer to access the NewUpRghtCorner function for GraphA. The x and y arguments are simply the coordinates of the press and tap gesture.

Table 11.15 Listing of OnDraw from TouchGrapherView.cpp

```
01    /* This is a listing of OnDraw */
02    void CTouchGrapherView::OnDraw(CDC* pDC)
03    {
04        CTouchGrapherDoc* pDoc = GetDocument();
05        ASSERT_VALID(pDoc);
06        if (!pDoc) return;
07        // TODO: add draw code for native data here
08        if (pDoc->JustStarting == "Yes") StartUpDisplay();
09        pDoc->JustStarting = "No";
10        pDoc->GraphA.ShowGraph(pDC);
11        pDoc->GraphA.PlotLines(pDC, &(pDoc->Curve1));
12        pDoc->GraphA.PlotLines(pDC, &(pDoc->Curve2));
13    }
```

Table 11.16 Listing of OnGesturePressAndTap from TouchGrapherView.cpp

```
01     /* This is a listing of OnGesturePressAndTap */
02    BOOL CTouchGrapherView::OnGesturePressAndTap(CPoint ptPress,long lDelta)
03    {
04        CTouchGrapherDoc* pDoc = GetDocument();
05        pDoc->GraphA.NewUpRghtCorner(ptPress.x, ptPress.y);
06        RedrawWindow();
07        return true;
08    }
```

The OnGestureZoom function is somewhat more involved. As we have seen in previous examples, the zoom gesture function continually cycles as long as a zoom gesture is being detected. And, to continually resize the graph, we need to incrementally adjust its size at each cycle of OnGestureZoom. The CGraphs function StretchGraph provides the incremental capability. We mentioned it in Section 9.2 for processing inputs from the arrow keys. In this case Table 11.17 shows the StretchGraph function being applied to our GraphA in line 09. It uses ZoomInc as both the x and y arguments so the graph grows equally in height and width. ZoomInc is defined from lDelta in line 05 reflecting the zooming or pinching action. Lines 07 and 08 limit the magnitude of

Table 11.17 Listing of OnGestureZoom from TouchGrapherView.cpp

```
01   /* This is a listing of OnGestureZoom */
02   BOOL CTouchGrapherView::OnGestureZoom(CPoint ptCenter, long lDelta)
03   {
04        CTouchGrapherDoc* pDoc = GetDocument();
05        int ZoomInc = lDelta;
06        int ZoomIncLim = 5;
07        if (ZoomInc > ZoomIncLim) ZoomInc = ZoomIncLim;
08        if (ZoomInc < -ZoomIncLim) ZoomInc = -ZoomIncLim;
09        pDoc->GraphA.StretchGraph(ZoomInc, ZoomInc);
10        if (abs(ZoomInc) > 1) RedrawWindow();
11        return TRUE;
12   }
```

ZoomInc for any cycle of OnGestureZoom. Line 10 allows redrawing of the window only for a significant zoom. This is intended to limit the tendency for flickering during the redrawing process.

11.4 Managing Multiple Graphs on a Touch Screen

Our final graphing example returns to the idea of managing a number of graphs and allowing a user to focus on any one of them. We described Grapher+ in Section 9.3. In this section we present its touch screen equivalent which we have called TouchGrapher+. This project was developed in a full screen mode using the same project options as described for the Scribble project of Section 10.6.2. As the project starts its window is maximized so it fills the display screen and is convenient for a tablet application. It has also been developed to operate easily with a touch screen approach. While at the same time, it has been configured to be readily compatible with mouse clicks and mouse movements.

You can find TouchGrapher+ in *Chap11\5_TouchGrapher+*. Bring it into the development environment with a click on TouchGrapher+.sln and build and execute it. The opening window is as shown in Figure 11.6 and nicely fits the screen of a tablet display. The enlarged tool bar buttons are intended to facilitate touch interaction. An individual graph can be selected for display with a tap of your finger.

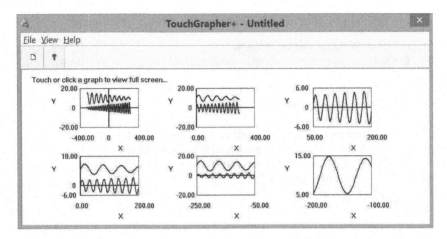

Figure 11.6 Initial Display of TouchGrapher+

The single graph display mode is shown in Figure 11.7 where the graph fills the screen along with a few prompts. At the center above the graph is the invitation to swipe the screen to move on to the next graph. Swiping will work in either direction. Also, there is a red rectangle with a "Return" prompt. Touching Return will go back to the full six graph array. Similarly, a touch of the green rectangle will move on to the next individual graph. The program operates by touches. But mouse clicks have also been left active to click on the red or green rectangles and a mouse swipe (left button down) will also move to the next graph. In the single graph display, a two finger tap will reposition the graph, a press and tap will rescale the graph by moving the upper right corner and zooming is also active.

11.4.1 Strategy for programming TouchGrapher+

We can now look at the programming details for TouchGrapher+ which relies on the class structures created in CGraphs and CCurves first discussed in Chapter 9. Table 11.18 shows the OnNewDocument function which starts the program. The document class contains member variables Curve1 and Curve2 from the CCurves class as well as an array

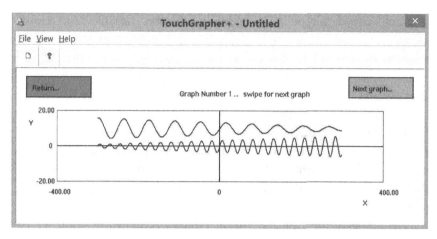

Figure 11.7 Display of a Single Graph… Swipe for the Next

Table 11.18 Listing of OnNewDocument from TouchGrapher+Doc.cpp

```
01    /* This is a listing of OnNewDocument */
02    BOOL CTouchGrapherDoc::OnNewDocument()
03    {
04        if (!CDocument::OnNewDocument()) return FALSE;
05        // TODO: add reinitialization code here
06        // (SDI documents will reuse this document)
07        AllGraphs = "Yes";
08        double xPlot[500];  double yPlot[500];
09        int Npoints = 300;  int i;
10    for (i = 0; i < Npoints; i++)  {
11        xPlot[i] = -300 + 2 * i;
12        yPlot[i] = 10 + (1 + (5. / 300) * (300-i)) * sin(.1*xPlot[i]);
13        }
14        Curve1.AdjustCurve(Npoints, xPlot, yPlot);
15    for (i = 0; i < Npoints; i++)  {
16        xPlot[i] = -300 + 2 * i;
17        yPlot[i] = (1 + (5. / 300) * i) * sin(.25*xPlot[i]);
18        }
19        Curve2.AdjustCurve(Npoints, xPlot, yPlot);
20        return TRUE;
21    }
```

of graphs called "Graph". The additional member variable "AllGraphs" identifies whether the multiple graph or single graph display is to fill the window. In Table 11.18, line 07 initializes AllGraphs so that the multiple graph display is in the initial window. After the variable declarations of lines 08 and 09, the for loop within lines 10–14 defines the first of the curves as a shrinking sine wave about a value of y = 10. Then lines 15–19 define the growing sine wave that we saw previously in Section 11.3. Notice that we have not yet initialized the graph array. This will be done in the document class function GraphUpdate, to be discussed shortly, which sizes the graph arrangement to nicely fit the current window.

The OnDraw function for TouchGrapher+ is shown in Table 11.19. Line 09 is the call to GraphUpdate. This prepares the graph array for lines 10–18 so that all of the graphs can be drawn appropriately into the window when the AllGraphs display is selected. The for loop of lines 11–15 can be seen as cycling through the six graphs which present different views of the data in Curve1 and Curve2 as defined by OnNewDocument. Lines 16 and 17 provide the simple prompt for a user to "touch" a graph in order to see it full screen. We will return to discuss the last half of OnDraw shortly, but first let's look more carefully at the GraphUpdate function which can be seen in Table 11.20.

Table 11.19 Listing of OnDraw from TouchGrapher+View.cpp

```
01   /* This is a listing of OnDraw */
02   void CTouchGrapherView::OnDraw(CDC* pDC)
03   {
04       CTouchGrapherDoc* pDoc = GetDocument();
05       ASSERT_VALID(pDoc);
06       if (!pDoc) return;
07       // TODO: add draw code for native data here
08       CString Buffer;
09       pDoc->GraphUpdate(m_SizeX, m_SizeY);
10   if (pDoc->AllGraphs == "Yes")  {
11   for (int i = 0; i < 6; i++) {
12       pDoc->Graph[i].ShowGraph(pDC);
13       pDoc->Graph[i].PlotLines(pDC, &(pDoc->Curve1));
14       pDoc->Graph[i].PlotLines(pDC, &(pDoc->Curve2));
15   }
16       Buffer.Format(L"Touch or click a graph to view full screen...");
```

Table 11.19 (*Continued*)

```
17      pDC->TextOut(25, 15, Buffer);
18      }
19   if (pDoc->AllGraphs == "No") {
20      m_FullGraph.ShowGraph(pDC);
21      m_FullGraph.PlotLines(pDC, &(pDoc->Curve1));
22      m_FullGraph.PlotLines(pDC, &(pDoc->Curve2));
23      Buffer.Format(L"Graph Number %d ... swipe for next graph",
24              m_FullGraphNo + 1);
25      pDC->TextOut(m_SizeX / 2 - 100, 50, Buffer);
26      pDC->SelectObject(&m_RedBrush);
27      pDC->Rectangle(m_RedRect);
28      Buffer.Format(L" Return... ");
29      pDC->SetBkColor(RGB(255, 0, 0));
30      pDC->TextOut(34, 37, Buffer);
31      m_GreenRect.SetRect(m_SizeX - 185, 20, m_SizeX - 25, 70);
32      pDC->SelectObject(&m_GreenBrush);
33      pDC->Rectangle(m_GreenRect);
34      Buffer.Format(L" Next graph... ");
35      pDC->SetBkColor(RGB(0, 255, 0));
36      pDC->TextOut(m_SizeX - 180, 37, Buffer);
37      }
     }
```

Table 11.20 Listing of GraphUpdate from TouchGrapher+Doc.cpp

```
01   /* This is a listing of GraphUpdate */
02   void CTouchGrapherDoc::GraphUpdate(int SizeX, int SizeY)
03   {
04      int GWidth = SizeX / 7;   int GHeight = SizeY / 4;
05      CSize GSize(GWidth, GHeight);
06      int CenterGraphX = (SizeX - GWidth) / 2;
07      CPoint GPos(GWidth, int (1.5 * GHeight));
08      Graph[0].AdjustGraph(GPos, GSize, -400, -20, 400, 20);
09      GPos.SetPoint(CenterGraphX, int(1.5 * GHeight));
10      Graph[1].AdjustGraph(GPos, GSize, 0, -20, 400, 20);
11      GPos.SetPoint(SizeX - 2 * GWidth, int(1.5 * GHeight));
12      Graph[2].AdjustGraph(GPos, GSize, 50, -6, 200, 6);
13      GPos.SetPoint(GWidth, SizeY - int(.75 * GHeight));
14      Graph[3].AdjustGraph(GPos, GSize, 0, -6, 200, 18);
15      GPos.SetPoint(CenterGraphX, SizeY - int(.75 * GHeight));
16      Graph[4].AdjustGraph(GPos, GSize, -250, -20, -50, 20);
17      GPos.SetPoint(SizeX - 2 * GWidth, SizeY - int(.75 * GHeight));
18      Graph[5].AdjustGraph(GPos, GSize, -200, 5, -100, 15);
19   }
```

In the GraphUpdate function the arguments are the size of the current window in x and y coordinates. These are passed as shown in line 09 of OnDraw as the view class member variables m_SizeX and m_SizeY. They are updated in the OnSize message handler as the window is established or any change of window size takes place. The graphs, as seen in Figure 11.6, are arranged in two rows of three each. Based on the size arguments, the width and height of each of the six graphs are set by lines 04 and 05 to be one seventh of the window size in width and one fourth in height. The CSize object GSize carries this information. Line 06 sets the x coordinate of the center graph in both rows. Line 07 then defines the x and y coordinates of the lower left of the first graph (Graph[0]) using the CPoint object GPos. Line 08 uses the CGraphs member function AdjustGraph to position and size Graph[0] using GPos, GSize, and the desired x and y scales of the graph. In this case, x ranges from -400 to +400 while y ranges from -20 to +20. After setting Graph[0], the function moves forward in lines 10–18 to set Graph[1] through Graph[5] in a similar way. The CPoint member function SetPoint is used to adjust GPos for each of the graphs and the x and y scales for each are set to specific new values.

Based on the discussion of GraphUpdate above, the operation of the OnDraw function for displaying the array of graphs (lines 09–18 of Table 11.19) should be clear. We will now consider the display of a single graph as shown in lines 19–37 of Table 11.19. This sequence begins at line 19 for situations where the document variable AllGraphs has been set to "No". This occurs after a screen touch or mouse click on one of the graphs has been detected by the message handler OnLButtonDown. Line 20 of OnDraw displays the graph selected by the screen touch. The specific graph m_FullGraph has been defined in OnLButtonDown. Lines 21 and 22 then plot Curve1 and Curve2 onto the chosen graph displaying the desired view of the curves. The remainder of the OnDraw function presents the various user prompts. Lines 23–25 show the "swipe for next" prompt. Lines 26–30 show the red box and the "Return" prompt. Notice that line 29 sets the background color of the text so that it is red and matches the color of the red rectangle. Lines 31–36 display the green rectangle and the "Next graph" prompt. In this case, notice that line 35 sets the matching background color for the text.

11.4.2 Touch screen interactions in TouchGrapher+

The discussion of OnDraw and GraphUpdate above explain the basics of the two displays shown in Figure 11.6 (the array of graphs) and Figure 11.7 (a single graph). In this section we will focus on managing the user interactions to choose a graph for the single display and to change the graph display by swiping or by touching the red or green rectangles.

The coding which controls the movement between displays is contained in the message handler OnLButtonDown which is shown in Table 11.21. Line 06 declares a TestRectangle which is used for testing touch (or mouse click) locations in this function. Notice that we have not distinguished here between a touch and a mouse click so that the basic operations of this program are available in either a touch or mouse mode. Lines 07–22 of Table 11.21 process touches or mouse clicks received while the array of graphs is being displayed. The if statement of line 07 begins the code sequence for AllGraphs = "Yes". The for loop of lines 08–21 cycles through each graph of the array, testing to see if the touch is within one of the graphs. Lines 09–12 identify the rectangle containing the graph being tested by finding its upper left and lower right coordinates within the window. These are then used in the SetRectangle function of line 13 and the touch point is tested on the graph rectangle in line 14. Lines 15–20 handle the preparation of a selected graph for full screen display. Line 16 sets AllGraphs to "No" and sets the member variable m_FullGraphNo to the current graph number. Line 17 uses this to set the view class member variable m_FullGraph (a CGraphs object) to the current graph from the array. Lines 18 and 19 adjust the position and size of the graph to reasonably fill the current window.

In the case where a single graph is being displayed and a touch or a mouse click is received, lines 23–34 process that input to consider the possibility of a touch in the red or green rectangles. In lines 24 and 25, if the touch is inside the red rectangle, AllGraphs is set to "Yes" so that the

Table 11.21 Listing of OnLButtonDown from TouchGrapher+View.cpp

```
01    /* This is a listing of OnLButtonDown */
02    void CTouchGrapherView::OnLButtonDown(UINT nFlags, CPoint point)
03    {
04        // TODO: Add your message handler code here and/or call default
05        CTouchGrapherDoc* pDoc = GetDocument();
06        CRect TestRectangle;   BOOL RectTest;
07    if (pDoc->AllGraphs == "Yes") {
08    for (int i = 0; i < 6; i++) {
09        int ULx = pDoc->Graph[i].m_xBP;
10        int ULy = pDoc->Graph[i].m_yBP - pDoc->Graph[i].m_yDisplayLength;
11        int LRx = ULx + pDoc->Graph[i].m_xDisplayLength;
12        int LRy = pDoc->Graph[i].m_yBP;
13        TestRectangle.SetRect(ULx, ULy, LRx, LRy);
14        RectTest = TestRectangle.PtInRect(point);
15    if (RectTest) {
16        pDoc->AllGraphs = "No";   m_FullGraphNo = i;
17        m_FullGraph = pDoc->Graph[m_FullGraphNo];
18        m_FullGraph.MoveGraph(100, m_SizeY - 100);
19        m_FullGraph.NewUpRghtCorner(m_SizeX - 100, 100);
20        }
21        }
22        }
23    if ((pDoc->AllGraphs == "No")) {
24        RectTest = m_RedRect.PtInRect(point);
25        if (RectTest) pDoc->AllGraphs = "Yes";
26        RectTest = m_GreenRect.PtInRect(point);
27    if (RectTest) {
28        m_FullGraphNo++;
29        if (m_FullGraphNo == 6) m_FullGraphNo = 0;
30        m_FullGraph = pDoc->Graph[m_FullGraphNo];
31        m_FullGraph.MoveGraph(100, m_SizeY - 100);
32        m_FullGraph.NewUpRghtCorner(m_SizeX - 100, 100);
33        }
34        }
35        m_LeftDown = "Yes";   m_LeftPosition = point;   m_SweepX = 0;
36        pDoc->UpdateAllViews(NULL);
37        CView::OnLButtonDown(nFlags, point);
38    }
```

full graph array will be displayed once again. Lines 26 and 27 provide a test for a touch within the green rectangle. For a green rectangle touch, line 28 increments the graph number to move on to the next graph. Line 29 makes sure that m_FullGraphNo does not exceed our array size of 6 and lines 31 and 32 update the size and position of the new graph to fill the display. For a screen touch that does not satisfy any of the cases tested previously, line 35 prepares for the possibility of a swipe that will move on to the next graph in a single graph display. This will be detected as the OnMouseMove function takes effect. Finally, line 36 results in the execution of OnDraw to update the display.

The possible use of a swipe operation to change graphs in the single graph display is managed by the OnMouseMove function shown in Table 11.22. We will discuss its operation in terms of a single finger screen touch. But, note also, that mouse movements with the left button down will also activate a swipe movement in this context. In the OnMouseMove function, line 07 checks to see if the left button is down. With contact of a single finger on the screen, the m_LeftDown variable will have been set by the OnLButtonDown function. When the line 07 if statement is satisfied, the full operation of OnMouseMove takes place. Line 08 detects the increment in horizontal movement of the finger touch and line 09 updates the latest touch position. In line 10, the graph is incrementally moved so that it appears displaced when the window is redrawn. Then, line 11 increments m_SweepX which is used to store the total x movement since the finger touch began.

When m_SweepX reaches 100 pixels (either positive or negative), the display moves on to the next graph. Until this point, the graph image simply appears to move under the finger touch. Line 12 checks on the magnitude of m_SweepX and will allow a change in graph at the present limit of 100. Line 13 prepares for a graph change by determining the sign of m_SweepX so that line 14 can make the appropriate change in graph number. Lines 15 and 16 check to hold the graph number between zero and five. The member variable m_FullGraph is then set by line 17 to represent the next graph to be displayed full screen. Lines 18 and 19 size the graph appropriately for the window and line 20 sets M_LeftDown to "No" bringing an end to this mouse movement cycle. Of course, line 22 redraws the window.

Table 11.22 Listing of OnMouseMove from TouchGrapher+View.cpp

```
01   /* This is a listing of OnMouseMove */
02   void CTouchGrapherView::OnMouseMove(UINT nFlags, CPoint point)
03   {
04        // TODO: Add your message handler code here and/or call default
05        CTouchGrapherDoc* pDoc = GetDocument();
06        int Inc = 0;
07   if (m_LeftDown == "Yes")  {
08        int dx = point.x - m_LeftPosition.x;
09        m_LeftPosition = point;
10        m_FullGraph.DMoveGraph(dx, 0);
11        m_SweepX = m_SweepX + dx;
12   if (abs(m_SweepX) > 100)  {
13        Inc = - m_SweepX / abs(m_SweepX);
14        m_FullGraphNo += Inc;
15        if (m_FullGraphNo == 6) m_FullGraphNo = 0;
16        if (m_FullGraphNo == -1) m_FullGraphNo = 5;
17        m_FullGraph = pDoc->Graph[m_FullGraphNo];
18        m_FullGraph.MoveGraph(100, m_SizeY - 100);
19        m_FullGraph.NewUpRghtCorner(m_SizeX - 100, 100);
20        m_LeftDown = "No";
21        }
22        RedrawWindow();
23        }
24   CView::OnMouseMove(nFlags, point);
25   }
```

In the single graph display mode the OnGestureZoom function is active and the graph can be pinched or zoomed. The position of the graph can also be changed with a two finger tap changing the lower left coordinates of the graph position and a press and tap changing the upper right corner and resizing the graph. These functions work with only small modifications of the OnGesturePressAndTap function shown originally in Table 11.16 and the OnGestureZoom function shown in Table 11.17.

11.5 Exercises

1. In the ZoomDraw project, a two finger tap returns the drawn image to the original screen position with the display origin at the standard upper left corner of the window. Add a press and tap gesture to the

project which will move the display origin to the window center. This will allow convenient drawing when there are negative values for x and y coordinates.

2. Add the function OnGesturePressAndTap to the Touch2DShapes project. A press and tap gesture should reposition the shape to its original coordinates and size but rotated 90 degrees (so that it is horizontal instead of vertical). Can you make this rotation take place about the shape center rather than the local origin?

3. The TouchMiniRobot project uses the function OnGesturePan to control the animated MiniRobot. Add mouse functions (including OnMouseMove) as necessary to also allow control of the animated MiniRobot by a single finger swiping gesture.

4. In TouchGrapher, a single finger touch does not produce a response. Modify the TouchGrapher project so that a single finger touch toggles Curve1 off and on in the display.

5. The TouchGrapher+ project displays two curves on various graphs. Use OnNewDocument to add a Curve3 of your choice to the collection of curves. Be sure Curve3 fits nicely on the graphs. Add a yellow rectangle labeled "Curve3" to both display windows and modify the project so that a tap or click in the rectangle will toggle Curve3 off and on in both the "all graphs" and single graph displays.

Appendix

The Companion Media Pack

The Companion Media Pack for this book is available from the website of World Scientific Publishing. The download process is described in Section A.1 below. The media pack contains the complete project files for all of the example projects in the book and also a series of executable files selected from the example projects which illustrate the scope of the book's contents.

The files for the example projects are located in the folder "AllExampleProjects". They are referenced throughout the book and provide the programming code necessary for compiling and building each example project to obtain an executable file. The code for each project is discussed in detail in the text in a tutorial format. These example projects provide the basis for developing competency with Visual C++ and the ability to write meaningful programs including graphics and touch screen capability.

The media pack also contains selected executable files in a folder labeled "ExampleExecutables_AtoZ". These executables have been compiled and linked in "release form" and may be executed directly on your computer, with or without the installation of Visual C++. They illustrate the progress that takes place as we move through the chapters increasing the programming level at each stage.

All of the example projects have been updated for the environment of Visual C++ Version 2013. Based on experiences of well over a decade with previous versions of Visual C++, it is expected that the example programs available in the media package will be upward compatible and that readers will readily adapt to modest changes as new versions of Visual C++ are released. In the event that future versions of Visual C++ do require adjustments of the example projects we intend to provide that information and, if necessary, access to updated versions of the projects. Information on updating may be found on the World Scientific website or may be obtained by Email to the author at mayne@buffalo.edu.

A.1 Downloading the Media Pack

Begin the download process of obtaining the Companion Media Pack by entering the World Scientific website using the url http://www.worldscientific.com/r/9435-supp. When you enter the site, you will be asked to login. If you have not previously registered on the World Scientific site, a simple (free) registration process will be required. Once you have successfully logged in and have reached the page for *Introduction to Windows and Graphics Programming, 2nd Edition*, select the "Supplementary" tab. This tab contains a direct link to the Companion Media Pack. Clicking on the link will allow you to download the zipped file containing the example projects and example executables. If, at this point, entry of a specific access token is requested, you may use the url shown above.

   If your computer automatically places downloaded files in a folder named "Downloads", you will want to relocate the zipped file to a convenient permanent directory before unzipping. The zipped file is named book9435_Companion-Media-Pack.zip and after unzipping, it will produce an unzipped folder of the same name. We suggest that you rename the folder "IntroToWindows&GraphicsProgramming2ndEd" and save a permanent copy of this folder on your hard drive so that it will always be available in original form. Make additional working copies of the material as you move forward with the projects in the book.

   Figure A.1 shows the open folder "IntroToWindows&Graphics Programming2ndEd". When you have successfully reached this point (after downloading, unzipping and renaming), you are ready to begin the adventure of Visual C++ programming described in the text. The two subfolders named "AllExampleProjects" and "ExampleExecutables_AtoZ" are indicated in Figure A.1 along with a ReadMe file presented in Word format and also in pdf format. The ReadMe file describes the media pack in further detail. After reviewing the ReadMe file, we suggest that you continue by exploring the

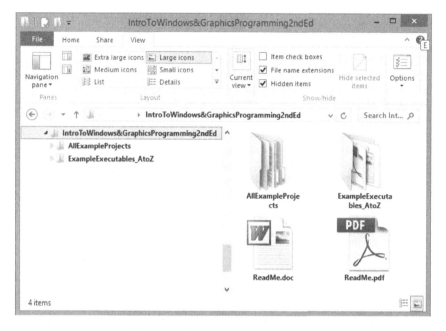

Figure A.1 Contents of the Media Pack

executables subfolder. It is organized by chapter and presents executable files that will help you browse chapter by chapter through the book's projects. ReadMe files for each chapter provide a few user guidelines for the examples and screenshots of the operating programs. By trying these example executables yourself, you can understand the progress to be expected as you work your way through the chapters.

The subfolder "AllExampleProjects" contains all of the example projects in the book. The projects are organized by chapter. Proceeding through the example projects on a chapter by chapter basis is the focus of the tutorial material presented throughout the book. Further details on organizing and using the example projects are presented in Chapter 1, Section 1.7. But, of course, you will want to start at the beginning of Chapter 1 to become familiar with the Visual C++ environment before considering the individual project folders.

Index